HARDPRESS.NET

HOME OF HARD-TO-FIND BOOKS

A Physician's Holiday
by Sir John Forbes

Address:
HardPress
8345 NW 66TH ST #2561
MIAMI FL 33166-2626
USA
Email: info@hardpress.net

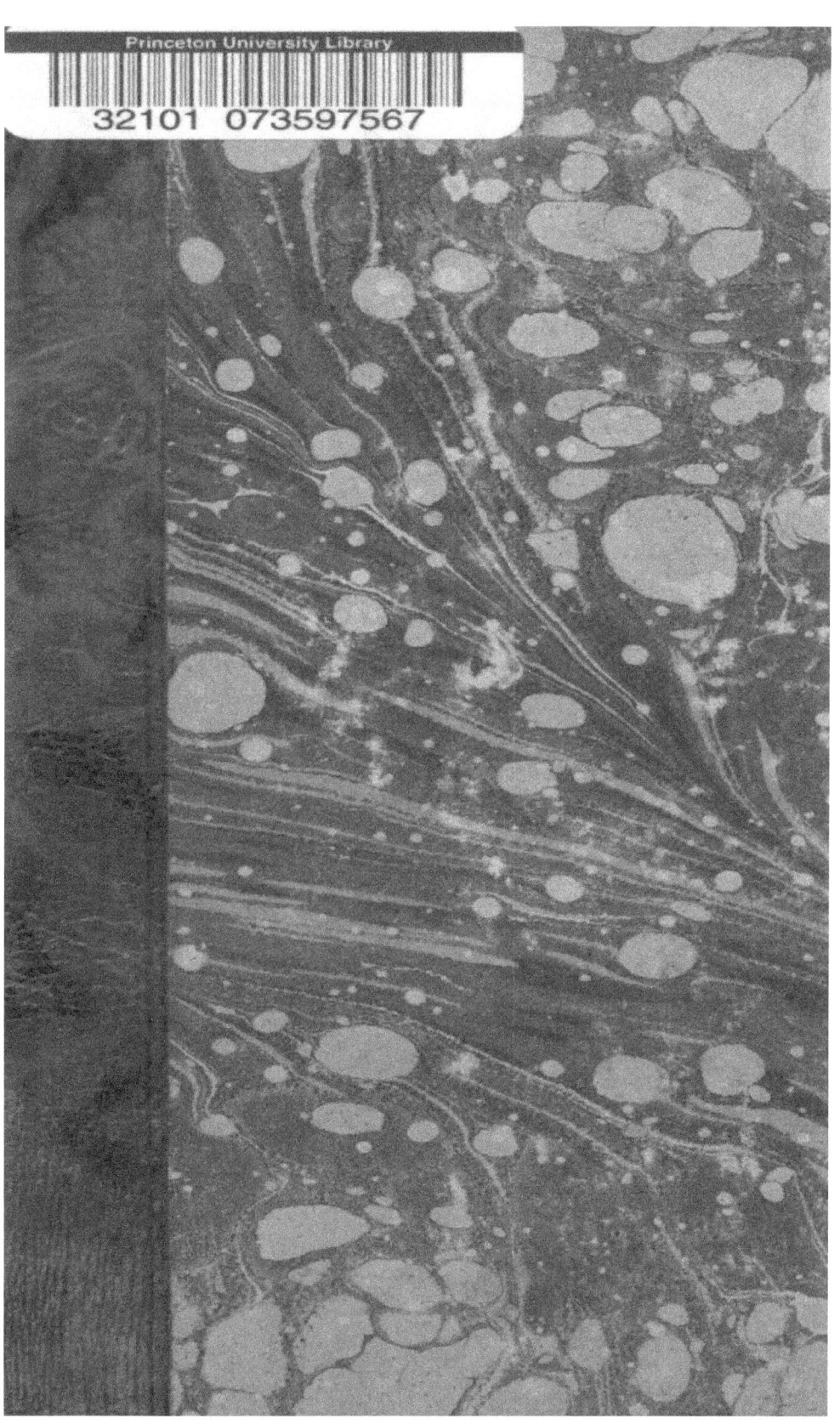

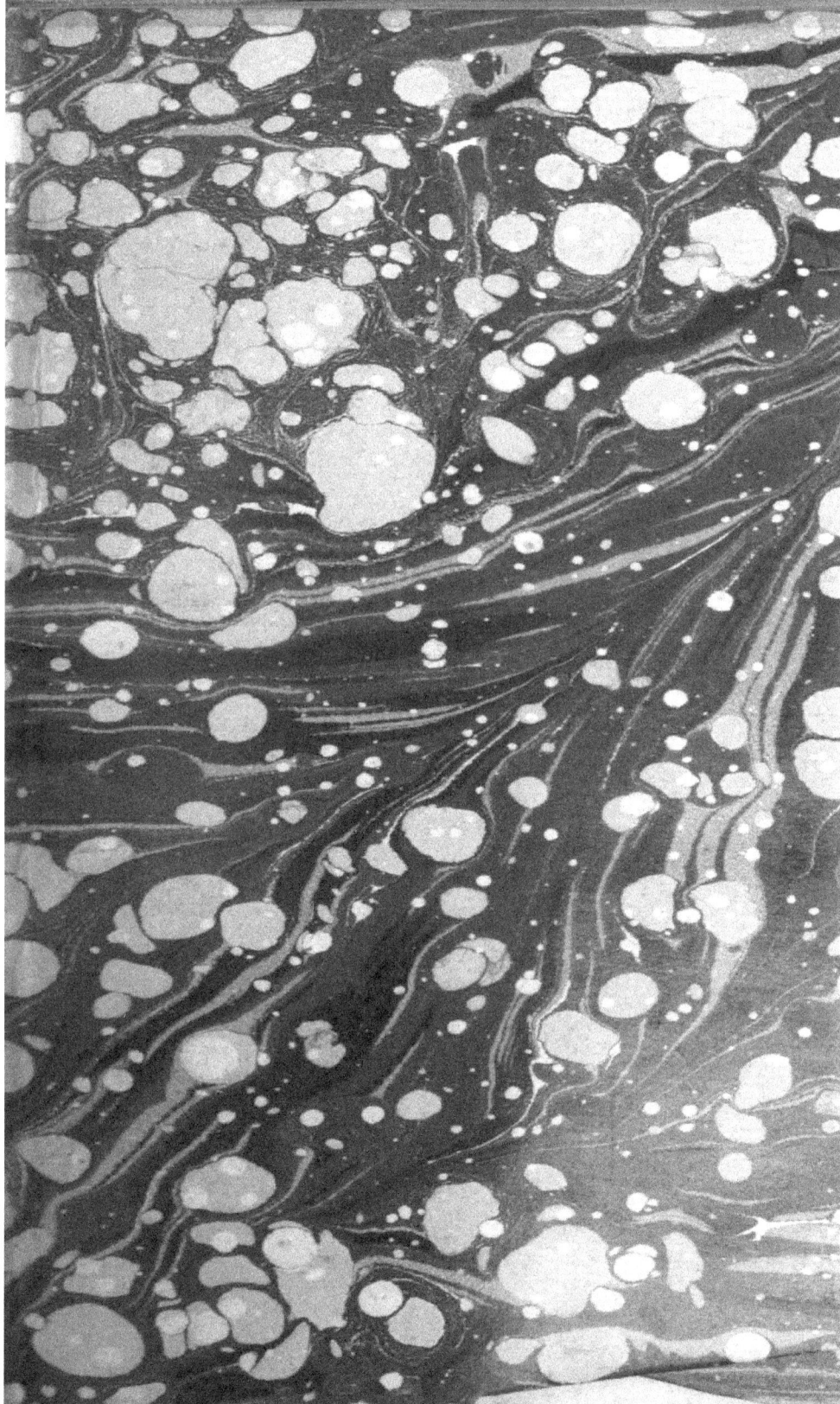

1.12

581/

A Physician's Holiday

OR

A MONTH IN SWITZERLAND

IN THE SUMMER OF

1848.

BY JOHN FORBES, M.D. F.R.S.

WITH A MAP AND ILLUSTRATIONS.

"I, curre per Alpes."—Juv.

LONDON

JOHN MURRAY, ALBEMARLE STREET.

JOHN CHURCHILL, PRINCES STREET, SOHO.

MDCCCXLIX.

"Ut fertilibus agris non est imperandum : cito enim exhauriet illos nunquam intermissa foecunditas : ita animorum impetus assiduus labor frangit. Vires recipient paullum resoluti et remissi . . . . Indulgendum est animo : dandumque subinde otium quod alimenti ac virium loco sit : et in ambulationibus apertis vagandum, ut caelo libero et multo spiritu augeat attollatque se animus. Aliquando vectatio iterque et mutata regio vigorem dabunt."

SENECA, *De Tranquillitate Animi*, cap. xv.

Distempered nerves
Infect the thoughts : the languor of the frame
Depresses the soul's vigour. Quit your couch,
Cleave not so fondly to your moody cell ;
Nor let the hallowed Powers that shed from heaven
Stillness and rest, with disapproving eye
Look down upon your taper, through a watch
Of midnight hours, unseasonably twinkling.
Take courage, and withdraw yourself from ways
That run not parallel to Nature's course.
Rise with the lark ; your Matins shall obtain
Grace, be their composition what it may,
If but with hers performed; climb once again—
Climb every day, those ramparts ; meet the breeze
Upon their tops, adventurous as a bee
That from your garden thither soars, to feed
On new-blown heath.

WORDSWORTH, *The Excursion*, Book iv.

Dedication.

TO

ALEXANDER FORBES, ESQ.

MY DEAR BROTHER,

During the period of our long and wide separation, now, alas, of more than thirty years, I have been so accustomed to communicate to you all my thoughts and feelings, and all the little incidents of my uneventful life, that the small work now addressed to you will only seem one of my Monthly Letters on a larger scale. Part of it, indeed, as you will find, has already reached you in that way; and it is probable, but for the interest you took in the portion of the narrative so communicated, it might never have been completed, or, at least, might not have assumed the formal shape in which it now appears.

Whatever reception my little book may receive

b

from the Public—and my expectations in this respect are of the most moderate kind—I am sure it will have a warm welcome from yourself, as being the record of one of the most pleasing passages in a life with all whose concerns you have so deeply sympathised, and which your unbounded and unvarying kindness has so much contributed to make a happy one. Fortified by this conviction, I shall be much less solicitous, though by no means indifferent, as to the judgment passed on my performance by other readers.

I am,

My dear Brother,

Most truly and affectionately yours,

JOHN FORBES.

LONDON; May 1st, 1849.

CONTENTS.

CHAPTER XIII.

CHAPTER XIV.

CHAPTER XV.

CHAPTER XVI.

CHAPTER XVII.

CHAPTER XVIII.

CHAPTER XIX.

CHAPTER XX.

CHAPTER XXI.

CHAPTER XXII.

CHAPTER XXIII.

CHAPTER XXIV.

CONTENTS.

CHAPTER XXV.

CHAPTER XXVI.

CHAPTER XXVII.

CHAPTER XXVIII.

CHAPTER XXIX.

CHAPTER XXX.

CHAPTER XXXI.

ILLUSTRATIONS.

Pp. 260, 294, for Chap. XIV, XV, read XIX, XX.

A PHYSICIAN'S HOLIDAY,

OR

A TOUR IN SWITZERLAND.

CHAPTER I.

INTRODUCTORY.

VARIOUS FORMS OF THE PHYSICIAN'S HOLIDAY—THE AUTHOR'S
—HIS MOTIVES FOR REPORTING IT—NATURE AND CONTENTS OF
THE BOOK—APOLOGIES—HINTS TO TRAVELLERS IN SWITZER-
LAND—NECESSARY PREPARATIONS.

It is well known to be the custom with Physicians
in London to absent themselves from town for some
weeks in the end of summer or beginning of autumn,
with the view of recruiting their health after the
labours of the preceding nine months, and laying in
a stock of strength and spirits for the ensuing busy
season. The modes of spending this period, and
the localities in which it is spent, are, of course,
extremely various. They who are fortunate enough
to possess country houses of their own, go to them,
and there indulge in farming, gardening, tree-fell-
ing, walk-making, or any other of the well-known
rural contrivances for letting the brain lie fallow,
and killing time in an easy way.

1

Sporting doctors fix the day of their departure from town either on the 12th of August, the 1st of September, or the 1st of October, according as their love is, respectively, for grouse, partridge, or pheasant; and their destination is determined accordingly, to the hills of Scotland, to the northern moors, or to the stubble fields nearer home. The salmon-fisher retires to the river-side inns of Wales or Scotland. The lover of trout must be content to postpone his amusement to the spring, unless he knows where the grayling haunt in the streams of Lancashire or Yorkshire.

Some physicians join their yachting friends in a trip to Jersey, Lisbon, Malta, or the Azores; some make a voyage in a trading ship to Hamburg or Drontheim; while others of this class, but of humbler aims, appease their thirst for water by making the periplus of our own islands in the common steamboats. A few revive the associations of their youthful days in quietly traversing some of the northern *links*, from breakfast to dinner-time, in philosophical pursuit of the golf-ball.

Others whose love of art is too potent to allow them to go quite beyond the sphere of patients, transport themselves to Brighton, Ramsgate, Matlock, or other places of water, maritime or inland, where they may take a fee now and then, as well as fresh air and a walk in the country, and may return to town at a moment's warning, or once a week at least, to see one or two very old friends, or two or three very urgent cases, and then go back to their oppido-rural retreat, in better spirits, and with renovated relish for both work and play.

The busier juniors and less-endowed seniors must content themselves with doings of a humbler sort; such as a residence for a few weeks in some railway village within twenty miles of London, whence their hospital or dispensary can be visited twice or thrice a week. Many must even be content with a hebdomadal trip by the express-train of Saturday afternoon, to visit their distant friends in the country, under solemn protest that they must return on Monday morning.

A philosophical friend, whose active brain will not allow him to desert his books and his apparatus, even for the woods and fields which he loves so much, takes his holiday sometimes in quite a different style: he sends his horses to grass, shuts up his front-windows, retires to his library in the rear, and leaves strict injunctions with the footman to inform all inquirers, patients especially, that he has gone on his annual holiday.

A travelling trip to Wales, to Scotland, or to the Continent, is one of the commonest forms of holiday-making for the London physician, and assuredly one of the best. This takes him thoroughly away from his business and books, changes everything without and within him, climate, air, exercise, habits, studies, ideas; and generally, within the period of five or six weeks, works such a thorough revolution in soul and body, that he returns to his home a new man, sunburnt and buoyant and keener and defter in his vocation than ever.

In what particular direction the traveller may go, how far, or with what special object or objects beside that of mere relaxation, will depend on the character of the individual mind, and the personal circumstances and relations of the man. Some go short distances, some great; some go fast, some slow; some do much active work, both bodily and mental, some merely lounge along their route with both their bodily and mental eyes only half open. One set of these holiday-makers thinks it best to let the written troubles of the brain be effaced spontaneously by time alone; another prefers driving the old notions out by forcing in new ones, on the principle of the pop-gun.

Of the former class of travellers I know one who will hardly accomplish his hundred miles of distance in half as many days, and whose delight it is to interpose a week between each successive stage of his progress, such week being mainly spent in a gentle daily walk to some easy height in the neighbourhood, which may command a quiet view of the open sea or secluded valley, and where he may stretch himself unmolested on the green turf until the hour arrives for his return to his gay hotel or village inn, as the case may be.

Of the latter class, the most prominent member is one who is among the very first, as well in professional station as in intellectual endowment and varied knowledge, and whose annual delight is to speed to the uttermost end of the earth that can be reached and returned from, within the period of the inexorable holiday. Year after year, has he thus visited, in succession, not merely all the nearer countries of Europe, but the most remote; and has repeatedly gone beyond these, to the east, to the south, and to the west. Norway, Russia, Asia Minor, Egypt, Algeria, Greece, Spain, Canada, the United States of America, have been thus swept over —if with the wing also with the eye of the eagle— and yet the old Library in the West End is infallibly regained on the very day fixed on for the termination of the holiday ere yet it had begun. Could my Publisher prevail on *him* to write out his ' Holidays,' there would be then something of a stamp that would enable many, for a time at least, to make holiday at home.

But, alas, " non cuivis adire Corinthum :" some have no better holiday than the change in their annual round produced by the holidays of others. Meek-eyed men of this class—and some, perchance, with locks neither so black nor so brown as they once were—may be seen, each autumn, sitting musingly on the banks of the channels that once held rivers, and wondering at the non-arrival of the golden rills that were wont to feed them so copiously.

It was in the category of continental travellers that I had the good fortune to enrol myself in the holiday season of 1848; and, on returning from my trip, I feel myself so renovated in health, strength, and spirits, and retain such a vivid impression of the exciting pleasures enjoyed during its continuance, that I cannot repress the desire to communicate to others, more especially to my brother-craftsmen, something of what I saw, did, and felt during the brief period of my absence from home.   In yielding to this desire I am partly influenced, as just hinted, by the wish to relieve my own " stuffed bosom," but mainly by the hope that, in so doing, I may induce some of my town-tied friends to do as I have done, and enjoy as I have enjoyed.

It is not, assuredly, from the belief of having anything particularly new to communicate, that I sit down to transcribe and enlarge my notes.   Most of the ground I have gone over, and most of the scenes seen by me, are among the best-known in Europe; and I make no pretensions to the power which can give to familiar things the gloss of no-velty, or make a desert blossom as the rose.   I fear, also, that neither the grave matter-of-fact reader who refers to books of travels for important or solid information only, nor the man who skims their pages for the sake of the exciting personal incidents they may contain, will find much to gratify them in this little book.   It gives, I believe, a faith-ful account of what was seen and what was done by the travellers; and a good deal was both seen and done; but though every successive day was to them productive of great gratification, the sources of their enjoyment were mainly the beauties and wonders of the external world.

Nevertheless, I am not without hope that among those who are not over-fastidious in their estimate of books, a small proportion, at least, may find something not altogether without interest in mine. If I have not great confidence in my own powers, I have infinite faith in the merits of my subject. As we can hardly have too much of Shakspeare or Dante, so I think we can hardly have too much of Switzerland. In both cases, the commentary may be sometimes tedious; but much will be forgiven in the satisfaction experienced in being yet again led to study the original. And it can hardly happen that a sincere and zealous admirer, whatever be his capacity, shall altogether fail in bringing to light some little beauty hitherto unobserved or less noted than it deserves to be. Even some of those who have trodden the same ground, may not be unwilling to go over it again in the company of one who, however dull, will certainly not detract from their enjoyment by much carping or criticising of what he sees; while to those who have never been in Switzerland, I feel that it would be an injustice to the incomparable scenes it presents, to believe, that *any* attempt to delineate its beauties could be altogether uninteresting, so long as it keeps nature and truth in view.

It is to the last class of readers that this volume is especially addressed; and it is from them

that it looks for toleration at least, if not en-
couragement.   One of its aims being, as already
stated, to entice some among them to follow the
writer's footsteps, it will be found to contain, in
addition to notices of scenery, and the scanty tale
of events that befell the travellers, many common-
place and minor details which, it is hoped, will be
useful to them, but which, without this prospective
relationship to the reader, might seem both frivolous
and unnecessary.   I here refer chiefly to the details
respecting the time occupied in travelling, the distances, modes of conveyance, expenses, inns, &c.
Although Murray's incomparable Handbooks leave
little to be said even on these matters, still I cannot
but think that the plain narrative of an actual
journey, fairly and honestly setting forth all that
the travellers did or saw on particular days, in particular places, will convey a much more impressive
lesson——even though inferior in actual merit——than
any general or abstract account to be found in the
Guide-books.   The detailed narrative of proceedings
on the road, from day to day, will show the inex-
perienced, by actual examples, what they may expect
in the way of difficulties or facilities on their journey;
what may be done within a given period of time, and
at what expense; and what means for accomplishing
particular objects may be most suitable in individual
cases.   As the travellers, in the present instance,
were of different ages, the reader may, moreover, see
what was easily done by the vigour of youth, and

what was found not beyond the power of a healthy sexagenarian: " quid ferre recusent quid valeant humeri." It may be here added, that it has been from the writer's desire " to teach by example" those among his brethren whom he hopes to allure into continental travelling, that the journal of the proceedings " up the Rhine" has been printed with the rest; although this route is so well known, and has been described much more frequently than that through Switzerland.

The party engaged in this journey consisted of three persons; one (THE PHYSICIAN) whose age has just been mentioned, and two healthy young men between twenty-three and twenty-five. In planning our excursion, the number THREE was fixed on advisedly, as in many respects the best for such a trip as ours; and the events of the journey proved that this arrangement was a wise one. In the first place, this number, like that of a small dinner-party, allows all the members to participate in any conversation that may take place, or in any inquiry or investigation that is going forward, without inconvenience, and without any necessity for spiritless second-hand repetitions, or for episodical discussions got up in self-defence. In the second place, it is very useful to have a majority always at hand in matters of action that admit dispute. Lastly, Three is an economical number: one porter or one mule can carry three knapsacks, but not four; and one

1 §

char will take three persons—but not four—at the same hire as one.

The usual preparations were made for active pedestrian work, and the usual precautions taken to meet all contingencies of locality and weather. As I foresaw at the time of preparation, and as was thoroughly demonstrated afterwards, we burthened ourselves with a most unnecessary amount of luggage. In addition to a knapsack, each traveller had a large portmanteau containing stores enow for a dozen persons, or for a journey of a dozen months in place of one. To be sure, it was not intended to use these except as stationary magazines, to be forwarded by the Diligence from place to place, so as to await the travellers on their arrival at certain central stations or head-quarters. The main inconveniences of the arrangement were, therefore, first, the trouble of directing the baggage hither and thither; secondly, the very considerable cost of transporting it over so long a tract of country and by such various conveyances; and thirdly, the great additional trouble and delay occasioned by the examination of it at the different custom-houses. I have no hesitation in affirming positively, after the experience of our trip, that a healthy and robust pedestrian traveller in Switzerland, need carry with him only one package, and this in the shape of a water-proof knapsack of moderate size. If provided, as he should be, with either an umbrella or water-proof overcoat or cloak (now to be had of extreme lightness), he need take no other exterior clothing, except perhaps a spare pair of trowsers and a second light coat to be used as occasion may require, either singly as a walking-coat or as an over-coat, and a spare pair of shoes for indoor use. The articles of *interior* clothing, both for day and night use, need be neither numerous nor bulky; and the dressing apparatus should be reduced to corresponding tenuity. One important item in the inventory must not be forgotten, as it is rarely to be met with in the inns, viz. Windsor soap.

The traveller in Switzerland need apprehend no difficulty as to clean linen, as he will find at every inn the most immediate assistance in this way. If he will only on his arrival at once summon the *Wäscherinn*, and give her his own directions, or give positive orders to the chambermaid or chief waiter, he will have his linen ready at the earliest hour in the morning, or even the same evening. We never met with the slightest difficulty in this respect. In one case (at Meyringen) we found the linen taken off when dressing for the table d'hôte at six, all ready in our rooms on retiring to bed at nine.

While on the subject of clothing, it is hardly necessary to repeat what all the Guide-books state respecting the necessity of the coat or shooting-jacket being of very light but strong materials (*cloth* not *linen*), and provided with numerous pockets; or of the shoes being roomy, with very thick soles, and, where glaciers are to be crossed, with a good sprinkling of nails. No covering for the head can compete

with the thin small-crowned broad-brimmed beavers
now known by the name of *wide-awakes*, as they
shade the face thoroughly from the sun, protect the
neck from rain, and, being extremely light and
perfectly flexible, are in every way portable and
commodious, and supersede all necessity for any
additional hat or for a clumsy hat-box.

As almost a necessary help, certainly as an indispensable luxury, I would further advise the procuring
of a good opera-glass, provided with a temporary
case like a cartridge-box suspended over the shoulder
for ready use.   This is much superior to a telescope
however portable, as this latter is only useful in
looking at very distant objects, and involves a good
deal of time and trouble in its adjustment every
time it is used, while the opera-glass is useful on
all occasions, is powerful enough for all practical
purposes, and may be kept always adjusted for the
eye, or may be so adjusted without trouble or loss
of time.   I mention this more particularly, because,
from having met with only one person in our whole
tour provided with one, I fancy its great advantages,
more especially to persons at all short-sighted, are
not sufficiently appreciated.   I found it so very useful
in the examination of the grander and more distant
scenes, that my gratification (on innumerable occasions) would have been seriously lessened had I not
possessed it.

The traveller who has more particularly in view
scientific researches and observations, will, of course,

be specially provided with instruments suited to his purpose, according as he is a geologist, botanist, zoologist, or physical geographer; but I think every one should be provided with a small pocket compass and pocket thermometer, as they will be found useful on numerous occasions.

All these are home supplies; and when to these you have added, on arriving at the field of action, the pocket drinking-cup and the indispensable and admirable ALPENSTOCK, you may regard yourself as fully furnished for the task in hand.

But this said ALPENSTOCK, or Alpine-staff, deserves a paragraph to itself, as it is truly an instrument of singular value, although it is nothing but a long plain staff, with an iron pike at its lower end, precisely like the old *Pike-staff* of the Highlands of Scotland, which was in common use in the end of last century. The Alpenstock varies in length, from five to six feet or more, and when used is grasped not like a common walking-stick, at the end, but at that height best suited to the arm of the individual. Its points of superiority over any common walking-stick are manifold. In the first place, its great length permits the actual column of support to the body to be made long or short, according to the circumstances of the locality; secondly, it admits of the length of this support being varied instantaneously, and with extreme facility, by allowing the shaft to slip through the hand at every progressive step; thirdly, by means of its sharp iron pike it is enabled to take an imme-

diate and firm hold on whatever it impinges, turf,
mould, rock, stone, or ice.   Owing to these peculiarities, the assistance derived from it in ascending,
still more in descending mountains; in scrambling
along rugged, shelving, or steep paths of all sorts; in
crossing rivulets, crevices in the ice, &c., is very great;
indeed, much greater than could be believed before
actual trial.   It is like another pair of legs to a
man; and if it does not make him quite equal to
a Chamouni mule, it greatly lessens the envy with
which, without it, he would contemplate the proceedings of that clever and cautious animal.   Therefore let no man think of visiting the Alps without
an Alpenstock.

Before concluding these prefatory remarks, it may
perhaps be reasonably expected that I should give,
in my professional capacity——even though only a
Holiday Physician——some hints as to the way in
which the traveller should conduct himself, generally,
in order that he may not only run no risk of diminishing his actual stock of health, but may stand
the best chance of improving it, if at all deteriorated.
And, in truth, valuing TRAVELLING as a means both
of preserving and restoring health so highly as I do,
and having, on the present occasion, derived such
great benefits from it in my own person, if I omitted
to do this I should feel as if I were guilty of a sort
of professional *lèse-majesté*, to say nothing of personal
ingratitude.   I shall therefore touch briefly on this
matter in the next chapter.

CHAPTER II.

INTRODUCTORY.

PERSONS LIKELY TO BE BENEFITED BY TRAVELLING — HOW IT BENEFITS—DIFFERENT MODES OF TRAVELLING—SANITARY HINTS TO TRAVELLERS — CLOTHING — DRINK — FOOD—REGIMEN OF INVALID TRAVELLERS.

IT may be stated, without any risk of being mistaken, that there are very few residents in large towns, particularly in our large manufacturing towns and in London, whom such a tour as is described in the following pages, will not benefit in a very marked degree. It will enable a large proportion of such persons to lay in a fresh stock of health sufficient to last through the year, in spite of all the exhausting influences of confined air, sedentary occupations, and that overtasking of the mind to which so many of them are exposed, and which is the fruitful source of so many diseases.

A journey of this kind, properly conducted according to the circumstances of the particular case, will be still more beneficial to that numerous—I had almost said that innumerable—class of invalids who, although unaffected by any fatal or even dangerous disease, are yet so disordered and distressed by chronic functional derangements of various kinds, and by consequent debility, that their condition is much more

to be pitied than that of the victims of the severest
diseases of an acute kind.   To these unhappy persons, whether their malady be, in popular or learned
phrase, 'bile,' 'liver,' 'stomach,' 'dyspepsy,' 'indi-
gestion,' 'mucous membrane,' 'suppressed gout,'
'dumb gout,' 'nerves,' 'nervousness,' 'hypochon-
driasis,' 'low spirits,' &c. &c., I will venture to recommend such a tour as that described in this little
book—*mutatis mutandis*—as more effectual in restoring health than any course of medicines, taken
under the most skilful supervision, *at home*.   And,
to say truth, such a journey may be made to fulfil
almost every indication of cure applicable to such
cases, which, however varied in appearance, are, in
reality, extremely similar in their more essential
characters.

A Course of Travelling of this sort—to speak medically—carried out in the fine season, in one of the
healthiest localities of Europe, in a pure and bracing
air, under a bright sky, amid some of the most attractive and most impressive scenes in nature, in
cheerful company, with a mind freed from the toils
and cares of business or the equally oppressive pursuits, or rather no-pursuits of mere fashionable life,
—will do all that the best medicines can do in such
cases, and much that they never can accomplish.

It is now well known to all experienced and scientific
physicians, that chronic functional diseases of long
standing, can only be thoroughly cured by such general and comprehensive means as act on the whole

system, and for a certain period of time, influencing the nutrition in its source, not merely by the supply of wholesome elements, but by keeping the nutrient function active and vigorous over the entire fabric, by an equable distribution of blood and nervous influence, and consequent energetic action of all the secreting organs. When drugs are useful in such cases, they are so only as subsidiary means calculated to fulfil some special, local, or partial indication. It need therefore excite no surprise that a COURSE OF TRAVELLING, calculated as it is, or at least may be made, to fulfil all the foregoing requisites, should be held forth as one of the most important methods of curing many chronic diseases. But as I am not now addressing the sick, but the well, or at most those who, though classed as invalids, can, without hazard, comport themselves as healthy travellers, I shall, in the few remarks I am about to set down, make no reference as to what should be the proper proceedings of persons labouring under formal disease. They must consult their physicians. I address those only who have not and need not physicians.

The traveller in Switzerland may indulge, to a certain extent, in all the modes of travelling now in use. The railway, to be sure, will stand him little in stead. In steamboats he may traverse all the large lakes ; and he may cross the few smaller ones not provided with steam, in a boat with the oar or sail. Switzerland is provided with excellent roads, and may

be traversed in carriages from one end to the other.
Horses or mules take up the traveller where the
carriage has no further access, and bear him up and
over mountains which, at first sight, seem impassable
for any beast of burden ; but they at last come to
a standstill, and nothing can convey the pilgrim further to the object of his desire but his own feet and
hands, aided by the trusty Alpenstock.

The only one of these modes of transit that is
equal to all exigencies is the latter ; the pedestrian
can go wherever carriage or mule can go, and if he
cannot cross lakes without help, he can at least walk
round them.   For such travellers, therefore, as are
robust and vigorous, who have plenty of leisure at
command, or who may prefer the economy of money
to that of time, pedestrianism, with the occasional
aid of the steamboat, offers every requisite, and may
be made most conducive both to enjoyment and
health.   To the generality of travellers, however, the
combination of all the modes of transport mentioned
will be found much preferable on every account.
Many of the broad and beaten highways of the
country can only be regarded as ordinary thoroughfares ; and the districts through which they lead do
not, in themselves, merit further inspection than can
be made in a carriage drive through them.   To take
a long, hot, and dusty walk over such a road, is
clearly an unnecessary waste of time and labour.   If
any single spot or object on the way merits notice,
the carriage can stop while this is being done ; and

on reaching the end of any stage, the further progress may be made either in the same way or on foot, or a temporary halt may be called, according to the nature or sight-worthiness of the locality.

But a point must soon be reached where no carriage is available; and they whose object is really to see the peculiar features of the country, whether grand or lovely, must henceforth trust to the horses or mules, or to their own legs. The experienced, well-breathed, and robust traveller will naturally and properly prefer the latter mode, as at once pleasanter, more efficient, and quicker. A good walker will always beat a horse or mule in ascending a mountain, while he can, at his pleasure, leave the ordinary track for better views, shorter cuts, &c. On the other hand, if the ascent is very steep or very long, or if the traveller should be naturally not very strong-winded, or not yet brought into good walking condition, it will be better for him to take the horse or mule. He will thus be in a much better condition to enjoy the scenery than if his attention were much absorbed by his own physical exertions or sufferings.

In many of the finest parts of the country a point is reached where even the mule must stop; and here every one must trust to his own powers, or, at most, to the occasional aid of his guide. It would, however, be a great loss of enjoyment as well as of the chances of health, if the traveller were invariably to mount the mule or horse, where the road is quite practicable for them. An occasional walk, both in ascending and descending mountains, in crossing bridges, skirting precipices, &c., is often unavoidable; and such walks, especially in descending mountains, should be taken even when not absolutely necessary. A good plan for those who have passed the vigour of youth or manhood, or are not otherwise robust or well trained, is, to ride a portion of the day's journey, and walk the rest : as, for instance, to ride up the mountain, and walk back; to ride to the top of a Pass, and walk down the other side.

Over-work in the way of walking is as destructive to enjoyment of scenery as it is in itself painful or injurious to health. Under the influence of great fatigue or exhaustion, a man's thoughts are too much occupied with his own sensations to permit him to attend pleasantly to what is without and around him. On the other hand, a timid horseman, especially in difficult and dangerous paths——and many of the paths are such——is apt to be either so much engaged in directing his beast, or is so much impressed with the dangers of his position, as to be in a still worse predicament for enjoying nature than the over-tasked pedestrian. Here, as in so many other cases, the middle course is the best ; and that course is the mixed one, of riding and walking. Nevertheless, I am still of opinion that walking, if not carried beyond the pitch of the traveller's powers, affords the best scope for the appreciation of external nature, as well as for calling forth the greatest amount of personal enjoyment generally.

As in the fine season when Switzerland is visited, the heat of the sun in the valleys is extreme in the middle of the day, the traveller under these circumstances must be prepared to graduate his amount of clothing accordingly; the transference of the coat or the waistcoat, or even of both from the traveller's back to his arm, or to the hand of the guide, will often be found a great relief. So long as the strong exercise is continued, the freest perspiration may be at least disregarded, if not encouraged; but when a temporary halt is made under the shade of trees, or a longer stay is necessary for refreshment and rest, the discarded garment should always be resumed, to prevent the too rapid evaporation and consequent chill. And this is equally necessary on the traveller reaching some exposed Pass or mountain-top after a hard hot walk up its side.

The state of perspiration resulting from exercise short of exhaustion, is a most wholesome one, and so long as the circulation continues vigorous, temporary exposure to a colder air will do no harm; but when exercise has ceased, such exposure continued for some time may be injurious by inducing a chill, and should therefore be avoided or obviated in the manner mentioned, by putting on more clothing, and buttoning this close round the body; evaporation being thus prevented, the natural heat of the body will keep the damp linen in contact with it of the same temperature, and thus no deleterious impression of chill will be produced.

It is hardly necessary to recommend partial ablution, at least, with cold or tepid water, on reaching the place where the night is to be passed. Indeed, provided the pedestrian feels himself still vigorous and warm, ablution of the whole body, if practicable, will be found not merely refreshing but most wholesome. It is unnecessary to say that the same process should be adopted before setting out in the morning.

The consideration of the external application of cold water naturally leads to speak of its internal use. With the Alpine pedestrian, toiling hour after hour in the sun's rays, in the deep valley or up the mountain's steep sides, the supervention of thirst is almost a necessary result of the great loss of fluid by the skin and lungs, and is a natural hint for the resupply of them. It would be strange, therefore, if the due gratification of this natural and irresistible instinct were injurious to health, much more if it were highly dangerous, as it is generally considered to be. The prevalent dread of drinking cold water I believe to be an entire mistake; and so far from regarding it as a thing to be forbidden to the heated pedestrian, I consider its use to be no less wholesome than it is delicious.

I am well aware of the fact that dangerous and fatal results have followed the sudden ingestion of cold water by travellers and others who had been undergoing great bodily exertion in hot weather. In recommending the use of it to the Alpine traveller, I must, therefore, guard myself against all risk of leading him into danger. It is its moderate and rational use I sanction and advise, not its immoderate and irrational use. The circumstances and bodily condition under which dangerous consequences have resulted, or are likely to result, from drinking cold water, seem to be the following : first, the exhaustion of the strength from previous over-exertion and consequent depression of the heat-producing and cold-resisting powers; second, the sudden application to the stomach of a large quantity of very cold water, when the system is in this state. And so long as the pedestrian eschews this combination of circumstances, I believe he may freely indulge his taste by filling his drinking-cup at every spring he passes in his way. So far from the simply heated state of the body being here an element of danger, I believe the hotter the individual is, provided he is not exhausted, and provided he does not drink an excessive amount of water, the safer is the practice. But he should content himself with a small cupful at a time, should drink this slowly, and, as a rule, rather drink often than much. This is more especially proper when the water is very cold ; and for this reason the pedestrian should always consider this quality of coldness when he is indulging his thirst, the rather as there is considerable variety in the degree of temperature of the springs he meets with.

When no other supply is at hand, the traveller may, if in the condition of vigour above mentioned,

drink with perfect safety of water just melted from
the glacier, as I have myself repeatedly done; but
in this case he should drink very slowly, sipping
rather than drinking, so as not to chill the stomach
too rapidly, and not in large quantity, rather renewing his draught after a time than quite satiating
his thirst at once. In drinking water of the temperature of 33° under such circumstances of extreme
bodily heat, I have been surprised to find how very
little its extreme coldness was felt either in the
mouth or stomach : it seemed to the sensations hardly
to exceed the ordinary temperature of summer water.

Much that has been now said respecting water, will
apply to *milk* when used as a beverage, as it frequently
is, or may be, in the numerous mountain chalets
the pedestrian meets with in his journey. It must,
however, be recollected that milk is not like water,
a mere innutrient diluent ; but that it becomes partially solid in the stomach, and supplies a considerable quantity of nourishment to the system. In
moderate quantities it is not merely refreshing, but
supporting ; but taken in excess it is oppressive, not
passing off speedily from the system like more watery
fluids.

In regard to this matter of drinking cold fluids
when the body is heated, I should be sorry to draw
positive conclusions on a matter of this importance,
either from theory or from my own limited experience; I think it right, therefore, to corroborate
my opinion by the practice of the guides : each of

these carries his leather or wooden drinking-cup in his pocket, and never hesitates to take a moderate draught from the passing springs as his thirst prompts him, and without any injurious result, as far as I know.

Another important and much-mooted question, in reference to the refreshment of the traveller by drink, is, whether he should preferably make use of the pure water, or mix this with spirits or wine when these are procurable. The general opinion is decidedly in favour of the latter proceeding; and I believe the most general practice with travellers is to provide themselves with a supply of liquor for this admixture. Wine constitutes an invariable item in the bill of fare of a luncheon or dinner on the mountains; and it is very common to meet pedestrians with a small flask suspended round the neck, containing brandy or kirschenwasser. Here, also, I expect that the middle measure will be found truer and wiser than either extreme.

Although thoroughly convinced that, as a general rule, total abstinence from all spirituous admixture with the traveller's natural beverage, is what is the wisest and best proceeding; and although there can be no doubt whatever of the extreme disadvantage and danger of using such admixture habitually, or even frequently, on a journey; I admit that in the case of men accustomed to the daily .use of wine or spirits, and unaccustomed to water as ordinary drink, the occasional admixture of a

2

small proportion of spirits or of wine with the water, may be not only safe but beneficial. At the same time, I have an equally strong conviction, that men accustomed to the exclusive use of water as a beverage, will, *ceteris paribus,* be found, on an Alpine journey, more than a match for those who seek to support their strength with even a moderate use of wine or spirits.* In my own case, I must say that my previous habit of drinking nothing but water, proved to me of the greatest possible advantage during my tour in Switzerland. While it rendered me perfectly independent and regardless of the state of the stores and cellars of mine hosts, and allowed me to dispense with the additional incumbrance of bottles, &c. in my longest journeys, it allowed me to gratify my thirst, without risk and with the greatest relish, on all occasions, at Nature's own fountain.

And assuredly Switzerland, of all countries, is the best for the water-drinker, as the boundless supply of the most delicious water, in every part of it, is one of its striking features. Every village, however small or insignificant, can boast of its public fountain, ever flowing and overflowing with water of the purest quality, and deliciously cool ; while every road and every footpath in valley, hill, or mountain,

* In questioning the guides of Chamouni and the Oberland as to their experience of the value of strong drink in winter excursions among the snow, I found them unanimously of opinion that spirits are injurious ; but they believed the moderate use of wine beneficial. It is to be recollected that the wines in use in Switzerland are very weak.

is ever and anon cheered by the murmur of copious springs of the same sort. There may be some merit for a man to be a water-drinker in many of our English towns, where the quality of the water is so bad; but, in Switzerland, the virtue of abstinence from strong drinks, seems to bring its own immediate reward in the deliciousness of the substitute there always at hand. In the whole of our six weeks' tour—and here I must in justice include the Rhine——never but on one single occasion, in-doors or out-of-doors, did we meet with water that was not merely good but excellent.

Before concluding these perhaps too professional remarks, I may as well say a few words on the matter of Food, in reference to Swiss travelling. Here, as in the case of drink, the materials are at once excellent and superabundant. Switzerland may be regarded as the country for travellers *par excellence,* and, accordingly, arrangements for their convenience are universally studied. Nowhere is there such a profusion of inns, and in very few countries are the inns so good. In every place ordinarily visited by travellers, in every valley, at every Pass, on many mountain-tops even, there are capital hotels to be found, provided not only with every necessary, but with every luxury of diet. It is only in the more remote and less-frequented districts, beyond the beat of the ordinary tourist, that the traveller runs any risk of meeting with a bad bed or a bad dinner. As to dinners, speaking generally, the danger is decidedly on the other side, namely, that they are too good, too tempting, for the happy medium of moderation.

In all the better inns, that is, in the great majority, there is not merely a table-d'hôte dinner at the ordinary dining hour of one or half-past one, but there are two more, at four or five and at eight, expressly for the English! At these tables-d'hôte, the variety and profusion of food is amazing, extending to a dozen, or dozen and half of different dishes, for the most part good in kind, and delicately dressed. It is well for the pedestrian traveller that if the toils of to-day prepare and qualify him to be a plentiful participator in all this extravagance, the toils of to-morrow are calculated to enable him to appropriate and dispose of it with less risk than would otherwise be the case. How the sedentary citizens, or mere lounging travellers, can get on under such a burthen as one is really frightened to see them take to themselves, is, I confess, not a little marvellous to me as a physiologist. But as the wind is tempered to the shorn lamb, so, it is to be presumed, the digestive machine may be magnified and fortified to its Herculean task.

The ordinary and, I believe, the best practice, is to take a cup of coffee and some bread and butter early in the morning, say at five or six, before starting, and then to take a more substantial breakfast on arriving at the place of midday rest; and complete the journey in time for a late dinner. In the case where the ascent of a mountain occupies all the earlier part of the day, it will be necessary for the travellers to carry something for luncheon with them; and it will occasionally happen that this must serve for the whole day, the resting-place not being reached till very late. But when a meal is thus taken in the middle of a day of laborious exercise, it must always be comparatively light; otherwise the subsequent journey will be less easily performed. The same holds good of wine: a glass or even two may invigorate those accustomed to such drink, but more than this will be found injurious.

To the traveller who has been accustomed to simple fare, and unaccustomed to stimulant drinks, the valleys and mountain pasturages of Switzerland will always supply a wholesome and delicious diet in the excellent butter, milk, cheese, and honey which there abound; and I believe that travellers, generally speaking, would get on much better than they do, if they depended more on these simple viands than on the more solid and more tempting dishes of the tables-d'hôte. Were the bread in Switzerland always as good as the butter, the honey, the milk, the cheese, and the water, the traveller need seek for no more delicious fare than these supply.

As invalids and, among the rest, dyspeptic or bilious invalids, constitute an important section in the list of those whom I have recommended to travel, it may be expected that I should have something special to say respecting *their* diet and general

mode of living,   This, however, is not the case ; or
if I would lay down any rules, they would all be
comprised in the single word MODERATION——moderation in strong food, and still more in strong drink.
So far from recommending rigid adherence to a precise and peculiar diet, I do not hesitate to say that
one of the great advantages of travelling, in cases
of this kind, is that it affords a most favorable
opportunity for breaking through the trammels
of such a system.   Nothing is so easy as to coddle
and pamper the stomach into intolerance of all the
more common kinds of food, by adherence to certain rigid formulæ of diet ; and when this exclu-
siveness is once thoroughly established, it is hardly
possible to break through it in the patient's usual
sphere, although, while it exists, firm or stable
health can never be attained.   The institution of
such a system of diet may be very proper in the first
instance, in order to give relief to urgent symptoms,
to correct still greater errors in the mode of living,
or to give room for a rational system of cure ; but
when it is made a permanent regulation, and when
it and its universal accompaniment, the daily pill
and potion, are relied on as the exclusive means of
health and strength, nothing can be more delusive
or more injurious. Instead of enjoying real, vigorous, independent health, the votaries and victims of
such a system can only be said to live a sort of ne-
gative, artificial life, as if by Nature's sufferance not
her sanction——and, for a man's life, one surely both

afflicting and degrading. Out of such a thraldom it is barely possible for an invalid to escape *at home*; but it is far from impracticable, if the case is not of very long standing, to do so abroad——that is, during an active tour.

Almost the only way of breaking such a chain, is the way in which the analogous chains and circles of the magicians used to be broken——namely, by simply willing and daring to do so. What was felt to be impossible in London, and what, if attempted, would have really been unsuccessful in accustomed air and haunts, amid habitual occupations or no-occupations, will be found perfectly practicable to a traveller amid the mountain valleys and breezy Passes of Switzerland. The bracing air, the brilliant sky, the animating scenes, the society of cheerful and emulous companions, and, above all, the increased corporeal exercise, will soon produce such a fundamental alteration in mind and body, in spirits and stomach, that what would have been felt like poison, will be here not only harmless but wholesome. Therefore it is, that I advise invalid travellers——those at least of the bilious, dyspeptic, hypochondriac, pill-taking class—— to follow no special regimen, but to eat the food that others eat——with the sole provisos, that they seek for and see the sights as others do, take all the exercise their strength will admit of, and remember the golden rule of *moderation* at all times, but more especially in the commencement of their emancipation.

Those who have had opportunities of observing what coarse fare becomes perfectly digestible by the most pampered stomachs, under the rough treatment of the hydropathists, amid the bracing breezes of Graefenberg or Malvern, and with the accompaniments of cheerful society, encouraging promises, no wine, and plenty of walking, will not be much surprised at the recommendation just made; any more than the invalid patrons of the Alpenstock need be surprised to hear of the wonderful cures effected by the water-doctors.   Both systems substitute action for inaction; the toil of muscle for the toil of brain; exposure for coddling; the roughness of the ruder times and humbler classes for the luxuries and over-refinements of an advanced civilization: and the return to a natural condition of the system, that is, to Health, is the consequence.

CHAPTER III.

OSTEND—BELGIUM—KÖLN—UP THE RHINE—COBLENZ—
UP THE RHINE—MAINZ.

August 3, 1848.——We left London in the mail-train, at half-past eight in the evening, and reached Dover at eleven. We went immediately on board the Princess Alice steamboat to deposit our luggage and make arrangements for passing the night, as she was to sail at one.

Aug. 4.——Sailed shortly after the appointed hour; and, after a very smooth passage, reached Ostend about half-past five. The morning was showery. As the train for Cologne, whither we purposed going that day, started at seven, we were somewhat anxious lest the proceedings of the authorities respecting passports and the examination of luggage should interfere with our plans. But the officials seemed to act as if it was their duty to have regard to the railway hours. The examination of the pass-ports was set about almost immediately on our landing, in a small office near the quay, and the luggage was inspected in a large apartment adjoin-ing. The inspectors of the passports were said to be unusually precise, on account of the political condition of the country at the time; and some of

2 §

the passports were found unsatisfactory. These special examinations considerably retarded the general
proceedings. The examination of the passengers'
luggage was less rigid, being evidently, in most
cases, more a matter of form than otherwise. Still,
as the number of passengers was considerable, we
found that the time of our dismissal from the hands
of the inspectors, did not leave sufficient leisure for
a formal breakfast before the departure of the train.
So we proceeded to the railway at once, contenting
ourselves with such extemporaneous fare as we could
procure from an old lady at the station, who seemed
to be well aware of the prevalence on her beat of
such necessities as ours.

We took second-class tickets on the strength of
the reputation of the foreign railways for superior
accommodation in this department ; but though we
found that the carriages were considerably better
than the English carriages of the same class, the
want of cushions was soon discovered to be a serious
drawback in so long a journey, and we, therefore,
exchanged our tickets for those of the first-class
long before we reached the extremity of the Belgian
territory. All travellers by the English railways
are well aware of the greatly increased fatigue in
travelling in a second-class carriage, in comparison
with that experienced in one of the first-class ; and
the fact is readily explained by the much greater
amount of muscular exertion necessarily called forth
in the former case, in order to preserve the body's

equilibrium. I may here remark, that in all the other railways on which we travelled, whether Prussian, Badish, or French, we found the second-class carriages as well stuffed and cushioned as those of our first-class; and no traveller need, therefore, on this account, go to the expense of a first-class ticket even during a long journey.

As the weather in England had long been cold and wet, we apprehended that we were about to experience a similar state of things on the Continent, as it rained the whole day until about four o'clock. The weather, however, cleared up at that time; and during the whole of our future journey it continued, with very short and partial exceptions, delightfully fine. This condition of weather is a most important element in travelling, not merely as affecting the traveller's progress and his personal comfort, but as influencing his judgment and opinions of men and things. Many a fine scene has lost its just fame, not so much because it was witnessed by the traveller in bad weather, but because the bad weather, which may be termed Nature's ill-humour, had put the traveller in bad temper.

> " It is the soul that sees : the outward eyes
> Present the object, but the mind descries ;
> Our feelings still upon our views attend,
> And their own natures to the objects lend."

The weather cleared up as we approached Liege; that is, just where the country becomes worth

looking at.   Nothing can be less attractive to the
traveller than the rich, but flat, plains of western
Belgium; while few railway tracts present more
charming scenes than the country from about Liege
to some way beyond Aachen or Aix-la-Chapelle. Here
the railway passes through a succession of hills and
valleys finely wooded and picturesquely grouped, with
frequent tunnels, bridges, and steep ascents.

We did not reach Cologne (Köln) till nine o'clock
—sufficient proof of the slow rate of travelling on
this railway, as the distance from Ostend to Köln
cannot be so much as 220 miles.   Our baggage was
examined at the railway station.   The inspectors
being numerous, we were detained as short a time
as could be expected, and the examination was not
at all strict.   We found omnibuses belonging to
several of the principal inns waiting at the station,
which is a good way from the body of the town:
we chose that of the Bellevue, on the other side of
the river, in Deutz, which we found to be a most
commodious and excellent hotel, as we had expected
from its repute.

Aug. 5.——A fine day.   We were occupied all the
morning in seeing Köln; and we did not, therefore, follow the more usual course of taking the
railway to Bonn, and embarking there on board the
steamboat, but joined her at once at Köln.   This
gave us more time to see the place, as the steamer
did not sail till three; but we lost the opportunity
of seeing Bonn, except from the river as we passed.

Köln is a fine old town, constructed on the best plan,——this is on no definite plan; with narrow picturesque streets and lofty white houses. This whiteness of the houses, so observable in all the German and Swiss towns, strikes the English traveller as a remarkable and agreeable feature. It arises from no superior cleanliness, but from the absence of brick in the exterior of the houses, and still more from the absence of our coal smoke, and the presence of a drier climate. The new parts of London, where brick exteriors are not seen, and where the same kind of cement is used as on the Continent, show nothing of the brightness and cheerful whiteness of the Rhine cities. The great height of the houses on the Continent compared with those in England, particularly in London, also gives them a character of dignity and grandeur, in which ours, though often superior in architectural merit, are so very defective. The cause of this greater elevation is to be found in the habit of continental nations to establish separate domiciles under the same roof. An Englishman, on returning from the Continent, requires some time to reconcile him to the stunted appearance of the houses in the London streets.

The object of universal attraction at Köln is, of course, the cathedral. We went over it, outside and inside, above and below. No one can fail to admire its beauty and symmetry, and the exquisite finish of some parts of the interior ; but, on the whole,

it made a less strong impression on me than I was
led to expect from its fame.   It seemed greatly inferior in point of solemnity and grandeur to York,
Durham, Lichfield, and even other of own cathedrals.   No doubt, the general impression was im-
paired, not merely by the unfinished condition of
the fabric, but by the interior being, at the time of
our visit, partially shut up and partly occupied by
scaffolding.   I hope all this augurs favorably for
the completion of this long-neglected pile.

The steamboat started punctually at three, with a
small number of passengers, and with the wind as well
as the current against us.   But as the afternoon
was fine, and everything we saw was new to us, we
were well pleased even with our journey to Bonn,
although the river's banks show nothing that is
either grand or very beautiful.   The country on
either side, however, cannot be said to be quite flat;
and there are plenty of villages on the banks backed
by well-cultivated fields.   It is the surpassing beauty
of the scenery further on, rather than its own de-
merits, that gives this portion of the Rhine so de-
preciating a report in the books of travellers.   We
had already a foretaste of these superior charms in
the lofty and picturesque summits of the Seven
Mountains (Siebengebirge), which gradually rose on
our view as we advanced, and which were now on
our right hand, now on our left, as the steamboat
turned with the windings of the river.   These mountains, with their jagged sides, and the ruined castles

on their tops, seemed to our eyes, yet new to mountains, not merely picturesque but grand, although none of them reach the height of 1500 feet above the sea; and if they seemed marvellously dwarfed when seen on our return from Switzerland, the impression first received from them was not less real than if they had numbered thousands instead of hundreds of feet in elevation. As seen from the river, Bonn has nothing particularly to recommend it; and as the object of our journey was rather to see Nature than Art, we the less regretted our incapacity to judge if it was more worthy of inspection in its interior and burghly properties.

At Bonn the character of the river, or rather of its banks, changes entirely, and changes wonderfully for the better. Indeed all the way, as long as daylight lasted, and this did not fail us till we had passed Andernach, it seemed to us hardly possible that any river scenery could be finer. The stream was no longer bordered by low, unpicturesque, cultivated fields, as becomes a river of the plains; but at once assumed the character of a bold Highland Water, bounded and hemmed in by fine hills on either side, through the winding intricacies of which it seemed every now and then as if there could be no outlet. Although thus inclosed, and as it were dominated by its lofty barriers, it seemed never threatened or hampered or hindered by them, but to possess them merely as kindred portions of the general beauty of which it formed a part. The hills on either side, with their tops and shoulders covered with trees, and their breasts and base dotted and lined with terraces of neatly-trimmed vines,—here coming sheer down to the water's edge, there retiring to make room for a rich green meadow, or white village with its glittering spire; every upper peak and every bolder rock jutting from the gentler slope, crowned with its ruined castle; and still the broad stream beneath, sweeping on in the same unvarying flow: all this ——presented as it is to the eye, not for minutes but for hours, not for a mile or two but for fifty miles and more——constitutes a picture of such varied beauty as is but rarely witnessed elsewhere.

As our boat pursued her upward course, regardless of the current, amid the ever-changing scene, we sat on the deck with the omnipresent 'Murray' and the 'Rhein-plan' in our hand, expecting, and not in vain, for some fresh ruin on every summit, and some new village on every meadow; and still they came, one after another, like the scenes in a diorama, almost as fast as we could refer to them, and much too numerous to be remembered. Among the earliest met—indeed only a few miles from Bonn——and last forgotten, were, of course, the famous Drachenfels, and Rolandseck and Nonnenwerth, rich and attractive as they are in other charms beside those that meet the eye. "The castled crag of Drachenfels" is almost brushed by the steamer, as its precipitous sides come down to the very edge of the stream. Like many other places on the Rhine and in Switzerland, it is associated in the mind of every English traveller with the poetry of 'Childe Harold,' whose Pilgrimage fortunately led him here, though the poetry in this particular instance is less felicitous than usual. The castle of Roland and the island of the fair *Nonne* which it overlooks, have a deeper and more universal hold on the imagination and feelings, from their indissoluble association with the tenderer legends of the dim times of old.

In looking up to the noble ruin, which still preserves all the forms of a castle, and seeing how closely and thoroughly it overlooks the lovely island of the convent—each in its form and locality seeming so suited to the character and objects of the respective parties, as the legend sets forth—we willingly yield to the fascination which Nature and Romance have alike thrown around the scene, and hardly doubt the truth of the melancholy tale which will make them famous for all time.

> " The tale is old, but love anew
> May nerve young hearts to prove as true."

Although no longer a convent, the antique many-windowed mansion of Nonnenwerth remains in perfect preservation—still looking up, as it were, "aus der Mitte düst'rer Linden," as Schiller describes it, to its castle on the rock.*

---

* The legend of Roland, though well known, may not be known to all. If any excuse were needed for repeating it here, I hope it will be found in Schiller's beautiful verses, which few will re-

After passing Nonnenwerth, the river continued for
a time still closely invested by its lovely and romantic banks, with their woods and vineyards, castles and
villages, varying with every half mile of our progress;
or, if there was sometimes a sameness, it was still the
sameness of beauty.   We stopped at all the larger
towns, as at Königswinter, Unkel, Remagen, Linz,
&c., and we took up or landed passengers at several
of the larger villages without touching the shore.
The signal of embarkation or landing was made by a
flag from the shore, and by a bell from the steamer,
gret to read once more. Roland, the nephew of Charlemagne,
rejected by a beloved mistress, yet not hopeless of eventual acceptance, temporarily to drown his cares went with his followers
to the Holy Land.   But love soon drove him home; and the first
greeting he had on his return was the news that his hoped-for
bride had taken the veil in the convent of Nonnenwerth.   In his
misery of despairing love he forthwith retired from the world,
and built the hermitage or castle of Rolandseck, in order that he
might at least see the bower of his lady-love, if not herself.   He
spent his life in watching the convent from his window, and here
he died; and here his dead body was found, still at the window of
his cell, in the attitude of the watcher.   The catastrophe is
beautifully told in Schiller's verses :

" Blickte nach dem Kloster drüben,
    Blickte Stunden lang
Nach dem Fenster seiner Lieben
    Bis das Fenster klang,
Bis die Liebliche sich zeigte,
    Bis das theure Bild
Sich in's Thal herunter neigte,
    Ruhig, engelmild :
Und so sass er, eine Leiche,
    Eines Morgens da ;
Nach dem Fenster noch das bleiche
    Stille Antlitz sah."

and the boat took up or discharged her freight in the middle of the stream with the least possible delay. There appeared to be a very considerable intercourse, in this way, between the different towns and villages. The fare for such short passages is very small.

At Unkel the bounding cliff encroaches on the bed of the river so as to give rise to a slight rapid at one side; and just above this, on the other side, the beautiful Apollinarisberg, with its splendid new Gothic church and convent, form a striking object in the landscape. Opposite Remagen are the singular cliffs of Erpelerlei, with their hanging gardens of the vine; and, a little further on, Linz, with its beautiful Pfarrkirche on one height, and the black ruin of the Ockenfels on another. At Remagen the river again expands, or rather its bounding hills recede on the left bank, giving greater space for meadow land and villages. The most conspicuous landmarks in this tract are the ruin of Argenfels on the right bank, and the renovated castle of Rheineck, one of the few castles now inhabited, on the left, and lastly, the ruins of Hammerstein, also on the right. Before we come to these, however, the rocky boundaries have again closed on the river. We stopped, of course, at the considerable towns of Andernach and Neuwied,——the former old and picturesque, the latter new and common-place; but by this time the declining night and the coming on of a cold wind, with rain, made the scenes less distinct, and the observers less attentive. It was fortunate that we had fine weather during the earlier part of our journey, as what we now failed to see was much less worth seeing. We arrived at Coblenz between nine and ten, and took up our abode at the *Riese* or Giant, a large and excellent hotel close to the landing-place.

Aug. 6.——Another fine day. Coblenz, although fair to look at from the river, and though containing some fine old houses, is an ugly town in its interior. I walked through it before breakfast, and went into the Church of the Virgin (Liebfrauenkirche) during morning mass. It is a very old but a very ugly building, both outside and inside. Mass was well attended, and the congregation were, for the most part, comfortably accommodated on benches. The still older church of St. Castor, near the mouth of the Moselle, was closed, being under repairs. It also has a very plain outside, but one would have liked to see its interior, if merely to stand on the spot where, it is said, the grandsons of Charlemagne, in the year 843, met to divide the empire.

After breakfast, having obtained the necessary ticket of admission from our landlord, we visited the famous Ehrenbreitstein. It is itself well worth seeing as one of the finest examples of a fortress, reposing on its precipitous rock, huge and massy, and seemingly impregnable; and from its ramparts we have splendid views of the city of Coblenz and its fortified neighbourhood, of the junction of the Moselle and Rhine, and of the course of the latter for a considerable way both up and down, including the beautiful castle of Stolzenfels. An old soldier showed us round the fortress, which is evidently a show-place.

The steamer from Köln reached Coblenz about twelve o'clock, and proceeded on her way upwards as soon as we and other passengers had got on board. We were fortunate in our weather. The day was bright and sunny, yet agreeably cool : all this, while enhancing the charms of the landscape, gave the observers increased relish to enjoy them. And, certainly, nothing of the kind could excel the scenes we passed through ; they were even finer than those of yesterday, at least for a considerable part of our course. With all the beauty of these, they had more grandeur and more romantic interest, from the still greater approximation and steepness of the bounding hills, and the increased number of castles and castellated ruins on the heights. The general character of the scene was, however, as before—a beauty not to be questioned, inspiring a delight not to be resisted.

Immediately above Coblenz is the modern castle of Stolzenfels, belonging to the King of Prussia, and where he entertained our Queen on her visit to the Rhine. It is an elegant building, delightfully situated on a rock projecting from the wooded face of the hill, with a charming little village at its foot. The river Lahn joins the Rhine nearly opposite. We touched at all the principal places—Oberlahnstein—Rhens—Braubach—Boppart—St. Goar

—Goarhausen — Oberwesel, Kaub— Bacharach—
Lorch—Bingen, &c.   At Boppart the channel of
the river becomes still more contracted, more gorge-
like, and it retains this character, in a considerable
degree, all the way to Bingen.   During our whole
course we passed old castles without number.   The
only one of these now inhabited is that of Rheinstein,
near Bingen, which, like that of Stolzenfels, has been
recently restored by the King of Prussia in a very
splendid manner, and is now used as a summer
residence by some of the royal family of Prussia.
The most magnificent ruin is that of Rheinfels,
near St. Goar, which has only been dismantled as a
fortress about fifty years.

After passing Bingen the river spreads wider, and
the hills retire on both sides, giving the scenery
more of the tame character it presented below Bonn.
At Bingen we took in a large accession of passengers,
most of whom seem to have gone there on a pleasure excursion, with the boats from Mainz in the
morning, and to be now returning to their homes
with us.   Passing the famous wine-districts of
Rudesheim, Geissenheim, Johannisberg, &c., we
reached Mainz about seven, and took up our abode
at the Rheinische Hof.   As we had dined on board
the steamer, at an excellent table-d'hôte, we had
time to stroll about the town in the twilight.   The
streets were filled with people enjoying the fine
evening.

CHAPTER IV.

August 7.——Before breakfast I took a drive
round the environs of Mainz. The new gardens,
laid out on a rising ground opposite the mouth of
the Main, are only worth seeing from the beautiful
view they afford of the junction of the two rivers,
the city, and the distant hills. More interesting
spots are those where the shattered remains of the
Tower of Drusus (Augustus's son-in-law) and of the
great aqueduct that supplied the city with water, re-
call the memory of the wonderful people who erected
them. There are said still to remain upwards of
sixty pillars (out of 500) of the aqueduct, but I only
saw eight or ten, sufficient, however, to show the
greatness of the work. The pillars are worn by
decay into the shape of pyramids. After breakfast
we visited the cathedral, a splendid structure of
great antiquity, built of the red sandstone of the
country. It is, to my taste, especially its dome, a
most beautiful piece of architecture. Unfortunately,
it is closely surrounded by houses, and the view of

it thereby much obstructed. The interior is not fine in an architectural point of view, but is very interesting from the great number and variety of the ancient monuments with which it is filled. Many of these are admirably executed. Like so many of the Rhine cities, Mainz has greatly suffered from war, and this cathedral has had more than its share of evil in this way.

Mainz is a very handsome town : the houses are large and lofty; many of the streets are extremely picturesque, from their narrowness and the antique character of the architecture, and some are very handsome from their width. Among the finer modern buildings, the theatre deserves notice. It is remarkable for its size and its semicircular front. In the adjoining square is the statue of Gutemberg. Mainz is built close to the Rhine, the natural banks of the river being replaced by lofty and extensive quays, which give an imposing aspect to the place. It communicates with the opposite bank by a bridge of boats.

We left Mainz at eleven by the railway, travelling through a very uninteresting country to Frankfurt, where we arrived about half-past twelve. Being anxious to see Danneker's famous statue of Ariadne, and knowing that it was not to be seen after one, we drove at once, baggage and all, through the town, to the place where it is exhibited, and arrived just before the doors were shut. It is a fine piece of sculpture. The woman's figure is good, but there seems to me something ludicrous in the way in which she rests on the back of so small an animal. The town was so full, owing to the presence of the congress, that we had some difficulty in gaining admission at the hotels; but we were at last accepted at the *Weisser Schwan*, where we arrived just while the table-d'hôte was in progress, and took our places among some fifty or sixty who were assisting at the same interesting ceremony. Here, as everywhere else, we found those dinners excellent, blameable only in being much over-sumptuous, and somewhat puzzling at first to the English traveller from what seemed an unnatural perversion in the chronological order of the dishes.

Frankfurt is a fine town, with many splendid streets and much good civic architecture. Its beauties are, however, mostly of a modern character, and, therefore, less interesting and picturesque than Mainz. On setting out on our journey, we had made a resolution not to visit museums and picture-galleries——things better unseen than seen imperfectly, as must have been the case with us; and as Frankfurt boasts of no fine churches we had plenty of time to see all that we wished to see. We visited the cathedral, however, but found nothing to repay us for the trouble. We also visited the old Stadthaus, called the *Römer*. It has a miserable exterior, and its interior is not much better; but it has an historical charm about it, as the place where the German emperors were elected in former times.

3

The room in it called the *Kaisersaal,* is adorned
with a series of portraits or fancy-portraits of all the
emperors.   These are of recent execution, and are
interesting as illustrations of the costume of the different periods, and of what the artists considered as
the peculiar character of the individuals.   Many of
them are well painted.

We made the circuit of the town; but as it lies
in a plain, there is little to be seen around it but
a series of garden-houses lining the road or boule-
vards, very much like the outskirts of an English
town.   The street or quay along the river Main is
fine, as well as the principal street in the centre of
the town, called the Zeil.   There is a good bronze
statue of Goethe, by Schwanthaler, in a small mall
near the centre of the town; and one of Charlemagne, in the centre of the bridge over the river.

Aug. 8.——A beautiful morning.   We breakfasted
at five, in order to be in time to join the train for
Heidelberg, which started at six.   The railway is an
excellent one, and seems in every respect well ma-
naged.   The tract over which it passes is perfectly
flat, being along the alluvial valley of the Rhine.
This alluvial plain, which began to form at Mainz
on the cessation, or rather on the secession from
the river, of the mountains heretofore so closely
bounding it, is here of great extent, the ranges on
its two sides being more than fifty miles apart.
The road, until we get beyond Darmstadt, is very
uninteresting, but afterwards it is quite the re-

verse. The railway takes nearly the same course as the old carriage-road, called the *Bergstrasse*, running the whole way at a little distance from the base of the beautiful mountain-range called the Odenwald. This range is almost identical in its characters with the mountain-ranges which border the Rhine so closely from Bonn to Bingen, having all the charms and striking features of that romantic tract——the same richly-wooded hills, crowned with their frequent castles, and looking down on the sheltered villages at their base, smiling amid their well cultivated fields. There could hardly be a better course for a railway, combining, as it does, the flatness of the rich plain with the constant and near prospect of the finest mountain scenery. We reached Heidelberg at ten o'clock.

Intending to proceed with one of the afternoon trains to Baden Baden, on our arrival at the Heidelberg terminus we transferred our luggage to the Baden station, and went into Heidelberg. After breakfasting at the Badischer Hof, we walked along the splendid street of Heidelberg——for it has hardly more than one——up to the celebrated castle on the hill at its south-eastern extremity. This is a magnificent ruin, well worthy of being seen for its own attractions, but still more for the delightful view from its terrace, of the city of Heidelberg and the beautiful valley and river lying immediately below it. The Neckar has here all the characteristic beauties of a highland river, rapid, bold, and tortuous, and hemmed in with mountains; it is also seen, farther on, after leaving the gorge of Heidelberg, as a lowland stream, winding its lazy way through the alluvial plain all the way to the Rhine at Mannheim.

After seeing the castle, we provided ourselves with asses kept ready for the occasion, and rode up by a very excellent path, shaded throughout with wood, to the top of the Kaiserstuhl, the highest point of ground in the neighbourhood, and which is sur-mounted by a lofty tower built purposely to facilitate the view from it. Although the day was fine, yet there was a slight haze in the plains, which prevented our seeing things clearly in the extreme distance. We did not see the spire of Strasburg Cathedral, visible from hence in a clear day, but we had never-theless a magnificent view, and to a great extent around. Chains of mountains were seen on every hand; the Odenwald and Taunus to the north and north-west; the Schwartzwald or Black Forest to the south; and the Haardt mountains, the northern continuation of the Vosges, on the west, beyond the Rhine. The vast valley of the Rhine lay stretched, a perfect flat, before us, with the river, like a thin streak of light on a dark ground, winding in the midst.

Looking down on this vast plain from our present position, noting its marked alluvial aspect, and the striking contrast it presents to its mountain boun-daries, and considering the nature and direction of these boundaries, and their more or less perfect approximation at both extremities of their course, it is impossible not to receive the immediate impression that it must have been, at some former period, the bottom of an immense lake extending lengthwise from Basel to Mainz, two hundred miles; with the Swartzwald and Odenwald ranges for its eastern shores, and the Vosges and Haardt mountains for its western. These ranges, or their associated chains, are not far apart in the district of Basel; and we have seen them at their southern limits gradually approximating, until at last, at Mainz and Bingen, they absolutely unite, all trace of the alluvial plain disappearing, and nothing remaining but a rocky channel just wide enough for the transmission of the stream. Whether this lake was drained suddenly by some convulsion rending asunder its southern barrier, or whether the draining was gradually effected by the progressive wearing away of the rock until the river descended to its present level, or whether both agencies co-operated, I leave for geologists to decide,—if they have not decided already, as is most likely. I can, however, entertain no doubt that, once on a time, the spectator from our station on the Kaiserstuhl, could have seen only a magnificent lake where the valley of the middle Rhine now spreads to the sun its green pastures and cultivated plains.

We left Heidelberg for Baden Baden, by the railway, at four. Our course was still pretty close along the base of the mountains—now the Schwartzwald—for the greater part of our way. As was the case at Heidelberg, when we came opposite to Baden we left our former track, turning at right angles into the mountain-valley in which this beautiful and fashionable town is built. We arrived at seven o'clock, and took up our abode at the Hôtel de l'Europe, a splendid establishment. In the evening we strolled into the famous gambling house, called the *Conversationshaus*, but we found there only a very scanty supply of performers. The political troubles of the time had ruined the trade.

Aug. 9.——After breakfast we proceeded to visit a summer palace of the Grand Duke, called Schloss Eberstein, about eight or ten miles distant. We drove through the valley of Lichten, and by the convent of Lichtenthal, to the hills lying to the east of the valley of Baden. We soon came to the end of the valley, which continues richly wooded and richly cultivated until it terminates in the ascent of the hills everywhere surrounding it. Up these hills there is an excellent carriage-road which winds gently and gracefully amid its continuous shade of magnificent trees, the white Tannen, until it brings us in view of the Murg; then turning down the northern brow of the hill, it leads us, by a gentle descent on its western side, to the castle of Eberstein. This castle, so called by courtesy, though it has now few of the attributes of a castle except its site, is built on one of the most charming spots that can well be conceived, on the flattened top of a rounded promontory rising precipitously from the valley of the Murg, and backed by an amphitheatre of lofty hills wooded to the very top.

Berg Eberstein thrusts forwards its steep and shaggy base into the very centre of the narrow valley through which the Murg runs, thus at once narrowing the extent of the valley, and making the river take a sudden bend to the eastward ere it resumes its former direction. By this means, the castle not only overlooks the stream at its base, but commands the same complete view of it and its valley, both up and down, as if it were built *over* the stream, and not at one side of it. And few scenes, I think, can excel in richness and quiet beauty those which are here presented to the eye, making New Eberstein the very *beau idéal* of a summer residence. Additional liveliness was given to the landscape by the numerous rafts of timber which were floated down the stream, the shallowness of which, in many places, made considerable exertions necessary on the part of the conductors to avoid running aground. Besides the near views, we had also, through the opening in the hills made by the Murgthal, a fine prospect of the valley of the Rhine backed by the Vosges mountains. The so-called castle is small. Its interior has been recently renovated, and is neatly fitted up in the antique style. It contains an armoury, and some pieces of antique sculpture worth seeing. Our time not permitting us to proceed further into the Murgthal, we returned by the same route, and then strolled about the town till dinner-time.

We of course visited the sources of the hot springs in the Schneckengarten, behind the Pfarr-kirche. They are several in number, and the hottest is of the temperature of 155° Fahrenheit. When uncovered they smoke like a cauldron, and may well have suggested the irreverent name (Hölle) by which this part of the town is distinguished. The water is conveyed through pipes to supply the baths in diffe-rent parts of the town. We took one before dinner at one of the Hotels : the temperature by my ther-mometer was 96° Fahr., and this was stated to be the temperature commonly used.——The church is a large and antique structure well worth seeing : it con-tains some good monuments and tolerable pictures ; it has a fine ornamental roof, and is extremely clean, and neatly fitted up. The great pump-room (Die Trinkhalle) is a very handsome structure which has only been erected a few years. In front it has a wide handsome portico running its whole length, protecting the frescoes with which the exterior wall is covered. These are all illustrative of popular legends of the Black Forest, and were executed, I believe, by Götzenberger. I know not what judg-ment the learned pass on these frescoes ; but some of them, at least, are very obviously of inferior de-sign and execution : as a whole, however, the effect is pleasing.

It is impossible not to be delighted with the whole exterior aspect of Baden Baden, with its handsome houses scattered here and there amid rich green meadows interspersed with fine trees, and its over-hanging hills beautifully wooded and crowned with ruins.   Even without its social allurements—per-haps more so without these—it would be an attrac-tive place of residence.

We took our departure in the train for Kehl, which left at seven.   The railway follows the course of the little river which drains the valley, the Oesbach, and soon joins the main line.   Here we changed carriages, and also further on, where the Kehl railway joins the great Baden line.   At Kehl we provided ourselves with a conveyance to Stras-burg, which is about four miles distant.   Kehl is on the right bank of the Rhine, and in the Baden territory.   The Rhine is here parted into two streams by an intermediate island, and consequently there are two bridges, both of boats, to be crossed. The French custom-house is on the island, and we stopped at the first village to have our baggage examined by the *douaniers*.   This process was speedily and very civilly gone about, and no inquiry was made for passports, either here or at Strasburg. We arrived at the Hôtel de Paris, a large but rather indifferent house, about ten o'clock.

Aug. 10.——After breakfast we proceeded to inspect the town.   Strasburg is a fine old city, exactly in the German style of Mainz and Frankfurt.   It has the great disadvantage of being built on a perfect flat, in the midst of an extensive plain surrounding it on every side.   It contains some very handsome

3 §

houses, white, lofty, and antique, like its fellow cities
of Germany; but nothing really attractive but its
glorious minster, and, perhaps, Marshal Saxe's monument in St. Thomas's church.   The former has
attractions, even in itself, to justify a long journey
for the sole purpose of visiting it.   Although it is
chiefly celebrated for its matchless spire, the highest
in the world, it is hardly less distinguished for its
grand interior.   Altogether it is one of the most
eminent of those architectural marvels of the middle
ages which still remain, in all their completeness, to
put to shame our modern attempts in the same field
of art.   The main fabric of the church was founded
so early as the beginning of the eleventh century,
and required one hundred and sixty years for its
completion.   The spire was not begun till the
church was finished : it was designed and partly
built by Erwin Von Steinbach, and required the
same lengthened period for its completion as the
church itself.   It is said to have been finished in
1439.   Like so many other cathedrals, this still
remains unfinished, the second spire of the original
design being yet to be built.   It is only on mounting to the top of the church, that the incomparable
lightness of structure of the spire can be seen :
it is a piece of open stone-work from top to
bottom.   We ascended to the top of the tower,
but did not mount into the spire.   The view is
extensive, but the mountains seen from it, the
Vosges and Schwartzwald, are too distant and too

little elevated to constitute either a grand or beautiful prospect.

At the time of our visit, the vast interior space of the cathedral was filled by the magnificent voice of one of the choir assisting at the ceremony of the mass. We did not fail, of course, to attend at twelve o'clock, to witness the wonderful performances of the famous clock, which is certainly a very ingenious piece of mechanism, but rather too ludicrous in its effect for its solemn locality. A great crowd was collected to see the show and hear the cock, which crowed marvellously well for a bird whose lungs are a pair of bellows. While waiting in the crowd, I entered into conversation with a young French soldier who stood near me; and his simple story, frankly and unaffectedly related, in reply to my inquiries, was a fair specimen of that disenchantment of war's glories which we so constantly find on looking into the private life and feelings of war's main agents. The poor fellow was only one-and-twenty; was a fine, tall, well-made man, and would have had a handsome face, but for the dreadful disfigurement of the smallpox. About a year and a half before, he had been drawn for the conscription, much to his sorrow, and had been sent from his native village, in the west of France, to this garrison. Shortly after his arrival he was seized with smallpox, from which he recovered, after a very long illness, and with his present disfigurement. As the talk at this time was all of war, I asked him whether he was not anxious to join the army then said to be assembling on the frontiers of Italy, to resist the Austrians in Lombardy, and so enter on the same career which, in the days of Napoleon, had made marshals and princes of men like him. He shook his head with a mingled expression of incredulity and disgust : the only thing near his heart was the hope that he might, after a time, be allowed to get back to *home!*

The upper and middle classes in Strasburg speak both French and German, but the more common language is the latter, and the lower class of people speak nothing else.

We took our dinner at the table-d'hôte of the Hôtel de Paris, and started for Basel (Bâle) by the train which leaves at twenty minutes past four. This is an excellent railway, about eighty miles in length, and running throughout on the perfectly level surface of the great Rhine alluvium. The train passed through no places of importance, except Colmar and Mulhausen. On leaving Strasburg it took a direction somewhat from the course of the Rhine to the south-west, and soon brought us near to the range of the Vosges mountains, along the line of which our whole subsequent course to Basel lay.

The plain through which we passed is extremely fertile, and without one uncultivated spot, except a few small plantations of copsewood at very distant intervals. We kept very nearly at the same distance from the base of the mountains the whole way, perhaps about two or three miles; and it would not be easy to over-praise the diorama which was presented to us as we passed along. It was remarkably similar to that already noticed on the other side of the Rhine, from Darmstadt to Baden, but was, if anything, still more beautiful. One thing greatly in favour of the present scene was, the state of the weather and time of the day. It was a most lovely afternoon, and during the first part of our journey, the sun shone brightly on the eastern slope of the hills, so as to exhibit all their charms to the greatest advantage.

Like the eastern boundary, this chain of the Vosges may be said to be composed of a basic mountain-mass, broken at its top and on its sides into a continuous series of conical hills, covered with wood, and ever and anon crowned with castles in various degrees of dilapidation and decay. The lower parts of the chain are cleared of wood, and converted into cultivated fields crowded with villages, which are very conspicuous with their lofty spires and whitewashed walls. Although quite below the base of the hills, they are built on ground still someway above the level of the plains, and therefore come well into view from the railway. Their great number and size show a very extensive population, which at first sight seems out of all proportion to the extent of the immediate district. But as there appears to be no habitations except in these villages, and as the plain between the mountains and the river is many miles in extent, the seeming anomaly is explained. As the train passed along, and the villages came into view one after another, they appeared to be hardly more than a mile apart. The prospect was the more charming from the contrast presented between our perfectly flat position on the railway, and the bold and sunny scenes hung up, as it were, for our special inspection and admiration. It was impossible to look on this beautiful barrier, unbroken as it is by a single lateral valley to show what is beyond, without feeling a desire to penetrate into its recesses, and explore the rich and picturesque valleys which, doubtless, it incloses.

About Colmar we had an addition to our party in the carriage——but only for a stage or two——in the person of a pretty young damsel, who made herself very agreeable to us all by her good humour and clever talk. She lived in one of the villages which so charmed us, but which did not appear to her quite so charming as they did to us. She complained— neither in sorrow nor in anger — still she complained ——that the country was not so good a country as it looked, at least for persons who are at all educated, or whose occupation is not merely manual and rural. She said the progressive subdivision of property had reduced all to one level. All, she admitted, had enough to eat and drink, and wherewithal to be clothed ; but only this,——there was no money not merely to buy luxuries and accomplishments, but not even to educate, except in the humblest style ; there was, in a word, no gentility, no meet sphere for minds raised by nature or culture above the one low level. This exposition of our clever and merry fellow-traveller, somewhat disenchanted my fairyland-scape and its happy villages; but still it was some-thing if the great majority were comfortable and even happy according to their views. We had many conjectures after our companion left us, as to who and what she was; but we could not agree in our opinions.

We arrived at Basel, or Bâle, at half-past nine, and drove to the Trois Rois. This is a magnificent hotel, built so close to the Rhine that the walls of its river-front are literally in the river. The grand Speisesaal or *salle à manger*, occupies this side of the house, and leads into an open gallery running its whole length. The river is here deep, and there is something at once beautiful and striking in seeing and hearing, as you walk the gallery, the noble stream still rushing along against its base, only a few feet below you. With the exception of the Schweitzer Hof at Luzern, which commands the incomparable view of the Lake and its surrounding mountains,—and perhaps, also, the Couronne at Geneva,—this hotel is the most delightfully situated of any we met with in our tour; and, as far as we could judge from a couple of nights spent in it, it seems as desirable for its special qualities as an inn, as for its charming locality.

As the professed object of our tour, as I have

already stated, was to see the country, not the towns —our allotted time would not allow us to do both, we resolved to start for Schaffhausen early next morning, without making any attempt to see Basel. Accordingly we arranged over night, through our landlord, with a voiturier, to take us to Schaffhausen the following day.   Our voiturier or Kutscher was one of those travelling freebooters who go about Switzerland with their own carriages and horses, picking up tourists wherever they can, and going with them wherever they will.   He engaged to carry us to Schaffhausen in one day, a distance of fifty-four or fifty-six miles, with the same pair of horses, on condition that we started early.   For this we engaged to pay him 60 francs (French), with the usual *Trinkgeld* contingent on our satisfaction with his performance.

As we were now going to start on our tour in earnest,—our journey hitherto being merely pre- liminary,—we selected from our grand luggage- stores all that was indispensable for travellers and nothing that was superfluous, and filling our knap- sacks therewith left our trunks to be forwarded by the Diligence to Luzern.

CHAPTER V.

August 11.—A most lovely morning. We had arranged to start at six, but did not get away until half-past. We crossed the Rhine by the bridge at Basel, and pursued our course, by an excellent though somewhat hilly road, close along its right bank. The Rhine at Basel changes its course entirely, now running east and west, instead of north and south as we had hitherto tracked it. It still continues to be the boundary of the Baden territory, into which we entered very shortly after we had crossed the bridge. The road continued to run close to the river's bank for about thirty-five miles,—that is, until we passed the small town of Waldshut. As the stream takes there a considerable bend to the south, the road pursued its former direction across the bight of land, and did not again touch the river until it reached Schaffhausen.

So long as we kept the Rhine for our near companion, the drive continued beautiful. The scenery was less grand than a good deal that we had seen lower down, but still it was far from tame, and was agreeably varied. Generally speaking, the side of the river on which we travelled was much flatter, or rather much less elevated, than the left bank, which presented to us all along the same charming prospect of lofty and wooded hills, which had bounded so much of our previous routes; while the noble stream, now almost on a level with our path, now far below it, but hardly ever out of sight or hearing, kept by us like a cheerful companion, vivifying and brightening each new scene that was presented to us. I think any one who has made the journey from Basel to Waldshut, as we made it——in an open carriage, and in a beautiful summer's day,——would feel that it is not one to be readily foregone.

We first stopped at Säkingen, a small town about sixteen miles from Basel, to refresh our horses. This has the air of having been formerly a place of greater distinction; and it was so, if, as I presume, it was the Säkingen in Suabia, the abbess of which is said to have had once the whole canton of Glarus as an appanage. I saw no signs, however, of an abbey; but the church seems of a size and style disproportioned to the present extent of the town. Although recently repaired, it is evidently old, and contains many monuments, and the usual stock of paintings and gaudy decorations of a Catholic church. There were a few women in it at their private devotions.

At the further end of the town there is a cemetery close on the banks of the river, and half surrounded by it, into which I strolled after leaving the church. In a small open chapel at one end of it I found two men and three women at their prayers, kneeling before a large image of Christ.   One of the men was reading the prayers aloud from a German prayer-book, with great correctness of pronunciation and emphasis, and with much apparent earnestness and devotion. The prayers, which were addressed alternately to the Virgin, Christ, and our Heavenly Father, and in the order of frequency here set down, seemed to possess the fine old nervous style of the English Liturgy. The people were all of the humbler class, very plainly yet neatly dressed ; and the reader, I was informed, was a layman of the village, in the same rank of society.   There was something very impressive in this exercise of devotion at such a time, in such a place, and by such persons ; and it was impossible, while listening to the solemn and earnest words of the humble man who officiated, and the unaffected responses of his hearers, not to feel that the devotion could not be wrong in them, whatever opinions might be held respecting some of the objects of it.

Säkingen, like every other town and village in Suabia and Switzerland, has, of course, its fountains in the public street, pouring out into stone reservoirs a never-ceasing supply of the most delicious water, and refreshing the traveller's ear by the very sound before he can see them.   The day being hot and the realms of ceremony being far passed by, some of our party, after taking refreshment in the inn, very naturally resorted to the fountain at its door to make amends for the absence of finger-

glasses within.   One of our number availed himself
of this luxury not only here, but at a village further
on, Dogern by name, where we also stopped, and,
being a wearer of rings——which no traveller should
be——he laid them on the fountain brim, and there
left them!   The loss was not discovered until we
had advanced some miles on our journey beyond
the place of the last ablution, and then it could not
be recollected at which of the two places the finery
had been left.   Consequently, although the rings
were of considerable value, we made no retrograde
step to recover them, but contented ourselves with
sending despatches to the innkeepers of the respective villages from the small town of Thiengen, where
we dined.   But the ring-bearing ring-loser, as might
have been expected, heard no more of his property.

About midway between Säkingen and Waldshut
we passed the small town of Lauffenburg, built
partly on our bank of the river, but principally on
the left.   It is here where the road from Basel to
Schaffhausen, which takes the Swiss side of the
Rhine, crosses the stream and joins the road we
travelled.   It is here, also, where the Lesser Falls
of the Rhine are to be seen.   The steep hill which
we had to ascend before reaching the town, indicated
the probable extent of the Fall, which, however, is
more of the nature of a rapid than a fall.   The river
rushes down a rugged slope, with much sound and
fury, but makes no positive leap or fall.   But it is
well worth the traveller's while to stop for a few

minutes to examine it, and to take a view of the wider scenery of which it forms a part. Boats can both ascend and descend the rapid, but they require to be freed from baggage and passengers. It was in descending this rapid that Lord Montagu, of Cowdray, in Sussex, was drowned.

Waldshut is a neater and more town-looking place than we had yet passed through since leaving Basel. A short way beyond it, just where the road turns off from the river bank, the Rhine receives its great Swiss tributaries, the Limmat, Reuss, and Aar, which, having previously united their streams under the name of the Aar, here mingle their white waters with the greener Rhine. The road from Waldshut to Schaffhausen, during the greater part of its course, presents nothing worth notice, the country being mostly open and well cultivated, with little wood or variety of surface. As it approaches the Rhine it reassumes its more picturesque character; but we had little opportunity of seeing this on the present occasion, except, indeed, by moonlight, as we did not reach our destination until near ten o'clock. We did not go on to the town of Schaffhausen, but proceeded at once to Weber's splendid hotel, which stands directly fronting the great Rhine-fall.

Later in the evening, we walked out on the terrace in front of the hotel, to enjoy the view of the falls by moonlight. The evening was as lovely as the day had been; warm, cloudless, and without a breath of wind. The huge white mass of tumbling foam lay straight before us, the only bright spot in the dimly-lighted landscape, and attracting and fixing the eye exclusively on itself. No sound was heard but the one continuous roar of the water, softened by the distance, and seeming to fill the whole air, like the moonshine itself. There was something both wild and delightful in the hour and its accompaniments. The mind yielded passively to the impressions made on the senses. A host of half-formed, vague, and visionary thoughts crowded into it at the same time, giving rise to feelings at once tender and melancholy, accompanied with a sort of objectless sympathy or yearning after something unknown. The ideas and emotions most definite and constant were those of Power and Perpetuity, Wonder and Awe. What was now impressing the senses and the mind seemed a part of something infinite which they could neither comprehend nor shake off : the same mass, the same rush, the same roar, day and night, year after year, age after age, now and for ever! A fanciful ideologist of the Hartley school might explain all this by supposing that an unmanageable idea—that of *Eternity* to wit—had got into some cranny of the brain too small and weak either to contain or sustain it, and had thus given rise to a sort of intellectual *Fall*, just as has here betid the Rhine, struggling in its rocky channel and overleaping its broken barriers. Hence, in both cases, the whirl and confusion, the hubbub and hurlyburly.

Aug. 12.—Weber's Hotel is admirably situated, exactly in front of the falls, and at about the same elevation as themselves, on the right bank of the river. The valley of the Rhine is here narrow, so that the inn is hardly more than a furlong from the Fall, if so much : the sudden bend of the river to the south, almost at right angles to its former course, immediately on descending the precipice, allows the hotel to stand, as I have stated, exactly in front of the Falls. Our bedroom window looked on the river, and we went to sleep and waked with the same everlasting sound in our ears. The morning was extremely fine, and immediately after breakfast we proceeded to make a closer inspection of the great object of our visit. Descending the little hill on which the hotel stands, and which is nearly all included in its own grounds, we crossed the river in a ferry-boat, and mounted to the little village which occupies the angle where the river makes its turn. A gentleman, a professional artist and teacher of drawing, has cleverly built his house in such a position as to monopolise all the good near views of the Fall. Accordingly, every visitor must pass through his rooms and into his private galleries, within doors and without, to see the sight, and must pay toll in the transit.

In the gallery within the house we are placed close to the fall, but raised considerably above it : in the outer or lower gallery we stand quite close to the fall, indeed over a portion of it—about its

mid descent.   The former view is the finest, or at
least the most pleasing, as from it you can look
down and see the whole extent and process of the
fall in tranquillity and comfort.   The latter view,
however, is, by much, the most striking and awful,
as here you seem almost to be involved and to take
part in the mighty work that is going forward.
The roar is quite deafening, and gusts of wind from
the concussion of the water shake the gallery on
which you stand, and wet you with a continued
shower of spray.   The enormous mass of water
shoots over the precipice almost above your head,
and is dashed and tortured into whirls and globes
of foam close to your feet.   The eye and the ear
become, in a short time, in some manner fascinated
by the objects before them, and the mind seems to
imbibe the impressions conveyed to it as if it were
stunned or stupified.   Standing and gazing and
listening here, one seems to understand the possibility of that mental state which is said to have led
to voluntary death under circumstances of terrible
danger or in positions offering the means of in-
stantaneous and facile destruction.

In regard to the general effect of these Falls on
the mind, I think I might say that they impressed
the intellect much less than the feelings.   The first
view was somewhat disappointing, particularly as to
the dimensions of the Falls, both in breadth and
height; and as I gazed I felt a sort of critical calcu-
lating spirit rising within me; but this was speedily

subdued by something in the inner mind beyond reasoning, and there only remained behind, such ideas and emotions as I have vainly attempted to describe. Milton makes his Adam and Eve tell us that they "feel they are happier than they know :" the spectator of the Rhine-falls feels they are grander than he thinks.

We renewed our contract with our freebooter Kutscher, after some misgivings respecting the weal of the poor horses : he engaged to convey us to Zurich, distant about thirty miles, for a napoleon, with the wonted Trinkgeld. We left our magnificent inn at eleven, and reached Zurich about seven.

Shortly after starting, we came once more into the territory of Baden, which here runs up to the Rhine in a sort of nook, which is only five or six miles in extent. We then entered on the territory of Canton Zurich. The road the whole way, though hilly, is admirable, almost better than is generally found in England. Indeed, all the public roads in this and the neighbouring cantons are excellent ; they have been made, or rather re-made, within the last twenty or twenty-five years. The country through which we passed, speaking generally, possessed no features of grandeur, but was decidedly beautiful, richly cultivated, and well wooded, with a finely varied surface, hilly but not mountainous. The farms seemed in some places of considerable extent, contrasting, in this respect, with most of the other districts of Switzerland which we afterwards passed through.

The direction of our route was nearly south the

4

whole way; and as the Rhine, after its bend at the
Falls, takes the same course for ten miles or so, the
first part of our journey ran parallel with the river,
but at the distance of two or three miles from it.
Indeed, we scarcely saw it until after it had resumed
its original westerly course; and as this was at right
angles to ours, we saw it only to cross it: this we
did at the small town of Eglisau, by a fine wooden
bridge.   The brief glimpse we had here once more
of this glorious river, so long our companion, made
us regret still more to leave it behind us: it was
beautiful in the extreme.   The banks on both sides
consisted of hills of considerable height, richly
wooded to the top, and coming so close together
at the base as to leave a narrow channel for the
river to pass through.   The channel, however, was
not so contracted as to hamper the stream, otherwise than somewhat to deepen it; and as the fall of
the ground was moderate, and the bottom apparently
smooth, the current, though rapid and strong, was
perfectly calm and noiseless.   The water was of
deep green, and as the sun shone into it you
could see almost to the bottom.   Altogether, I
think it would not be easy to find a more charming
scene, on a small scale, than that which meets the
traveller's eye as he looks down from the brow of
the hill into the valley of the Rhine at Eglisau.

About five miles beyond this we stopped at the
small town of Bulach to refresh our horses and ourselves.   The inn was small but very clean, and we

made a passable dinner on the usual dish of extempore soup, chops name unknown, and trout and potatoes. We entered into Zurich by a long hill of gentle descent, and in descending, had full time to admire its fine site on the shore of its beautiful lake. We drove through the town, across the bridge on the Limmatt, and put up at the famous Hotel Bauer.

As the evening was very fine we took advantage of the remaining light to see as much as we could, our purpose being to leave Zurich early next morning. Our first step was to ascend to the belvedere on the top of the hotel. From this we had an excellent view of the whole town, with its lake and river. We had also the good fortune to see a most lovely sunset lighting up the lofty mountains on the west, the chains of the Utliberg and Albis. Zurich is situated at the northern extremity of the lake, just where the Limmat issues from it, like a true lake-river, full grown and beautifully clear. It is in the valley formed by this stream, and on the shores on both sides of it, that the town is mainly built; but it also climbs the base of the surrounding hills to a considerable extent, at least on the eastern side. The environs are very fine, richly cultivated, and, like the whole shores of the lake, crowded with white neat-looking houses.

In Switzerland, any river discharging the waters of a lake, is supposed to be a continuation of the main river entering it at its further or higher end, however distant, and the latter usually takes the

name of the former.   Thus the Rhine retains its
name after passing, or being supposed to pass,
through the lake of Constance ; the Reuss after
traversing the lake of the Four Cantons; the Rhone
after traversing the lake of Geneva ; the Aar after
passing the lakes of Brienz and Thun.   It is thus
that the river, which here leaves the lake of Zurich,
obtains its title, although the word *Limmatt* has disappeared from the map as the name of any higher or
primary river.   This was the name formerly borne by
the unruly stream which conveyed the united waters
of the *Linth* and *Matt* into the upper extremity of
the lake, and which, since the grand engineering
feat of Escher, is known as the *Linth-Canal.*   The
name of the river is obviously a compound formed
of the names of its two primary branches.

I was fortunate enough to meet with a literary
friend here, one of the professors of the Zurich
University (Dr. Hasse), who, among other civilities,
planned for us an important alteration as well as
an extension of our intended route, for which we had
afterwards good reasons for being grateful.

Before bed-time we walked once more into the
town, at least that part of it adjoining the lake.
It was a most lovely evening, and the lake and town
looked beautiful in the moonlight.   As we stood on
the bridge over the Reuss there passed us a band of
young men, twenty or thirty in number, marching
in line, arm in arm, and all singing, in good style
and with great earnestness, a German song.   I was

informed by a townsman who stood near us as they passed, that they were members of a society which made nocturnal demonstrations of this sort a part of its transactions. Many of the singers wore conspicuous beards, all were neatly dressed, and there was no sign of intoxication in any one of the party. I naturally inferred that they belonged to one of those political or patriotic associations so fashionable of late years among the young men on the continent, and which have been distinguished by the epithet "Young" prefixed to the name of their country. I afterwards learnt that my inference was correct, and that the singers were, in fact, members of the ZOFINGER-VEREIN, or ZOFINGER UNION, a true "Young Switzerland" Society, which originated with the students of Zurich in the year 1819. The society takes its name from the small town of ZOFINGEN, where the first general meeting of the society was held; and the members call themselves ZOFINGERN, Zofingers. They are chiefly students and young men. The society in 1847 consisted of 275 members, belonging to ten different cantons. Their motto or symbol is "Vaterland—Freundschaft—Wissenschaft." The society inculcates the composition and singing of patriotic and social songs as a means of reviving and preserving a spirit of nationality and union in the country. There is a special song-book of the Verein published by Tschudi of Zurich, himself a Zofinger, containing numerous patriotic songs, one of which,

I doubt not, our zealous friends were now singing. It is curious that the first air in this collection is our " God Save the King," which seems to be adopted as the national anthem of the Swiss also. I subjoin a few of the verses which are here set to it, as it may interest some readers to see the style of a republican national song.   The original consists of seven verses.   I think the three which I here transcribe cannot fail to remind the readers of Burns, of his ' Bannockburn,' nor (I think) greatly to the disadvantage of the Swiss poet.

DEM VATERLAND.

Rufst du, mein Vaterland?
Sieh' uns mit Herz und Hand
    All' dir geweiht !
Heil dir Helvetia !
Hast noch der Söhne ja,
Wie sie Sankt Jacob sah,
    Freudvoll zum Streit !

Da wo der Alpenkreis
Nicht dich zu schützen weiss,
    —Wall dir von Gott,—
Steh'n wir den Felsen gleich,
Nie vor Gefahren bleich,
Froh noch im Todesstreich,
    —Schmerz uns ein Spott.

Frei und auf ewig frei
Ruf' unser Feldgeschrei,
    Hall' unser Herz !
Frei lebt wer sterben kann,
Frei, wer die Heldenbahn
Steight als ein TELL hinan,
    Nie hinterwärts !

CHAPTER VI.

August 13.——After an early breakfast at our excellent hotel, we went on board the steamboat lying at the quay, which sailed at eight. It was bound for Smerikon at the farther extremity of the lake, but we took our passage only to Horgen, a small town about ten miles distant on the western shore, and in the direction of the lake of Zug and the Rigi mountain, whither we were bound. The morning was beautiful, without a cloud, and the waters of the lake of the same bright blue as the sky. The ZÜRICHERSEE is a fine piece of water, and its boundaries are everywhere cheerful and rich,——green, however, more with cultivation than with woods, and nowhere rising into grandeur. The shores on both sides are lined with many pretty villages close by the water, and the whole slope of the hills is dotted with cheerful-looking white houses. We reached Horgen in about an hour.

The steamer was crowded with passengers. The great majority were persons of the lower classes, but they were all neatly and cleanly dressed. There was a full proportion of women, and all of them decked out in holiday attire, showing the characteristic costumes of various cantons. Some of these were very elegant; some simply odd; some very ugly. Among the ugly costumes were those of some women from Baden, whose heads were decorated with high-crowned, bright-yellow hats, precisely like men's hats. These women were going on the pilgrimage to Einsiedeln. Most of the women were very plain,——a term which, I fear, applies very generally to the sex in Switzerland, at least to the labouring class, in which we must reckon ninety-nine hundreds of the population. Nothing is such an enemy to good looks as hard work, and of this the women have here more than their share. The men, or a considerable portion of them at least, have many intervals of comparative ease, in hunting, in soldiering, in mule-driving and as guides; but the poor women are always at home and always at work, in-doors and out-of-doors. In consequence of this, they generally look older than they are. I questioned some of my male neighbours in the steamer, as to the probable age of several women we were looking at, and was told they were only forty or fifty, although I should have guessed them at ten or even fifteen years more.

On arranging for our passage on coming on board, we found we could engage for the whole journey by land as well as water; accordingly we

took our places all the way to Arth at the foot of
the Rigi, to which we were to be conveyed from
Horgen by means of a Diligence in connexion with
the steamboat. On landing we had to wait about
half an hour before the diligence was ready to start,
seemingly to afford time for breakfast. There were
passengers enow to occupy two supplementary carriages as well as the diligence. As is customary
in Switzerland, every one received a ticket and took
his place in the carriage according to his number.
By an early application to the conductor, I was fortunate enough to get my place with the driver, outside, and was thus enabled to have a complete view
of the country passed through, as well as to get some
local information from my companion, although he
was by no means a favorable specimen of a Swiss
driver. His language was a strong patois, and it
was only by hard work that our sole mutual medium,
German, enabled us to understand each other.

I may here remark, however, that with a knowledge of this language and French, no one will find
much difficulty of understanding or being understood in any part of Switzerland. In almost all the
cantons, if not in all, the language of the common
people is a broken German, and all the more intelligent of the men make themselves very well understood by one who knows German. At the inns,
the waiters all understand French as well as German ; and in every inn of any note, there is always
one or two waiters who understand and speak

4 §

English very fairly.   In the cantons of Geneva and
Neuchatel, also in some parts of the Vallais, Pays
de Vaud and in Piedmont, French is more generally
spoken; but the prevailing tongue of the main body
of the population throughout Switzerland, is German,
or, at least, a form of German; and it is impossible to
travel through the country, with either comfort or
much advantage, without a greater or less knowledge
of this language.   French alone will enable you to
make your way very comfortably through the hotels
and with the gentry; but without knowing German,
you will never know the people, nor obtain that
amount of local information which is essential to a
traveller.

There is a very fine new road all the way from
Horgen to Zug, though very steep in many parts,
especially for the first half of the journey, where it
climbs up the side of the Albis.   The ascent commenced immediately on leaving Horgen, and continued to zig-zag up the face of the hill for at least
four or five miles, the horses being obliged to walk
all the way on account of the steepness.   The whole
of our progress upwards was through a series of
lawn-looking slopes, highly cultivated and richly
wooded, the near beauties of which were greatly enhanced by the glimpses we had, at every turn of
the road, of the splendid sheet of water below us,
and the green hills on its further shore.   Our
descent from the brow of the hill was almost as
long and steep as our ascent had been, and the road

ran for some time in almost an opposite direction to that we had recently come. It took this course in order to gain the bottom of the valley of the Sihl before it traverses the chain of the Albis to join the Limmatt. We tracked the downward course of this stream for some time until we reached the bridge, after crossing which we turned sharply to the left, and then turned our course towards Zug, almost at right angles to the path we had been previously following. The valley of the Sihl reminded me of some of the Scottish valleys, with its clear and brawling stream, its rich but narrow meadows, and its finely-wooded banks.

We soon came in sight of the ZUGERSEE and the lofty mountains bounding its southern extremity, the Rigi group. On approaching the margin of the lake the ground became flatter, and we entered the old town of Zug, situated at its north-eastern extremity, by a gentle descent through well-cultivated and well-wooded meadows. Zug is a small town with some very antiquated towers and droll-looking streets, lying on the very margin of the lake. We stopped only a short time here, just long enough to enable us to see the church and the outlines of the place. The church is a fine large building, more modern-looking than the rest of the town, and presenting a full share of images, pictures, and altar decorations. On my return from the church, in which I only found a few women, and while waiting in the market-place till the horses were got ready,

I entered into conversation with a tradesman's wife, who was sitting with her child at the door of her shop, and I was not a little pleased with her common-sense remarks on the late war, on which subject I had questioned her. "It is governments," she said, "that make war—not the people; the people always wish for peace, and to be let alone." I could not help thinking of Goldsmith's verses:

"How small, of all that human hearts endure,
    That part which laws or kings can cause or cure!"

The road to Arth runs close to the very margin of the lake the whole way, on a small ledge of ground between it and the range of mountains which here bound it. This space is in some places so narrow as merely to afford room for the road; in others it widens into green slopes of more extent, yet still very narrow. Through its whole course it is shaded by trees, fruit trees and others, and overhung by magnificent hills wooded to the very top. These hills, which are formed by the back of the Rossberg, become steeper and steeper as we approach Arth. This is a very small town jammed, as it were, into a corner, by the Rossberg, the Rigi, and the lake. We arrived here at about half-past one, and after taking a slight luncheon to fit us for our purposed ascent of the mountain, we set out on our journey a little after two o'clock, two of us walking with our knap-sacks on our backs, the third on horseback; I was one of the walkers.

As the day was extremely hot, the thermometer

standing at 79° in the shade, we took due care to apportion our apparel to "the corporal feat" we were undertaking; a precaution always very necessary, and soon found to be particularly so on the present occasion. Our course for the first two miles, as far as the village of Goldau, was along the high road to Schwytz, with very little ascent : we then turned sharp to the right, with our faces to the Rigi. For a mile further, the path lay through cultivated fields, and the ascent was moderate; but then we were fairly on the spurs of the mountain, and the path became suddenly very steep. The path was also very rough from loose stones (the mountain is of pudding stone), and was in many places crossed by wooden steps, partly, I presume, for aiding the ascent, and partly for preventing the path being carried away by the rains. The first third of the ascent is so very steep as to be quite like a stair, even although the path takes a zig-zag direction in the greater part of it.

Without ever considering that this was my first essay in pedestrianism since leaving London, and making no due allowance for the great heat, I very thoughtlessly started on my walk at full speed. But I was soon made aware of my imprudence, and painfully reminded of the " non sum qualis eram" which meets the sexagenarian on so many occasions. The process of ascending after a short time gave rise to an oppressive constriction on the chest, with breathlessness, and a severe throbbing in the head. It was obvious that the muscular effort necessary to raise the body up an ascent so very steep, propelled a greater volume of blood upon the organs of circulation than they could easily dispose of; and in order to relieve them it was found necessary to make frequent stops, and even to lie down occasionally on the ground for a few minutes. This speedily relieved the oppression, and enabled me to proceed comfortably for a time. I was not at all tired or fatigued, in the ordinary meaning of these terms, but simply oppressed in the circulation and breathing; and when relieved by temporary rest, I could immediately proceed as vigorously as ever.

After going on about a mile I gave up my knapsack to a little girl of eleven, who had joined us at the bottom, and continued to accompany us, in hopes of being allowed to relieve me of my burthen. I for a time refused her request, being willing to prove my own powers, but at last was glad to consent, and felt considerably relieved on doing so. My little aide-de-camp was delighted to have the burthen transferred to her shoulders, and trudged and tripped along, whistling merrily, evidently caring nothing for it or the mountain.

The steep staircase-ascent continued for about two miles or rather more, and was succeeded by a tract, of about a mile in length, where the ascent was greatly less steep, and in some places quite level, or even with a small descent occasionally. So soon as I got upon ground like this I got on capitally, as I felt not the least fatigue of limb from the previous exertion. This easy path, which conducted us along the side of a beautiful ravine, was followed by ground of increased steepness, augmenting as we advanced towards the top of the mountain, but never approaching the steepness of the early ascent. About a mile or mile and a half from the summit I once more resumed my knapsack, as I was anxious that my little porter should be able to return home before it was dark. We reached the top about half-past six.

On arriving at the inn on the highest point called Rigi-Kulm, after a hurried toilet we walked out to see the view for which we had taken all this trouble. At this time I felt no fatigue, and no remains whatever of oppression on the chest. I could have then walked with perfect ease a much greater distance than I had done already, *on level ground:* a proof that my failure as a hill-climber depended on the cause already mentioned. In my subsequent trials I experienced a somewhat similar difficulty in like circumstances, but never to near the same extent ; and I can easily account for the greater distress on the present occasion, by the fact of my being much less prepared for this than for my other attempts. I had had no active walking since leaving England, and was, consequently, not in good condition to make the effort I did, on so steep a hill and in so very hot a day.* My fellow-traveller could have

* I give these egotistical details purposely, as a warning to others whose breathing and circulatory machinery may be likewise disproportionate to their general muscular vigour and their will.

easily reached the summit an hour or hour and a half sooner than we did together; but he very kindly waited for his more breathless senior.

The measured surface distance from Arth to the Rigi-Kulm is said to be nine miles. The actual vertical height of the Rigi, according to Keller, is about 5900 English feet above the sea, and about 4400 above the lake of Zug.

All along the path as we mounted there are many little chapels containing either figures or paintings; in one of them about midway, larger than the rest, there is a horrid figure of Christ carrying the cross, as large as life. They cease to be seen about two or three miles from the top, at a little village containing a small church devoted to the Virgin, called Mary of the Snow (Maria zum Schnee).

The evening was very fine, but though neither cloudy nor misty there was a slight haze in the air, which rendered the view of the more distant mountains indistinct; but the view was still very magnificent, and very varied. It was, however, much finer when seen, as we saw it, at sunrise on the following day, when the horizon was as clear as the nearer landscape. What most struck us, on the present occasion, were the snowy mountains towards the south-west, including, I believe, the Rothhorn, and the higher mountains of the chain which join on to Mount Pilatus and the lakes of Luzern and Zug. Both of these lakes washed the base of our mountain, but on different sides; the latter lay almost immediately below us ; the portion of the Rigi on which we stood rising sheer up from its waters. Several light, airy clouds, perfectly white, floated in mid-air between us and the lake, and added much to the beauty and picturesqueness of the scene. To the north of Mount Pilatus, but in a westerly direction, in the line of the setting sun, there was also an extensive prospect of wide plains and distant hills, spreading out in a sunny but indistinct haze, and losing themselves in the horizon. To the south, at an immense distance, we had the enormous snowy peaks of the Bernese Alps, indistinctly seen in the evening, but very clear in the morning, and rising high above the clouds. We also saw, in the morning, the snowy range of Alps to the east and southeast of us, including the mountains of Glarus, the Dödi and the Glärnish. Close to us, in the same direction, is the Rossberg, and far beyond it a snowy peak, which is said to be Mount Sentis, in the distant canton of Appenzel.

There can be no doubt of the grandeur of this view : yet, while fully admitting its magnificence and splendour, it appeared to me, on comparing it with some others seen afterwards, to lose in impressiveness from its very extent and variety. The mind seemed somewhat distracted by the great number of the objects it had to contemplate, one after another, and in every direction ; and the consequent impression was less profound than if the observation had been more concentrated. Yet, most assuredly,

no one who has seen the sunrise on the Rigi, or, I
should rather say, who has looked round the horizon
as it was rising, will ever regret having made the
ascent.

We waited on the Kulm a short time after the
setting of the sun, and then retreated to dinner.
There was a slight breeze, and the air felt quite cold
——presenting a very striking contrast with the intense
heat of the valley when we began to ascend.   The
thermometer stood now at 52°.   The hotel is quite
new, having been built only this summer.   It is on
the site of the old, and is considerably larger than
its predecessor.   It has a large eating-room on the
ground-floor, and numerous small bedrooms above.
We sat down to an excellent dinner, presenting the
usual profusion and variety of a German or Swiss
table-d'hôte.   There were about twenty-five persons at table, only five of whom were English.   We
retired before ten o'clock, with an understanding
that we were all to be summoned in the morning in
good time to see the sunrise.

CHAPTER VII.

August 14.—We were roused shortly after four by the loud notes of an Alpine horn, blown in the gallery of the house; and all the party were soon assembled on the highest point of the Rigi-Kulm. The morning was bright and without a cloud, show-ing all the views much more distinctly than on the preceding evening. The air was, however, very cold to our feelings, and we required all our coats to keep us warm while awaiting the sunrise. The thermometer showed the same temperature as last night, 52°. The sunrise was glorious, and the clearness of the atmosphere enabled us to observe distinctly the beautiful phenomenon—so often seen afterwards—of the gradual illumination of the snowy peaks according to their height, and the pro-gressive descent of the line of light on them as the sun ascended. After satiating and almost tiring our eyes by long and manifold speculation of the grand scenes on all sides of us, near and remote, we returned to the hotel, and having completed our

toilet, partook of a very fair breakfast of coffee, &c.,
and then started on our return to Goldau about half-
past six.

Deep beneath us and before us, as we left our
inn, lay the large town of Luzern and the small
town of Kussnach, at the extremities of their respective arms of the Waldstättersee ; the former at
some distance, the latter immediately below us.   I
regretted not being able to visit the latter, so famed
a spot in the history of William Tell.   Looking
down upon it, at the very base of the steep yet sloping
mountain that overhangs it, it was easy to understand the nature of the catastrophe that has sometimes befallen it from the sudden melting of the
snow on the mountain.   In the year 1778, the
small brook which runs through the village, was
suddenly raised thirty feet above its usual level ; it
destroyed five-and-twenty houses, and drowned about
sixty persons.

Besides the hotel on the Rigi-Kulm, there is a
smaller one half a mile lower down, called the Staf-
felhaus.   It is now more occupied as a lodging-
house than as an inn, invalids coming up here for a
month or two in the summer to enjoy the benefit of
the bracing air and the goats' milk.   As we passed
through the village of the church of Mary of the
Snow, there were a great many persons standing
and sitting about, and in a small open space near
the church several booths were set out, containing
the usual wares of a country fair on a small scale.

I went into the church, and found that mass was being performed to a rather thin assemblage. The church though small, is really large when we consider its site; it is decorated with the ordinary finery of such places. In our way downwards we met several small parties of pilgrims coming up, and others passed us going down. They were on their way to or from the famous Einsiedeln in Schwytz and our neighbour Mary of the Snow; all solemn and grave, and with earnestness of purpose in their determined walk. The descent was perfectly easy, and the walk through the greater part of it was delightful. The valley or ravine down the side of which we passed, with its steep walls of mingled rock and wood, and its small stream leaping from cliff to cliff, looked beautiful in the morning sun which shone directly along its course. We felt occasional inconvenience in the steeper parts, from the loose stones in the path.

We reached the small village of Goldau at nine, and put up at the Swan, a clean, comfortable house, with good fare and moderate charges. The landlady is the mother of no less than thirteen children, all of them grown up; and we were served at breakfast by a couple of her tidy daughters. The inn is one of the new houses built on the ruins of the Rossberg, and will be found a very desirable residence for a few days, for any traveller having time fully to explore the very interesting country that lies around it. The church close by, as well as the inn, and indeed all the houses of which the village of Goldau now consists, indicate by their looks a recent origin : they have been all erected since the fall of the Rossberg, on the 2d of September, 1806. This fall, and the attendant and resulting circumstances, must be reckoned among the most remarkable phenomena of a physical and local kind that have taken place on the surface of the globe within the memory of man. On the day named, a huge portion of the surface of that side of the mountain which slopes towards the village of Goldau, computed to have been full three miles in length, a thousand feet wide, and a hundred feet in depth, suddenly slid off from the subjacent rock, and rushed down into the valley, overwhelming this large village and two others, dashing huge rocks beyond the valley up to the base of the Rigi, and damming up a considerable portion of the lake of Lowertz several miles distant. The space covered by the fallen masses is three miles in width, and four or five in length ; and the masses themselves are heaped into huge hillocks, several of them some hundred feet in height. Three hundred houses were destroyed, and 450 of the inhabitants killed. Dr. Zay of Arth published an account of this catastrophe the year after its occurrence.* Amid much extraneous matter he notices many interesting occurrences. The whole process of the fall occupied only three or four minutes. Dr. Zay says, that the

---

* Goldau und seine Gegend ; wie sie war and was sie geworden. Von Dr. Karl Zay, Dr. in Arth ; Zurich, 1807.

mass of earth and stones which rushed into the lake of Lowertz, five miles distant, produced such a prodigious wave that the water rose at once from sixty to seventy feet beyond its usual level, overwhelming everything on its shores. The village of Seewen at its further extremity, and Steinen on its northern shore, but at a considerable distance from it, were inundated and damaged. During the fall, enormous blocks of stone appear to have been projected like cannon-balls to a great distance through the air. The wave raised in the lake carried everything before it. As evidence of the statement being correct as to the height of this wave, Dr. Zay says that he himself still saw, the day after, some hay on the spire of the small chapel of Schwanau, which had been left by the water at this elevation. At a village on the shore of the lake, the force of the water moved to some distance a huge stone, weighing more than a hundred quintals—" mehr als 100 schwere Zentner."

In leaving Goldau, on our way to Steinen, our road lay for several miles upon the new surface thus created, and partly on what had once been a portion of the lake of Lowertz. The whole still looks unnaturally angular and sharp and desolate enough, though Nature has evidently made some progress, chiefly through the agency of her vegetable ministers, in the work of restoration. In a hundred years more, the scene will have been restored to its pristine beauty ; perhaps even to a superior beauty, on account of its more varied surface ; and the traveller will then see here, what may be seen everywhere, in the moral as well as the physical world, how the losses of the past are the gains of the present :

> " Das Alte stürzt, es ändert sich die Zeit,
>   Und neues Leben blüht aus den Ruinen."

In looking up to the Rossberg, where the gap made by the fall still looks raw and bare, I could never cease to feel surprise that sufficient impetus should have been attained by the loosened mass, to project it to such an amazing distance, and with such astounding force and rapidity. The mountain itself does not look very high, and is in reality only about 3250 feet above the valley of Goldau ; and its slope towards its base is not very steep. I say I always felt surprise on looking at the mountain ; although the results are exactly such as a physical investigation of all the conditions would lead us to expect.

We covenanted with our worthy hostess of the Swan, for an open carriage and pair of horses to take us across the country to Rapperschwyl, on the lake of Zurich; and we started on our journey about half-past ten, under the guidance of a fine young man, one of the six sons of the house. As usual, I took my place on the driving-box beside him. Instead of following the main road towards Schwytz, keeping the lake of Lowertz on our left hand, we took the direct road to the small town of Steinen, keeping the lake on our right hand. This made a great saving as to space, but the road was for some distance of a kind I never saw before travelled by a carriage; it was, indeed, more a footpath than a road, and rough in the extreme. It improved as we advanced, and became very good before we reached Steinen. Here we came into the high road from Schwytz, which, though extremely hilly in some places, was tolerably good during the rest of the journey: at Steinen it was deemed good enough to claim a toll—and a high toll, too, viz., eight batzen. From a mistake, we here neglected the opportunity of paying our respects to the memory of one of the Fathers of Swiss Freedom, Walter Stauffacher, whose birthplace Steinen is, and where there is a chapel dedicated to his memory still standing, and in good preservation, though built in 1400.

From Steinen the road was a continued and steep ascent for full five miles, up the side of a beautiful mountain valley, or hollow in the hills. This valley is very fertile, and well cultivated, not only in the bottom, where there is a small stream, with its bordering meadows, but up the sides of the hills to a considerable extent; when not cultivated, the hills are finely wooded. Near to the top of this valley is the small town of Sattel, where we stopped to bait our horses. It can boast of a large church, with a neat cemetery around it; internally, it is richly adorned with images, paintings, gilding, and all the usual tawdry decorations. On the front, under the portico, there are some glaring frescoes, more startling in effect than attractive in design or execution.

5

In one of these over the door, the subject of which is the last judgment, a long-tailed and long-horned imp is seen carrying a poor naked sinner pick-aback, holding him by the legs under his own arms,* and hastening with him to the place of punishment, which is seen blazing at an awful rate just before them, with a dozen or two of men and women amid the flames. In the interior of the church we found upwards of twenty pilgrims at their devotions, all on their way to and from Einsiedeln.

This church of Sattel seems a sort of halfway-house between Einsiedeln and the Kloster Church on the Rigi. I observed, however, that those who entered the church only remained there a very short time, and coming out at the door opposite to that they had entered by, pursued their pilgrimage. Having learnt that next day (Tuesday) was a great festival dedicated to the Virgin (viz. the Marie-Himmel-fahrt), I naturally concluded that the thronged pilgrimages seen by us were made on this account; but I was informed by an intelligent priest that this was not the case, the pilgrimages, such as we witnessed them, taking place at all seasons. Yesterday and the day before, both in ascending and descending the Rigi, we had encountered troops of

---

* Precisely as in Dante :—

> " E vidi dietro a noi un diavol nero . . . .
> L'omero suo, ch'era acuto e superbo,
> Carcava un peccator con ambo l'anche,
> Ed ei tenea de' pie ghermito il nerbo."
>
> *Inferno,* Canto xxi.

these pilgrims, men and women, trudging in both directions; and as our journey to-day lay in the very track that must be taken by travellers between the Rigi and Einsiedeln, we had the best opportunity of observing their proceedings.

Between Goldau and Rothenthurm, at which place the path to Einsiedeln turns off from the main road, I think we must have seen between three and four hundred pilgrims, either going or coming. They were all of the lower orders apparently, but all were cleanly and neatly dressed, and some of the women rather gaudily : not a ragged or dirty gown or coat, or dirty shirt, was to be seen among the whole number. The day being very hot, the men almost invariably had their coats off, which they carried on their shoulders, generally by means of a stick or umbrella.* All the young women were bare-headed, but neither men nor women were bare-footed. The pilgrims were generally seen in small groups of four or five; and as they were met or passed by us, they were heard very earnestly repeating some prayers or psalms, in a quiet manner, and with a low tone, but still very distinctly. Frequently some one of the party carried a book, from which he or she was reciting. There seemed to be generally one leader who gave the initiative, and who was followed by the others as if in response. Most, if not all, had strings of beads in their hands. Every now and

* Umbrellas are remarkably numerous everywhere in Switzerland, indicating the frequency of unexpected showers.

then the men who walked with their heads covered, lifted up or took off their hats for a few minutes, in a grave and reverend manner, as if the passage then being recited was of more than wonted sacredness.

My companion on the driving-box who, though a Catholic, was certainly not a bigoted one, looked without much complacency on these scenes. He himself and all his family made the pilgrimage to Einsiedeln as well as their neighbours, but he evidently regarded it rather as a troublesome custom than as a piece of necessary or heart-felt devotion. My friend was, however, far from orthodox on other points. For instance, he did not hesitate to state that he thought the Protestants better than the Catholics in many respects; and he named as instances the greater care taken of the poor by them, the smaller number of beggars in the Protestant cantons, the better state of cultivation in the same, &c. He regarded the great number of holidays in the Catholic church as a very serious evil, interfering very injuriously with industry and good husbandry. He made use of a phrase in talking on this subject which I fancy must be proverbial, from its emphatic alliteration : *Immer beten immer betteln* ("Aye praying aye begging"), he said, was the characteristic of the people of the Catholic cantons. This circumstance of superfluous church-going and supernumerary holidays I heard accused by many persons of different ranks and faith in Switzerland, as a very serious drawback to the prosperity of the Catholic states; and I must add that my own observation led me entirely to concur in the opinion.

Soon after leaving Sattel we reached the ridge that overlooks the valley of Rothenthurm : when here we were only a short distance from the field of Morgarten, the first and one of the most glorious of all the heroic battles of the early Swiss. It lies on the left hand, at the northern base of the ridge we were now crossing, on the borders of the small lake of Egeri, which is partially seen from hence.

It is a great misfortune in travelling through any country to pass by without inspection the scenes of great actions; and this misfortune must constantly be incurred by persons circumstanced as we were, who, in one sense, might be called *travellers against time*, inasmuch as our " Holiday" had a limit not to be overpassed. And Switzerland probably possesses such scenes in greater number and of more intense interest than any other country of the same extent on the face of the earth, except perhaps Greece; and even Greece can hardly be allowed to present to the traveller, over all the hills and plains of her glorious land, spots more dignified by heroic deeds or more hallowed by the devotedness of genuine patriotism, than the battle-fields of Switzerland,— Morgarten, Sempach, Grandson, Morat, St. James, Naefels, &c.

On descending the hill from the ridge of Sattel we come into a common-looking, tame valley, the

only one in Switzerland that I have seen which cannot boast of some beauty.   It is bare and wild, like
a Scottish moor : a considerable portion of it is an
actual moss, furnishing turf and peat for fuel.   The
small town of Rothenthurm lies in this valley, and
cannot be said to exhibit anything to redeem the
character of its locality.   The old red tower from
which the town derives its name is, however, still
standing, a marked specimen of primeval architecture, and doubly interesting to the antiquary, as
the residence of the famous or infamous Gessler.
My Goldau friend knew it only by the name of
Gessler's tower.   As already stated, the road to
Einsiedeln turns off here over the hills to our right,
about a mile beyond the town.

A few miles further on we come upon the banks
of one of the branches of the Sihl and into a fine
country once more.   We soon arrived at the main
stream, a river of considerable size, the course of
which we followed for some time on its left bank,
and then crossed it by the bridge of Schindelegi.
We then came in sight of the lake of Zurich from
the shoulder of the Ezel range of hills, and turning
to the right descended to its shores, opposite Rapperschwyl, by an excellent road some miles in length,
leading through fields richly cultivated and finely
wooded, like all that bound this beautiful lake.
We reached the village adjoining the bridge of
Rapperschwyl at half-past four.   Here we took leave
of our courteous driver, with mutual good will and

much shaking of hands by all parties; and, with knapsacks in hand, proceeded on our way to Rapperschwyl across the wooden bridge which here traverses the lake from side to side. This is a piece of rude work, but apparently very efficient. It has no side rails, and the pieces of wood constituting the roadway are laid loose side by side, without other fixture. There is a drawbridge in the centre to allow the steamboats to pass. The bridge is about 1700 paces or about three quarters of a mile in length. It reminds one of the wooden piers at Ryde in the Isle of Wight and at Southend at the mouth of the Thames; but it is much shorter than either of these, and very inferior in its construction—more especially to the latter.

We proceeded through the curious old town of Rapperschwyl to the Pfau (Peacock) Hotel, which is built quite in the country, and is an excellent inn. The present landlord is one of the medical practitioners of the place. After dinner we walked down to the side of the lake. The evening was perfectly calm and warm, and the lake looked beautiful in the declining light. We here witnessed one of those glorious sunsets which can only be seen in perfection amid mountains and lakes, where the beauties of the earth reflect and emulate those of the heavens.

CHAPTER VIII.

August 15.——The *Pfau* is a well-provided and pleasant inn : losing the best position, the shore of the lake, it has the next best, that of the meadows outside the close and crowded old town. The professional landlord is a sensible plain man who took charge of the inn on his brother's death. He does not allow his supervision of the hotel to interfere with his medical practice. I spoke to him respecting the removal of certain nuisances presented by even the best Swiss inns, which seriously depreciate their other excellencies. He, and indeed all the other landlords, readily admitted the evil, and it is to be hoped that for their own interests, as well as for the comfort of their guests, they will make an effort to abate them. I amused some of the fraternity by threatening to head a new *Sunderbund* movement against those who would not abate the nuisance.

Our purpose being to proceed to the baths of Pfeffers by the lake of Wallenstadt, we had to wait for the arrival of the steamboat from Zurich, to convey us to the end of our own lake at Smerikon; and she did not arrive till ten o'clock. There is here a small pier built for the accommodation of the steamboats, which renders embarkation very comfortable, as the vessels come alongside of it. At this there was now lying another steamboat, which had just arrived from Smerikon, and was on her way to Zurich: she bore the appropriate name of *Escher von der Linth*. We reached Smerikon at half-past eleven. The lake and its boundaries retain the same general characters here as at the other extremity— those, namely, of gentle beauty and richness unmixed with either wildness or grandeur. The range of the Ezel, however, which bounds the southern shore opposite Rapperschwyl, gives the scenery a somewhat more impressive character at this end of the lake.

There were not a great many passengers. Among them one couple, doubtless yet within the limits of the honey-moon, attracted a good deal of notice, from the absorbing earnestness of their affectionate attentions to one another. In the simplicity of their devotion, they seemed unaware that their innocent caresses might be the subject rather of merriment than respect in a company of strangers. Shall I set this down as an illustration of the unsophisticated manners of the land? We had also on board two Roman Catholic priests, whom we found very agreeable and intelligent companions. One of them could make himself understood in English: he also spoke French well, and rather posed us by his volubility

5 §

in Greek and Latin. These priests were on their way to the baths of Pfeffers.

Having covenanted on board the steamer for transport all the way to Ragatz, we were provided with a conveyance on landing at Smerikon. We at first got into an omnibus which took us to the small town of Uznach, about three miles distant ; we then were transferred to an old-fashioned stage coach, which took us on to Wesen at the western extremity of the Lake of Wallenstadt. I was fortunate at Uznach, to obtain an outside place beside the driver. This enabled me to see the country much better, but I did not profit much by information obtained from my companion, as he proved to be rather a stupid fellow and understood but little of either German or French. I, however, got the names of places from him ; and that was something.

The country all the way from Uznach to Wesen is very beautiful, and the latter part of it grand and picturesque. On leaving Smerikon the road turns somewhat from the lake, and, making a considerable bend under the base of the mountains, leaves the flat valley of the Limmatt spreading to a considerable distance on the right. On approaching Wesen it returns to its former direction, forced thereto by the encroaching sweep of the range of hills whose base it had been following. During the whole of its circuit the road winded through a lovely tract of country. The range of lofty hills or mountains on our left hand, was beautifully wooded to the top, while its base and its gentler slopes, sometimes to a considerable height, were richly cultivated. Our path was shaded or overhung with fruit-trees; and on our right extended to the base of the opposite mountains the rich and level valley traversed by the Limmatt, or rather by the Linth canal. As we approached within some miles of Wesen, the valley of the upper Linth, leading into the canton of Glarus, opened upon us with all its magnificent array of snowy mountains glittering in the sunshine—some close at hand, some filling up the distant horizon. This was the first near view we had had of the true scenery of the Alps, and we saw but few things in our future journeys that exceeded it in grandeur and beauty. Within a couple of miles of the lake of Wallenstadt, the ranges of mountains on either hand approximate so as to leave only a narrow valley between them; at the same time, their sides become much more precipitous and rugged, particularly on our left, presenting vertical cliffs of rock instead of wooded slopes. Seen from the gorge of this picturesque ravine, the snowy summits of the Glärnish, directly in front, and apparently close to us, and almost filling up the whole background of sky left by the mountain range on either side, were truly grand. This prospect was only closed by the rather sudden turn of the road to the left, just before it terminated at Wesen.

While proceeding on our course from Uznach we could see, at times, far on our right hand, the waters of the Limmatt, in their new course, stretching in a straight line towards the Zürichersee; but when we reached the gorge of the mountains, we then came close to the watercourse and followed its banks for some distance. The first glance shows what it is; as it forms so strong a contrast, by its smooth formal banks and perfectly straight direction, with the natural free course of a mountain-river. Yet if the Linth canal gives to the eye nothing but the formal stiffness of art, it conveys to the mind so strong and agreeable an impression of the power of man to modify nature for beneficent purposes, as to leave no room for regret to the most enthusiastic admirer of the Beautiful. Looking at the vast benefits produced by it, the ingenuity and simplicity of the means by which these benefits were brought about, the perfection of the arrangement adopted to answer the intended objects, and, lastly, the pure and philanthropic motives in which the scheme originated, it is impossible not to feel a glow of delighted wonder in contemplating the Linth canal, and emotions both of reverence and love towards the memory of the man who planned and executed it. The following is a brief outline of the facts relating to this undertaking.

In the original state of this locality, the lake of Wallenstadt transmitted its superfluous waters to the lake of Zurich by means of a small river named the Matt. About two miles after leaving its parent lake, this small stream was overtaken in its tranquil course by one of the most impetuous torrents in Switzerland,

the Linth. This river, originating in the snowy glaciers of the lofty mountains that inclose the upper
borders of the great Glarus valley, and flowing
through a steep tract of country thirty miles in
extent, furnishing constant additions to its mass,
brought down with it such a vast collection of stones
and gravel as not only obstructed the course of the
Matt, but elevated its bed, as well as its own, considerably above the original level of the valley. The
consequence was twofold : the waters of the Wallenstadttersee, thus partially dammed up, overflowed
their banks during the snow-melting season, at both
ends of the lake, inundating the towns of Wesen and
Wallenstadt and their respective neighbourhoods ;
while the large and level valley lying between this
lake and that of Zurich, was ever and anon flooded
and ravaged, and thus rendered both sterile and unwholesome by the alternate fury and stagnation of
the waters.

Conrad Escher conceived the happy idea of reme-
dying these evils, and did remedy them most completely by a feat of engineering skill as beautifully
simple as it was effective. Turning the Linth from
its natural course as it passed by the Wallenstadttersee, he opened a new path for its waters directly
into the body of the lake ; then cutting a large and
straight channel from it to the other lake, he made
this the single substitute for the two primary channels of the Matt and the Linth. The consequences
were exactly such as he had anticipated. The wild

and wasting Linth from henceforward not only deposited its stony burthen into the quiet depths of its new reservoir, but left all its pristine force and fury there also.   The water which it added to the original contents of the lake, now left it, in union with those of the Matt, as pure and tranquil as the last had always been.   The valley thus freed from inundation and drained into the very stream which formerly wasted it, was at once restored to a state of security and wholesomeness, apt and ready for cultivation.

This great undertaking was completed in the year 1822 ; and the six-and-twenty years that have since elapsed have gradually extinguished all traces of the old desolation, and left the valley of the upper Limmatt one of the richest spots in Switzerland.   The reward conferred on the author of this noble work, was as grand as it was simple, emulating in its severe and naked dignity the honours awarded by the republics of old : the significant words "OF THE LINTH" were added to his original surname ; and it will not be denied that modern times can show us few if any titles more honorable than this.   The descendants of Conrad the Engineer still bear the honoured name of ESCHER VON DER LINTH : may they

"Bear the addition nobly ever."

The only local indication extant, of his countrymen's sense of the benefits conferred upon them by Escher, is a marble tablet dedicated to his memory let into the rock on one side of the gorge of the valley.   Let us hope that this may be hereafter converted into a monument as magnificent as that which records Swiss fidelity at Luzern : an appropriate emblem would be A DRAGON CHAINED.

Wesen is a small town jammed into a corner at the mountain's foot, at the left hand or northern angle of the lake.   We found the steamer waiting for us at the small quay : we went on board at once, and she sailed immediately.   This lake which is said to be twelve miles long and three broad, though its dimensions on Keller's map are considerably less, made a greater impression on me, on both occasions when we traversed it, than any other of the Swiss lakes.   The Vierwaldstädtersee is certainly much more varied and beautiful ; but no part of it, not even the bay of Uri, can compete with this in point of grandeur and picturesqueness.   The whole of its northern boundary is one continuous cliff of perpendicular rock coming sheer down into the water so as not to leave the possibility of even a footpath between, and rising so high as to shut from you nearly the whole sky on that side of the heavens.   The face of the rock is much too steep to admit of anything like general vegetation, but every cleft and crevice, every projecting point and shelf, each coign of vantage whereon it is possible for roots to fasten, has its little colony of pines, their white shafts and green pyramidal heads shooting gracefully upwards against their rocky background, and thus adding the charm of life and beauty to a scene which would otherwise

be too stern and severe. Over all, apparently beyond the grasp of vegetation, tower the sunny peaks
of the Leistkam range, and the still more magnificent Kurfürsten with their fantastic pinnacles, as if
looking down into the lake, although situated at a
considerable distance from it.

On the right hand or southern side of the lake,
the rocks are much less precipitous and lofty, and
proportionally more wooded. They retire sufficiently
from the water's edge to allow of a road all along
the shore, while here and there they retreat far
enough back to leave space for a small village and
a few sloping meadows.

It will be observed that the character of the two
rocky walls of the lake, is precisely that of the gorge
we passed through on approaching it ; bespeaking an
identity of origin, and showing a difference only in
the depth of the chasm that separates them. On
the south side also, the bounding range is overlooked by lofty mountains, some of them snow-
covered ; but they are at greater distance than
those on the other shore. Both times on which
we sailed or rather steamed along this singular lake,
the weather was remarkably fine, the sun high, the
sky cloudless, the water blue and bright, so that the
impressions communicated by its wilder features
were in a great measure softened if not counteracted; but I can easily believe that, under different
circumstances,—in a dark, gusty, autumnal day,
cloudy or rainy, or amid the gloom of a thunder-

storm,—all aggravating and enhancing the native sternness of the place,—the effect would be exclusively gloomy and awful, if not appalling.

Although the traveller who knows something of the history of that wonderful people the Romans, is hardly surprised at meeting with memorials testifying to their *once*-presence in any part of western Europe or Asia, I confess I hardly expected to find them in such a spot as the Wallenstadttersee : and yet we did so. A very intelligent passenger in the steamboat, a native of the country and evidently well acquainted with its history, antiquities, and physical geography, pointed out to us places on the northern shore of the lake which are known to have been Roman stations or spots indicating local distance. This lake, it would appear, constituted a portion of one of their lines of route to and from Germany, and was thus traversed by their boats. And it is interesting to find that the route is used for precisely the same purposes, and no doubt on the same grounds of convenience, at the present time. In fact, it would appear that the very origin of the small town of Wallenstadt at the extremity of the lake, is the consequence of the transport of merchandise to and from Germany and Italy, through the Grison country ; a trade which has existed many years. How different the means of transport whereby we were traversing it, from the rude boats of the Romans, and how different the two classes of traversers and their objects !

A few of the passengers dined on board, and as the dinner was laid on deck we joined the party and fared not amiss. In this land of equality we would not have been much surprised to have the conductor of our Diligence one of the company, even if he had been a less respectable man than ours proved to be. As it was, we took advantage of the privileges of bread and salt, and secured for ourselves the exclusive right of the outside seats of the Diligence, into which we were accordingly installed in due time.——The captain of the steamer is one of the finest men I ever saw, erect and tall, and with a magnificent beard : he wore an order on his breast, which I found he had received in Holland, having formerly been an officer in the Dutch army.

We reached the end of the lake in about an hour. We found the Diligence waiting for us on landing, and it started immediately for Ragatz. The small town of Wallenstadt is about half a mile from the lake, built, like Wesen, close under the mountains on our left. It is a poor place ; and the flat ground between it and the lake gives evidence, in its rich but marshy-looking meadows, that the river which feeds this end of the lake (the Scez) does not always keep within its banks. We tracked the course of this river to the south-east for seven or eight miles, keeping on its right bank and between it and the mountains. This valley of the Scez still preserves the general characteristics of those we had lately passed through ; but it is wider. The mountains on the left preserve their relative superiority to those on the opposite side : they are indeed to the full as lofty and almost as precipitous as those which border the lake, and they have much of the same sterile grandeur, but intermixed with more frequent spots of living beauty. The road was up-hill all the way to the small town of Sarganz, but the ascent was not steep until we actually reached it.

Sarganz is a very picturesque-looking place, built on the summit of a small hill sloping to both sides, and overlooked by a curious old castle perched on a rock just above it. The eminence on which the town is built extends across the valley to the mountains on the other side, in the direction of the course of the Scez which here turns away, at the south-west, nearly at right angles to that portion of it which we had hitherto traced. The streams on the further side of this transverse ridge we found running in an opposite direction to join the Rhine, to which river we gradually approached after leaving Sarganz. The country between Sargans and Ragatz is less picturesque and beautiful, the valley being much wider and the bounding mountains further off and less lofty.

In starting in the morning it was our intention to stop at Ragatz, to visit the baths of Pfeffers and then return to Wesen, but we received so tempting a report of the country beyond, and particularly of the Via Mala, from our friend the conductor, that we altered our plan and proceeded in the Diligence

to Chur in the canton of the Grisons, which place
we reached between eight and nine. We had come
close to the Rhine before reaching Ragatz, tracking
its left bank. About a couple of miles beyond Ragatz
we crossed over to its right bank, by a fine new
wooden bridge, and then kept it close to our right
hand all the way to Chur. Very shortly after
crossing the Rhine we crossed the Landquart also,
a large and impetuous stream which, after a lengthened course and rapid descent through the Grison
district termed Prätigau, here joins the Rhine.
The road from this spot to Chur runs along the
valley of the Rhine, every part of which is both
grand and beautiful except the Rhine itself, which
here presents that unpleasant aspect which a mountain river so often assumes on reaching a flat
country—namely, a wide or ill-defined channel and
far-spreading irregular banks strewed with stones
and sand. The road also frequently crossed similar
patches of stones and gravel brought down by the
torrents from the mountains on our left. As a
whole however, the valley, as already stated, is both
grand and beautiful. The ranges of mountains on
both sides are lofty, more especially on the left
bank, which is here bounded by the great Galanda
chain. The valley is sufficiently wide to leave
space for cultivated grounds of considerable extent.

On arriving at Chur we put up at the hotel of
the White Cross, which is I believe the best inn in
the town, and is tolerably good. We took our

evening meal in one of our own bed-rooms, on account of the Speisesaal being occupied by some ten or twelve officers of the Lombardo-Sardinian army, who had reached this place over the mountains after their discomfiture by the Austrian forces. They had left their soldiers behind them, and were making the best of their way, some towards France, others to Bellinzona in the canton of Tessino.

We had very indifferent rest in our inn, owing to the over-zeal of the Chur watchmen, whose practice it is to perambulate the town through the whole night, twelve in number, and who, on the present occasion, certainly displayed a most energetic state of vigilance. They not only called but sung out every hour, in the most sonorous strains, and even chanted a long string of verses on the striking of some: and as the Weisser Kreutz happens to be in a central locality, with a street both in back and front, we had rather more than an average share of this patriotic and religious demonstration. I suppose the good people of Chur think nothing of these chantings, or from habit hear them not : but a tired traveller would rather run the risk of being robbed in tranquillity, than be thus sung from his propriety during all the watches of the night.

Through the kindness of a friend I have obtained an accurate version of these elaborate night-calls, and I give in a note the words, as an interesting illustration of manners. Although the words are in modern dress, and the verses are very similar to what are chanted in different parts of Germany, there is little doubt that they are, like the custom itself, really very ancient. It could only be in the undoubting and unquestioning simplicity of the faith of the old time, that a ceremony and formula so entirely religious could have been excogitated. It speaks well for the faith and temper of the present day, however, that this nocturnal and matutinal clamour, even though religious, should still be tolerated by the children of Chur.

WATCH CHANT AT CHUR.

I.—NIGHT.

Hört ihr Christen, lass't euch sagen
Uns're Glocke hat Acht geschlagen.
　　,,　　　　,,　　　Neun　　　,,
　　,,　　　　,,　　　Zehn　　　,,
　　,,　　　　,,　　　Elf　　　,,
　　,,　　　　,,　　　Zwölf　　　,,
　　,,　　　　,,　　　Eins　　　.,
Acht, nur ach zur Noah's zeit
Waren von der Straf' befreit.—*Achte!*
Neun verdient des Dankes nicht,
Mensch, gedenke deiner Pflicht!—*Neun!*
Zehn Gebote schärf Gott ein,
Lasset ihm gehorsam seyen.—*Zehne!*
Nur *Elf* Jünger waren treu ;
Gieb, Herr, dass kein Abfall sey!—*Elfe!*
Zwölf Uhr ist das Ziel der Zeit :
Mensch, gedenk der Ewigkeit!—*Zwolfe!*
Eins, O Mensch, nur Eins ist Noth :
Mensch, gedenk an deinen Tod!—*Eins!*

II.—MORNING.

Stand auf im Name Jesu Christ,
Der { helle Tag / Tag nun bald } vorhanden ist;
Der helle Tag der nie verlag;
Gott geb uns allen ein guten Tag!
Ein guten Tag, glückselige Stund',
Das wunsch ich euch von Herzen's Grund.
    Funfi zähl Funfi!

TRANSLATION.

I.

Hear, ye Christians, let me tell you
Our clock has struck eight,
    „   „   nine, &c.
Eight, only eight in Noah's time
Were saved from punishment.—*Eight!*
Nine deserves no thanking—
Man, think of thy duty!—*Nine!*
Ten Commandments God enjoined:
Let us be to Him obedient.—*Ten!*
Only *Eleven* Disciples were faithful;
Grant, Lord, that there be no falling off!—*Eleven!*
Twelve is the hour that limits time—
Man, think upon Eternity!—*Twelve!*
One, O man, only one thing is needful:
Man, think upon thy death!—*One!*

II.

Get up in the name of Jesus Christ,
The { bright day / day soon } is near at hand;
The clear day that ne'er delayed;
God grant us all a good day!
A good day and happy hours
I wish you from the bottom of my heart.
    Five, O! reckon Five, O!

CHAPTER IX.

JOURNEY TO TUSIS—SUNRISE ON THE ALPS—REICHENAU—TUSIS
—THE VERLORENES LOCH—RONGELLEN—VIA MALA—PARTED
FRIENDS—RETURN TO CHUR—A DOWN-HILL DRIVE—
SYMPTOMS OF ITALY—CHUR—THE CATHEDRAL—ST. LUCIUS
—RETURN TO RAGATZ.

August 16.——Having taken places overnight in the
Diligence for Tusis, and having, by a small official
bribe, secured the coupé as affording the best opportunity of seeing the country (there were no outside
places in this Diligence), we started at five o'clock
after a hurried breakfast. The day was only just
dawning, but we soon had daylight and a fine day;
and the scenes we passed through, and still more
perhaps those we did not pass through, deserved
both. We kept close upon the right bank of the
Rhine until we reached the small town of Richenau
at the distance of six or seven miles. So far the
road has but a very slight ascent, the river running
with only moderate rapidity along the foot of the
Galanda mountains. These are here extremely precipitous and lofty, rising into bare craggy peaks, and
exhibiting frequent patches of snow on their shoulders
and in their clefts. The chain on our left hand was
considerably less bold. During this part of our
journey our course lay directly in the line of the

valley of the Fore-Rhine (Vorder Rhein), and through
the opening thus afforded we had straight before us,
or rather a little to the right hand, on the distant
horizon, a most magnificent view of snowy mountains. From the direction in which they lay, as well
as their height, they must have been either the Tödi
and Scheerhorn in the cantons of Glarus and Uri, or
the Oberalp which divides the valley we were looking
down from the canton last named. As we proceeded
on our course we saw their snowy peaks gradually
illumined as they caught the rays of the rising sun,
and when they had become fully illuminated, their
brilliant brightness, relieved as it was against a sky
without a cloud, was literally excessive. I was so
struck with their appearance that, in recording the
circumstance in my note-book, I put down at the
time " approaching in brilliancy to that of the sun
himself—fully as brilliant as the full moon." Let no
one therefore, in journeying from Chur to Reichenau,
fail to look down the valley of the Vorder Rhein and
up—high up—to the sky beyond.

At Reichenau the two great branches of the Rhine,
the Vorder and Hinter Rhein, unite almost at right
angles, the former running nearly east, the latter
nearly north. As our road to the Via Mala lay
along the left bank of the Hind-Rhine, we had to
pass two bridges before we could reach it, namely,
one across the main river just after the union of the
branches, and another across the Fore-Rhine just
before the union. These bridges are fine lofty

6

structures of wood, housed in, as almost all the Swiss bridges are, and tend by their proximity to each other, as well as by their general aspect, to enhance the picturesqueness of this most oddly-placed town ——with its three valleys and their three rivers, and their bounding mountains, all ending, abutting, and uniting within its narrow limits. From Reichenau to Tusis, a distance of ten or twelve miles, the road is up hill, and generally very steep, the whole way. We kept our branch of the Rhine close on the left hand, and rarely out of sight. The range of mountains on the other bank are throughout lofty and precipitous, and that over the spurs of which we were passing, is also lofty but much less so. The distance between the two chains is not great, so that the valley retains a good deal of the ravine-like character of which we had lately seen so much. This valley is tolerably well cultivated and rather populous. We passed through a good many villages and small towns, and did not fail to remark the great number of old castles with which the peaks and hill-promontories on either side are crowned——sufficiently indicative of the feudal grandeur and power that bore sway in the valley of Domleschg before the gray-coated peasants had fought for and won the freedom they have since enjoyed.

We reached Tusis at eight o'clock, and breakfasted at the Eagle Post-House where we found very tolerable accommodation. This inn, like all the houses of the village, is quite new, the old inn and the whole place having been destroyed by fire two years since. The village is now being rebuilt, a little below the site of the old, along the side of the road, and is no doubt a great improvement on the former, as the new houses are remarkably good, and many of them of large size.

The church is not yet finished; but the work-men were employed in covering its oriental-looking cupola with its smart coating of burnished tin. Spires of this form, viz. a slender shaft rising from a square tower and swelling out into a small angular cupola covered with shining metal——are general in the canton of the Grisons, and are found in some other parts of Switzerland. They have a very becoming appear-ance, and give a great degree of lightness and live-liness to the villages in which they exist, especially when the sun is reflected from their bright tops.

Leaving our knapsack at the inn, we set out at nine o'clock on foot to view the Via Mala. The day was very fine, and we had a delightful walk. The extent of this was a little beyond the third bridge, between four and five miles from Tusis, to which we returned at half-past twelve. Immediately at the end of the village we crossed a fine stone bridge over the impetuous Nolla which here joins the Rhine. There is a fine view up the valley which it descends, bounded by the lofty peaks of the Piz Beveren. The Nolla is an impetuous torrent, and treats the Rhine and its valley much in the same way as the Linth treated the valley of the Limmatt before it was tamed by the genius of Escher. Marks of its ravages are too conspicuous all along the borders of the Rhine below Tusis; and although efforts are being made to keep the river within its banks, they seem, as yet, only very partially successful. On crossing the bridge of the Nolla we come at once upon the base of the cliffs which, at first sight, seem effectually to preclude all further progress; but as we advance, a huge gap in the mountain is found to give outlet to the Rhine and entrance to the passenger. This opening, instead of enlarging as we advance, decreases, and the rocks on both sides become at the same time so precipitous, down to the very bottom of the chasm, that all further access would be clearly denied to human foot but for the interference of art to break through or remove the obstacle. And for ages this was the case; all approach to the regions beyond being only attained by a circuitous and lengthened course up the valley of the Nolla and over the mountains on the right hand. For this reason this part of the defile of the Hinter Rhein was designated *Das Verlorenes Loch*, the Lost Hole or Pit, a name which it still retains. So unexplored was this chasm only a hundred and fifty years since, that Bishop Burnet, in his interesting Letters from Switzerland, written in 1685-6, speaking of it, says that the Rhine runs through it, " but under ground for a great part of the way." To obtain direct access to the valley beyond, at length, in the end of last century, the obstructing barrier of rock was pierced through by a tunnel, a bridge at the same time being thrown over the Nolla, and the road improved generally; and since that time the whole extent of the ravine, though still called the Via Mala, is not merely easily accessible, but can boast of one of the best roads in Switzerland, perfectly safe, and with only a very moderate ascent.

For the first half mile after entering into the defile, the bounding cliffs are less steep and a good way apart; but as we approach the part where the tunnel admits us into the Verlorenes Loch the ravine becomes very narrow, consisting of two huge perpendicular cliffs separated by a very narrow space, like a rent or fissure in the rock, which it probably is, with the Rhine dashing along its stony bed far below, and only a strip of blue sky visible above. The tunnel is not extensive, being only a little more than 200 feet long, 14 feet high, and 18 feet wide. It answers its intended purpose admirably, but it is a rude enough piece of work in itself, and when we passed through it, was dirty as well as dark. Looking back from its entrance through the vista formed by the ravine, we have a charming view of the hills beyond Tusis; and the extensive ruins of an old castle standing on the very pinnacle of the lofty cliff which forms the right-hand boundary of the vista, present a striking object to the eye. This ruin is called Rhealt or Rhæalta, and has the legendary fame of having been built by a certain Tuscan or Etruscan chief of the name of Rhætus or Rhetius, some centuries before our era.

The ravine continues narrow, and the road partly
hewn from the cliff at a great height above the
stream for some distance beyond the tunnel; but
turning a little to the right, we then come upon an
open space where the rocks on the right hand
retire backwards, giving space for a lovely green
slope of some extent, with its cultivated fields and
cottages.   This is the valley, if it may be called so,
and village of Rongellen, down the slope of which
the road from Tusis formerly came to join the Via
Mala.   Its gentle beauty contrasting with the scenes
amid which it is placed, or through which we had
just passed, struck us forcibly and agreeably.   In
looking on it, and I may say very many other similar
spots in Switzerland, one is reminded of the expression of one of our poets, applied, I believe, to this
very country, of " Beauty sleeping in the lap of
Horror."

After passing Rongellen, the ravine contracts
again, and retains the same gloomy, wild, and savage
character to its extremity.   Generally speaking the
road runs on a narrow ledge of rock, in most places
natural, but sometimes formed by art in the rock,
high above the stream, on which you look down as
from a gallery almost overhanging it; the cliffs on
both sides shooting directly upwards to an amazing
height.   At the time of Bishop Burnet's visit in
1685, the solid pathway did not exist continuously
as at present.   " The Way (he says) is cut out in
the middle of the rock in some places; and in
several, the steepness of the rock being such that a

way could not be cut, there are beams driven into it over which boards and earth are laid."*

The width of the ravine varies considerably, but everywhere in this part of it it is narrow——in some places so narrow as to be spanned from side to side by a stone bridge of a single arch, perhaps not more than thirty feet wide. There are two bridges of this kind in the narrowest part of the ravine, built in spots where the ledge on which the road is constructed, ceases entirely on one side in abutting against a vertical cliff, and commences on the opposite side: it is to reach from the point where the one stops to that where the other commences, that these bridges are erected. The first two bridges, and particularly the second, are built at an immense height above the stream, not less than 400 feet, it is said. A striking illustration of the narrowness of the chasm through which the river here flows, as well as of the vast increase which a river in a mountainous country like this can at times receive, is mentioned in Murray's Handbook, page 239. The author there states that during the great inundation of 1834, the river rose within a few feet of the bridge ——a perpendicular rise of four hundred feet! In looking over this bridge, the stream of the Rhine beneath seems contracted into a small rill, partly from its distance, but much more from the actual narrowness of the fissure in the rock through which it flows: it presents to us only its *narrow edge*. In

* Letters on Switzerland; Rotterdam, 1686.

one place this fissure seems quite obliterated as you look down upon it, from its having an oblique instead of a vertical direction; one portion of the rock overlapping the other, and thus hiding the stream from view. A configuration precisely similar to this, and on a still larger scale, occurs in the fissured rock through which the Tamina flows above the baths of Pfeffers.

It was easy to see, in glancing from cliff to cliff as we walked along, that it was precisely the same mass of rock that constituted the wall on either side; the same inclination of strata, the same interruption by beds of other rock, and, in the narrower parts (so I fancied at least), the mutual adaptation of prominences and hollows opposite to one another, giving patent evidence that they had once formed a continuous whole. It was from rocky chasms like these, perhaps from these very chasms, or from those of Pfeffers and the Münsterthal, which are exactly similar, that Coleridge derived his admirable simile of broken friendship, which cannot fail to come to the traveller's recollection as he looks on them:

> "Alas, they had been friends in youth:
> They parted—ne'er to meet again!
> But never either found another
> To free the hollow heart from paining:
> They stood aloof, the scars remaining,
> Like cliffs which had been rent asunder;
> A dreary sea now flows between;
> But neither heat, nor frost, nor thunder,
> Shall wholly do away, I ween,
> The marks of that which once hath been."

It must not be imagined that because I have said so much of cliffs and rocks, that the mountain-boundaries of this singular ravine, are all bare precipices. Many of them certainly are too vertical, and of too solid a face to admit the possibility of vegetation; but others, and indeed by far the greater number, are by no means so. On the contrary, with the few exceptions named, the most precipitous cliffs are fringed with pine trees, not in a continuous mass, but scattered here and there in patches from top to bottom, wherever a ledge will support them or a fissure admit their roots; and in many places their beautiful white stems, and graceful heads of green, are seen rising vertically against the face of rocks where we would deem it almost impossible for them to find a footing. This partial clothing of the cliffs with living verdure, softens in a considerable degree the gloomy wildness of the scene.

Before we reach the third bridge, a handsome modern structure built to replace one destroyed by the overflow of the river in 1834, the ravine loses all its wildness and grandeur, and gradually opens into a comparatively tame valley (the valley of Schams), presenting no special attractions. Accordingly, we here reversed our march, and returned on our steps to Tusis. Although we had found the ascent but slight on our upward path, we were very sensible of its advantages in returning, and therefore proceeded at a rapid pace, so as to complete the whole distance in an hour or thereabouts. As the day was very

6 §

hot, we were glad, on reaching our inn, to rest for
an hour, winding up our labours of the morning with
one of the most refreshing beverages the traveller
can take—good strong coffee reduced by a plentiful
allay of cold milk.

We started on our return to Chur in one of the
long narrow chars of the country, drawn by one horse
and without springs, except the leather substitutes
by which the seat is suspended.   For this we paid
twelve francs.   Our horse turned out to be good,
and our driver better.   At least, in all my experience, I never met with so resolute and fearless a
charioteer.   The road, as we have seen, is all down
hill from Tusis to Reichenau, steeply down-hill indeed, and full of turnings; but down the steepest
pitches, and round the sharpest angles on we went
at full trot and full swing, as if there had never been
such an event as an upsetting, or such things as
broken knees and broken bones equine and human.
Luckily, none of these fell to our lot to witness or
to suffer; and we reached our destination of Chur
considerably before the covenanted time, viz. in two
hours and a half.   In all the active part of these
proceedings our good horse had the whole merit, as
the driver hardly twitched the reins or used the whip
from first to last, but left him to take his own pace
and his own course as to him seemed good.

All the way from Ragatz to Tusis we had had
indications of our nearer approach to the Italian
border in many little circumstances and incidents,

and even, as I fancied, in the qualities of the sky and the looks of the people. For instance, the insignia of the fire-insurances nailed up on the houses, instead of the names of Berne, Geneva, or Lyons, now bore the word " Milano ;" and many of the signs over the village shops were printed conjointly in German and Italian : and on the toll-house by the bridge at Reichenau, we read in Italian only, " Qui si paga la Razzia." Throughout the portion of the canton of the Grisons which we had yet seen, the frescoes on the churches and other houses were much more frequent than we had observed elsewhere. They were almost all of a religious character, and the majority had reference to the Virgin Mary. Along the roads, as is usual all over the Catholic cantons, there were numerous crosses ; and on the transverse bar of many of them, were different series of figures, cut out in wood, having more or less direct reference to the events of the crucifixion——such as, the ladder, the nails, the scourge, Peter's cock, &c.——On many of the houses we also remarked a wooden framework projecting from the gable-end under the eaves. This we found, on inquiry, was a provision for drying the fruits for which this district is celebrated. The framework is thrust out or retracted, according to the state of the weather.

On arriving at Chur we engaged another carriage, with a single horse, to convey us to Ragatz, for which we paid ten francs and Trinkgeld. While it was

getting ready, we strolled out into the town, and paid
a visit to the old cathedral, or church of St. Lucius.
It contains much that deserves notice, not merely
in its architecture but otherwise.   Some parts of
the building are very ancient, dating, according to
our cicerone, from the sixth or seventh century ; and
there are stone figures and other pieces of sculpture
obviously of very early date from their grotesque
rudeness.   The church is much ornamented with
old pictures and images, as well as others of more
recent execution.   Some of the pictures are said to
be by Holbein and Albert Durer ; and a very fine
piece of carved wood, richly gilt, representing a
complex mass of figures, is said to be the production
of the younger Holbein.

The patron saint of the church is St. Lucius, who
is said to have been an English king, who travelled
hither in the second century and converted the natives to Christianity.   He commenced his missionary
labours as a hermit, having built his hermitage on
the site of the present church : hence his honours
as Patron Saint.   We were shown among the holy
relics some of the bones of this ex-king of England,
as likewise some of those of his sister, who suffered
martyrdom for her religion, being burnt to death at
Chur.   These relics are richly adorned with gold
and gems, and are preserved in a secure place in
the church, along with some curious old church
plate of considerable value.

The town of Chur is of considerable extent, containing between 5000 and 6000 inhabitants, the great majority of whom are Catholics. It presents a somewhat warlike aspect as we approach it, being defended by a high wall, and a moat, now empty, with old-fashioned towers and gateways. It stands on a small space of ground in the mouth of a gap in the mountains which surround it on three sides. The streets are narrow, but there are many good houses in them.

Most of our Swiss travellers, as well as the author of Murray's Handbook, call this place by its French name of *Coire.* This is wrong, as it is invariably termed Chur by the natives, who do not speak French. Besides, this last name is unquestionably the proper one, seeing that it is generally admitted to be a simple modification of its original Roman name Curia or Curia Rhætorum, given to it on account of its having been the temporary residence of the Emperor Constantius in the fourth century.

The voiturier from Tusis, though, as we have seen, a parlous driver, was rather a dull fellow and possessed little knowledge of the country. The driver from Chur to Ragatz, however, was a very intelligent young man and spoke German very tolerably. He had been rather better educated, being the son of a schoolmaster in the canton of St. Gall. He was fully informed respecting the nature of the government, the produce and economical wants of the country, the details respecting the military, &c.; insomuch that I could not help respecting both his

character and acquirements.   He was a servant of
the *Weisses Kreutz*, and I put down in my note-
book a memorandum of the *diet* supplied to him and
his fellow-servants, as a specimen of the mode of
living in this country.   The allowance will be admitted to be liberal.   They are allowed two meals
of meat daily, besides soup, with vegetables for
dinner (chiefly beans) and an unrestricted supply of
bread.   They have a pint of wine for dinner and
half-a-pint for supper.

We reached Ragatz at seven, and put up at the
splendid hotel, the Ragatzer Hof.   On coming down
stairs to our tea at eight, we found about thirty
ladies and gentlemen at supper.   They were all
patients lodging at the hotel for the benefit of the
waters, and were now taking their evening meal under
the supervision of the Physician or Bad-Artzt.   To
judge by their proceedings and their noisy mirth,
they were not very seriously ill.   They all retired
at nine, and we soon followed their example.

CHAPTER X.

August 17.——For the first time since we reached
the Rhine we had a bad day——a continuous heavy
rain all the morning, becoming less heavy as the
day advanced, but not ceasing until the evening.
Having waited for some hours, in hopes of improvement in the weather, our indoor patience was exhausted, and ordering one of the small cars, we set
out to visit the old baths of Pfeffers.   The road to
these lies through the ravine of the Tamina, or
Taminbach, a furious torrent which, on leaving its
mountain path, passes through the village of Ragatz
to join the Rhine.   Crossing a bridge under which
it passes at the end of the village, we ascended close
by the edge of the river, on its left bank, all the
way to the baths.   Indeed, the configuration of the
ground leaves no choice in the matter, as by no other
route could a road for a carriage or even for a horse
or mule, be possible; the ravine through which the
river flows, being the sole opening into the chasm of
the mountains where the baths are situated.   The

present road which is, like that of the Via Mala,
formed, in a great measure, out of the rock itself, is
very good and the ascent not very steep.   It was
formed in the year 1839 ; and the following year
the wooden tubes which convey the thermal water
to Ragatz were laid down : they run along its border
next to the torrent.

This ravine even at its outer extremity presents
a very picturesque and striking scene, and its character of wildness and wonderfulness is greatly enhanced towards its upper end.   It is, in fact,
another Via Mala ; on a greatly reduced scale, no
doubt, but possessing all its striking characteristics
in a remarkable degree.   Had we not seen the real
Via Mala previously, it would have made a still
stronger impression on us ; but even after seeing
the greater gulf, this was to us wonderful.   In
respect of what may be truly called *horror*, the
upper part of the ravine of the Tamina even exceeds
that of the Hinter Rhein in its wildest spots.   But
still, I think, the traveller, with the view of gra-
duating, and so enhancing his enjoyments, should,
if practicable, visit Pfeffers before entering the
Verlorenes Loch.

Like that of the Via Mala, the road to Bad-
Pfeffers runs quite close to the bank of the river,
and thus serves as a sort of gallery for viewing the
scenery through which it leads.   Owing to the
smaller scale of the whole, this road is only in a few
places raised greatly above the stream ; more gene-

rally it is only a small way above its level, and this circumstance gives another striking feature to the ravine, which that of the Via Mala may be almost said to want—I mean the close proximity of a furious torrent lashed into one mass of foam just under your eyes, and stunning you with its incessant roar. The bed of the Tamina consists of large blocks of stone, and as its general inclination is very steep, the stream through its whole course retains the character just given to it, and may almost be said to exhibit a succession of rapids. As enhancing this feature, the heavy rains we had had over night and in the morning, were an advantage; as also in producing an increased display of waterfalls from the cliffs. The road conducts us to the door of the bathing establishment : it could not possibly reach further, as the ravine may be said to terminate here, leaving beyond a mere crack or vertical chasm in the rock, into which no vehicle or animal drawing a vehicle, or even a foot passenger could enter, in its original condition. The only access to this chasm is through the house. This is a dismal old-fashioned place, but of large size, being capable of containing some hundreds of patients.

The first establishment on this spot was erected in the year 1630 by the then Abbot of the Monastery of Pfeffers; the present house was built in the year 1704 by one of his successors. The springs themselves were discovered so far back as the beginning of the eleventh century, it is said by a man in search of the young of ravens which built their nests in the cliffs. The water was not, however, made any medicinal use of till the middle of the thirteenth century, when some wooden buildings were erected on the spot. These were the only accommodations for invalids in use for a period of four hundred years, when the present house was built, and the waters conducted to it from the springs. Invalids seeking the benefit of these previously, had access to them only by being lowered down the cliff from the open chasm above. In the year 1838 the monastery was suppressed, and it and all its possessions came into the hands of the Government of the canton of St. Gall; these baths among the rest.

The main part of the building consists of a series of rooms, opening on one side into long, low-walled galleries running the whole length, one above another. As the resident Bad-Artz, to whom I addressed myself, was at dinner with his patients of the first class, we proceeded at once, with a guide from the establishment, to view the primary source of the spring in the rocks beyond. For the permission to do so, we had to pay a small fee each. We descended to the basement floor and passed out through the huge cellar-like place, termed the Trinksaal or pumproom, into which the water for drinking purposes is admitted. On emerging from this gloomy abode, which forms a singular contrast with the gay and

brilliant halls of the German watering-places, we
come at once upon the still-roaring Tamina, struggling in its solid bed of rock, and just emerging
from the dark chasm beyond. Crossing this by a
small wooden bridge we immediately entered the
"rifted rock" on a narrow gangway of wood, attached to and suspended against the face of the cliff
on the right bank of the torrent. This gangway,
which answers the double purpose of a support to
the wooden pipes through which the water is conveyed, and a path to visitors, is sufficiently wide to
allow one person to walk comfortably, and is defended, through its whole course, by a handrail on
the exterior side. It is literally *suspended* in its
place, on iron bolts driven into the rock, the cliff
both above and below it being so perfectly vertical
and smooth as to furnish no natural support. The
torrent, for the most part immediately under you,
sometimes a little on your right hand, is nowhere, I
should think, at a greater depth below you than fifty
or eighty feet, and as it dashes along even more
furiously than in the open ravine, you may judge of
the tremendous roar kept up by it in this rocky
and vaulted inclosure.

Whatever may be thought of the rocky beds of
other mountain streams, it will hardly be doubted
by any visitor of this truly forlorn gulf (verlorenes
Loch) of the Tamina, that it is the result, at least
in the first instance, of a rending asunder, by some
sudden force, of the rocky mass in which it lies; as

it possesses very strikingly every mark of such an origin, and only in a secondary degree those indicating the slow action of a stream of water on its bed. The chasm is everywhere extremely narrow in relation to its height; in some places it cannot be more than twelve or fifteen feet wide; and its average width can scarcely be more than twenty or thirty feet; while its height may be three or four hundred. The walls of the chasm are scarcely ever vertical in their whole depth, but inclined, one over the other, at a considerable angle. In some places, the one wall overhangs the other so much that the sky above is entirely excluded, and this for a considerable space, by the natural configuration of the parts; in others, the size of the upper fissure has been originally so small, that it has been entirely closed up by the accidental fall of rocks and rubbish from the heights above. On these accounts the whole chasm is very dark, giving one much more the feeling of being in a cave or a mine, than by the natural banks of a river. The shelving direction of the walls of the chasm is sometimes the same at its bottom as at its top, so that in looking down we can only see a bare rock, the stream being hid by the overlapping of one of its rocky sides. Altogether the place is very extraordinary and very dismal, and is surely well entitled to rank high in the category of things which have been vulgarly denominated Wonders of the World.

The little wooden gallery extends no further than

the hot spring, but the chasm continues beyond it as before. I did not make any admeasurement of the distance we had come, but I should think it could not be much less than a furlong. The springs which are three in number, but no doubt all having the same primary source, flow from the rock on the right bank of the Tamina, at a place where the opening over head is a good deal larger than usual, and where, consequently, there is a tolerably good light. The upper spring, termed the Herrenbad, is the smallest, and does not flow constantly all the year through. The lowest, next in size, is seen issuing from the bottom of the rock and flowing into the Tamina : it is named the Grumpen. The middle spring is by far the most copious, and is the only one used. It is termed the Cauldron (Chaudière), a name to which it seems well entitled from the steam that is constantly rising from it. The entrance to it is by a small horizontal gallery cut in the rock, having a wooden door at its outer extremity. This gallery, according to our guide, extends inwards about twenty feet, but the reservoir into which the spring flows, and which is a narrow well about fifteen feet deep, is only a few feet inside the door. I found the water here of the temperature of $98\frac{1}{2}°$ or at most 99° of Fahrenheit. This is somewhat less than 30° Reaumur, which is the temperature usually ascribed to it. The water is beautifully clear, and has little or no taste. It, in fact, contains much less of mineral or saline impregnation than most of the waters in ordinary use. Its most copious ingredient is carbonate of lime, and it contains extremely minute portions of the salts of soda and magnesia as well as silica, and a trace of iron. The source is by no means copious, the whole of the mainspring being carried off by one wooden pipe to supply the two establishments, which it does in the following proportions : to Bad-Pfeffers, 855 ; to Ragatz, 570.

On returning to the house, we looked into the different baths. Some are single, some for two persons, some large enough to contain eight or ten. These last are for the poor patients, a certain number of whom are received into the establishment gratis. All the baths seemed tolerably clean and in good order, but they partook of the gloom——real material gloom from insufficient light——which involves the whole establishment. The house is capable of containing a great number of patients, but at the period of our visit (towards the end of their *season*) there were not so many as fifty of all classes. There is a resident physician here during the season, who superintends all the proceedings. Most of the patients drink the water as well as bathe in it ; but they do not appear to make use of the bath prolonged for hours at a time, as at the baths at Leuk.

Considering the nature of the mineral impregnation of this water, and the manner in which it is here used, and considering the nature of the locality and the circumstances under which it is used, it is impossible to believe, without very strong evidence, that a residence at Bad-Pfeffers can be of material use in most chronic diseases. In the case of nervous invalids, a considerable number of whom are found among the patients, I cannot but think that injury, not benefit, must be derived from a residence here. The close confined atmosphere of the whole ravine out of doors, with no means of escaping from it by paths which an invalid could climb, the hot and damp air of the house within, with its low roofs and dark galleries, must surely aggravate all sorts of nervous affections. It seems nevertheless possible that these baths may still retain their fame even in these cases, on the authority of a dogma very prevalent at watering-places, and not unknown to the practice of medicine generally, namely, that though not benefited at the time when the course of treatment is in progress, they will be so after it is over. I think I could venture to predict that most of the nervous patients of my colleague, the Bad-Arzt at Bad-Pfeffers, will find themselves *better* after they have left it : whether they may find themselves better than before they came to it, I will not so confidently assert.

Being desirous of seeing the old monastery in the village of Pfeffers, now converted into a lunatic asylum, we dismissed our char, and, notwithstanding the continuance of the rain, set out to reach it by the nearest path across the mountain. Our course lay for some time up the same side of the ravine as before, but at a level considerably above the river, and through a thick wood. From our path we looked down into what seemed the bottom of the ravine, but what was, in fact, only the roof of the deeper ravine, the interior chasm in which the river flowed. Here we could neither see nor hear the Tamina. After proceeding a short distance in this direction, we turned to the left, descended the hill, and crossed to the other side of the valley, the road passing directly over the chasm in which we had so recently been. So completely was the top of the chasm here covered in by an accumulation of stones and soil, that the place where we crossed looked like the natural bottom of a riverless valley, covered with grass and shaded with bushes. At a little distance on either side of us, however, we could see the lips of the gaping chasm, and could hear the roar of the torrent rising up from its subterranean abyss.

The ascent of the opposite bank of the ravine was extremely steep, a considerable portion of the path being a sort of ladder, or at least a stair partly formed of wood and partly cut out of the rock. This steep ascent continued the greater part of a mile. On reaching the top we came into a carriage road, which led us by an easy descent to the village of Pfeffers. This road, in the other direction, led up to some high valleys in the line of the Tamina; but I know not how far it continued. The Tamina itself had already run a lengthened course perhaps of twenty or thirty miles, before it entered the chasm of

Pfeffers : it takes its origin in the glacier of Sardona, belonging to the chain of mountains that bound the canton of Glarus to the east. It runs along the Kalfeuserthal.

There is nothing in the village of Pfeffers worth seeing. The old monastery is a large building, and seems extremely suitable for the purpose to which it is now applied. It is remarkably well fitted-up, and is very clean. The establishment having been only very recently opened, there were only forty patients in the house, but it is calculated to take a great many more. It is arranged for both the rich and poor. We were told by the resident surgeon that there were no persons in restraint, and we saw none in our progress through the wards.

The descent to Ragatz was easy, being, indeed, by a carriage-road. We reached our inn in sufficient time to allow us to examine the water department before the dinner at five. There is a large establishment of baths, to which you enter by a covered passage leading from the inn. They are, like their fellows at the old baths, somewhat gloomy, but sufficiently neat and clean. The water is deliciously clear, but I found it too cold for comfort, the temperature being only 93°. From some cause or other it had thus lost nearly six degrees of heat since it left its source. This must be owing to some mismanagement, as I think so great a loss could not necessarily be experienced in a column of water of this size passing through such bad conductors as thick wooden pipes,

7

for so short a distance as two miles and a half, and
at so rapid a rate.   If, however, this is the case, or
if the loss of temperature, though not necessary, is
really so, the great superiority of the new baths as to
locality, must be entirely counteracted by the circumstance, as baths of this temperature must be inap-
plicable, or at least much less efficacious, in many
diseases for which we are accustomed to recommend
warm bathing.   I named the circumstance to the
Bad-Artz, but he seemed to consider the depression
of temperature as owing to some temporary cause.

The Ragatzer Hof is an excellent inn, capable of
receiving upwards of one hundred persons.   It belongs to the government of St. Gall, and is let, together with the exclusive right to the baths, for a very
high rent.   There were not more than twenty or
twenty-five Curgäste or patients in the house when
we were there; but, as already remarked, the bathing
season was drawing to a close.   The Speisesaal is
very elegant, and could easily accommodate a hundred guests at a time.   The master of the hotel is
an intelligent young man, who speaks English very
well.   He supplied us with good entertainment, and
we had no reason to consider the charges as otherwise
than fair.   We retired early, in hopes of a fine day
to-morrow, as we had it in view to travel as far as
the baths of Stachelberg, in the valley of the Linth.

CHAPTER XI.

August 18.—The early morning was rainy, and the lofty range of the Falkniss, fronting us on the other side of the Rhine, was covered low down with a thick cloud portending, as we feared, a continuance of bad weather. We were, however, happily mistaken, as the rain entirely ceased within three quarters of an hour after we set out on our journey, the sky soon after becoming clear and the weather very fine, and so it continued the whole day. We had taken places over night in the Diligence to Wesen; and as we had to wait its arrival from Chur whence it starts, we did not set out from Ragatz before seven. We were still fortunate in securing places on the top, and the speedy clearing of the weather made us feel their value. We travelled by the same road, and indeed by the same Diligence, as in our journey to Ragatz. We saw, therefore, the same scenery, though in a reverse point of view; but this difference of view made no great difference in the prospect on the present occasion.

That which most struck us was the fineness of the range of mountains stretching out on our right hand, and directly before us. The first of these ranges, the Balfries, abuts closely on the town of Sarganz, and runs to the north and east to join the range to which the Kurfürsten belong, which, as we have seen, bounds the lake of Wallenstadt on the northern shore. The highest mountain in the former range (the Kamek) is about 7600 English feet, while the Seven Electors (Kurfürsten) are 7400. The peaks of the latter shone beautifully bright before us the whole of our journey, until we came under their very base at Wallenstadt.

Both on the former journey and the present, when crossing the little *Col* on which Sarganz stands, I could not help regarding the configuration and bearings of the surface of the district in relation to the opinion that has been entertained—promulgated first I believe by Von Buch—that a very little alteration in the level of the Rhine might divert it from its present course through the gap in the mountains to the east of Sarganz, and send it more directly to its final destination, by the lakes of Wallenstadt and Zurich. The height of the ground that separates the valleys on either side of Sarganz is said to be only about twenty feet; consequently, it is argued that if anything was to lower this, or to elevate the bed of the Rhine in the same degree, the river would take this course as the more direct one. It has even been supposed that this, in past ages, was the actual course of the river. Whether all or any part of this opinion is true or probable, it will strike any one travelling along the two valleys that to effect such a change by artificial means might not be impracticable.——As we proceeded on our course beyond Sarganz we profited from the rains of yesterday in the increased extent and frequency of the cascades, which we saw falling from the cliffs on both sides of the valley. The whole country looked also greener and fresher from the same cause.

We arrived at Wallenstadt about ten, and immediately embarked in the steamboat which we found waiting for the Diligence. The voyage along the lake was delightful, and its grand beauties struck us as forcibly as on the former occasion. Here, also, we had an improvement in the waterfalls from the previous rain. On arriving at Wesen, we stopped at what seemed the principal inn, L'Epée, facing the landing-place. The house is small, but the accommodation and supplies were tolerably good. The mistress is a very shrewd, clever person, who had been educated in Savoy, and who speaks French very well. We bargained with her for a conveyance to take us to Stachelberg at the top of the valley of the Linth; and were supplied with a one-horse char on moderate terms. We started on our journey about twelve. The day had now become extremely hot; and this satisfied us of the justness of our decision not to walk this journey.

Indeed, in passing along a valley like this, the scenery is fully as well seen from a carriage as on foot.

Passing over the bridge on the Linth canal, and also the original bed of the Linth, and leaving on our left the embankment which keeps the stream in its new direction into the lake, we turned directly up the Linththal, close by the base of the mountains bounding it on the west, and dividing it from the canton of Schwytz. These are lofty, and present almost a vertical cliff along the road, but are not high enough to prevent the snowy peaks of the Glärnish to be seen above them. The loftiest of these nearer mountains, forming the immediate boundary of our road on the right hand, are successively the Rauti and the Wiggis, the elevation of which is about 6200 and 7200 English feet. For some distance we see nothing of the Linth, as it runs on the other side of the valley, or is rather kept there in its new course to the lake; but when we have passed the small town of Näfels (famous for its glorious battle-field) we then approach the original current, and from henceforth never leave its banks so far as to be beyond the sight of its foam or the hearing of its roar. It is, indeed, a most furious torrent, presenting scarcely any alternations of tranquillity in its course from its source to its termination. In the few quieter parts where it flows with an unbroken stream, it still preserves the whiteness so characteristic of glacier water.—We reached Glarus in about two hours.

The town of Glarus is of considerable extent, and contains upwards of 4000 inhabitants. It is situated in the most extraordinary locality, at the bottom of a rounded valley closely hemmed in on all sides by lofty mountains almost vertical in front, and with many of their heads covered with snow. Vulgarly speaking, you would say, and truly, that it lies *in a hole,* if you could allow yourself to give this name to a scene so striking and magnificent. It gives one a shudder to look up to those snowy mountain barriers from which, when in the town, you see no outlet; more especially when you think of the place in winter; as the landlord of the inn told us, the snow lies more than four months in the streets, and the sun is only visible for four hours in the day. The same authority assured us that Glarus, nevertheless, is neither particularly cold nor damp, the very same barriers that shut out the sun, shutting out the winds and keeping the clouds aloft at the same time.

The mountains that more immediately impend over Glarus are the Schilt and the northern base of the Glärnish, the snowy heads of which seem to look down into the very market-place. They rise upwards of 7000 feet above the town, which indeed lies at a very low level for Switzerland — being only about 600 feet above the Mediterranean. Glarus is evidently a bustling place, containing several cotton-factories, and probably supplying a good many of the workers for the numerous mills that are built

along the river here and there, all the way to
Stachelberg. There is a curious fresco on one of the
houses in the market-place, representing a savage
man of portentous size, who is indicated, by a written
legend on the painting, to be a sample of the population inhabiting the country a certain number of
centuries before the birth of Christ. The authority
is unfortunately not quoted in the record.

From Glarus onwards the road keeps close on the
banks of the river, and generally at a considerable
elevation above it; it is very good and not very
steep, but yet constantly on the ascent, as shown by
the unvarying precipitancy of the stream. Shortly
after leaving Glarus we passed through two small
towns or large villages, Mitlodi and Schwanden,
close to the last of which the Linth receives a large
accession in the junction of the Sernft which, after
a long sweep through its mountain valley, communicates with our stream at right angles. About
two or three miles further on, the road crosses to
the right bank of the Linth, at Luchsingen, and continues on the same side all the rest of the way. The
Linth-valley is through its whole extent of considerable width, except at the town of Glarus and a few
other places; and it contains many green and well-
wooded lateral valleys and rich slopes stretching up
the spurs of the mountains. It exhibits every appearance of industrious cultivation, and seems rich
in meadow produce. Everywhere as we went along,
the people were busy gathering in their second crop

of hay, which seemed plentiful. We had occasion to observe the same operation in progress all along our previous route, and then and now could not but admire the extremely rich green of the meadows, and also the excellence of the mowing, which left every surface as smooth and even as the finest country-house lawn in England. We saw no corn in this valley; and we had seen very little since leaving Zurich. Here, however, as elsewhere, there were frequent patches of hemp and some of flax, which seem favorite productions of the Swiss in all their cantons. We passed a considerable number of cotton-factories, which seemed to be built in most places where the flatness of the ground allowed the waters of the river to be drawn off laterally.

The mighty range of the Glärnish, with its numerous heads crowned with snow, long continued close to us on our right hand, changing its profile every half mile, but never losing its grandeur or its beauty. And when, at length, our advance up the valley and the direction of our course left it behind us, we were then greeted by the yet mightier and more majestic Tödi, climbing the blue sky right in our front, its angular and flattened head clothed in one unbroken mass of snow, and now shining with astonishing brilliancy in the western sun. Though still at a great distance from us when first seen— probably fifteen miles—it seemed almost to overlook our path.

About a mile and a half below the village of

7 §

Linthal, we left the main road almost at a right angle, and crossing the Linth on a flat wooden bridge, drove up to a splendid-looking house standing in a pretty pleasure-ground close at the foot of a peaked mountain on our right. This is the Stachelbergerbad, or Hotel of the Baths of Stachelberg, where we purposed to pass the night. We were immediately struck with the romantic beauty of the spot, which subsequent observation tended only to enhance. The hotel is so situated as to command a view both up and down the valley; and this view from the upper rooms is almost as varied as it is magnificent. The valley itself is charming; with its rich green meadows on every side, climbing the spurs of the mountains until stopped by the woods that overhang them; the Linth seen rushing between its wooded banks and receiving, close by the hotel, its two mountain tributaries, one on each side, the Durnagelbach and the Brummbach; and the village of Linthal, with its two church-spires, lying snug amid its fruit trees at the mountain's base. But the mountains that surround and overhang the valley are the great objects of attraction. They are all of great height, many of them, besides the Tödi, being covered with perpetual snow. In fact, the Tödi is merely the loftiest of a chain of snowy mountains which constitute the south-eastern boundary of this portion of the Linththal. One of these, the Haustock, seemed close to the hotel as we looked at it from the windows.

Plate III.

It was only about half-past five when we reached Stachelberg; but even then this part of the valley had already lost the sun and lay in partial twilight. The snowy mountains, however, and especially the Tödi, were bright in the sunshine, even low down on their sides. Later in the evening, between seven and eight o'clock, the view of these mountains was still more striking, when their snowy peaks were seen shining high up in the heavens as bright as we had seen them in the daytime, while all the valley, and indeed all the mountains but themselves, lay in comparative darkness.

Although not of the first order of Swiss mountains, those which border the Linth-valley are of great height. The Glärnish is about 9400 English feet above the sea; the Haustock about 10,000, while the Tödi is 11,800, that is, about 7600 above the baths of Stachelberg. It is only within these ten years that the Tödi has been ascended. It has been now climbed to its highest point at least twice, if not three times.

On arriving at the hotel, we immediately proceeded to take a walk a little further up the valley while daylight lasted. The evening was charming, and felt delightfully mild and cool after the heat we had experienced in the middle of the day. Immediately beyond the shrubbery in which the hotel stands, we cross the little mountain-stream of the Brummbach, just before it enters the Linth. A short way further on, on the same side of the Linth, there is a very large factory worked from a feeder from the Linth, which is here for a short space confined within the banks of a straight artificial bed. I here found the temperature of the water 49°. Crossing the Linth by another bridge, we walked on to the village of Linthal, which is prettily situated under the base of the mountains on the right bank. It is a small place, but contains two churches— one Roman Catholic and one Protestant— and two inns, with a town-hall and some business-looking houses, stores for cheese, &c.

In this village, as indeed all along the fields in our way to Stachelberg, we had frequent indications of the prevalence of cretinism in this valley, in the huge goitres, idiot-like looks, and ill-shaped bodies of many of the persons we met with. We saw some of these wretched beings at the doors of the cottages of Linthal, and they came crowding after us to beg in the streets. Among them there were several quite dwarfish in size. One girl in particular, who was said to be nineteen, and who had a look of age even beyond this, was not taller than a child of six or seven.

After our return I went with the landlord to inspect the bathing establishment which is attached to the hotel. It consists of twenty-four single baths of wood, each supplied with two taps, one for common hot water, the other for cold mineral water. The mineral water is not heated, partly from the apprehension of driving off its special ingredients,

and partly because it is deemed too strong for bathing in its undiluted state.   It is generally used in
the proportion of one part to two of common water.
The spring is about a mile distant, in the base of
the high sharp-peaked rock (the Stachelberg) overhanging the hotel.   It is situated in a cleft in the
limestone rock, and is so scanty as only to furnish a
stream of the size of a quill, affording about a pint or
two per minute.   It is perennial, and is never frozen.
The water is, in the first instance, conducted into a
large tank immediately below the spring, and is
thence conveyed in wooden pipes to the reservoir in
the bath-house.   At the time of our visit, the conducting tubes were so much out of repair that the
people were obliged to convey from the spring in
vessels a portion of the water used for the baths, and
all that was used for drinking.   The water belongs
to the class of alkaline sulphurous waters, and, besides sulphur, contains some carbonate of lime and
sulphate of soda and magnesia.   It also contains
some free carbonic acid gas.

For that class of invalids for whom our Harrowgate
water and sulphureous waters in general are recommended, I cannot but think that this particular
spring ought to have great attractions.   The water
is as good as elsewhere, and the local adjuvants are
superior to those of many other places.   The hotel
is comfortable and clean, and the landlady and the
youthful landlord, her son, are highly respectable
and most attentive.   Such a residence, indeed, ac-

cording to my view, must be highly beneficial in itself, without any reference to the waters. The fine bracing air of so elevated a spot, and the boundless attractions of the district in which it lies, all enticing to constant and somewhat severe exercise, supply, of themselves, when aided by proper diet, all the elements necessary for the cure of a large proportion of chronic diseases. The waters, no doubt, also, used either externally or internally, will prove a valuable auxiliary in some cases; but while the place possesses so many other advantages, the waters I think, as a general rule, may be regarded as only of secondary importance. At any rate, I think the rule laid down by the poet of mineral waters, may be safely followed in this case at least——not to take too much water nor too little exercise :

Nie verleite der Rath des unberufenen Klüglings
Dich, in den köstlichen Gaben der gütigen Nymphen zu schwelgen,
Trinke gemach und wandle dabei—so lautet die Regel.*

Though there was much in the Linththal, in its tributary valleys, and in their bounding mountains, that was most attractive and demanded inspection, our inexorable holiday allowed no indulgence in wishes of this kind. We, therefore, adhered to our original intention of crossing the Klausen Pass on the following day. We could not even spare time, with so long a journey before us, to go up the

* Neubek. Gesundbrunnen.

valley so far as the Pantenbrücke, though well worth visiting, and only about five miles above the baths. But besides this, and the yet higher glens at the foot of the Tödi——not to name the climbing of the Tödi itself——I have every reason to believe that the ascent of several of the minor mountains and *Alps*, and the exploration of the valleys which furnish streams to that we were in, would well repay the delay requisite for their examination. The Sernft-thal, or valley of the Sernft, in particular, affords a highly interesting excursion. It is shut in by mountains on every side, and is only accessible through the narrow rocky pass through which the river flows for half a league before joining the Linth at Schwanden. Above this pass the valley spreads out to some extent, and contains several small towns or villages, namely, Engi, Matt, and Elm.

CHAPTER XII.

August 19.——Our plans having been arranged over
night, we were summoned at four. The morning
was beautiful, the air mild (though the thermometer
at five stood at 51°), and the sky cloudless; and we
had a repetition of the magnificent scene of last
night, of the illumination of the Tödi and Haustock
in the regions above, while all below was yet in
comparative gloom. The process of lighting-up,
however, was now in some measure reversed, the
light gradually descending on the snowy peaks until
the whole were bright, instead of gradually ascending, as in the evening, until the whole was dark.
I hardly know which of the two was most beautiful.

Having breakfasted, we started on our journey at
six. We had engaged one man to carry our luggage all
the way to Altorf, and another to take charge of the
horse which was to carry me to the top of the Klausen
Pass, and then return. My two companions were

to walk the whole way. After advancing about a mile along the base of the hills on the left bank of the Linth, we turned off at right angles, and immediately began a steep ascent, of the zigzag kind, up a wooded hill. On emerging from the thick wood, which may have been in about an hour and a half, we came upon a much more open and less steep slope, bounded with a lofty range of mountains on either side, and exhibiting a fine example of rich Alpine pasture, or what is called an ALP in Switzerland. Although still well-wooded, this slope, or rather series of slopes, had many spaces of considerable extent almost free from trees ; and even where these grew thickest, there was everywhere plenty of pasture-ground among them, occupied by large herds of cattle and also by goats. It would not be easy to find a more charming scene for a ride or walk, or one more truly pastoral than that which we were now travelling. Although it was, as I have said, bounded on either side by a lofty range of parallel cliffs, showing very little verdure and but scantily sprinkled with trees, and although there was a brawling stream washing the base of the bounding ridge on our left hand, we advanced a long way on our path before we could properly say that we were traversing a valley. It was rather a sloping indentation in the mountains than a valley properly so called.

After advancing for some time through this kind of country, we made a slight descent down to the banks of the stream, and then we entered on a much flatter and wider and much less wooded space. This is what is properly called the Valley of Urnerboden, although the whole track we had been traversing since we reached the top of the steep mountain path, is usually so designated. As we advanced, our path led us close under the cliffs on the right hand ; the river still continuing at the base of the opposite range. This comparatively flat and open valley was probably a mile wide, and extended many miles in length. It is bounded at its further extremity by the lofty ridge called the KLAUSEN PASS, which is merely the union, at a somewhat lower level, of the two ranges of inaccessible cliffs which had formed the lateral boundaries of the valley all along.

Nothing could be more shut in from the rest of the world than this Alpine Valley of Urnerboden. As a natural consequence of its very extensive and rich pasture-grounds, it contains numerous herds of cattle, many chalets or summer huts, and a considerable population during the summer months. I went into one of the chalets in the first group we came to, lying close under the base of the bare cliff. We here found an old woman busy at her spinning-wheel, and her husband who came from his dairy labours to greet our arrival. We were very kindly received, and immediately presented with bread and cheese and goat's milk, of all of which we partook. The cottage was extremely small and rude, but less dirty than others I had seen. On looking about among the old man's furniture, which was of the most primitive fashion, I found two or three books of a religious kind, and one which contained an epitome of the laws of the canton of Uri where we now were. The old couple seemed very cheerful, and were very grateful for the small bounty we offered for their hospitality.

About a mile further on, we arrived at what must be regarded as the capital of Urnerboden, as it contains some twenty or more chalets in one group, a kind of hostelry or wine-hut, and a small chapel, built of stone, and having a little belfry and bell. Finding that the priest resided in one of the wooden houses——the only one of two stories in the place——I waited on him and requested permission to see the interior of his chapel, and also to speak with himself. His housekeeper, who was a tidy, middle-aged woman, much deformed in her person, accompanied me to the chapel. This is a small place, capable of containing sixty or eighty persons, tolerably neat, and having the usual altar ornaments. It has also several pictures, one illustrating some of the great doings of its patron saint, and some others on Scripture subjects. On my return to the priest's house, he came down stairs, and cheerfully conversed with me for some time, while the housekeeper plied her wheel in the corner. He was a fine-looking man of perhaps thirty years of age, Johann Joseph Gisler by name. He belonged to the valley of Schächen on the other side of the Pass, but spent four months up here every summer. There was service in his

chapel twice every Sunday, and he said his ministrations were well attended. He never left the
valley, to go to the under world, during the period
of his residence here. The whole population of
Urnerboden, with the exception of two or three,
descended to the lower country in the winter.

I accompanied the good man to a cottage, a
short distance from his house, to visit a family who
were sick. I found in one small room, with its
door and windows closely shut, a mother and one
child in one bed and two other children in a second,
all of them labouring under dysentery. They were
attended by a young woman and by the father and
husband, a man upwards of six feet high, and certainly one of the finest men I ever saw. My pre-
scription was to open the door and windows, to
allow the forbidden luxury of cold water and milk,
for drink and food, and to apply fomentations to the
affected region; and I left my patients in full confidence of their recovery, though there was probably
not one grain of medicine nearer than Altorf. I
was much interested by this good priest of the
Alp of Urnerboden, who, in his humble and lonely
station, seemed to fulfil with such good faith and unaffected simplicity, the sacred duties to which he
had vowed himself; and when he took leave, after
accompanying me some distance from his cottage,
I could not help feeling more warmly than the
occasion might reasonably have been thought to require. But the sources of sympathy had been opened

on either side, and the imagination might easily be impressed both by the place and the circumstances of the meeting and the parting; and, besides,

"One touch of Nature makes the whole world kin."

I overtook my companions before they had made much progress up the steep ascent that ended in the ridge of the Klausen. This ascent had none of the rich verdure or wood through which we had hitherto passed, but was a bare, sterile hill covered with loose rocks fallen from the cliffs above, and showing other signs of our having gained a loftier level. The bounding cliffs on our left hand had now terminated in a mountain peak completely covered with snow, having on one of its skirts a small glacier from which the stream we had been tracking was seen to take its precipitous origin : its glacier source had been already sufficiently indicated by the low temperature which it had exhibited far below in the valley, viz. that of 40° and 41°. We reached the top of the Klausen at noon, and here we stopped to take some refreshment which we had brought with us, and to make new arrangements for the remainder of the journey. The day was still extremely fine, but the height to which we had now attained rendered the air cool, the thermometer in the shade being only 51°. The temperature of a spring in the same place, fed by the glaciers, was only 37°. We dismissed our horse and one of our attendants to retrace their steps to Stachelberg, and we transferred

to our remaining guide the knapsacks of the whole
party. The view from this ridge, which is about
6500 English feet above the sea, is not particularly
grand.

The valley of Schächen, which extends all the
way to Altorf, takes its origin at the western base
of the Klausen Pass, and into this we now proceeded
to descend by a path which soon became extremely
precipitous, and continued so for a considerable
time. All the party were now pedestrians; and we
reckoned on having only about twelve or fourteen
miles before us, and all down-hill. On reaching
the bottom of the steep descent, we found the foaming Schächen already a stream of considerable size,
although so near its source; a circumstance indicative of its snow-source in the adjoining mountains.
Shortly after entering the valley we passed on our
left hand the falls of the Stäubi, a magnificent and
beautiful cascade falling from a steep cliff of great
height. The mass of water was sufficient to form a
large stream, which we crossed by a wooden bridge,
in its way to the Schächen. Its glacier origin was
testified alike by its white colour and its temperature,
which I found to be only 37°.

In looking at this fall we were particularly struck
with the manner in which the water seems to descend in a succession of distinct globes, and gradually lengthening columns of foam, which the eye
cannot help fixing on and following as they fall.
This appearance I have since found described so

exactly by Laborde, that I must quote his words. His description is taken from the Staubach, which, however, did not present the peculiar appearance to us when we saw it ; probably because it contained but little water at the time of our visit. But the following sentence conveys to the mind most accurately and vividly what we admired at the Stäubi : " The leisurely and graceful manner in which its light vapoury columns dispose themselves, one over the other, in the first stage of their descent from the edge of the precipice, is very remarkable : each of these, after the first rupture of its waters by the action of the air, takes the appearance of a white star followed by a long tail." It may also be compared to a more vulgar object, a ball of wool thrown down from a height, and ravelling out into a long train as it falls.

The valley of Schächen bears a considerable resemblance to that of the Linth, and is very beautiful. As we descend, it becomes at first wider and more richly wooded, and then again contracts ; but everywhere its flatter fields exhibit the greenest and richest pasture, and the bounding mountains are clothed with trees to the borders of the stream, which retains its rapid and foaming course through its whole extent. We kept for a considerable time on its left bank. Some way below the Stäubi we passed over the remains, yet raw and bare, of a Bergfall or avalanche of earth, which had descended in the year 1833 from the mountain on our left hand, and temporarily blocked up the river, which indeed is still partially dammed by it. Nearly opposite there are two small villages, both conspicuous by their churches. We now crossed the river; and further on we rested half an hour and took some refreshment at another village called Spiringen. Here there is also a church and of greater size; and there are a good many houses, both of wood and stone, scattered about among the trees. The landlord of our little hotel had been one of the soldiers of the Sunderbund in the late disturbances: but he looked with no complacency on the proceedings of his party, being evidently attached to the views of the reformers. He told us that his father had been one of the guides that helped to direct the course of the Russian army in the year 1799, when Suwarrow led them up the valley of Schächen over the Kinzig Kulm into the Muotta Thal. Below Spiringen the valley becomes more contracted and hilly, but still richer than before. Our road at times led us high above the river, and up and down hills (the spurs of the mountain on our right) of considerable steepness.

After keeping for a long time on the right bank of the river, we crossed again to its left, at a beautiful spot some distance above BURGLEN, where the valley was clothed with walnut, chesnut, and other fruit trees. We were now in the land of WILLIAM TELL, and, consequently, on classic ground. We stopped a short space at Burglen, his birthplace, and visited the little chapel which was erected, a hundred and fifty years after his death, on the spot where his house stood. This chapel is still in good repair, though some of the rude frescoes that cover its walls are somewhat effaced. Its little wicket of open ironwork is kept locked, and the key deposited in a house adjoining. The frescoes are not of a religious character, but represent some of the incidents in the life of this heroic peasant ; yet the building is truly a religious one, and consecrated to the devotions of the pious wayfarer.

It is a striking indication of the more general prevalence of religious feelings among the people of those simpler times, that remarkable events even of a purely political character, were then commemorated in immediate connexion with the exercise of the Christian rites. Where we would erect pillars and statues, endow schools, or establish Exhibitions, our more pious progenitors built chapels and oratories. It was, accordingly, by such monuments as these that the patriotic exploits of the great fathers of Swiss freedom were commemorated ; and it is, pro- bably, owing, in a considerable degree, to their spe- cial connexion with what has always been felt as man's first duty, that they have been kept so fresh to this hour, in the memories of their humblest descendants.

On leaving Burglen, we crossed once more to the right bank of the Schächen, and now turned directly away from it to pursue our course to Altorf. This stream, which soon after passing Burglen, joins the

8

Reuss at Attinghausen, has both a bright and a
melancholy fame in the annals of Switzerland.   On
its banks both Tell and Walter Furst were born,
and in its furious waters the former is said to have
lost his life in attempting to save that of another.
At Attinghausen, the house of Walter Furst is still
standing, and held in the veneration it deserves.
Here also are still the ruins of the castle of that
good knight, the banner-bearer of Uri, who, as the
only noble who sympathised with the patriots, plays
so interesting a part in Schiller's Wilhelm Tell.
But our time did not permit us to go so far as to
visit either.

It was exactly six o'clock when we arrived at
Altorf.   We put up at the Adler or Black Eagle, a
tolerably good inn, where we slept.   This inn is
close by the famous tower of Tell, and consequently
near the two fountains which mark, or are believed
to mark, the spots whereon Tell and his son respectively stood on the grand day when the bold bowman in cleaving the apple sealed the doom of his
country's oppressors.

In our hotel at Altorf we were again saluted,
during the vigils of the night, but in a very miti-
gated degree, with some of the same patriotic and
pious strains which had so disturbed us at Chur.
As chanted here, however, they were far from un-
welcome.   The only other place, I think, where we
heard these *Wächterrufe*, was Neuchatel.   These calls
are very interesting relics of the old times, and must

be considered indicative as well of the simple habits, as of the pious feelings of the people of old. I am indebted to the same kind friend who furnished me with the Chur-chant, for the following additional notices respecting these watch-calls in Switzerland.

In the town of Glarus the following are the evening and morning chants :

I.—EVENING CALL, AT TEN P.M.

Ich komme auf die Abendwacht,
Gott gebe euch alle eine gute Nacht :
Löschet Feuer und Licht,
Dass euch Gott behüth ;
Losset was ich euch sage—
Die Glocke hat zehn geschlage.

II.—MORNING CALL, AT FOUR A.M.

Steht auf im Namen Herr Jesu Christ,
Dieweil der Tag erschienen ist :
Die Sonne kommt über die Berg' herab—
Drum wünsch ich Allen ein guten Tag.
Losset was ich, &c.

———

I.

I come upon the evening watch :
God give you all a good night :
Quench fire and light,
That God may you guard :
List to what I tell you—
The clock has struck ten.

II.

Get up in the name of the Lord Jesus Christ,
For the day has appeared :
The sun comes over the mountains down—
So I wish you all a good day.
List to what I tell you, &c.

The following, in the Swiss patois dialect, is chanted in some places in the canton Zurich, but not in the town of Zurich itself, where the watchman's call is no longer heard :

> Jez stohni uft der Obedwacht,
> Behüt is Herr in dieser Nacht :
> Gib dem Lib und der Seele Rhu,
> Und fuhri is alli gen Himmel zu.

> Now stand I on the evening watch :
> Protect us God in this night :
> Give to body and soul rest,
> And lead us all to heaven.

The Chur-chant as well as that of Glarus, which are both in the common German, have probably been modernised by some modish reformers of the night-watch ; but they are all very ancient. The one just given in the vernacular Swiss is probably the identical call chanted centuries back.

Of the great antiquity of these chants we have some strong evidence. In the small town of Stein, on the Rhine, in the canton of Aargau, there is a chant now in nightly use, which dates as far back as the fourteenth century. Its precise origin, as well as its original words, have been handed down from father to son, and both are of unquestioned authenticity. This is the story : Some time in the fourteenth century, at a period when there were very frequent contests between the towns and the feudal lords of the country, a plot was concocted to deliver Stein into the hands of the nobles of the vicinity, in which plot some traitorous citizens were engaged. The night of attack came, and all was arranged for the admission of the enemy by the traitors at two o'clock in the morning; the watchword agreed on between the parties being " Noch ä Wyl" (Noch eine Weile —Yet a while). An industrious shoemaker, however, who lived close to the gate, and whom some urgent work kept up so late, overheard the whispered signal and the sound of arms also outside, and, rushing to the watchhouse, gave the alarm, and so defeated the meditated assault and saved the town. Ever since, the nightwatch at Stein, when he calls the hour of two, must chant out the old words which saved the little burgh from destruction five hundred years since—" Noch ä Wyl! Noch ä Wyl!"

The same antiquity and also the inveteracy of old customs to persist, is strikingly shown by the fact, that in some parts of the canton of Tessino, where the common language of the people is Italian, the nightwatch-call is still in Old German.

CHAPTER XIII.

August 20.——After breakfast I took a short walk about the town, which is a small, quiet place, but contains some good houses, and shows in its general clean and fresher aspect, the beneficial consequences of the fire which destroyed it in 1799.

Close before our inn, in the market-place, there is a venerable old tower of common and even rude architecture, which is said to have been built anterior to the date of Swiss freedom. Its exterior walls are ornamented with rude frescoes representing the one grand subject of all the pictorial legends of Uri, the tyranny of Gesler and his fellows, and the terrible vengeance of Tell. Close beside this tower there is a public fountain, understood to mark the spot where Tell's son stood when his father clove the apple on his head ; and further down the street there is another, considered to be the spot where the matchless bowman stood in his agony. I measured the distance between the two fountains, and found it to be about 120 paces ; a distance, I apprehend, quite within the range of a cross-bow.

We took a carriage to Flüelen, a small town on

the border of the lake, about two miles beyond Altorf. Here we found one steamer about to sail for Luzern, and another whose arrival was soon expected, but which would not sail for a considerable time afterwards. We, of course, wished to proceed by the first, but found we could not do so, on account of some silly quarrel between the proprietors of the boats, and which, strangely enough, had been adopted by the cantons ; the one boat not being permitted to carry passengers from Flüelen to Luzern, nor the other from Luzern to Flüelen. This arrangement annoyed us at first, but we soon found reason to be well satisfied, as, owing to it, we were enabled to visit the famous TELLENPLATTE, which we must have otherwise been contented to look at from the lake as we passed. The captain of the interdicted steamer having given us a hint that he could take us up a little further on in the lake, we and three or four young men, in the same predicament as ourselves, got into a boat, and were rowed along the lake in the direction of Luzern.

We had sufficient time, before the steamer reached us, to see the chapel of Tell ; and it was not without some excited feelings that we leaped from our boat upon the famous PLATTE or small rocky shelf on which tradition records that he leaped, 500 years ago, from the boat of Gesler. It was something to see with our own eyes and feel with our own feet, here as at Altorf, that what tradition records to have been done might have been done. Nothing could

be easier than for an adroit and athletic steersman
so to direct his course as to enable him to jump on
shore on this the sole point in the neighbourhood
where his foot could rest. The little chapel is
erected just above the ledge of rock, in a small niche
of the cliff. We found it open. Its interior is
covered throughout with rude frescoes illustrating
the history of Tell and his heroic companions. The
pictures are somewhat injured by time; but considering their antiquity, it is surprising to find them
so perfect as they are. This chapel was erected, it
is said, not more than thirty years after Tell's death,
but I presume the paintings are of much more recent date, though still old. The following remark
of Laborde, written in reference to this very spot,
is most just, and every one who travels in the land
of Schwytz and Uri will feel its force:

"There is something in the grandeur and magnificence of the scenes which surround you in this
classic country, which gently but irresistibly opens
the heart to a belief in the truth of the page upon
which the events which have hallowed them are
recorded. Whatever a man may think, and however
he may be inclined to question the strength of the
evidence upon which the relation of these facts rests,
while in his closet, I should think there are but few
sufficiently insensible and dogmatical to stand firm and
bar their hearts against the credulity which steals over
them while contemplating the spots themselves."*

* Alpenstock, p. 77.

And in respect of William Tell, more especially, we may well say as Byron said of Homer on the plains of Troy :

> "Oh, cold were he
> Who here could gaze denying thee !"

In a short time after we had left the chapel and returned to our boat, the steamer came up and took us in tow until she arrived at her first halting-place, Brunnen, in canton Schwytz. Here, I suppose, the local jurisdiction of the two other cantons ceased to be valid, and therefore we were received on board. This Brunnen was the place where Gesler landed after his boat was launched back into the lake by the " potent foot-thrust " of William Tell at the PLATTE.* We had come along the same track precisely, and in a boat to be sure rude enough to have been used by Gesler, but with what a difference in the locomotive power !

In our way, we had, of course, pointed out to us by our boatmen, the famous trysting-place of Grütli amid its green trees, on the other side of the lake ; not without regret that we must so pass it. When opposite to it, we were agreeably startled by the young men in our boat, who had accompanied us from Flüelen, suddenly bursting out into a pleasing strain which they sang in concert, and apparently

---

* "—Schwing' ich selbst
Hochspringend auf die Platte mich hinauf,
Und mit gewalt'gem Fussstoss hinter mich
Schleudr' ich das Schifflein in den Schlund der Wasser."

W. Tell, Aufz. iv, sc. 1.

8 §

with feeling as well as taste. It was one of the new national songs of their country, and had for its theme the very spot we were looking at. I inferred, as well from their general appearance as from this badge of patriotism, that the singers were students and members of the ZOFINGEN-VEREIN ; and I was not mistaken. I subjoin, in a note, a portion of their song, which, with the verses already given (p. 78), will help to illustrate, at once, the present state of feeling in Switzerland, and the quality of the poetry now popular.

GRÜTLI.

Von Ferne sei herzlich gegrüsset,
Du stilles Gelände am See,
Wo spielend die Welle zerfliesset
Genähret von ewigem Schnee.

Gepriesen sei, friedliche Stätte,
Gegrüsset du heiliges Land,
Wo sprengten der Sklaverei Kette
Die Väter mit mächtiger Hand.

Hier standen die Väter zusammen
Für Freiheit und heimisches Gut,
Und schwuren beim heiligsten Namen,
Zu stürzen die Zwingherrenbrut.

Und Gott, der Allmächtige, nickte
Gedeihen zum heilige Schwur;
Sein Arm die Tyrannen endrückte,
Und frei war die heimische Flur.

Drum, GRÜTLI, sei freundlich gegrüsset ;
Dein Name wird nimmer vergehn,
So lange der Rhein uns noch fliesset,
So lange die Alpen bestehn.

We can hardly say that we saw much more of Brunnen than of Grütli, as we merely landed on its little beach to walk to the steamer. But it, as well as Grütli, recalls the memory of deeds glorious as those of the battle-field. If it was at Grütli that the deliverance of their country was peaceably planned by the Swiss patriots, it was at Brunnen that that country was established as an independent nation, by the solemn federation of the three forest cantons on the 8th of December 1315, three-and-twenty days after the victory of Morgarten.

Our next stoppage was at Gersau, once an independent republic, and the smallest in Europe, now belonging to the canton of Schwytz. It is a romantic-looking spot, with its small strip of rich mountain land above it, crowded with neat cottages, which were now shining brightly in the sun from amid its green fields and fruit trees. We reached Luzern at eleven o'clock.

The whole of our voyage from Altorf to Luzern was delightful. Nothing could exceed the summer beauty of the day, and the same may be said of the scenes which it lighted up. That arm of the lake which extends in a northerly direction from Flüelen to Brunnen presents, more especially at its southern extremity, much bolder scenery than elsewhere, the bounding mountains on both sides being bare perpendicular cliffs resembling those of the Wallenstadter See, but less lofty and grand. At Brunnen, the lake makes a sudden turn to the left hand, so as to shut out entirely that portion of it which we had already passed through. The shores also become much less precipitous and lofty, and, instead of bare cliffs, present us with cultivated meadows and finely-wooded hills, of the greatest beauty.

We had a great many passengers on board, a considerable proportion being country-people taking advantage of the holiday. Many of these were gaily dressed in their Sunday attire, and looked picturesque in their cantonal costume. I cannot say, that I saw much beauty among them. I found much good nature, however; as my female readers will admit when I tell them that some of the damsels were so very civil as to derange their smart headdress, in order that I might inspect the fine silver ornaments which they saw I was curiously admiring. This is only one instance out of many I could name, which prove at once the good nature and simplicity of the Swiss.

On arriving at Luzern, we took up our abode at the Schweitzer Hof, a magnificent hotel built on the very shore of the lake, and commanding a glorious view of it and the surrounding mountains. From our windows we could reckon at once upwards of twenty lofty peaks in our front and on both hands, all hemming in the beautiful sheet of water lying at our feet. The rugged and lofty Pilatus was the nearest to us; and, shortly after our arrival, he gave us a taste of his quality in the form of a thunderstorm, which added much, for the time, to the grandeur of the scene before us. It passed speedily off, and left the skies clear and brilliant as before.

The town of Luzern is a poor place, at least when compared with the towns of Germany, and we had therefore no great temptation to inspect it minutely. Its position in relation to its lake and its river, the Reuss, is exactly like that of Zurich in relation to its lake and the Limmatt. But the Reuss is a finer river and the bridges across it are much more picturesque and more extensive. They contain many quaint old pictures, painted on the walls of the house-like structures which inclose them. The water of the Reuss is beautifully clear, and of the same rich sea-green colour as the lake. It flows tranquilly but with great rapidity.

The great lion of Luzern is THE LION sculptured on a sandstone-rock adjoining the town, in commemoration of the Swiss guards, who may be said to have suffered martyrdom in defence of their master, the King of France, in the beginning of the French Revolution. It is truly a magnificent work of art, admirable in conception and execution, and touching forcibly both the imagination and the feelings. It is cut in high relief on the face of the living rock, and represents a lion wounded by a spear and dying, yet still seeking to protect with his body the shield of France. The lion's figure is of immense size, 28 feet by 18. The original idea of the monument was suggested by General Pfyffer, one of the surviving Swiss, but was worked out and modelled by Thorwalsden. Above the sculpture is inscribed the motto : *Helvetiorum Fidei ac Virtuti ;* and, below it, the names of the officers who fell, and the few survivors. One of these still remains, and holds the office of curator of the monument. He is a hale old man of about seventy, and was a drummer in the corps when the conflict took place, the 10th of August, 1792. He attends here during the summer months, dressed in the ugly old uniform of the Swiss guards. During the rest of the year he works at his trade, which is the unheroic one of a tailor.

We joined the late or English table-d'hôte at four o'clock. It was not very numerously attended, and one half of the party was probably English. After dinner we walked to the top of a small hill on the north side of the town, from which there is a fine view of the lake.

CHAPTER XIV.

August 21.——Being busy all the morning with
our little economical arrangements as to baggage,
bankers, letter-writing, &c., we did not leave Luzern
till half-past ten.   Our destination was Meyringen.
We took a char to Winkel, a small place on one of
the angles of the lake, only four or five miles distant from Luzern.   Our road lay along the western
side of the lake, but at some distance from it, the
range of hills which borders the water being interposed between us and it.   The valley through which
we passed was green and woody, and all the sweeter
from being frowned over by the gaunt Pilatus.   We
reached Winkel in three quarters of an hour, and
immediately embarked in a rowing-boat for Gestad,
near Alpnach.   We had three rowers whose fare
was only a franc a-piece, and who were much pleased
when we gave them something more at the end of
the voyage.   One of them was a splendid specimen
of a Swiss mountaineer, just such a man as we could
fancy the men to have been whose actions made

classical the very spots we had recently been and still were traversing. Our men rowed well, and as they were also enabled to hoist sail part of the way, the wind down the lake being favorable, we reached our destination in about two hours. The day was in every way delightful; and such was the charm of the scenery all around us, that it was impossible not to regret that our voyage was so soon at an end.

This portion of the lake exceeded in beauty the finest spots we had passed through the day before; and, for my own part, I can scarcely imagine that, in point of mere beauty, *any* lake-scenery could excel this. In one place, just before passing the narrow strait at Stanzstadt, we had a splendid view of the lake all along its north-eastern arm, to an extent probably of fifteen miles or more; but at other times the expanse of water was comparatively small, so as to bring the beauty of the shores directly within our grasp. There was, at the same time, great variety in the scenery, owing to the twisting course of the shores, both on our left hand where the hills were wooded to their base, and on the right, where Pilatus sent his naked flanks sheer down into the clear blue water. Such scenes hardly need the charm of historical legend or romance to heighten their impression on the mind; but these were also here in abundance. I was gratified to find that our boatmen were acquainted with the story of the castle of Rotzberg; and looking on the manly frame and fine countenance of our chief rower, as, standing up in the boat, he swept us past the ancient ruin, the thought came naturally into the mind that the bold lover of Anneli might have been such a man ; and of such a stamp might have been the Twenty who on the first day of the year 1308 wrested the fortress from the hands of the Austrian garrison.

On reaching the village of Gestad, we hired a char at the White Horse to take us to Lungern. The landlady tried hard to make us take two horses instead of one ; but after some sharp remonstrance, backed by the threat of walking the distance, she at length acceded to our wishes, and we started with the single horse and char, for which we were to pay twelve francs and Trinkgeld. About a mile and a half beyond Gestad, we passed through the village of Alpnach, once famous for its slide or slip for launching timber from the top of the mountain into the lake, on the same principle as ship-launching. It has now nothing to distinguish it but a very smart new church. From thence we proceeded, by a fine level road, to Sarnen, situated at the northern extremity of the lake of that name. That part of Unterwalden, or rather Obwalden, through which we passed, is a fine open valley, richly cultivated and thickly spread with all sorts of fruit trees. The fields are large and green ; and finely mowed as they were, the whole country looked like a succession of gentlemen's parks in England, with the pleasing addition of glorious mountains in the background

on every side.   We kept on the left bank of the
river which unites the lake of Sarnen with the bay
of Alpnach, but at a considerable distance from it,
until we arrived at the town of Sarnen, when we
crossed it.

Sarnen is a small town, prettily situated at the
end of the lake, near the base of the ridge of mountains which bound the valley on the east.   On the
right hand as we enter the town from the Alpnach
road, stands a small isolated hill termed Landenberg, another of the classical spots of Swiss history.
Here stood the castle of Beringar, one of the tyran-
nical bailiffs whose oppression caused the revolution,
and which shared the same fate as the Rotzberg,
and on the same auspicious new-year's day.   There
are no remains of the ancient castle, and its site is
now occupied by a public building of very plain appearance.   We did not stop here, but halted a little
further on at the village of Sachslen, in order that
we might pay a short visit to the handsome church,
which contains the remains of the celebrated Nicholas
Von der Flue, still revered as a saint, and justly
famous as a patriot.   We did not desire to see his
bones, which are however still preserved in the
church, and exhibited to the public, richly decorated,
on high days and holidays.   We should have been
better pleased, had our arrangements permitted us,
to visit the valley of Melchthal where he lived and
died, and where also we should have seen some more
of the spots where the lowly but noble workers of

Swiss freedom lived in the heroic times. This valley was the abode of Arnold of Melchthal, one of the three men of Grütli, whose resistance to the servant of the Bailiff of Landenberg, when sent to take possession of his oxen, was the cause of his father being deprived of his eyes, and one of the immediate causes of the revolution. The river Melch, after traversing its valley-in a northerly direction, joins the Sarnen stream just before we enter the town.

From Sachslen our road lay close along the eastern shore of the small lake of Sarnen, which is about three miles long, and also close under the mountains which here closely bound it. The lake itself has not much to recommend it ; but the bordering ground through which our road lay, and the range of hills on our left hand, are both exceedingly beautiful. The hilly slopes, across the base of which we passed, looked like, or rather were, an almost unbroken succession of gardens or orchards —that is, rich, green meadows, interspersed with walnut, chesnut, apple, and plum trees, covered abundantly with fruit. The mountain range above was also beautifully wooded, in most places up to the very top.

Accustomed as we are in England to see walnut, chesnut, and plum trees used either for ornament, or at most as affording a mere temporary luxury, I was at first surprised at observing such a profusion of these trees in Switzerland, covering ground which I thought might be more beneficially employed for other kinds of husbandry. I found, however, on inquiry, what I ought to have anticipated among so thrifty a people, that the fruits of all these trees constitute an important part of the produce of the country. Walnuts are employed to a great extent as supplying the main part of the oil made use of by the inhabitants for purposes of light : it is also used, but sparingly, as an edible oil. The country cottagers raise the oil employed by the people in the towns; and this, indeed, constitutes no inconsiderable portion of their little trade. The oil is extracted by compression in a mill, after the walnuts have been individually broken by hand, with a common hammer. Chesnuts are much used as food, simply roasted, also in soup, &c. In many parts of Switzerland, and still more abundantly in Piedmont, the produce of the plum trees are dried in the sun, and are exported in great quantities. They constitute our *French plums*.

On arriving at a small village at the extremity of the lake of Sarnen, where the stream from the Lungern lake flows into it, we left our carriage to walk up the steep ascent called the Kaiserstuhl. This ascent is about two miles in length, and leads in zig-zags through a thick wood. From its summit we had a fine view of the lake of Sarnen and the country through which we had passed; and before us, and close below us, lay the remains of the lake of Lungern, sadly altered from its original condition.

Previously to the year 1836, when the Lungern-see was undermined, and the greater portion of its waters drawn off into the lake of Sarnen, it and its surrounding scenery constituted one of the loveliest spots in all Switzerland. The case is, however, very different now. The mountains and village, to be sure, remain, but the lake itself, once celebrated for its great depth and the exquisite blue colour of its water, has lost much of its extent and still more of its beauty. Nature has not yet had time to efface, in her own charming way, the disfiguring scars inflicted on her by the hand of art. Owing to the great depth of a portion of the lake, a good deal of water still remains in its original hollows, below the level of the tunnel; but it gives evident marks, in its black bounding rocks and coarse bordering meadows, that it is only the ghost of what it was. A very considerable quantity of land has been gained at the southern end of the lake, and is now in a state of cultivation; but it has a tame, artificial look about it, totally unlike that of a natural Alpine valley, and quite out of keeping with the fine wooded steeps which rise around it, and which a poet might describe as mourning the loss of the blue waters which so long mirrored their beauties. The tunneling and eventual tapping of this lake was a work of great labour and cost; but the reclaimed soil will eventually far overpay both, in the estimate of the economist, at least; and this being the case, I suppose in this worky-day world of ours, the reclama-

tion of the landscape painter or lover of nature ought
to go for nought.

On our way up the Kaiserstuhl we sometimes saw
in the valley below us, and sometimes only heard
the precipitous stream which now takes its subter-
raneous origin from the bottom, or what was once
the bottom of the lake, instead of flowing over the
top of the Kaiserstuhl, which was formerly its barrier
on this side. From this point to the small town of
Lungern the road lies close along the eastern border
of the lake. In some places this border is now a
steep and lofty cliff, high above the lake that once
lay level with it, and the old high-water mark of
which is still very visible on the rocks all around.
As we advanced, however, the banks became less
steep, and sloped gently down to that portion of
the old bottom of the lake which is now dry land.
This, though still bearing indications of its recent
change, is mostly green and cultivated, with a good
many young fruit trees and new cottages scattered
over it.

At the bottom of the Kaiserstuhl we had engaged
a man, at his own urgent entreaty, to carry our
knapsacks from Lungern to Meyringen; and as he
took the start of us going up hill, we found, on
our arrival at the Golden Lion of Lungern, some
refreshment in the shape of coffee and milk, and its
accompaniments of excellent honey and butter, all
ready for us. We arrived at a quarter to five, and
as we had a good long walk before us, we made no

longer stay here than was absolutely necessary. The afternoon being very warm, we prepared for our foot-journey by lessening our clothing, and I soon found the advantage of doing so. The village of Lungern lies at the very foot of the Brünig, so that the ascent began at once. This became immediately very steep, the footpath leading up it in zigzags through a thick wood. This hard pull lasted for about a couple of miles, and I was glad on reaching its top to rest by the small chapel which crowns it, and from which there is a beautiful view of the country we had passed through.

We now descended a steep hill on the other side, which formed the northern boundary of one of the loveliest of those secluded mountain valleys which are so charming. This valley is perhaps a couple of miles long, and nearly half as broad. It is surrounded on all sides by beautifully wooded hills, which on the east and west sides terminate in bare mountain cliffs of great height. There was a very small stream flowing through it towards the south, but owing to the form of the ground we could see no outlet to it. The valley was clothed in rich green meadows, interspersed with trees of great size, and dotted over with hay-chalets. I saw no dwelling-houses, and I believe there were none, as it was evidently only a summer Alp for the feeding of cattle, and growing hay for winter consumption in the valleys. It was almost flat at bottom, and, with its precipitous walls all round,

looked somewhat like the crater of an old vol-
cano. The ascent out of the valley at the further end was considerably less steep than at its
other extremity. On reaching the top we had a
glorious view of the Oberland Alps, their snowy
summits shining bright in the evening sunshine.
Some of these seemed close to us on the other side
of the valley ; others at a greater distance.

We now turned to the left, and pursued our
downward course to Meyringen along the side of
the mountain-ridge of the Brünig, which bounds
the valley of the Aar to the north. This ridge,
like most of those we had seen, is clothed with wood
along its sides and base, with bare craggy peaks
above. The descent was steep at first, but gradually
became more gentle, and the last few miles were
quite in the flat of the valley along the right bank
of the Aar. By this time it had become nearly
dark in the valley, as we did not reach the village of
Meyringen until twenty minutes to eight, after a
smart walk of two hours and forty minutes. We put
up at the *Wilde Mann*, or Hôtel du Sauvage, where,
among other good things, we got for supper some
excellent trout from the lake of Brientz.

CHAPTER XV.

August 22.——Having arranged our plans over-
night, to visit the falls of the Aar at Handeck and
return to our inn, we were called at five o'clock,
and, after taking some coffee, started at about half-
past six.   The whole party engaged horses for this
journey, paying nine francs per horse, with two
guides.   After proceeding up the valley eastward
for some distance, we crossed the Aar by an inclosed
wooden bridge of recent construction, the former
having been carried away a few years since.   Then
turning to the right, we ascended the hill called the
Kirchet, which here divides the valley of Oberhasli from that of Meyringen or Unterhasli, leaving the river to pursue its way in its narrow ravine
at some distance on our left.   An excellent and
broad carriage-road, only just finished, conducted
us to the top of the Kirchet, and there abruptly
stopped, leading, literally, to nothing; as there is
neither town nor village on this side of the hill.

9

From this point we had a charming view, immediately below us, of the valley of Imgrund, which is the name given to the lower and flat portion of the great valley of Oberhasli.   The descent into this is much too steep for a carriage-road; and, indeed, we had to get off our horses during a part of the way.

The valley of Imgrund may be about two miles in length and half as broad: it is quite open and flat, and extends on both sides of the Aar, but mostly on its left bank.   It is well cultivated, and contains a small village with its church, which bears the same name of Grund.   Advancing along the Aar, we soon left the meadows behind us, the mountains coming close to the river on either side, and converting the open valley into a wild mountain-ravine, which form, with the exception of two or three small patches of opener ground, it preserves the whole way to the Handeck.   On an average, this upper valley or ravine is not wider from cliff to cliff than half a mile, and in many places it seems narrower.   The mountain-walls of it are very precipitous; in many places quite perpendicular, and consist almost entirely of bare rock.   Trees grow here and there along the borders of the river, where there is room, and also in some fissures in the cliffs; but the general aspect of the ravine is wild and savage.   The bottom of the valley is everywhere strewn with huge blocks which have fallen from the cliffs.   They also in many places fill up the bed of the stream, and thus, by partially obstructing or diverting its course, add not a little to the turbulence which the natural rapidity of its descent over a rocky bed necessarily occasions. In the whole of its course from the Handeck Falls to the open valley at the foot of the Kirchet, I do not believe that it can show a single fathom of green unbroken water, so furiously does it dash and foam and roar along its steep and rugged path. I found the temperature of the water to be 43°, a degree of cold sufficiently indicative of its glacier origin, but also of its admixture with smaller streams heated by the sun in their course to join it.

The path, as may be believed, was extremely rough. It was often also very steep; and, in many places, it wound so closely round the brow of precipices of great height as to be really dangerous —the safety of the rider being entirely dependent on the sure-footedness of his horse. On such occasions prudence would certainly counsel the rider to get off; but this was not always done. But the poor beasts were prudent if the riders were not, and picked out their nice way with marvellous precision, and we experienced neither stumbling nor starting. Our path crossed the river several times by small wooden bridges, of rather rude and insecure structure. I remarked, in crossing some of them, that we got into a pretty strong current of cold air, produced by the impetus of the water below us. But, for the most part, our path lay much too high above

the course of the stream to allow us to partake of
this refreshment, which we should have been very
glad of, as the day was extremely hot.   Many of
the mountain peaks, particularly those on the left
or western bank of the river, were covered with
snow ; and at one spot, below the village of Gutannen, we crossed the path of an avalanche which had
fallen in the spring, and the remains of which yet
filled the bottom of the ravine—the river finding its
way in a tunnel which it had formed beneath it.

In the two or three spots where the ravine became wide enough to give space for a few meadows
and cottages, we were struck by the extreme pains
taken by the inhabitants to take advantage of every
inch of possible pasture.   Wherever a man could go
or hand could stretch, there the grass was cropped
and added to the heap to be carried home anon.
In some places we saw the mower actually on his
knees, working away with his short scythe or hook.
Wherever there was spread out anything like a
field, it was shaven as close and fine as the best-
kept lawn.   The people were at work on their second crop.

All along this valley, wherever we saw any houses,
we were sure to be beset by children of all ages as
beggars.   We had, indeed, seen too much of this
begging habit of the Swiss before, particularly in
the canton of Schwytz ; but we had latterly been
less troubled by it.   What struck us as odd,
here and elsewhere, was the contrast between the

appearance of the houses out of which the beggars came and the beggars themselves. The houses were all large, well built, and in good repair, looking more like the abodes of substantial farmers than of beggars. In England, Scotland, and still more in Ireland, there is always some harmony between the huts of the beggar and his trade ; but here it seems otherwise.

We arrived at the village of Gutannen a little after nine, and found the materials of a good breakfast at the little inn. At this place the valley is of some width, and there is a good deal of comparatively flat and cultivable land. At a short distance above the village, however, the valley reassumes its ravine-like character, becoming even more rugged and steep, but at the same time more wooded than lower down. We crossed the river more than once before we reached our destination, the Handeck Falls, where we arrived at half-past eleven.

We first viewed the cascade from beneath, but we could not get near the bottom of the gulf into which the water falls, owing to the precipitous character of the rocks on both sides. Still, the view is grand even here, although much less so than from the top of the Falls. There we can see at once the whole descent of the water into its basin below, and more or less perfectly from three points of view, viz. from the face of the cliff on either side of it— particularly the left, and from a small wooden bridge thrown across the stream just before it precipitates

itself over the ledge of rock. The whole body of
water shoots at once into the abyss from the edge
of the cliff, a depth of probably 300 feet at least,
and reaches the bottom almost without touching the
face of the rock. It is stated in Murray's Handbook that "it reaches more than half-way down in
the form of an unbroken glassy sheet before it is
tossed into white foam." This certainly was not
the case when we saw the Falls, as the stream was
already all broken and white when it took its leap.
Perhaps the difference of appearance depends on the
quantity of water at the time ; but whether the increase or decrease of quantity produces the one or
other, I cannot tell.

A singular feature in this Fall is the union of
two cascades into one. Just at the point where the
Aar precipitates itself, the Adlerbach rushing down
its rocky path on the left bank, shoots over a portion of the same cliff, but nearly at right angles to
the other, and the two joining in mid-air, about
half-way down, dash together into the gulf below.
As might be supposed from the great mass of water
and its high fall, the whole space between the rocks
is filled with a continuous misty spray which, at certain hours of the day, chiefly from ten to twelve,
gives rise to the well-known phenomenon of the local
rainbow when the sun is clear. We were fortunate in
making our visit at the proper time, and witnessed this
beautiful appearance in great perfection, sometimes
spreading over one cliff, sometimes another, in broken

segments, and occasionally crowning the steaming abyss with an almost complete circle or glory. We had previously seen the same phenomenon at the Falls of the Rhine, and subsequently at the Reichenbach and elsewhere, but in none of these did it come near what we now witnessed, either in extent or completeness.

It must have been surely in this Fall, and on the very spot where we were standing, that Lord Byron, in his Manfred, saw his vision of the witch of the Alps. No other place could seem so appropriate as this for such a manifestation; uniting, as it does in a singular degree, wildness, grandeur, loneliness, and a sort of dreamlike, mysterious beauty. Having the imagination once prompted by the poet's delineation, a common spectator might almost be forgiven for trying to picture to himself in the sunny obscurity of the abyss below, his own prosaic outline of the " Beautiful Spirit with her hair of light and eyes of dazzling glory, which make tame the beauties of the sunbow bending over her." At any rate, the least imaginative man could easily fancy the poet himself beholding all this—and more—when, standing where we stood, he saw

> " ——————— the sunbow's rays still arch
> The torrent with the many hues of heaven." *

---

* It would appear, however, from Lord Byron's letters and journals, that it was the *Staubach* that supplied him with the materials for the fine description of which these lines form a part. He seems not to have visited the Handeck Falls, during his Swiss journey. This only shows that genius can supply all defects out of its own stores.

Wishing to get a nearer view of the Fall than I could from the wooden bridge, I very sillily got down under the right extremity of this, where the rock shows a flattish ledge, intending to look over the precipice, but I found the granite so very slippery from the spray that I was no sooner down than I was glad to get up again, not without a little salutary fright. The rock was not merely slippery, but a good deal more shelving than I had anticipated; and although the space I had to return was hardly my own length, I found my footing so insecure that I was very well pleased when I got hold of the bridge again. I would, therefore, advise any one who had no desire of going to visit the witch of the Alps in her own domicile, not to get nearer the channel of the stream than the bridge itself. By the way, this bridge, at the time of our visit, was in a very shaky and dilapidated state, the foot-boards being quite loose and the rails partly broken off.

There is a small inn close by the Falls, where our guides put up their horses; but although we spent nearly two hours here, we did not visit it or make proof of its quality. After walking down the very steep descent immediately below the Falls, we mounted our horses and set out on our return to Meyringen. Although the horses had so long a rest at the Handeck, our guides wished us to put up again at Gutannen, under pretence of refreshing them. We objected to this, and wished to continue our course through the village, intending to proceed onwards. After some altercation, however, we were forced to submit; and, leaving our horses, walked on a little way in advance, and there waited their coming. They did not detain us very long; but one of our party was so disgusted with the conduct of the men, that he walked on, and never mounted his horse again all the way to Meyringen, where, indeed, he arrived before his mounted companions. The two men, as we afterwards found, were not regular guides, but peasants not accustomed to such expeditions. Their subsequent conduct was also bad. On reaching the bottom of the valley of Imgrund, we found ourselves accompanied by the loose horse, but without any guides; and so we were forced to follow the known path homewards, instead of visiting, as we intended, the rocky ravine through which the Aar makes its way through the Kirchet barrier into the valley of Meyringen, and the Finster Aar Schlucht adjoining this. We thus missed, as I am given to understand, a singularly picturesque scene, very well worth going out of the way to see. We had plenty of time to do so, as we reached Meyringen at six.

As on the day before, we had an excellent dinner at our Wild Man. There were a few guests there before us; and afterwards another small party or two arrived, one of which was English. In the Speisesaal or dining-room there is a cabinet for the display of the carvings in wood so common throughout Switzerland, and the artist-proprietor

9 §

himself attended for the purpose of displaying them
to the company, in hopes of obtaining purchasers.
He was not altogether disappointed in this respect.
I presume the artist pays the landlord in personal
service for permission to have access to his guests,
as he waited on us as actively and adroitly as the
other servants.   On the whole, we were very well
pleased with our quarters at this hotel.   The landlord and servants were very civil and attentive, and
everything was good of its kind.   The bill seemed
somewhat high, but I am not sure that it was extra-
vagant.

The valley of Meyringen has magnificent and
picturesque boundaries, bare-peaked or snow-covered
at top, and beautifully wooded at their base ; but
the flatter grounds between them are a good deal
disfigured by the ravages produced by the numerous
torrents that fall into it, by several extensive land-
slips by which it has been visited, and by the frequent overflowings of the Aar.   The width of the
valley varies from two to four miles, and its length
is about fifteen : it runs nearly east and west, and
is bounded on the west by the lake of Brientz, into
which the Aar discharges itself.   The small town or
village of Meyringen consists of a long range of
houses scattered along the base of the cliff that
bounds it on the north, and has a population under
a thousand.   It has several inns besides ours of the
Savage.

CHAPTER XVI.

August 23.——We had the pleasure to find, on waking, that our usual luck as to weather had not deserted us : it was a lovely morning. Our plans for the day were to cross the Great Scheideck to Grindelwald, inspecting in our way the Reichenbach Falls, the Rosenlaui Glacier, and the Upper Grindelwald Glacier. For this purpose we engaged one regular guide, and a couple of horses with one driver; the former to proceed through the Oberland with us, the latter to return after conveying us to the top of the Scheideck ; one of the juniors of our party preferred walking the whole way. We were to pay nine francs for each horse, and the usual fee of six francs per day to our guide Johann Brütschgi. We did not set out until seven o'clock, and after taking breakfast.

After proceeding for a short distance on our yesterday's tract, on crossing the bridge we turned to our right at once, and made directly for the range

of mountains which we had the day before left on
our right hand. It is in rushing down the southern
face of these that the small river Reichenbach makes
the Falls so called. These we had seen at a distance
all along from Meyringen, and we now made our
approach to them through a fine slope of cultivated
fields, with the village of Zwirgi at the top. Leaving our horses here, we walked through some meadows to a small house built on a bank almost in
front of the Falls, and so close to them that it is
necessary to keep the windows shut in order to keep
out the spray. This is a very fine cascade, but inferior to the Handeck as well in beauty as in extent.
The sun, however, shining brightly upon it, the rainbows were very brilliant and of considerable size.
We were told that they are visible, when seen at
all, from six in the morning until noon. There are
two other falls lower down, but inferior to this;
the last being close to the bathing establishment
called the Reichenbach-Bad. The small room of
our Belvedere had the usual display of wood-carvings,
and we found that, over and above the price of our
little purchases, a small fee was expected for the
repair of the road which had led us to the falls.

On rejoining our horses we soon reached the top
of the steeper part of the ascent, and then proceeded,
on a gentler acclivity, along the banks of the Reichenbach, towards its sources, keeping the stream,
the greater part of the way, on our right hand.
This runs through a beautiful valley, bounded by

lofty steeps on both sides, narrow, but smiling and green and full of trees. The Reichenbach is plentifully nursed by lateral rills. Among these there is a very pretty cascade on the right hand as we proceed upwards, falling from a great height, but of very slender dimensions, and therefore named the Seilbach, or Rope-brook or Rope-fall. On descending from the Brünig we had remarked a singular cluster of bare peaks of great height in this direction, and yesterday we had seen the same on our right hand, as we passed up the valley of Imgrund. These are the Engel-hörner or Angel-Peaks, which rise from the ridge of mountains that divide the Oberhasli valley from that we were now traversing. On the present occasion they constituted a striking but only a secondary feature in the landscape which opened upon us on entering the upper valley of the Reichenbach.

On turning an angle in our path, the snowy peaks of the Wellhorn and Wetterhorn came suddenly into view, shining far up in the blue sky above us, yet directly in our front and apparently quite close to us. Of the snowy peaks, the one nearest to us was that of the Wellhorn, by some considered as a part of the Wetterhorn, and certainly belonging to the same chain, though stretching in a line at right angles with the other peaks. The Wellhorn is upwards of 10,000 English feet above the sea-level. The peaks of the Wetterhorn, properly so-called, shone beyond and far above this, rising to

the elevation of more than 12,000 feet.   The principal summit of this magnificent mountain presented
a striking appearance from the point where we now
saw it.   Its outline was perfectly symmetrical, and
it looked exactly as if a gigantic model of the great
pyramid of Egypt, cased in snow, had been placed
on this magnificent base.   Its other summits, which
to us seemed nearly of equal height, had symmetry
also, but of a different kind, as they rose up in the
more familiar form of conical peaks.

In passing along this smiling valley in the bright
sunshine, dressed, as we were, more like West Indians
than Europeans, we could not help being struck
with one of those contrasts of local climate which
meets the Alpine traveller on so many occasions.
In England and other northern countries we are so
accustomed to associate the idea of winter and wintry
things with the presence of snow, that we require
some little experience to reconcile in our minds the
seeming incongruity of opposite conditions existing
at the same time.   And nothing short of actual
experience will thoroughly satisfy any one that the
vicinity of immense masses and tracks of snow and
ice does not, in fact, greatly modify the temperature
of the local atmosphere.   But this experience is
speedily acquired in Switzerland.   In the present
case, for instance, all things immediately beside us
——trees, grass, shrubs, flowers, fruit——were quick
with summer life and rich in summer beauty, and,
obviously, no more influenced by the snowy moun-

tains by which they were overlooked, than if they had been basking in the sunshine of a land that never knew winter. In describing a scene like this, a poet might seek for its analogy in the moral world, and liken it to a beautiful affection based on natural goodness, which no coldness can chill, no harshness wither. It may probably make some of the readers of Charles Dickens think of young Florence Dombey and her father.

As the valley approached its termination at the foot of the Wellhorn, it became still more flat and narrow. Here we crossed the river (which I found to be of the temperature of 43°), and proceeded along its left bank until we reached the inn of Rosenlaui. This is built on a rising ground close to the river, and exactly fronting the glacier of the same name and the Engelhörner chain, whose bare and rugged peaks rise immediately beyond this glacier. Some of our party here partook of a second breakfast, while others amused themselves in examining some beautiful herbaries, prepared and here offered for sale by the landlord Mr. J. Brunner. These herbaries comprehend collections of the plants of the neighbouring mountains, and amount to upwards of three hundred specimens. They are very neatly prepared, and are sold cheap, the complete set, in a neat case, costing only 30 francs. Smaller cases are sold, as *souvenirs* of Rosenlaui, at a proportionally smaller price. Mr. Brunner is a fine robust young man, well acquainted with the mountains in his double capacity of chamois hunter and botanist. He has more than once ascended the Wetterhorn, and, in conjunction with some of his scientific friends, has given distinctive names to the different peaks.

In our way to view the glacier, we again crossed the river, and proceeded half-way up the hill on horseback. We walked the remaining part of the distance; the whole course from the inn not occupying more than half an hour. In our way we crossed over the Weissenbach, or ice-brook of the glacier, which, although so close to its course, was already a considerable stream. Where we crossed it (by a small wooden bridge) it was rushing along at the depth of 200 feet below us, in the bottom of a fissure not more than from three to six yards wide, and which it had evidently worn for itself in the slaty rock. Stones thrown into it—and we found on the spot a professed artist in this line whose special business it is to throw them—make a tremendous noise in their descent. This rocky channel is very curious, and the inspection of it makes me believe that the lower portions of the ravine of the Via Mala has also been worn by the stream itself, and is not a part of the primary rent which, no doubt, formed the ravine in the first instance.

We walked close up to the glacier with the greatest ease, and by a comfortable dry path, without any interruption from moraine, which, in fact, does not exist at the point where we approached it. Indeed, this glacier, as far as we saw, has none of the stones or rubbish upon it which forms the moraines; and this circumstance makes the natural cerulean or blue colour of its caverns more bright and clear. We went upon its surface to look into these, and were much struck with their beauty. All the exposed surface at the extremity of the glacier was in the act of melting, and streaming with water of the temperature of (nearly) 32°. The whole of its watery produce forming the Weissenbach, when joined by two other streams from the Schwartz glacier and Schwartzwald glacier, forms the Reichenbach. On the whole, the glacier of Rosenlaui, from its beauty, easy accessibility, and cleanliness, may be considered as a sort of show-glacier, and should on no account be passed unvisited by lady-travellers.

On mounting our horses we once more crossed the stream, now only the Schwartzbach, and began to ascend the valley along the western base of the Wetterhorn, which, for some distance, continues to present all the characters of a rich alpine pasture-ground, fine meadows interspersed with trees, and dotted over with hay-chalets. This, however, is soon succeeded by a very different scene, namely, a thick gloomy forest of pines feathered to the bottom, and almost shutting out the light from the path that is cut through them. It is truly a dismal-looking place, and well entitled to its name of the Schwartzswald. The only relief afforded to the passenger in traversing it, is the occasional gush of a clear stream crossing his path, or, yet better, a glimpse of the bright Wetterhorn shining through the gloomy vistas of the forest. It is here where the mountain sends down the glacier, named after the forest, the Schwartzwald Gletscher, and which gives origin, as already mentioned, to one branch of the Reichenbach. The other branch rises at the foot of the Schwartzhorn, a mountain lying to the north-west of us.

On reaching the southern edge of the pine forest, we came upon an open piece of rich pasture ground, intermixed with trees; but this was of small extent, and soon terminated in a wilder and barer region, covered with coarse and scanty grass, like an English moor. Before entering on this, we sat down on a bank, intending to rest for a short time; but hearing some claps of distant thunder, and seeing a black cloud beginning to darken the sky towards the south, we mounted our horses and made the best of our way up the ascent, in hopes of reaching the inn on the Scheideck, before the storm set in; but it was too quick for us. The clouds rolled onwards towards the Wetterhorn; and while we were still two miles from the top of the Pass, it burst upon us in a heavy shower of rain, accompanied by two or three loud claps of thunder from the cloud on the Wetterhorn—which, even on this fine day, seemed to justify its name of Storm-peak. We all made the best of our way for shelter, the horsemen pushing their beasts as fast as they could go, up the steep hill, and leaving the pedestrians to follow as they might. Thanks to the impenetrable mackintoshes of my companions, and my own trusty umbrella, we reached the inn without being much wet, except about the legs, though the rain continued the whole way, and did not cease until some time after we had gained shelter. In the inn, which is built on the very top of the Pass, we found assembled about a dozen travellers, who had found shelter also, and among others three English ladies belonging to a party of twelve, the other members of which we had met shortly after leaving Rosenlaui. They were proceeding from Grindelwald to Meyringen, two on horseback, and one carried on a hand-car, or litter.

After waiting at the inn about three quarters of an hour, the storm having passed by, though the sky still continued dark with a thick mist, we proceeded to descend the other side of the Scheideck towards Grindelwald. At first, we could perceive nothing before us but a sea of white mist, surging and rolling up from the valley, exactly as described in Manfred, and no doubt a precisely similar appearance to that which suggested the lines to Lord Byron :——

" The mists boil up around the glaciers ; clouds
Rise curling far beneath me, white and sulphury." *

---

* It appears from Lord Byron's letters and journals, as given by Moore, in his Life, that it was from the Wengern Alp that he

Although pleased to witness this phenomenon, we could not help regretting, at the time, that it shut out entirely from our view the peaks of the Wetterhorn, and only allowed us to see, by fits, the sheer cliff of its base, close by the side of which our path was now leading us. We soon, however, had ample compensation. A brief descent brought us below the level of the mist which, slowly rising, fixed itself, in a dense white mass, on the Wetterhorn, shrouding all the upper part of it precisely like a veil, and having its lower border defined as accurately along its brow as if drawn by a line. Sometimes this lower border or hem would gradually and slowly ascend, so as to leave the inferior and middle region perfectly clear; at other times, the process was reversed, the dark face of the mountain gradually disappearing beneath the descending veil, To whoever looked on this magnificent spectacle, it was a ready and facile imagination, to conceive some Great Being enthroned on the mountain-top and raising and lowering the veil at will; and recollecting that it had immediately followed the sublimest and most awful of Nature's active operations, the Thunder Storm,—and on the very field of its manifestation,—it was no less easy to understand how phenomena of a like kind, presented to the men of ruder and simpler

saw this phenomenon, on the 23d Sept. 1816. "The clouds rose from the opposite valley, curling up perpendicular precipices like the foam of the ocean of hell during a spring-tide : it was white and sulphury, and immeasurably deep in appearance."

times, may have transformed the primary conception into speedy belief——belief that, on the shrouded Peak, and amid the darkness of the storm, the Great Author of Nature was Himself in bodily presence.

The descent from the Scheideck was easy, and we soon arrived opposite to the Upper Grindelwald glacier. We turned off our path to visit it, conducted by our own guide, and also by a local one who attends for this purpose at a neighbouring chalet, an old man of seventy-three, who has had by his two wives no less than twenty-five children, as he takes care to tell all his clients.

This glacier is very like that of Rosenlaui. We went a short way upon it, our old guide preceding us with a hatchet to cut steps in the steeper parts. On the surface it looks precisely like an old indurated snow-wreath, such as may be seen in Scotland filling the bottom of the glens in spring; but this rough snow-like appearance is produced by the disintegrating effect of the sun and rain, as its interior, as seen in its huge fissures and chasms, is a beautiful bluish ice, transparent and fine as that of the Wenham lake. Some of the fissures are open, and some closed at bottom. Looking into the former, we sometimes saw, and sometimes only heard, the strong torrents rushing on beneath us : the latter presented to us beautiful basins filled to the top with the purest water, which I found to be of the temperature of (nearly) 32°.

Like all those of the Bernese Alps, this glacier,

we were told by our guides, has been shrinking for some years past. We saw sufficient evidence of this in the large moraines lying all round its base, and at a considerable distance from it. The old man assured us that it had shrunk forty or fifty yards during the last twelve years, and he pointed out to us a huge fragment of rock which was formerly on the glacier but which now lay at the above distance from it. These icy masses are also undergoing continual and great changes in their interior. One of our party who had visited this glacier last summer, and who spoke much of a long subglacial cavern into which he had then entered, could find no traces of it on the present occasion; and on questioning our guide, we found that it had since fallen in and disappeared, its walls and roof and all having gone long since to help to fill the banks of the Black Lütschine.

We reached Grindelwald about six, and took up our abode at the Adler or Black Eagle inn, situated near the church at the east end of the village, if village it may be called, which consists mostly of separate houses sprinkled here and there among the fields. We had a table-d'hôte dinner at seven, and found it excellent both as to matter and form. We had besides soup (somewhat meagre) excellent roast beef, with good potatoes (dressed in their skins), haricôt of mutton with well-boiled vegetables, mutton cutlets, and roast-chicken, all well and neatly dressed and of excellent quality (I believe some of our party could speak of all from personal experience). We had also puddings and tarts, with dressed cherries, and also fresh plums and cherries, and various sweet-meats for our dessert. The wine was less approved of by those of our party who partook of it; but I observed that it was cordially taken by some of the other guests less fastidious than Englishmen. I mention all these particulars for the benefit of travellers, to show them what they may expect, not only at the Black Eagle of Grindelwald, but generally in Switzerland, at all the better order of hotels. The charge for the whole, including wine, was three French francs, or half-a-crown, per head.

The hotel is built exactly fronting the lower glacier, which looks as if it were merely divided from it by a couple of small fields; it is, however, in reality a mile or more distant, even as the crow flies. We retired early, having laid our plans for the morrow, viz. to visit the glacier and the Eismeer beyond, at the foot of the Eiger and Schreckhorn. For this purpose we engaged a second guide of local experience, and proposed setting out on our expedition after an early breakfast. We retired, however, in doubt, as the weather was not promising.

CHAPTER XVII.

August 23.——Alas, for the second time, our wonderful good luck failed us: the morning was miserably
wet, and the rain heavy; and we were told that it
had snowed all night on the mountains. We therefore made up our minds to wait until next day, in
the hopes of better weather, as we were very unwilling
to miss the exploration of the glacier. We breakfasted in the great Speisesaal, but as this is built
somewhat in the manner of a greenhouse, the whole
of one side and both ends being windows, we found
it rather cold, and therefore were glad to exchange
it for an adjoining room with a stove in it. Here
we found ourselves very comfortable, the temperature
being soon raised to 65°, though the air out of doors
was only 51°. The valley of Grindelwald is always
comparatively cold, on account of its height above
the sea, which is not less than 3350 English feet.
In consequence of this coldness of the climate, the

crops and fruit are considerably later here than in the adjoining valleys, though they are not less plentiful.

The rain continued heavy all the morning, and we made up our minds to lose a day, in other words, to spend it under a roof. Between eleven and twelve, however, the weather improved, and gave promise, in partial glimpses of blue sky, of our being yet able to accomplish our plans. We accordingly got ourselves speedily ready, and set out with our two guides, about noon,—all on foot. In order to reach the glacier we had to return a little way on our path of yesterday, crossing that portion of the Lütschine which takes its rise from the base of the Wetterhorn and upper glacier. The Lower Grindelwald glacier, in descending into the valley from the Eismeer or Mer de Glace, passes between the bases of the Eigher and Schreckhorn, the former known by the name of the Schlossberg, the latter by that of the Mettenberg: these rise precipitously on either side, and thus compress it into a comparatively narrow space, although, even at its narrowest point it is probably half a mile in width. It was up the spurs of the Mettenberg that we had to climb to reach the Ice Sea.

For some time the acclivity was very steep, fully as steep as the Rigi, but shorter. I felt it, however, greatly less fatiguing to the chest, and indeed suffered but little. The improvement I attributed partly to my increased practice in climbing; but also a good deal to the much greater coldness of the air on the present occasion. Our path at first led us

10

up the base of the mountain at some distance from
the glacier; then turning to the right brought us
close to its border, or rather close to the line of its
border, as we were at a great height above it. From
this point the path continued along the face of the
cliff, sometimes cut out of it, and everywhere occupying a mere ledge in the precipice, with the glacier
immediately below us and the sheer cliff above.
There was no footing for either horse or mule on
the greater portion of this scrambling path.

On a portion of the cliff close to our pathway, a
short space before we reached the Eismeer, our guides
called our attention to a rounded indentation in the
rock known by the name of *Martinsdruck*, and
pointed out to us, at the same time, an aperture in
the top of the mountain on the other side, called
Martinsloch, through which we could see the sky
beyond. The aperture was very visible; but at the
distance we were from it, we had some difficulty in
convincing ourselves that it was not merely a patch
of bright snow on the face of the black cliff. There
is no doubt, however, of its being an opening in the
rock; and, indeed, on one day in the year (the
13th Feb.) the sun's rays traverse it so directly
that they indicate its existence by a bright spot in
the shadow which the mountain casts on the valley
beneath. There is a curious legend attaching to
this "Impression" and "Hole" of St. Martin, which
I subjoin in a note.* In justice to its inventor, it

* "Once on a time, according to the tradition, the basin now

is but fair to admit that the *Druck* in the rock is really not a very bad cast of a gigantic back and lumbar region.

This same St. Martin seems to have had a propensity to meddle with mountain tops, as there is another *Martinsloch* in the Flimserberg in Glarus, through which the sun shines into the valley of the Sernft, near Elm, on the 3d of March. To be sure, there is a dispute among the learned, as to the justice of his claim to honour in this instance; some maintaining that St. Matthew not St. Martin was the veritable perforator, on the strong ground that the 3d of March is *the day* of the former saint. Old Scheuchzer tells us,[*] that the chief priest of Glarus (Glaronensium Pastor Primarius) was a very decided stickler for St. Matthew, contending that the name of the Hole should in reality be *Matthisloch;* but the people, as usual, carried the day against the philosophers, and *Martinsloch* it remains to this hour.

We had a fine view of the glacier below us, all

occupied by the Eismeer was filled with a lake, but the space between the Mettenberg and the Eigher being much narrower than at present, the outlet from it was constantly blocked up, and inundations produced which ruined the fields of the peasants in the valley below. At length St. Martin, a holy giant, came to their rescue ; he seated himself on the Mettenberg, resting his staff on the Eiger, and then, with one lusty heave of his brawny back, not only burst open the present wide passage between the two mountains, but left the marks of his seat on the one and drove his walking-stick right through the other."—*Murray's Handbook,* p. 81.

[*] Iter Alpinum, Anni 1704, p. 161.

the way; and looking back along its course to the green valley beyond, it presented a striking appearance. Through the greater part of its descent, its surface exhibits a sort of ice-forest——a continuous series of sharp icy pinnacles, set close to one another, and many of them of considerable height. This is the form that glaciers in certain positions constantly assume, in the process of melting, and it is a very picturesque one. These pinnacles are also very beautiful when the sun shines bright upon them, exhibiting something of translucency and blueness in their finer points and angles. We saw something of this on the present occasion, as the weather remained clear and fine during the two hours which it took us to reach the Mer de Glace.

We attained the object of our walk just above the point where the two mountain bases retreat backwards, and open out a wider space for the main body of the glacier to spread itself. On getting upon this we found our progress much more difficult and slow than I had anticipated; and we soon discovered that we had need of the aid and guidance of both our attendants. Although we had here none of the pinnacles which mark the glacier lower down, we had a good deal of the kind of surface which forms the base on which they stand, namely, a constant succession of round hummocks or narrow ridges of ice, with sides more or less steep and slippery, and separated from one another by pretty deep hollows or huge ruts, twisting about in all directions, with deep wells and chasms of every shape and size, some with water some without, traversing and obstructing the path on every side. But for the aid of our Alpenstocks to steady our footing on the slippery slopes and narrow ridges, and to enable us to leap across the cracks and hollows, we could have hardly advanced at all; and without the personal assistance of our guides, in the more difficult spots, even our Alpenstocks would have occasionally proved insufficient. Not that there were any extreme difficulties or imminent dangers encountered or overcome by us, nor even any obstacles sufficiently formidable to hinder a man of ordinary resolution from encountering them by himself : I mean simply to state, without exaggeration, that the route was not merely troublesome but difficult, and such as should, on no account, be attempted by a stranger, however active, without an experienced guide.

The first part of our course lay nearly across the glacier ; and about its middle we encountered the grand chasm or crevasse which constitutes the channel of its main glacier-stream (Gletcherstrom). This channel was in some places open at top for a considerable space, at other times it was vaulted over and quite concealed by the solid ice. Where open, it twisted about through the mass of the glacier, exactly like the channel of the Rhine in the rocks of the Via Mala, or of the Tamina at Pfeffers, or the Weissenbach seen by us the day before. It resembled them also very remarkably in its size, depth, and configuration—being quite narrow, and the sides occasionally overlapping one another, so as to hide the stream from view, though its channel was quite open at top.   When exposed, the stream, of considerable size, was seen at a great depth, rushing along its bed of ice with a tremendous noise and at an amazing rate, and shooting in beneath that portion of the mass which was yet unbroken.*   In no place had the stream sawn the ice quite through so as to have the solid earth or rock for its bed, which appears to me rather singular, considering the effect of such streams in cutting asunder the solid rock itself; an effect, by the way, which is admirably explained and illustrated by the phenomena of these rivers in the ice.   Where the chasms were the deepest, our guides favoured us with the usual exhibition of tumbling huge masses of stone into them, in order that we might see them darting from side to side in their descent, and hear the prolonged echoes they occasioned. Even on the middle of the glacier there was no difficulty of meeting with plenty of materials for such an experiment, as the whole of its surface was strewed with large stones and fragments of rock, fallen from the mountains on either side, here or far beyond us, and now in progress towards its sides or end to supply fresh matter to the moraine.

* I was rather surprised to find the stream make so much noise, as, where most exposed and nearest to us, the bed of ice on which it ran was quite smooth and polished.   It was, no doubt, the rapidity of the descent, its crooked course, and the narrowness and depth of the hollow space above it, that produced so loud a sound.

It was into this chasm that M. Monson, a Lutheran clergyman of Iverdun, fell, and was of course killed, in the year 1821. Our guides pointed out the very spot where he fell. It appears that the way in which this gentleman lost his life was this : fixing the point of his Alpenstock on the op= posite side of the chasm to that where he was standing, he leant forwards upon it in order that he might obtain a better view of the chasm. While in this position the point of his staff slid from its hold, and he was of course precipitated into the gulf head foremost. After twelve days, the body was recovered by a guide and a friend of the deceased, who were let down by means of ropes to a depth of 130 feet. Owing to the conservative influence of the cold, the body, though broken and bruised, was found quite *fresh* when brought to the surface.

An accident of a somewhat similar kind which once took place lower down on this glacier, had a more fortunate issue. An innkeeper of Grindelwald, of the name of Bohren, fell into a fissure upwards of 60 feet in depth ; but though his arm was broken in the fall, he contrived to make his escape, by crawling along the downward course of the subglacial river, until it reached the open air. Luckily, the distance was not more than threescore feet.

After we had been on the glacier a short time, the day became again clouded, with rain and sleet, so that we had only partial views of the mountains

around us.   We were, however, unwilling to return
without seeing more of them as well as of the glaciers, and therefore proceeded upwards along the ice
towards the cliff which juts out from the base of the
Vierscherhorn or Walcherhorn, and separates the two
great glaciers, viz. that of the Strahleck or Schreckhorn and Finsteraarhorn on the east, from that of
the Mönch and Eigher on the west.   Proceeding onwards we soon came directly in front of that portion
of the latter which descends from its own high level,
down a steep declivity, to join, at right angles, that
on which we were travelling.   As we looked up to
it from this position, the view of the glacier was
singularly grand.   It had exactly the aspect, and
excited in the mind the impression and feeling——as
if a gigantic river, a hundred times as broad as the
Rhine at Schaffhausen, and falling over a precipice
proportionally high, had been instantaneously frozen,
and fixed in all its fury and turbulence——a Titanic
waterfall, white and foamy, but eternally silent.   So
strong was its resemblance to a waterfall, or, perhaps,
I should rather say, so strongly did its appearance
excite the idea of a waterfall, that one almost required the aid of hearing to be convinced that the
huge icy mass above him was not in reality a tremendous rapid rushing down from some unseen and
unknown lake in the regions above.   The eyes were
fixed on it by a sort of fascinating terror as well as
wonder : the idea of danger, as from a torrent about

to overwhelm you, forced itself into the mind in spite of your conviction; the very silence of the scene seemed unnatural and awful.*

The above statement may seem exaggerated; but it is really not so, either as regards the scene itself or the ideas and feelings excited by it; and I am of opinion that few persons, possessed of only a moderate share of imagination, could be brought suddenly and unexpectedly, and without previous warning or expectation, into the presence of such a spectacle (as was the case with myself), without experiencing all that has been described—and more. The comparison of a glacier to a frozen river or torrent or cataract, is one likely to occur to any beholder; it however had not suggested itself to me when looking on those I had already visited or seen at a distance : and although I must have formerly seen this comparison both in Coleridge and Byron, I fortunately had entirely forgot it; so that the spontaneous excitation of the idea on the present occasion, was accompanied by all the additional force which perfect novelty gives to any mental impression. On referring to the poets since my

* It is probable that the fancied resemblance to a waterfall is, in the present case, heightened by the existence of some dark rocks projecting from the glacier in its mid-descent, exactly as we see in the falls of the Rhine. These rocks are never covered by either snow or ice, and are vulgarly supposed to be heated by some internal fire, which enables them to melt the ice as it touches them ; the fact is, their face is too steep to allow it to lodge.

return home, I was delighted to find the forgotten
idea expressed in their own glorious language:

> " Ye ice-falls, ye that from the mountain's brow
> Adown enormous ravines slope amain—
> Torrents, methinks, that heard a mighty voice,
> And stopped at once amid their maddest plunge!
> Motionless torrents! silent cataracts!" *

> " ———————— O'er the savage sea,
> The glassy ocean of the mountain ice,
> We skim its rugged breakers, which put on
> The aspect of a tumbling tempest's foam
> Frozen in a moment." †

Turning from this great sight to pursue our course,
we were so fortunate as to be soon after favoured
with another perhaps still more glorious.   Hitherto
all the great mountains surrounding us had remained covered with an impenetrable veil of mist,
so that we could see nothing but the base and brows
of those nearest to us, and we had almost given up
all hope of seeing anything of their loftier regions,
when, all at once, the clouds on our left hand began
to exhibit in one spot some tints of sunlight, and
then opening out their folds, one after another, displayed to us the very topmost peaks of the Schreckhorn in all their glory.   For some time I could
scarcely believe that what we saw was anything but
illuminated clouds of singular shape; so entirely
beyond the point where I should have thought of
looking for a mountain, were the snowy peaks that

---

* Hymn on Chamouni.   † Manfred.

now appeared; and when some of my companions shouted out "The Schreckhorn!" I began to look for it much lower down. The Schreckhorn, however, it was; and it remained long enough uncovered, or rather it momentarily uncovered itself sufficiently often, not only to leave no doubt as to its identity, but to show itself in as striking a point of view as, perhaps, a mountain-peak can ever be seen in.

The whole mountain to its very base was wrapped in a dense, whitish mist, so as to give no indication of its outline; nothing, indeed, being visible in that direction, but a continuous wall-like mass, extending from the earth upwards; well-defined at its base, but gradually lost in the general body of cloud that filled the upper sky. There was, consequently, nothing left whereby to measure altitude; and when the snowy summit broke through its covering, its height seemed vastly greater than if the whole mountain had been exposed. Nothing, I think, could be grander or more sublime than this view, more especially when the opened veil, remaining stationary for a moment, let us see the peaks set, as it were, in a framework of clouds, their interior edges rounded and curling, and brightly tinged with the same unseen sun which illumined the yet brighter peaks beyond.

This sight almost made amends for the loss of what we had hoped to see in visiting the Eismeer, namely, the whole range of the mountains which surround it, including the Eigher, the Walcherhorn, and, grandest of all, the Finsteraarhorn. The respective elevation of the loftiest of these mountains, in English feet, above the sea level, is, in round numbers, as follows : Eigher, 13,200 ; Schreckhorn, 13,350 ; Finsteraarhorn, 14,100. To see at one view all these majestic peaks rising around into a clear sky, in all their snowy glory, must indeed be a sublime sight ; but this we were not destined to see, on the present occasion at least. I feel assured, however, that there was something in the effect of the transient, half-seen, and mysterious vision of the Schreckhorn peaks which we had just witnessed, that could hardly be surpassed in one kind of impressiveness.

At any rate, we should have been most ungrateful had we not been contented with what the weather, dark and gloomy as it was, enabled us to do, seeing that to the snowy night and rainy day we were most probably indebted for yet another great sight which distinguished this eventful afternoon. This was nothing less than the fall of an enormous avalanche from the Eigher mountain, or rather from that part of its base which bounds the glacier to the south-west, and which is termed the Schlossberg. This took place when we had reached the upper border of our glacier to within a furlong or thereabouts, and were hastening towards a small goatherd's chalet niched in the base of the cliff just before us.

We were all suddenly roused and startled by a

tremendous noise behind us, like a continuous peal of distant thunder, which made us instantly stop; and while we were in the act of turning round, our guides, shouting "An avalanche!" pointed to the mountain behind us. We looked, and from beneath the lower border of the mist which covered it, and out of which the hoarse loud roar which still continued, evidently came, we saw a vast and tumultuous mass of snow rushing down and shooting over the edge of the sheer cliff into the air beyond. At first this had a pointed triangular or conical shape, with the small end foremost; but as the fall continued, it assumed the appearance of a cascade of equal width throughout. In this form it continued until its upper extremity had parted from the cliff, and the whole mass had fallen to the earth, renewing, as its parts successively reached the ground, and with still louder and sharper reports, the sound which had momentarily ceased while it was falling through the air. The whole of the process, which has taken so long to describe, was the work of a few seconds, half a minute at most; and all was over and gone, and everything silent and motionless as before, ere we could recover from our almost breathless wonder and delight. The excitement was then great; every one, as if suddenly freed from a spell suddenly cast upon him, talking, and exclaiming, and expressing his agitation in his own particular manner. What we had just witnessed —what we had seen, and heard, and almost felt— was, in relation to our perceptions, not a mere passive phenomenon, but *a work*, an active operation or performance, begun and ended in our presence; and it affected the mind as if it were really a result of voluntary power, an action in which the beholder could feel a sort of reflected sympathy, and take a personal interest. Hence the agitation and excitement, so different from the tranquil, solemn, and almost melancholy feelings with which we had just before been contemplating the "motionless torrent" of the glacier, and the unveiling of the silent Schreckhorn.*

The avalanche seemed to us to come down exactly in the line of our upward path on first crossing the glacier; and we had, therefore, mingled with our other emotions, a sense of danger narrowly and happily escaped. On examining the spot more closely, however, on our return, we found that the nearest part of our former path was probably half a furlong or more from the spot where the avalanche fell; and

---

* The state of feeling here experienced was somewhat analogous to that which is felt during the few last moments of a well-contested horse-race, when all is agitation and excitement, and scarcely any one can restrain himself from shouting, while the whole company is swayed about, in their eagerness to see, like a cornfield beneath the wind; or it is like that which accompanies and follows the triumphant close of some elaborate and difficult air by an accomplished singer at the Opera, when the whole house is at first breathless from delight, and then bursts out into an universal shout of delighted approbation. And it would hardly have astonished me if, on the present occasion, the spectators of the avalanche, after their pause of fearful delight, had clapped their hands in ecstasy and ended with "Bravo!"

I believe we should have sustained no damage had it taken place when our position was the nearest to it. Our guides, however, thought otherwise, and persisted in maintaining that if we had been there, or even on our path on the cliff at the opposite side of the glacier, we should have been destroyed by what they called the *dust* and *wind* of the avalanche. I was utterly sceptical on this point at the time; and, much to the horror of the guides, could not help expressing my regret that it had not descended when we were close to it. I still think my opinion correct; but I own that it was somewhat shaken by what I afterwards learnt of the effects of an avalanche which fell from the Weisshorn in the year 1821, and which I shall have occasion to notice in a subsequent part of our journey.

The avalanche which we had witnessed was admitted by our guides to be of extraordinary size to fall so late in the year; and the old goatherd whose chalet we were approaching when it occurred, said that it was absolutely the largest that had fallen from the mountain during the last twelve years. Our good fortune in witnessing it was therefore doubly great. On viewing from the opposite side of the gorge, on our way home, the mass of fresh snow which had fallen, we calculated its longitudinal extent to be more than a furlong; and its depth may be guessed by the fact that it filled up the whole angle between the base of the precipice and the ridge of the glacier adjoining, whose crevices it completely obliterated to some distance from its border, covering it with an uniform sheet of snow. The impetus with which so great a mass must have fallen from such a height, would necessarily occasion a great compression and commotion of the air; but whether it would have been sufficient to operate at the distance believed by our guides, is still to me very doubtful: it is certain that where we stood when it fell, no movement whatever, perceptible by the touch, was sustained by the air.

On reaching the goatherd's chalet, which is perched at the base of the cliff some fifty or a hundred feet above the glacier, we were glad to rest and refresh ourselves, though the accommodation was of the rudest. We, however, had brought with us something to eat, and we here found a plenteous supply of excellent goat's milk, as well as delicious water.

On our way back we took a somewhat easier path along the glacier, but it was at best both troublesome and fatiguing. We had, however, already gained both courage and skill by our short experience, and we descended a good deal quicker than we had ascended. We reached our inn at six, having been absent exactly six hours, into which we had, in spite of bad weather, been fortunate enough to crowd much more enjoyment than we could have possibly anticipated.

CHAPTER XVIII.

August 24.——We were summoned at half-past five by our trusty Johann Brütschgi, and on looking out at the window were delighted to find that our wonted good luck, as to weather, had not long de- serted us. The sun had not yet looked on our valley, but the atmosphere was clear, and the noble Eigher was seen towering before us into the blue sky, his snowy head already bright with sunshine. What with dressing and packing and paying bills, and breakfasting, we did not start on our journey till seven o'clock. As on our yesterday's excursion, we were also to-day all walkers ; our guide being loaded with our three knapsacks, and part of the personal apparel of some of us ; for the sun had now risen above the mountains and was promising us a hot day from a cloudless sky.

The first part of our journey from the village, until we had crossed the Black Lütschine, was a little down-hill, but we then began to ascend a path which soon became very steep, and so continued for the space of a few miles, when it became much easier, and, with the exception of a few short bits, did not again become very precipitous. The acclivity from the river was, like the other side of the Grindelwald valley, well wooded and cultivated, and interspersed with numerous neat wooden houses; and when we had reached some way up it, we had a splendid view to look back upon. Several of the grand mountains which had been hid from us yesterday, viz. the Wetterhorn, Schreckhorn, and Eigher, were now seen in all their beauty, their snowy peaks bright in the sun, and not a cloud upon one of them. The Finsteraarhorn was too directly behind the Eigher to be seen from where we were, and we had yet a good long space to traverse before the Mönch could come into the landscape. Splendid, however, as was the view now presented to us, I felt more and more convinced that our yesterday's vision of the Schreckhorn "in clouded majesty," was greatly more impressive than if we had seen it in all its naked glory; although I am aware that, when seen from near its base, it would necessarily appear much more lofty and imposing than when viewed from a distance as at present. In the former case, beside the apparent or, so to speak, the factitious augmentation of elevation from the mist, there was,

no doubt, a good deal in the *partialness* of the disclosure of the mountain, which, by stimulating the
imagination, led to an unconscious exaggeration of
its majesty and beauty. It was, as in the case of
beauty of another kind—

> " Che mezzo aperta ancora e mezzo ascosa,
> Quanto si mostra men, tanto è piu bella."

The whole of our course to-day, as on the day
before yesterday—that is, all the way from Rosenlaui to the Jungfrau—was along the base of the
great mountain-chain of the Bernese Oberland Alps,
which closely bounded our left-hand path with an
impassable barrier, while the mountains on our right
were at some distance from us, and of subordinate
height. From the lowest point, which is that
where the Black Lütschine turns its course westward
away from the mountains, the valley gradually rises
on either hand until it terminates, on the east, in
the Great Scheideck, and on the west in the Little
Scheideck. It was towards this pass that we were
now ascending a succession of slopes intermixed with
hollows formed by the rounded spurs of the mountains on our left hand. These slopes continued for
some time cultivated and wooded; but as we rose
in elevation, the vegetation became scantier and
coarser, and the pine trees grew gradually feebler
and dwarfish. At the bottom of the last acclivity
there is seen scattered over the slope of the valley,
on the right hand, the miserable remains of a pine

wood which has been destroyed by avalanches. This wood, however, never had vigorous life in it, as may be seen by the blasted look of the trees below it, which show no signs of having suffered from any other violence but that natural to their bleak exposure. Lord Byron notices these " blasted pines" in his journal (Sept. 23, 1816) : " Passed whole woods of withered pines : all withered ; trunks stripped and barkless, branches lifeless ;—done by a single winter: their appearance reminded me of me and my family;" and he copies the same idea, and indeed the same words, in his Manfred :

> " Like these blasted pines,
> Wrecks of a single winter, barkless, branchless."

In the course of our ascent, we met with more than one road-side cottage or chalet, which tempted us to rest by other attractions than mere benches, though these were set out in attractive order. At two of these, only a few miles apart, we were offered delicious refreshment in the shape of wild Alpine strawberries and cream, and we thought it no shame to prove the excellence of both the one and the other by an *experimentum crucis* performed by the whole party. At the first station, our repast was accompanied by the instrumental and vocal performance of two damsels who reside in a neighbouring cottage, and come to the resting-place for the special gratification of travellers. The instrument on which one of them played was a sort of nondescript guitar, and neither this nor the vocal organ, perhaps, discoursed very superior music; still there was something in the locality, the theme, and the occasion, which made the performance not a little interesting. They played, of course, the Kuhreien or Ranz des Vaches; but they played also another——the true *Heimweh-Lied*, or Home-sick lay of the Swiss, which would arrest the attention from its associations even if it were not in itself attractive. But, as sung by these girls, it seemed to be a very pathetic air; and, whether it was from its absolute quality, or from its manifold associations, I can answer for some of the travellers, at least, feeling a sort of Heimweh in hearing it. We, of course, gave the damsels some little gratuity; and I suppose they must have been especially well-pleased therewith, as they continued their song long after we parted from them, making us often stop to listen and look back to where we could still see them sitting and singing in the sun far below us in the valley.

On approaching our second station, and long before we reached it, we were saluted by the master of the chalet with more than one sonorous blast from his Alpine horn, which wakened the echoes of the Eigher, now quite close to us, in a very magnificent way. There was something picturesque as well as pleasing in this exhibition, as looking up from the slope far below, when roused by the first note, we saw the sturdy performer standing with

outstretched legs and arms on the green hill beside
his cottage, and directing the huge tube towards
the mountain side.   He made no attempt at any
air, but contented himself with sounding a few notes
only; but these were returned by the cliff wonderfully softened and most literally

> " ———————— in many a bout
> Of linked sweetness long drawn out."

These Alpine horns, as they are called, and which
I have only seen in their holiday use of awakening
the echoes for the benefit of travellers, are formed
of wood, a piece of hollow pine in fact.   They vary
in length, but are all long: that of our Eigher
trumpeter was full eight feet.

Through the greater part of our course to-day,
the base of the Eigher presented to us a bare and
almost vertical cliff, or rather series of cliffs, of
enormous height, often terminating in jagged peaks
of the most fantastic kind.   In one place the cliff,
midway from its base, presented an appearance so
strikingly like that of a castle with buttresses,
towers, and windows, jutting over a tremendous
precipice, that I required the use of the glass to
disabuse me of the notion that it was not so.   And
this is a delusion which the traveller among the more
rugged valleys of the Alps must often experience.
I was surprised to learn from our guide that this
part of the mountain was not named *Schlossberg*.
If ever any one merited this title, it surely was it.

Exactly on the top of the Lesser Scheideck Pass, there is a large building, of recent erection, intended for the accommodation of travellers; but it was shut up, on the present occasion, in consequence of the "bad season," that is to say, the paucity of travellers. We should not have stopped at it, at any rate, as our object was to reach the little inn built on the brow of the Wengern Alp, fronting the Jungfrau, and which was about a mile down the slope on the other side. Accordingly, after taking a last look at the beautiful valley through which we had passed, now spreading out to a vast extent behind us, green and glittering in the sun, and of the still more magnificent mountains which hemmed it in and overlooked it, we proceeded on our downward path, with the Mönch now close on our left hand, and the glorious Jungfrau straight before us, their snowy and cloudless heads majestically towering into the blue sky in all the brightness of the noontide sun. Keeping on the slope of the green mountain on our right, on a path which was separated from the base of the mountains on the left by a deep valley or ravine, we soon reached the small inn which is dignified by the name of the Hotel of the Jungfrau. We arrived exactly at noon, fresh and vigorous, and some of our party ready for yet another breakfast, after a walk of five hours.

In the course of our journey from Meyringen hither, the sight, here and there, of flocks of goats on the mountain-pastures, and the frequent direction

of our glasses to the cliffs, in hopes of seeing what
we were very anxious to see, some of the Gemsen or
chamois in their native haunts, led us often to talk
with our guide and others of the habits of these
wild animals.   The only specimen of these we had
yet seen in a living state, was a tame one which is
kept in a small hut in the village of Zwirgi, near
the Falls of Reichenbach, and is exhibited to the
passers-by for a small gratuity.   It was a pretty
little animal, showing sufficiently, in its clean limbs
and shape and its quick eye, that though in cap-
tivity, it was still one of Nature's legitimate children.
It was trained to show the activity and dexterous
delicacy of footing for which it is so remarkable in
its wild state, by leaping upon a high table at the
allurement of a piece of bread, and by standing,
with its four tiny feet all united, on the top of an
upright pole.   One has often heard and read of the
efforts made by goatherds to tame these animals
effectively, and which have always been baulked by
the sudden breaking out of the instinct through the
coverings of a civilization which concealed but did
not extinguish the native fires—

> "———————— ignes
> Suppositos cineri doloso."

Johann Brütschgi gave us a pretty history of one
of these attempts, which occurred within his own
knowledge only five years before.   The proprietor of
a large flock of goats on the greater Scheideck, had

rendered one of these creatures so tame, by training it almost from its birth, as to get it to mingle in the herd with its more civilized brothers, or rather cousins, and to go and come with them to and from the mountains, with perfect docility and seeming content. Like many of its companions it was decorated with a bell, suspended round its neck. After following for three successive seasons this domestic course, and having acquired a most satisfactory reputation for steadiness, it all at once, like the lady in Peregrine Pickle, under the influence of strong temptation unexpectedly presented, forgot all the lessons it had learned, and lost its character as a member of civilized society for ever. One fine day, when higher up on the mountains than was customary for the flock, it suddenly heard the bleat of its true brethren on the cliffs above, and pricking up its ears, off it started without one moment's consideration, and speedily vanished amid the rocks whence the magical sounds had come. Never from that hour was the tame Gemse seen on the green slopes of the Scheideck, but its bell was often heard by the hunters, ringing amid the wild solitudes of the Wetterhorn.

I cannot resist the temptation of here translating from the pages of old Johann Scheuchzer of Zurich, the painful account which he gives of the manner in which the young chamois are captured alive, and which he relates with all the *sang froid* of a naturalist dealing with his dead or nonsentient speci-

11

mens. "When these are only a few weeks old, and incapable of yet following their mother, they may be captured without any special artifice; but when they are somewhat older, the following stratagem is had recourse to. When the hunter has shot the suckling dam, he rushes forward, throws himself on the ground, and supports the dead animal the best way he can on its four legs. The kid seeing its mother once more in this position, comes forward to suck, and is then caught by the hunter and bound. Frequently it is not even necessary to bind the kid, as it will trot after the dead body of its mother hanging on the shoulders of the hunter!" The upshot of this miserable tragedy is usually such as I have above stated. "When taken home," continues Scheuchzer, "the young chamois is brought up with the milk of the domestic goat, and soon learns to keep with the flocks, going with them to the pastures on the mountains and returning with them to the fold. Sometimes, however,

"Naturam expelles furcâ tamen usque recurret;"

these nurslings, when they become older, desert the domestic herd, and seek loftier haunts more suited to their nature."*

The same traveller mentions another fact which had come to his knowledge, and which shows, by an affecting contrast, the insuperable love of the Gemsen for their mountains. It is only when they have

* Itinera par Helvetiæ Alpinas regiones facta, p. 156.

lost, through disease, that amount of intelligence with which they are gifted by nature, that they abandon their wild fastnesses and seek the haunts of man. In the year 1699, only four years before the date of Scheuchzer's journey, a chamois spontaneously descended into the valley of Engelberg in Unterwalden, and not only mixed with the cows and horses in the fields, but could not even be driven from them by stones. It was at length shot, and on its body being examined after death by one of the fathers of the neighbouring monastery, an hydatid or sac containing watery serum and sandy particles, was found pressing on the brain.*

The hotel of the Jungfrau is built on the slope of the Wengern Alp, on the edge of the cliff which forms the northern side of the ravine, named Trümlethenthal, and which separates it from the base of the mountain. It is directly in front of the Jungfrau, which looks as if it were quite close, although probably three quarters of a mile distant. As the site of the hotel, though seemingly so low, is really at a considerable elevation above the ravine, being nearly 6000 English feet above the sea, the view of the mountains from it is most perfect; and as we sat at our ease on the benches before the house looking at them, and watching the fall of the avalanches one after another into the ravine, it almost seemed as if we were looking on a performance of

---

* Ibid., p. 25.

art, instead of contemplating some of the grandest features and phenomena of nature.

The Jungfrau, though the fourth highest mountain in Switzerland, and upwards of 13,700 English feet above the sea, owing to the immensity of its mass and the comparative flatness of its top, like Monte Rosa and Mont Blanc, looks less lofty than it is ; while other mountains, as the Schreckhorn for instance, seem to be more elevated than they really are.   It is, however, evidently the queen of the magnificent group of mountains, which running from the north-east to the south-west, form the unbroken chain of snowy peaks which were now filling our horizon as far as we could see on either hand.   I will put down in order the names of all the loftier summits, such as I took them down at the time from the mouth of our guide, beginning at the left ; remarking only that the list must not be condemned as inaccurate because it may not quite accord with others, it being very common in Switzerland to find the same peaks in a group of mountains going by different names. Johann Brütschgi's catalogue was as follows: the great Eigher; the small Eigher; the Aletchhorn; the Mönch; the Jungfrau ; the two Silberhörner ; the Strahlen-berg; the Mittagshorn; the Grosshorn; the Breithorn; the Schwanenhorn ; the Schwalbenberg ; the Fräuen-grad.   All these peaks were, on this occasion, either perfectly clear and bright almost as the sun itself, or they were temporarily and partially clothed, not covered, by delicate wreaths of most lovely mist, so brilliantly white as to be distinguished from the snows on which it rested only by the configuration of its folds and its occasional motion.

During the period we remained at the hotel, which extended to a couple of hours, we had the pleasure of seeing many avalanches fall from the brow of the Jungfrau into the Trümlethenthal. For some time there was no appearance of the kind; but when they began, they came in quick succession: I counted no less than six within half an hour; and there were a few more. Though these avalanches were all small, and in no way to be compared with that we had seen fall from the Eigher, they were still exceedingly interesting to us from their novelty and beauty. They all came from the same part of the mountain, and appeared to arise but at a short distance above the cliff over which they were precipitated. The nature and course of the process was this: suddenly we heard a report like a small thunder-clap, which we found was produced by the rupture of the mass from the glacier and its brief descent along the rock; and by the time the eye had fixed on the exact spot, the lower portion of the moving mass had already reached the border of the cliff, and was beginning to shoot from it into the gulf below. In its fall it assumed exactly the appearance of a cascade, only whiter, and there was a pause of silence while it was passing through the air, speedily followed, however, by a second thunder-clap, much louder and longer than the first, as it reached and was accumulated on the ground below. As this ceased, there was seen to rise, and to extend to a great height, along the face of the dark rock, a fine white mist composed of the finer particles of the broken glacier and snow which had just descended. When the detached mass was small, and perhaps also under other conditions, there was no primary sound, and our first indication of what was taking place would be either the sight of the powdery cascade, or the sound it produced on reaching the ground; this sound was sometimes very considerable, even when that of the disruption was entirely absent.

While resting at the hotel, notwithstanding the bright sun, the air felt rather cold, and the thermometer in the shade was only 47°.

All around the hotel, and on the pastures both above and below it, there were large herds of cattle, chiefly cows; and we saw many more on the fine rich slopes as we pursued our way to Lauterbrunnen.

These cattle, and I may say the same of all those seen by us in the upland pastures in other parts of Switzerland, struck us as being particularly neat, clean, and healthy-looking, with much more of the slim make and breed of wild animals than our cattle. They were, however, far from wild in reality, allowing us to come near to them and even touch them, more readily than the cows in an English meadow. They are generally small, and, from their size as well as general appearance, remind one of the "black cattle" of Scotland, though I cannot but think them a finer breed than the Scotch. Almost every cow has a large bell suspended round her neck; and in passing along the valleys or wooded slopes of the mountains, it is very pleasing to hear the continuous tinklings of these bells from a large herd, more especially when coming to you, as they often do, from a considerable distance. It is also a beautiful sight to see the herd itself, consisting often of more than a hundred cows, thickly dotted over the open green slopes at the base of some bare cliff high above you, or appearing here and there amid the woody glades of some valley far below you. In eulogising the Swiss cattle living, I must not, in gratitude for many good dinners, omit to notice their good qualities when dead. On all occasions we found the roast beef—and this was a standing dish at every good hotel—very excellent in kind, and well cooked.

We left the hotel of the Jungfrau at two o'clock, by the same mule-path along which we had hitherto come, and which now led us by a continuous descent through pastures becoming gradually greener and richer and more wooded as we lowered our level above the valley. Very soon after starting, we took a sharp turn to our right and proceeded nearly at right angles to our former course, still coursing the base of the Wengern Alp, but now in a northerly instead of a westerly direction. The mountain had also changed its character as well as direction; as we had now a lofty perpendicular cliff close on our right hand, wooded at the base and on partial plots here and there on its breast, but for the most part bare. This range of cliff constitutes the barrier of what may be termed the upper valley of Lauterbrunnen on this its eastern side. From its base there is a gentle slope of some extent spreading towards the centre of the valley, but which, in its turn, terminates in another cliff or precipitous descent, forming the boundary of a lower and narrower valley, the special water-course of the white Lütschine. This lower valley is that which is more properly termed Lauterbrunnen, and possesses quite a different character from that through which we were now travelling. So steep and lofty was the cliff on our right hand that, like those of the Wetterhorn and Eigher, and many others, it had, at one spot, its special horn-blower to awaken the echoes for the benefit of travellers. And the spot was well chosen; as "the voice of the rock" was here particularly articulate and melodious, and well merited the few batzen that were paid for its awakening.

For some miles before we reached the point where we descended into the lower level, our path lay through an upland slope of meadow land, at once rich as pasture and yet well wooded. The fields were crowded with chalets intermixed with dwelling-houses. These last increased in size and number as we descended, until at length their frequency gave the green slope almost the appearance of a continuous village. The individual properties were evidently very small, and sometimes each had its cottage, and, at other times, one larger house accommodated several families. Some of the cottages we found empty, as the great mass of the population were in the open fields making their hay, in the bright afternoon sun; a circumstance which added not a little to the charm of the rustic landscape.

As on the present occasion, we had been frequently struck during our journey, and especially since we had entered the canton of Berne, with the great size of the houses of the peasantry; and it was some time before we discovered the real cause to be this union of families under the same roof. The same fact explains, in some measure, a circumstance formerly noticed, the apparent want of harmony between the dwellings and the habits of a certain portion of the community—I mean the issuing of a troop of begging children from a really handsome and well-appointed house.

It is probable, however, that a part of the superior aspect of the houses of the poor in Switzerland, may depend on the materials of which they are constructed. A poor man's cottage, built of brick or rough stones, and still more when built of mud or turf, and thatched with straw (as is the case in many parts of England, and generally in Scotland and Ireland), as it gets old or is out of repair, necessarily exhibits an appearance of dilapidation and

11 §

disorder but too much in accordance with what is probably the condition of its inmates. But the fine large wooden houses of the canton Berne, with their really elegant forms, their projecting roofs, numerous and large windows, straight lines and sharp angles, will never, when in a state of good repair, be taken by an English traveller for the abode of poor persons, much less of beggars : nay even when they get old and are verging on decay, they retain an external look and outlines which seem but little akin to the condition of poverty. It is, indeed, true that few of the people, even of the lowest class, in this country are really poor, or at least destitute——for in one sense they may be all termed poor; but if not paupers, they are certainly beggars ; and it seems somewhat of a contradiction to see beggars living in fine houses.

Many of the houses inhabited by the class of persons now referred to, are, as I have said, extremely neat ; and those belonging to the class above them, or, to speak more accurately, to such individuals of the same class as are in better circumstances——for all seem of one class here——are frequently not merely neat, but of elegant design and richly ornamented. Many of them seem new, but I believe many seem so which are not so ; the mere surface having been only renewed, while the old fabric remains untouched. This renovation of the surface by replacing the old shingles by new, is easily accomplished, without interfering with the substantial parts of the building; and it is the more frequently necessary, on account of the universal absence of paint, as a means of preservation, on the exterior of buildings. From the plentifulness of wood in the country it is found cheaper to renew the surface than to conserve it by paint.

There is one mode of ornamenting houses in Switzerland, and more especially in this canton, which is to me very pleasing; I mean the inscription in black paint, of long lines of words along the upper portion of the front above the windows, or on the pediment under the projecting roof. These inscriptions are generally short moral apophthegms or scriptural quotations; but sometimes they express merely the style and title of the founders or proprietors, the date of the erection, or other family or personal announcements. They are always in the German language, and painted as they invariably are in the picturesque and elegant letters of this old tongue, they reminded me—comparing small things with great—of the beautiful scrolls of Mr. Barry on the walls of the new palace at Westminster. I presume this mode of decorating houses is of very ancient date in Switzerland, as we find Schiller (who follows history closely) in his Wilhelm Tell, representing the house of Stauffacher at Steinen, as being thus distinguished:

" Von schönem Stammholz ist es neu gezimmert,
Und nach dem Richtmass ordentlich gefugt;

Non vielen Fenstern glänzt es wohnlich, hell ;
Mit bunten Wappenschildern ist's bemahlt
Und weisen Sprüchen." *

At the point were we descended from the upper
valley to the village of Lauterbrunnen, the declivity
is not rocky but a wooded hill ; it is, however,
almost as steep as a cliff, the path being zig-zagged
to a greater extent and in a more determined
manner than any we had hitherto travelled.   Nevertheless, it is not by any means a bad path, in regard to its formation, and is constantly trodden by
mules, both up and down.   The valley of Lauterbrunnen proper may be described in general terms
as a narrow and deep ravine, but a ravine of a gentle
character ; rich in trees and foliage, with a bare
perpendicular cliff of enormous height on the west,
and a wooded but steep and lofty mountain on the
east.   The rapid Lütschine, justifying by the colour
of its glacier-water its distinctive name of white,
sweeps along it, for the most part close to its right-
hand or eastern barrier, so as to leave on the other
side only a small ledge of flatter ground which is
richly cultivated.   As the valley winds along with
an equable but not very steep descent, nothing can,
in general, be seen but its own picturesque and
beautiful ramparts, its orchard-like and lawn-like

* Of good sound timber it is newly built,
  Well planned, well fashioned by the rules of art,
  Shining with windows, light and comfortable ;
  Painted with many-coloured heraldries
  And sayings wise.

fields, and its rich hanging woods; but every now and then when the traveller looks back, the Jungfrau or its adjoining peaks show themselves as it were blocking up the sky between the bounding cliffs on either hand, and adding their own peculiar glories to this most remarkable scene.

All the way down the upper valley we had seen the fall of the Staubach, like a narrow line of snow marking the dark cliff on the other side; and on crossing the bridge over the Lütschine, as we reached the village, we found ourselves close to it. At this time there was only a small supply of water, and we therefore saw it to disadvantage. It was, however, still very beautiful—one might almost say graceful and elegant also; but it had nothing of the grandeur of the Handeck or even of the Reichenbach. It is finely likened by Lord Byron to "the pale courser's tail" of the Apocalypse; and his description applies to it exactly as seen by us, namely, "a waving column of sheeted silver flinging its lines of foaming light to and fro;" but on this occasion it had nothing of the mysterious or sublime qualities which seem necessary elements in the haunt of the Witch of the Alps, and therefore I have, in a former page, claimed for the Handeck this distinction, as being the only place I saw in Switzerland where I think she would feel herself at home. She might, perhaps, pay a morning visit to the Staubach, just to see the rainbows and play with the hairs of the courser's tail, but I have no idea of her living there.

The village of Lauterbrunnen consists principally of pretty, detached houses, dotted here and there among the trees along the base of the cliff.   There is a neat church with a cheerful-looking spire, and a large hotel several stories high.   To this we were conducted by our guide, who was to leave us here, provided we could obtain a carriage to take us on to Interlachen.   For the second time since our arrival in Switzerland, we here encountered an attempt at imposition in a small way, on the part of the land-lord of the Steinbock.   Knowing that the distance to Interlachen was only seven or eight miles, the road good, and a declivity the whole way, we wished, for the sake of economy, to hire a one-horse char, and this without entering the hotel, as we purposed dining at the end of our day's work.   Whether to punish us for thus slighting his good things within doors I know not, but the landlord almost refused to let us have a carriage unless we took two horses, alleging that the road was bad, &c.; and it was only on the usual threat of taking none at all, and making demonstrations of continuing our walk, that the char was produced.   We had a good horse and an intel-ligent driver, and nothing could be a better com-mentary on the pretences of their master, than the rapidity with which they rolled us along the down-hill road the whole way, without making a single stop.   The valley retained its narrow ravine-like, yet rich and beautiful character, for several miles after leaving the village, until we came near the spot where our white Lütschine joined its black namesake* as it issued from the valley of Grindelwald, through a narrow gorge overhung by the huge cliffs of the Hunenfluh, the northern extremity of the mountain ridge which abuts on the Jungfrau under the name of the Wengern Alp. Here the character of the landscape began to change; the mountain barriers retreating on either hand, and at the same time losing their cliffy aspect, and assuming the gentler forms of wooded and rounded mountains.

The valley thus left flat and open, embosomed in its lofty but green and living barriers, is that of INTERLACHEN, one of the sweetest spots in all Switzerland. It is apparently surrounded on all sides by mountains, but is really open on the east, west, and south; at least as open as three narrow valleys debouching into it, and surrounded themselves by high mountains, can leave it. The southern valley is that of Lauterbrunnen, which we had just descended; the other two are filled respectively by the lakes of Brientz and Thun, which abut on either side at right angles to the former. Thus sheltered, yet not confined or close, the triangular plain of Interlachen, four miles probably in extent, supplies us with a perfect specimen of a Swiss valley in its richest and best form. It is one continuous sheet of green—green meadows everywhere shaded,

* The Grindelwald branch of the Lütschine is named *black* from its comparatively dark colour, arising from admixture with mud.

but nowhere overshadowed, with the lofty green trees
of an Alpine orchard—the chesnut, the walnut,
the plum, the cherry, the pear, the apple; and
brightened and rendered still more cheerful by neat
little villages and villas, scattered over it in every
direction.   In now entering upon it, we passed the
villages of Mühlinen and Wyldeschwyl, and proceeded through its entire width to the centre of its
northern limit, where it is bounded first by the river
Aar flowing from the lake of Brientz to that of
Thun, and then by the finely-wooded mountain
called the Harder, close at the base of which the
Aar runs.   Along this side of the valley, on the
left bank of the river, the village of Interlachen is
built, consisting for the most part of hotels and
lodging-houses, scattered all about amid the trees,
and respectively inclosed within their own plot of
garden ground.

We proceeded to the Belvedere, a very large
hotel in the centre of the village, just opposite the
opening into the Lauterbrunnen valley, and, consequently, with the Jungfrau right in front, and
ever seen from it filling up the gap in the dark
mountains with its skyey pinnacles of snow.   We
left Lauterbrunnen about half-past four, and reached
Interlachen at six.   The sun by this time had taken
his leave of the valley, behind the Abendberg and
Morgenberg mountains, but he still continued to
illumine the Jungfrau.   Long after this hour, when
the sun had gone down even to the loftiest peaks,

we were surprised to observe this mountain still retaining a wonderful degree of brightness, looking down upon us from its mountain path, as if only two or three miles distant.

I have stated that we parted with our guide at Lauterbrunnen, and that our car-driver from thence was an intelligent man. I ought to have stated that Johann Brütschgi was no less so; and indeed it is but doing simple justice to all the men of his class we had lately conversed with, to give them the same character. So far as we had hitherto had opportunities of judging, and speaking generally, I am bound to say that the common people of Switzerland are a fine race, physically and intellectually. Our intercourse with them was necessarily limited, and lay chiefly with that class of men who fill the station of husbandmen, guides, drivers, &c. With the few exceptions mentioned in their place, we found these persons remarkably intelligent and well-informed on all matters relating to the country. They seemed also straight-forward men, without any servility, and yet with nothing of that self-satisfied and obtrusive independence which has been said to mark the republican character. They spoke their minds freely but civilly, with unaffected and manly simplicity, showing only that degree of respect and deference which an honest nature spontaneously yields to superior knowledge. They were excellent companions, yet excellent servants; conversing with you without restraint, helping you without pretence; and annoying you neither by unmanly humility nor by ignorant impudence. They obviously felt that, in their station, they were as respectable as yourself, and they expected to be treated with that consideration which was their due: but their claim to such respect seemed to be founded on the conviction that they were fulfilling the duties belonging to their position in life, as you were fulfilling yours. It was always pleasant to travel with such men; and when the journey was over, it did the heart good to see them the first to hold out the hand, bidding you farewell with a cordial and honest shake, which seemed rather to express regard for the man than obligation to the employer. From what I have seen of men in the same class of life in our own country, I would compare my Swiss friends, more particularly in regard to intellectual development, with the miners of Cornwall and with the shepherds and mountaineers of Cumberland and Scotland: they are greatly superior to the class of agricultural labourers and common artisans in England.

As far as I could learn, the people of Switzerland seem still a very temperate race. During the whole of our tour, neither in town or country did we see anything approaching to intoxication: and, although they do not refuse wine or spirits when offered, they seem to have little recourse to either in habitual life. Beer seems unknown to the country people, and as a general beverage, wine is too dear for their means. Kirschenwasser, the only spirit generally accessible, and which, as its name implies, is made chiefly from the cherry, is only used on particular occasions. The form of strong drink most in use, is a kind of cider made from apples and pears; but their habitual daily drink, at meals, is water, milk and whey.

During the drive from Lauterbrunnen to Inter-lachen I heard a good deal from our driver respecting his position and relations, both public and private, of all of which he spoke without any backwardness or reserve. He himself lived in the hotel, but his wife had a house in the village. He received a fixed sum in wages during the winter, but was left in summer to depend on the Trinkgeld he obtained from travellers. The servants in the hotel have four meals a-day of good and plentiful fare. They breakfast at six on coffee, bread and milk; dine at eleven, on soup, meat and vegetables; have an after-noon meal at three, consisting of potatoes or other vegetables, with bread and cheese; and supper at seven or eight, of the same constituents. Here, as everywhere else in Switzerland, the commune sup-plies the lower classes with firing from the public woods, the parties cutting it for themselves, from trees marked for the purpose, and only to a certain but sufficient extent. My friend the driver is a voter for the representative of the district in the local parliament, and always exercises his privilege.

CHAPTER XIV.

August 26.——A lovely morning, though the thermometer in the open air was only 43° at half-
past five, when I was called. I breakfasted at
half-past six, and set out for the Abendberg on
horseback shortly after seven, leaving my younger
companions in their beds; they very naturally——not
being medical——preferring the charms of Interlachen
to the examination of cretins, which was the object
of my visit to the mountain. Retracing, for about
a mile, our path of yesterday, then turning to the
right, I soon began to find the road lose its flatness, and almost immediately entered on the ascent.
The Abendberg is one of the green barriers already
noticed as inclosing the plain of Interlachen. It
lies to the south-west of the village, its northern
base abutting on the eastern extremity of the lake
of Thun. Its elevation above the level of this lake
and the plain of Interlachen may probably be

3500 English feet, that is, about 5300 feet above the sea-level. The cretin establishment of Dr. Guggen-bühl is situated on the southern slope of this mountain, within probably a thousand feet of its summit ; it took me exactly an hour and a half to reach it from the village, at a good—rather fast—walking pace. The mountain from its base until we reach the hospital, is completely covered by trees, so that the steep zig-zag path by which we ascend is entirely shaded by them. They consist chiefly of fir of different species, and beech, and are all vigorous and healthy-looking trees. The woods belong to the local government, and are disposed of chiefly as firewood.

On emerging from the mule-path, which has also its termination here, I came at once upon a small open terrace, surmounted by a green slope stretching to a considerable distance up the mountain, and surrounded on all sides by the forest. It is on this small terrace, which looks like a step in the mountain, that the cretin establishment is built; and the green slopes above serve the double purpose of meadows for pasture and hay, and as an exercising ground for the patients. The spot is a remarkable one, and remarkably beautiful. It looks as if the wild forest had withdrawn itself on all sides, purposely to open a spot for the abode of man, yet remained sufficiently nigh to defend and shelter it, leaving it only exposed to the south and east, where exposure is desirable. It can hardly fail to remind the traveller, when its

green sunny fields first greet him on emerging from
the gloom of the forest, of some of those open yet
sheltered solitudes which Spenser is so fond of in-
troducing amid his forest-scenes.   The simple fact,
however, probably is, that the lesser steepness and
better soil of the spot, and its southern aspect,
induced some industrious husbandman to clear away
the forest to make it into pasture land ; and so it
has remained.

On arriving at the Institution, I found Dr. Guggenbühl would not be at leisure for a short time ;
so, leaving my horse at the house, I took the opportunity of mounting the open slope some half a mile
higher, in order to inspect the place still more completely.   On this short journey I had for companion
a young man of Interlachen, whom we had overtaken in the forest, and who was now pursuing his
further journey over the crown of the Abendberg to
the Alpine valleys beyond.   He was a saddler, and
carried a small pack of leather skull-caps of his own
manufacture, for disposal among the cowherds and
dairymen.   These caps cost about a franc each, and
are used by the milkers, who, partly from convenience
of posture, and partly with the view of promoting
the flow of milk, are in the habit of pressing the
head against the cow's flanks while milking.   I
mention this little circumstance as an evidence of a
degree of cleanliness on the part of these people,
which they have not always got credit for ; and also
in illustration of the industrious and simple habits

of the Swiss artisans, even at the present day. This young man told me that he might probably be two or three days among the mountains disposing of his goods, during which time he would sleep in the chalets, and live on the produce of the dairies. He seemed well-informed and was very neatly dressed. The day before, we had met at the Hotel of the Jungfrau another young man of the same trade, who had just returned from the United States and the Mexican campaign, with some money in his pocket. He, however, was about to start again for his adopted country, the great republic of the West.

In descending towards the house, I encountered midway, on the green slopes, some twenty of Dr. Guggenbühl's patients or pupils, climbing the hill for air, exercise, and amusement—all combined— under the superintendence of a well-dressed young man and two of the sisters of charity who belong to the establishment. They were all children, from the age of twelve or thereabouts down to three or four : one was carried by a servant, being incapable of walking. They were running and waddling and tumbling on the grass, and playing in their own way, with the servants, with one another, and with a fine good-natured dog who made one of the party, and who was probably of nearly the same intellectual caliber as some of his poor biped companions.

This little exhibition at once satisfied me of the enlightened character of Dr. Guggenbühl's views ; and I felt much greater pleasure in thus observing and examining the poor objects of his benevolent care, amid their humble enjoyments, and as it were in Nature's own presence, than if I had seen them cooped up in a ward or schoolroom, under restrictions which they probably could neither understand nor well brook. They were all neatly and cleanly but plainly dressed, and, like most individuals of the pitiable class to which they belong, were cheerful and apparently happy. The motherly care shown to them by the excellent sisters was delightful to witness. Sitting down in the sun on the beautiful soft grass, or trooping about you with that social instinct which seems so strong in idiots, with endless shaking of hands and the same monotonous greetings, repeated again and again, they seemed to renew the interesting scene I had so lately witnessed at the congenial establishment on Highgate Hill. And, indeed, I was much more struck with the similarity of the subjects, in the two cases, than I had expected. Several of Dr. Guggenbühl's patients unquestionably presented such characteristics of cretinism, in their dwarfish shape, peculiar configuration of head, and odd, old expression of countenance, as left no doubt as to their class ; but there were some of them regarded by Dr. Guggenbühl as cretins, whom my less-practised eye could in no way distinguish from the ordinary idiots of other countries ; and there were others whom he himself admitted to be simple idiots, though natives of Switzerland. Two or three of the children had come from districts where cretinism does not prevail : one was an infant from England.

On my return to the house, I found Dr. Guggen-bühl ready to receive me, and to receive me with that cordiality and kindness which form so marked a feature in his character. He showed me over the establishment, detailed his views, submitted to my inspection the most interesting cases, and put in operation before me some of his practical methods for developing both the physical and moral powers of the children.

Dr. Guggenbühl justly considers cretinism as a physical malady, consisting in an imperfect develop-ment of most of the bodily organs, and of the brain in particular, on the imperfection of which latter organ all the mental incapacity depends. Whatever be the special cause of the affection, he concludes that it is only by improving the bodily health generally, by strengthening and improving—that is, develop-ing to a higher degree of functional activity—all the organs of the system, and among the rest, and in an especial manner, the brain, that any rational hope of benefit can be founded. It was therefore a beautiful and most philosophical principle which he adopted as the indispensable basis of all his prac-tice, that, namely, of having the infant-cretin re-moved from the low, close valleys in which the malady generally originates, to the free, dry, cool, bracing air of the open yet comparatively sheltered and sunny slopes of the Abendberg. In such a locality, which

12

in itself is powerfully restorative, all the most effectual means of improving health can be applied with the best prospect of success; while they must have as obviously failed so long as the deteriorating causes were in full operation around.

These restorative means are the few simple ones which medical science has long recognised as alone influential—plenty of good food, exercise in the open air, friction to the surface, bathing, moderate mental exercise, cheerful occupation, comfort and happiness, with such small auxiliaries as medicine can supply in the form of drugs to promote healthy and correct unhealthy actions. The attempt to teach or to improve the mind in such cases, without improving the whole animal system at the same time, would be absurd, and could only be thought of by men who are utterly ignorant of human nature, that is, of animal nature. It would be as rational to try to extract music from a violin without strings or with slack strings, and with a cracked and broken frame, as to seek to develope and improve the mind of a cretin without previously strengthening and mending, and otherwise improving the qualities of his mental organ—the brain. When this is done, or even when this is doing, attempts may safely and with propriety be made to rouse the mental faculties and to improve and develope them; in other words, to teach : but not before. And it is by pursuing this natural, physiological system, heedless of the visionary dogmas of the metaphysicians, that Dr. Guggenbühl has already attained most gratifying and important results in the treatment of his patients and pupils.

Dr. Guggenbühl justly regards *all* the external influences with which his pupils are surrounded as of more or less importance in developing their slumbering faculties, well knowing that the restorative or curative power, which is but another name for nature, can only work efficiently when it works leisurely, uninterruptedly, and for a long period. It is, therefore, not without good reason that in selecting the Abendberg for his residence, he took into consideration, not simply its air and sun, its dryness, its sheltered exposure, and its facilities for exercise, but also its local charms, the beauty and grandeur of the scenes which lie around it and force themselves incessantly on the senses of the pupils, without any effort on their part or that of others. The green valley of Interlachen with its lofty yet living barriers of mountain forest, the series of mountains that stretch from this in every direction, the lakes of Brientz and Thun with their connecting stream, and, above all, the grand chain of the Oberland, with its snowy peaks piercing the blue sky close at hand——all these cannot be supposed to be without effect in exciting attention and interest, that is, in stimulating the material organ of the mind to action, and action of the best kind.

Heroic doctors, in their ignorance of the way in which alone Nature works, may attempt to cure a chronic disease by a *coup de main*; and, by mistaking temporary relief for real cure, may themselves suppose, or be supposed by others, to have done so; but every physiological physician knows well, that a morbid condition which may have been months or years in forming, can only be effectually and permanently removed by means which act slowly and for a length of time, not on one part only, but, more or less, on the whole system.   And so it is, and still more certainly, in the cases now under consideration; in the cure or amelioration of which nothing is to be neglected that can help to waken up the dormant faculties, in that gentle and imperceptible but uninterrupted mode in which Nature produces all her great and permanent changes in the organic world of life, and in the psychical no less than in the mere physical portion of her domains.

But Dr. Guggenbühl is far from trusting to these general influences alone, or to means directed to the improvement of the physical powers of the system at large; in conjunction with these he is in the constant employment of measures intended to act directly in developing the mental faculties.   These comprehend everything which is usually included under the term education.   When of a fitting age, all his pupils must attend the schoolroom for certain short periods of the day; and there they are carefully disciplined by his teachers and by himself, in exercising their feeble faculties of thought, and in acquiring such small modicums of knowledge as their respective capacities can grasp. The alphabet of letters and figures, syllabification, numeration, writing, outline or diagram drawing, spelling, reading, and such-like elementary processes, are among their first attempts ; while to those more advanced, a knowledge of things is communicated in that simple and natural method, by direct action on the senses or demonstration, which it is to be hoped will ere long entirely supersede, in schools for the rational also, that absurd system of teaching by the ear or by rote, which is no teaching at all, or a teaching only of sounds not ideas.

Dr. Guggenbühl was so kind as to examine, in my presence, three or four of his more advanced pupils in this species of instruction ; and it was delightful at once to see the amount of real knowledge that had been thus acquired, and the gratification which its acquisition and the conscious possession of it evidently conferred on the respective pupils. Not that the poor children knew much or could do much ; far from it ; but what they did, sufficed to show that the instrument was capable of action, and left no grounds for doubting that perseverance in the same course would lead to something still better. At the very least, the actual result showed the existence in the poor children of the quality of *teachableness ;* and this quality can be made subservient, in many ways, to the acquisition of *habits* which cannot fail to add to the comfort, health, and happiness of themselves as well as of their relations.

This has been sufficiently manifested by many cases at present in the establishment, and by others that have left it. And, indeed, when we merely see that those who could neither walk, nor talk, nor feed themselves, have learned to do so by instruction, we need not doubt that improvement may take place in matters involving only a little more cerebral or mental action.

The institution on the Abendberg is the private property of Dr. Guggenbühl, and originated in his own benevolent desire to benefit this wretched class of his countrymen. He has received some assistance, but not much, from the governments of Switzerland and from individuals; but his exertions are obviously cramped by inadequate means. He has only about thirty patients at present; but the house is capable of accommodating many more. As Dr. Guggenbühl's method is just as applicable to the improvement of the common idiot—although in simple idiotism accompanied with a good corporeal development, the obtainable results will be relatively less—he does not refuse to admit such into his establishment; and I am sure I am doing a great service to parents afflicted with any offspring of this kind, in recommending the Abendberg to their especial notice.

As I have already stated, I differ somewhat from my excellent friend the superintendent, in regard to the special nature of some of the cases now in his house; believing that more than one of those he regards as cretins, are in no respect different from the ordinary idiot of this and other countries. And in the course of my examination of such reputed subjects in different parts of Switzerland, I found some among them who, I think, should be classed in the latter category and not the former. This is, indeed, what might be expected. One hears little or nothing of simple idiotism, as distinguished from cretinism, in those districts where the latter malady is known to prevail : yet surely we may reasonably expect the ordinary proportion of such cases ; there being no country in which idiotism does not prevail to a certain extent. I infer that all Swiss idiots are classed as cretins.

This is not the place to enter upon the consideration of the causes of this great national affliction. They are, in fact, very imperfectly known. The most that can be said on this head is, that the more general features of the localities in which the disease is chiefly found, and the more general external circumstances amid which it occurs, may be considered as ascertained with some approach to accuracy. But even here we want positive proof; and we have no proof whatever as to the actual efficient or immediate cause of the affection. Every theory hitherto advanced is defective as not applying to all the cases.

It is by no means proved that cretinism has any essential connexion with goitre, beyond the general fact that they both commonly prevail in the same

localities in Switzerland. Innumerable goitrous subjects, however, even here, have no taint of cretinism,
either as to the general imperfect physical development, or the special cerebral defect; and many cretins have no goitre. This disease, moreover, under
the denomination of Bronchocele, is well known to
prevail in most countries of the world, chiefly in the
valleys of hilly districts, where yet no cretinism is
found. It is very common in England. The well-
known localities of cretinism as well as of goitre, in
Switzerland, are the deeper valleys and their outlets,
and it has been very generally admitted, of late, on
the strength of little more than this fact of locality,
that the main cause there operative in producing
them, is what is vaguely termed *confined air*, assisted
by the dirty habits of the people, &c. The old theories deriving these diseases from snow-water, water
having mineral impregnation, &c., have been generally abandoned as untenable. The water-theory
is of all others most improbable, seeing that snow- or
glacier-water is most rarely—if ever—used, while
that which is in habitual use is among the finest
and purest in the world, and exists in boundless
quantity.

Notwithstanding what has just been stated, of the
want of evidence as to the essential connexion of
goitre and cretinism, I am myself inclined to believe
that they may very possibly have an essential connexion, inasmuch as they may be both owing to the
same cause, or to a modification of the same cause.

I make no attempt to investigate the precise nature of such cause, nor do I propound even a conjecture respecting it, as the result of any special or enlarged consideration of the subject; but my present impression is that it is some form of that unknown local influence or thing, commonly recognised under the name of *miasma* or *malaria*, and which operates on the animal system as a poison, producing special modifications of function and special changes of structure, according to certain special conditions which, however, are like itself unknown. As the unknown thing which we term malaria or miasm of marshes, under certain circumstances gives rise at one time to simple ague, at another to a fatal remittent fever, &c., and produces at times a morbid enlargement of the spleen, at others disease of the liver, &c. &c.; so I can imagine that some other *malaria* or unknown thing or influence, of local origin, may be the cause of ordinary bronchocele, of the aggravated bronchocele or goitre of the Alps, and also of cretinism. There must be something more than stagnant or impure or heated air requisite for its production, as we find it frequently more rife in the larger than in the smaller valleys, as in the instances of the great valley of the Rhone and the valley of Aosta, which may be regarded almost as its head-quarters. Mere elevation above the sea, however, does not seem to exempt from it, provided the relations of mountain and valley still characterise the locality. Professor Forbes found the disease extremely prevalent on the south side of the Pennine Alps, in the Valpelline, at the elevation of 4000 English feet above the sea.*

It cannot therefore be questioned, under every view of the case, and even while we are still in total ignorance as to its efficient cause, that, in attempting the relief or cure of cretinism, removal from the source of its origin is a most important if not an altogether essential proceeding. I had myself sufficient evidence, not merely of the special preference of this affection for certain localities, but of the actual power of certain localities to produce it in families not otherwise predisposed to it. At Bonneville in Savoy, one of the surgeons pointed out to me a village near that town in a gorge of the mountain-range that bounds the Arve on the south, as the only place where cretinism prevails in that district; and he informed me that he knew a family who had had several healthy children while residing in a more elevated spot, and who, on coming to reside in this village, gave birth to several cretins: and similar instances have been mentioned to me by others, and are also noticed by writers on the subject. I saw cretins in the valley of the Arve, in the valley of Aosta, in the Vallais, in the valley of the Visp, in the valley of the Linth, &c.; but wherever I made inquiries respecting the prevalence of cretinism, I uniformly received the same assurance that it was everywhere on the decrease, and in so marked a degree that the belief of its final

* Travels in the Alps, p. 271.

extinction at no distant date seemed very general. Dr. Grillet of Sion, the very intelligent physician to the cretin hospital in that city, and who has made extensive statistical inquiries respecting this disease, regards the gradual diminution of cretinism as fully established.

The most marked evidence I myself obtained on this point was afforded me by the pastor of St. Nicolas, in the valley of the Visp. The population of his parish is 560 or 570. Among this number there are twelve cretins, all, save one, above the age of thirty; most of them upwards of forty; the exceptional case is seven years of age, and is itself the child of a cretin. It follows from this that there have been very few cretins born in the parish during the last thirty years. The pastor assures me that the child just mentioned is the only one born during the twenty years of his incumbency. He attributes the recent comparative immunity to the change of habits and manners that has taken place of late years. He says, the persons of the people, as well as their houses, are much cleaner than they used to be; the rooms better aired; and that the children are sent much more out of the valley into the mountains, there being now many more alpine chalets for summer residence than was the case formerly.

In my numerous inquiries respecting cretinism in Switzerland and Piedmont, I was much struck with the illustration it afforded of the influence of habit in modifying some of our strongest instincts and feelings. The mother of an idiot, even in the lowest class, in England, feels the imperfection of her child to be the greatest of personal misfortunes; she looks upon the affliction as of too awful a nature to be thought of except with a solemn humility; and does all in her power to conceal it from the world. I saw nothing of this in Switzerland. On the contrary, the neighbours and companions, and relatives, sometimes even the fathers and mothers of cretins, had not only no delicacy in showing them, but seemed to make their unhappy oddities a subject of mirth: they appeared to regard my inquiries and personal examination of the poor creatures as something essentially odd and ludicrous. I was really shocked to see and hear what I did on these occasions; but on reflection I was not much surprised: custom has in all times been found capable of smothering not only the natural instincts and feelings, but reason itself, even in the minds of the strongest.

Before taking leave of Dr. Guggenbühl's establishment, I was fortunate enough to enter into a conditional arrangement with one of his sisters of charity, to come to England to assist in conducting the business of the Asylum for Idiots, lately instituted, mainly through the influence of the Rev. Dr. Reed, and now in active operation at Highgate. The experience of this young woman acquired under the eye of Dr. Guggenbühl, cannot fail to be advantageous in the early stage of this establishment, which promises to be one of the most valuable charities in the country, as it is certainly one that is most wanted. The effects already produced in it, in improving the health, comfort, and habits of its inmates, are such as leave no doubt as to the immense importance of a systematic attempt to educate the idiot as well as the cretin; and I entertain no doubt that a very few years will prove this establishment to be a worthy rival of the Abendberg, in the same great cause to which Dr. Guggenbühl has devoted himself.

I returned to Interlachen by the same path—the only one—and arrived at the Belvedere at one o'clock. As the steamer for Thun, which was our destination this evening, was to start at four, we had only a short time for looking over the village. But there is little to be seen in it but a repetition of the same large, flashy garden-houses for the accommodation of visitors, scattered here and there among the trees, with now and then a deceptive cottage for various households, a reading-room, or shops. Among the latter were some devoted to the manufacture and sale of wood-carvings, which appeared to us superior to any we had previously seen. I regretted much that our plans would not allow us to take a trip on the lake of Brientz with the steamer which, by daily trips, now unites the valley of Meyringen with that of Interlachen and Lauterbrunnen.

The small town of Unterseen is a good deal nearer the lake of Thun than the village of Interlachen, but is still a considerable distance from it: it bears the same relation to the latter, in point of appearance, which any crowded old English town bears to the smart outskirts of Cheltenham, Bath, Leamington, or any other modern and fashionable watering-place. It consists of curious old-fashioned wooden houses, closely huddled together, on both sides of the Aar, which we found greatly increased in size since we last saw it at Meyringen. Not wishing to go on board heated by exercise, we took a small carriage from the Belvedere to Neuhaus. The Belvedere is an excellent hotel, everything being conducted on a large scale, and no fault to be found with the cookery, chamber accommodation, attendance, or charges. It had only the single fault referred to elsewhere, and which it shares with all the inns of Switzerland.

Neuhaus, the port of Interlachen as it may be termed, consists merely of a few small houses on the border of the lake, with a little pier for the convenience of embarkation and debarkation. We found the steamer lying alongside, and went immediately on board. She sailed shortly after four, and reached Thun in about two hours. The afternoon was clear and sunny, but by no means too warm, as there was a pleasant breeze on the water. The lake of Thun is inferior to that of Wallenstadt in grandeur, and to that of Luzern in beauty, but superior to the lake of Zurich in both. In respect of the views *from* it, however, it is superior to all these, none of them having any near or distant prospect to be compared with that on which we now looked back, where the snowy giants of the Oberland, the Mönch, the Eigher, the Jungfrau with her Silver Horns, &c., are seen over the tops of the Abendberg and Morgenberg; or where, further to the right, the Blumlis Alp or Frau, the Doldenhorn, &c., are seen bounding the horizon to the south-east and south. The more immediate boundaries of the lake are also fine. The northern shore is in some parts, at least towards its eastern end, almost as bold and precipitous as the Uri branch of the Waldstädttersee, becoming, as we approach Thun, subdued and softened to the quieter and richer character of that of Zurich. On the southern shore, again, we have close at hand the two magnificent and comparatively isolated mountains, the Niesen and Stockhorn, striking from their sharp and peculiar outline; the former rising up like a vast symmetrical broad-based pyramid, the latter shooting out diagonally into the western sky its huge terminal horn. The Niesen is 7800, and the Stockhorn 7200 English feet above the sea-level.

About a couple of miles after leaving the pier, our steamer passed close under the perpendicular cliff on our right hand, which forms the base of the Beatenberg or mountain of St. Beatus, a legendary countryman of ours, who, after great exploits in the

saintly line, finished his career as a hermit in a cave
which is still shown midway up the cliff, and from
which a small cascade descends into the lake. Whether it was in homage to the memory of the saint or
to evoke the echoes, I know not, but while close to
the shore, an organ kept on board for the purpose,
but of whose presence we were previously ignorant,
suddenly startled us by striking up a loud strain,
which rang wildly and beautifully among the cliffs
above.

I regretted not being able to visit the famous
cell which most probably is well entitled to the distinction claimed for it, of having been the abode of
a holy hermit in the old time; although there may
be some room for doubting whether his predecessor
was really a dragon, or whether he himself was in
the use and wont of navigating the lake on his own
cloak, without either wind or steam.

The description given of the cave of St. Beatus
by my learned brother, Dr. Scheuchzer, in his *Itinera*,
holds out sufficient attractions of a more natural
kind to induce the traveller, though neither of the
ecclesiastical or antiquarian order, to visit it.   " It
enjoys (he says) a pleasant outlook over the lake
and its opposite shore, which could not fail to delight
a man accustomed to the open air; while near at
hand the trees and their shade, and the songs of
the birds in the boughs, must be no less attractive.
The interior of the cave is divided into separate
spaces or apartments, among which is pointed out

the dormitory of the holy man. But above all to be admired, as recreating at once the eye, the mind, and the palate, is the copious and most limpid stream which wells forth from the interior of the cavern, flowing at first over its declivities with a gentle murmur, and then over the cliff without in the form of a distinct cascade. In a word (the doctor adds), if the most potent monarch had such a thing in his pleasure-grounds, even he would have no limits to his admiration, let alone a poor world-weary hermit."

I know not whether the honest doctor, like some more brilliant travellers I could name, was here indulging a little in fancy when he introduced the "songs of birds" (avicularum cantus) among the charms of his landscape; but this I know——and I may as well notice the fact here as elsewhere——that the nearly total absence of birds of every sort, was a thing which struck us as very remarkable in our Swiss tour. Not a rook, not a magpie, not a sparrow, not a wood-pigeon, not a blackbird or thrush, lark or linnet, not a partridge or quail, did we see; not a song, caw, croak, scream, or chirp did we hear from one end of the land to the other, with the following exceptions, which I noted as mark-worthy for their rarity :——On the top of the Col de Fours, in the Alps of Savoy, we saw a raven; in the Münsterthal in the Jura we saw an eagle; in some other place, but exactly where I now forget, we saw a hawk; on the brow of the mountains which bound the Klausen Pass we saw a few white game or ptarmigan; and on the slaty slopes of the Riffelhorn and Mount Breven, I saw a couple of stone-chats.

No doubt the naturalist will tell me that the period of my visit is not the time of the singing of birds, and that in August the whole feathered creation are particularly quiet in all countries. Still such a total absence of birds as was noticed by us in Switzerland, indicates their positive non-existence in the same proportion as in many other countries. And this is readily explained by certain obvious peculiarities of this. The severe and lengthened winter must render the sustenance of birds extremely difficult, if not impossible, in that season; while the infrequency of grain crops in the country must curtail the nutriment, even in the summer and autumn, of one large class of birds. Does the nightingale visit the beautiful valleys of Switzerland?

There were not many passengers on board the steamer, and not more than two or three English beside ourselves. There was one passenger, however, who attracted much attention, and deservedly; as he was certainly one of the most perfect specimens of his race. This was a magnificent young dog, of a jet black colour, of the largest size, yet extremely well-made. He was the most beautiful animal of the species I ever saw; but I notice him here because the captain, whose property he was, assured us that he was of a breed peculiar to the country.

The steamers on this lake and that on the lake of Brientz belong to a company of brothers of the

name of Knechtenhofer, one of whom was the captain of our present boat, and another master of
the Bellevue Hotel at Thun. To this hotel we proceeded on our arrival. It is situated on a gentle
rise of ground near the lake, in a neat shrubbery,
quite out of the town ; it is a large building, and it
proved to be an excellent resting-place.

After dinner we walked about the town, the
evening being very fine. The outskirts, with their
gardens, and the higher parts of the town, with the
church and old castle, are interesting ; the main
body of it is close and crowded, but with a good
deal of the character of an old German city. It
is traversed by the river Aar, after escaping from
its second lake, enlarged and purified. It is now a
very fine river, beautifully clear and still preserving
its rapid course. It leaves the lake in two branches.
Some of the main streets of Thun are curiously
arranged, there being a sort of terrace at either
side, some ten or twelve feet high, from which access
is had to the shops, &c., while the carriage-way is
immediately bounded by the cellars, &c., of which
the terrace is the roof. A similar arrangement is
seen at the small town of Unterseen. The situation
of the church is very fine, on a lofty terrace overlooking the town and the lake. The churchyard is
crowded with tombstones, and contains numerous
neat inscriptions, some on stone, but the greater
number on small metal plates supported on rods
attached to the graves.

CHAPTER XV.

August 27.—Having in prospect a rather long journey to the Baths of Leuk in the Vallais, we were early stirring, and indeed took our departure while it was still somewhat dark, at a quarter before five. The previous evening we had engaged a carriage with a couple of horses to take us on to Kandersteg, a distance of about twenty-five miles, for which we were to pay twenty-five francs. The night had been extremely warm, and the thermometer, which had been left in the open air, stood at 60° at half-past four. The morning was clear and calm ; and there seemed a fresh charm in the old scenery, as the gradually-dawning day shed its quiet light on the Stockhorn and Niesen on our right, on the tranquil lake on our left, and on the snowy peaks of the Oberland, now towering far in our front. The road lay close along the

borders of the lake for several miles, and then turned
with a gentle inclination away from it, in a direction nearly south.

About a couple of miles after leaving Thun, we
crossed the Kander by a handsome bridge, a very
short way above the point where it discharges itself
into the lake by its modern channel.   This channel
bears now very slight trace of its artificial origin,
looking exactly like a deep rocky gulley made by
nature by and for the passage of a large mountain
torrent.   The only thing about it having the look
of art, is the perfect straightness of its course as it
enters the lake.   The origin of this canal, its plan,
object, and its happy results, are almost identical
with those of the Linth canal; and as its formation
long preceded that of the Linth, there can be little
doubt that it was from it that Escher took his plan.
Previously to the formation of this new channel, the
Kander discharged itself into the Aar at some distance below the town of Thun; and as the last few
miles of its course, after leaving its mountain gorge,
were through a flattish country, it was constantly
overflowing its banks, when swelled by rains or the
melting of snow on the mountains, so as to injure
the district to a great extent.   On this account the
Bernese government, in the beginning of the last
century, caused this canal to be constructed, at great
labour and expense, and with complete success; the
whole of the devastated district being thereby at
once reclaimed and rendered perfectly secure.   When
Dr. Scheuchzer visited Thun in the year 1711, the

work was then in progress, under the direction of
the engineer of the canton, Samuel Bodmer; two
hundred and fifty men being employed on it. The
inhabitants of Thun were at this time under great
apprehension lest the lake thus reinforced should
rise above its previous level and flood their gardens.
But such fears have proved altogether visionary.
The only effect on the lake produced by it, since its
opening in the year 1714, is the formation of an
extensive stony delta on that part of the shore of the
lake where the river enters. This derivation of the
Kander, like that of the Linth, is truly a noble work
and one most creditable to the canton :——"opus
magnificentiâ Bernensi dignum" — as Scheuchzer
justly terms it. According to this author, the following are the dimensions of the canal : width at its
commencement, 272 feet ; greatest vertical depth,
152 feet; length, 3000 feet. The extent of river
thus diverted, measuring from the new canal to its
old junction with the Aar, is 42,000 feet, or between
seven and eight miles.

A mile or two further on we crossed the mouth
of the Simmenthal, between the Niesen and the
Stockhorn, a beautiful valley which one passes by
with regret. From this valley descends the Simmen,
to unite with and swell the Kander before it enters
on its new course ; and here also we passed two of
the ancient castles of the land, that of Spiez close
on the margin of the lake on our left, and that of
Wimmis on the right. All the way from Thun, the
country is well wooded and highly cultivated : like

the valleys of Unterwalden and Obwalden, it put us in mind of a series of gentlemen's parks in England.

On rounding the base of the Niesen, and turning to the south along the right bank of the Kander, we entered into the comparatively open and well-cultivated valley drained by this river. The mountains bounding it on either hand are for the most part wooded to the very top. We passed through a good many villages, some of considerable size, as Mühlinen and Reichenbach, the latter at the mouth of the Kienthal, which sends a branch to the Kander. We reached the small town of Frutigen, containing about a thousand inhabitants, at about eight o'clock, and here both men and horses sought refreshment. The postboy took us to the Posthaus, or Hôtel de la Poste, which we afterwards found was not the best inn ; indeed the house was inferior in every respect. As some excuse, however, for its imperfections, it is but fair to state, what we learned from our driver after leaving it, that the landlord was then confined to bed with a severe illness, under which he had laboured for many weeks. Having rested here about an hour, we proceeded on our journey, crossing once more to the right bank of the Kander, and so continuing until we reached the village of Kandersteg. As we advanced towards it, the valley gradually contracted on the river, and soon terminated altogether in a buttress of steep mountains surrounding it on every side except the north.

We arrived at the village of Kandersteg about eleven o'clock. It consists of a few wretched wooden houses—the inn being only somewhat less bad than its neighbours. As we stood in no need of refreshments here, we found the innkeeper not very well disposed to accommodate us according to our own views; and we had "an angry parle" in consequence. What we desired was, a man and horse to convey me and the knapsacks of the party as far as Swarenbach midway to the Gemmi: and the fight on our part was to get all this done by one man and one horse; and on the part of the belligerents of Kandersteg, to get it done by two men and two horses. After a hot logomachy, in barbarian Deutsch on either side, Kandersteg at length succumbed under the *in-terrorem* argument of *this or nothing*—either one horse and one man, or no horse and no man: we had legs to climb and backs to bear. Accordingly, after waiting a good while until the horse was brought from a field at some distance, we set forth, the owner being allowed to divide the baggage part of the burthen between himself and his horse, according to his pleasure.

A little beyond the village we crossed the Kander —already a considerable stream—once more, as it escaped from the gorge of the Gasternthal on our left; and proceeding along the banks of a smaller stream, the Ueschinen, which here joins it, we soon reached the base of the Gellihorn, which forms the abrupt termination of the valley we had been all the morning travelling up. This eastern border of the Gellihorn consists partly of a perpendicular bare cliff, and of a wooded steep somewhat less abrupt, which joins it to the root of the Altels, on the eastern side. It is in this wooded steep that the mule path is formed, in many places out of the solid rock.

The ascent began abruptly in the usual zig-zag fashion, and so continued, with occasional short intervals of gentler slope, until we had reached, at a great elevation, to what may be called the top of the pass. The ascent from this point was much gentler, but carried us still a good way higher; though, looking at the vast cliffy steeps of the Altels and Gellihorn that bounded us in on either side, we seemed, even at our greatest elevation, to be yet at the bottom of a mountain gorge. On looking behind us, however, we had very satisfactory evidence of the great height we had attained, in the extensive view we had of the valley of the Kander, stretching far away to the north at a vast depth below us. We had a still more magnificent view on turning to the east where the Doldenhorn, the Blumlis Alp and many other of the snowy peaks of the Oberland chain, were seen filling up the horizon.

The path for a long way up the mountain was shaded with trees; the entire pass from cliff to cliff being a continuous forest, with scarcely any open pasture ground. When, however, we reached the gentler slopes, the woods grew thinner, and left open pastures on which many cattle were feeding. We were now on the boundary line of the cantons of Berne and Wallis (or the Vallais), which was only marked to us by a common wooden wicket in the

13

mule path, pointed out by our guide.   The division
of the cantons was, however, indicated by something much more characteristic of the genius of the
respective governments. Hitherto our path, how steep
soever, was carefully planned, formed evidently at
much expense, and in excellent preservation : the
very instant we passed through the terminal wicket,
the evidence of man's industry and care ceased
abruptly, and we had now no other tract than what
had been beaten out of the native turf and mouldering
rock, by the feet of men and beasts.   And this was
only a foretaste of other contrasts of a more important
kind, which we were to meet with in the Vallais——all
in favour of Berne.

At this point we were about 6200 English feet
above the sea-level, and about 2700 above the village
of Kandersteg ; and we had come close to the base
of the Altels on our left hand, which, while raising
its snowy peaks into the sky to the height of more
than 12,000 feet above the sea, sent down its glaciers
into the valley close at our side.   This mountain
and its prolongations to the south, the Rinderhorn
(11,600 English feet above the sea) and the Plat-
tenhorn, continued to bound our left-hand path
with an impassable barrier for a considerable part
of this day's journey ; while the cliffy base of the
Gellihorn continued to do the same on the right.   On
reaching the height which brought us close to the
base of the Altels, we made a short descent into a
valley well named Wintereck, and which resembled

those we had passed through in crossing the Klausen and Brünnig only in configuration, as it was as wild and desolate as they were beautiful. It had, to be sure, a considerable extent of flat pasture land in it, but it was coarse and cold-looking; while the steep mountains which bounded it on either hand were wild and treeless, the slope at their base being covered with rubbish accumulated by the torrents and avalanches from above. A stream called the Schwartzbach ran along the foot of the Altels eastward, and we crossed another of considerable size, which joins it from the opposite side of the valley at its south-western extremity. How or where these waters make their exit from the valley, or whither they ran, we could not discover; but I believe that they find their way round the base of the Altels into the Kander, before it escapes from the Gasternthal. There were several chalets here; and we saw a good many cattle which belonged to the inhabitants of the valley below the Gemmi. The few women and children that came begging from the huts, looked very miserable and cretinish.

Leaving this green but dismal glen, we entered on a fresh ascent speedily ending in a true petræan desert which continued all the remainder of our way to the cliffs of the Gemmi. At its commencement there was a ragged wood of pines; but as we advanced, every form of vegetation gradually and at length almost entirely, disappeared; yet apparently less from the high level than from the nature of the surface, which consisted exclusively of loose fragments of slaty rock huddled one above another, without any appearance of earth or soil, and with scarcely a shrub or even a blade of grass to relieve the utter barrenness. The qualities of the path or rather no-path, through such a locality as this, may be imagined. And they became even aggravated when, in advancing, we came upon the banks of the little lake called the Schwarisee, lying in a deep hollow on our left hand.

At this place I was very near meeting with an accident which, had it taken place, might have been of serious consequence to myself. The young mare I had ridden from Kandersteg was by no means sure-footed, and withal rather skittish, especially when accidentally touched. She had repeatedly tripped in the course of the journey hither, and now as we were descending a rather steep and narrow path cut in the cliff bounding the lake, she gave a sudden fling behind, and at the same time made an awkward stumble in front, so that I had the greatest difficulty to keep my seat, and was, indeed, within an ace of being tossed over her head, taken as I was by surprise in the idle fashion that one sits on a walking horse. Had I been thrown off, I think I must have inevitably gone down the cliff, in which case it is pretty clear that the reader would not have been troubled with this tour in Switzerland. I hardly know whether I or the poor man who was the innocent cause of the accident by touching the mare with his alpenstock, was most frightened : probably he was better aware of the danger than I was.

I am induced to mention this circumstance chiefly by way of caution to others, as I am well aware that, on many occasions during this tour, I trusted too readily to the surefootedness of my beast in places where a stumble must have been fatal. Although it is unquestionably not very pleasant for a rider to be getting off his horse at every dangerous spot, still I believe this ought invariably to be done. The surest beast, horse or mule, sometimes stumbles, and the very possibility of this ought to be eschewed where the stumble must be fatal. It is well known that many travellers in Switzerland have perished from disregarding this caution.

At length we reached Schwarenbach, the solitary halfway house and, with the exception of the chalets in the valley of Wintereck, the only house between Kandersteg and Leukerbad. It is rudely but substantially built out of the slaty rocks amid which it stands. It is occupied by a man and his family, and serves the purposes of an inn, having even some sleeping accommodations. The official station of the custom-house officers being at this outlet of the Vallais, the house is inhabited even in winter. Just in front of it, in a deep hollow, lies the small gloomy tarn from which it derives its name, and which by no means tends to enliven the scene.

This house has got an ill-omened celebrity from having been once the scene of a terrible murder

which has been made the groundwork of Werner's
tragedy called the 'Vier-und-Zwanzigste Februar.'
The poet has, however, reversed the facts of the
case, the landlord and his family having been the
victims instead of the murderers.   The murderers
(two Italian vagabonds) were afterwards apprehended
and condemned and executed at Berne.

I here took leave of my guide and horse, preferring to walk the remainder of the journey.   At
first we were apprehensive that we should have to
carry our own knapsacks, but at last we obtained
the services of the landlord's two sons, lads of ten
or eleven, who gladly undertook to accompany us
to the baths.   Their father, however, chose to regard
their services in the light of a favour to us, and
charged accordingly.

The   same   petræan   desert   continues   beyond
Swarenbach, but is varied—it can hardly be said
to be improved—at the distance of a couple of miles
further on, by the appearance of the Daubensee, a
small lake, probably two miles long and less than one
broad, filling up the entire bottom of the valley and
forcing the path up along the base of the cliff on the
eastern side.   It is bounded by a range of naked cliffs
on both sides, that on the west side being terminated
by a ridge of rugged peaks of the wildest shapes.
This lake has a most dismal aspect, looking dull and
dirty, with flat, bare, stony, and muddy borders,
and with scarcely even a shrub around it to give it
life.   It is fed by the glaciers that overhang it on

both sides; and though a lively stream of some size from the Lammern glacier runs into it at its south-western extremity, it has no discoverable outlet whatever. In the Gasternthal, a short way above its opening into the valley of Kandersteg, there is a powerful waterfall issuing from a circumscribed open-ing half way up a perpendicular cliff. It is con-jectured by some that this may be the outlet of the Daubensee; but this is very improbable. I found the temperature of the water of the Daubensee, a foot under the surface, to be 49°. Its height above the sea level is about 7400 English feet.

In advancing on our path towards the Gemmi we rounded the southern end of the Dauben lake for a short space, and then proceeded directly south up a considerable acclivity, still of bare rock, but now of the solid slaty strata *in situ*. After scramb-ling about a mile over this rugged and slippery ground, we reached the culminating point of the Pass, and at once found ourselves in presence of a magnificent prospect. This was part of the great chain of the Pennine Alps, which were seen rising over the dark tops of a long range of intervening mountains, and filling up the sky to the south and east, with a barrier of snowy peaks of the in-tensest white. Descending a short space from the summit, we sat down on a ledge of the rock to con-template the view at leisure. It being only half-past three, the sun was still high : the sky over the distant mountains was of the true Italian blue, as it had

now good reason for being ; and the air was so transparent that the whole of the snowy region, peak
upon peak, was almost as distinctly visible as if it
had been only a few miles distant.   Not having now
a guide with us, we could only form conjectures as
to the individual mountains seen ; but a couple of
days' further journeying taught us to know them all
in their own localities.

Here the best authority is Mr. Engelhardt, who
tells us that he had crossed the Gemmi no less than
seven times, and never crossed it once without being
compelled, by the renewed charms of the landscape,
to make a drawing of these very mountains.   The
following is his account of them as seen from the
spot where we were now sitting : "As central
object in the view towers the Weisshorn, 13,898
feet above the see, according to M. Berchtold's
trigonometrical survey.   It is an irregular cone with
sharp peaks, that on the north-east being lower than
the others.   As it is in the same line of direction,
it entirely blocks the view of Monte Rosa from us,
which mountain lies about five leagues further to the
S.S.E.   Two peaks, the Brunekhorn and Schwartzhorn, lie directly to the north of the Weisshorn, and
unite with it, but at a level 2000 feet lower : they
seem to bear the same relation to the loftier mountain, as the Silverhorns bear to the Jungfrau, and
thus create a certain degree of resemblance between
the two.   To the East of the Weisshorn there is
another vast group of mountains, which rise up into

a series of pyramidal peaks, one above the other. These belong to the Saasgrat group. The loftiest and most distant of these peaks is that named the DOM, by M. Berchthold, and which he calculates at 13,674 feet above the sea; the second is termed by him the Swartzhorn; and the third and lowest is the Balfrein. This group of mountains is usually, but erroneously, taken for that of Monte Rosa. The loftiest peak, to the west of the Weisshorn, judging from its elevation and form, must be the Matterhorn, or Mount Cervin."*

All these mountains were either entirely cloudless or were only here and there partially wreathed with slight folds of those fleecy clouds of the upper sky, which, in the sunshine, look almost as bright as the snow itself. A good many small isolated clouds of this kind were now travelling the heavens at a higher level; and as they came, in succession, between the mountains and the sun, it was beautiful to observe how the brilliancy of the snowy peaks alternately waned and waxed. The masses of cloud being well defined, it was easy to trace the perfect outline of the shadows as they moved slowly along the snowy field; and as peak after peak emerged from the partial eclipse, each seemed to shine with greater brilliancy than ever. It was pleasant to sit in a sunny corner and look on a scene like this; and as we saw the place of our destination apparently close to us, and, as it were, at our very feet,

* Naturschilderungen, p. 73.

13 §

in the valley below, we were in no great haste to resume our Alpenstocks.

Every one must have felt that in looking stead-fastly on a spectacle like this, the eye at length seems to become fixed on it with a sort of fascination, and that it is impossible to avoid falling into one of those dreamy, half-concious moods, in which the common trains of thought take their own way without leave or licence from the higher powers. This must have been my case on the present occasion; as all at once, while still sitting in the sun and looking on the mountains, I felt that every impression of what was actually present had vanished, and the mind was exclusively filled with ideas of a totally different cast, ideas of desertion and desolation, of utter solitude and silence. I presume that fancy had been playing one of her ordinary tricks with the unconscious spectator, placing him in imagination amid the very scenes he was contemplating, and making him feel, for the moment, as if he actually suffered what he merely thought: otherwise a pro-spect of such grandeur, brilliancy and beauty, ought to have excited feelings of quite a different kind.

At length we set out, about four, to descend the Gemmisteig, or pathway of the Gemmi, on our way to Leukerbad: and a wonderful descent it is. As a work of art it greatly excels, in my mind, even the Via Mala; and taking its art and its nature together, it is exceeded by few things seen in Switzerland. Although the path is quarried literally out of the solid rock, and though this rock is literally perpendicular, there is neither danger nor difficulty in ascending or descending it. It consists of an unbroken series of short zig-zags, is four or five feet wide, and is everywhere defended by solid balustrades of stone. As might be expected, its steepness is extreme, much steeper than the steepest stair of a house; nine tenths of it, indeed, *is* a stair, the steps being formed in the solid slate. The height of the cliff, in direct perpendicular measurement, is about 1700 English feet, and the length of the path between the same two terminal points, is about 10,700 English feet, or two English miles; a discrepancy sufficiently illustrative of the great extent of the windings. Looking from the top of the cliff one would fancy that a quarter of an hour or thereabouts, might bring one to the bottom; it took us, however, a complete hour, of good hard walking, or rather skipping, to do so. The path is perfectly practicable for mules, and we met several coming up. Here as in all similar places the animal is taught to keep carefully to the side of the path furthest from the rock, in order that his burthen may pass clear of the cliff, the touch of which might not merely injure the goods but might throw both beast and burthen over the precipice.

The Pass of the Gemmi has been known and used from time immemorial. A marked proof of its existence so early as 1318, is the fact that, in that year, an army of 10,000 Bernese descended it previously to fighting the famous *Battle of Sighs* in

the valley below.   The path then used, however,
was quite different from the present.   It lay considerably more eastward, was much longer, and is
supposed to have opened into the valley above, to the
north of the Daubensee, somewhere about Schwarenbach.   Collinus of Sion, who wrote his work *De
Sedunorum Thermis*, about the middle of the sixteenth century, says that some traces of this road
still existed in his time.   At present there is not only
no remains of it, but its actual course is unknown.
The earliest notice we have of the present pathway
is contained in Munster's work entitled *Cosmo-
graphia Universalis*, published at Basel in 1550, but
he gives us no hint as to how long it had existed.
Munster's description will apply accurately to much
of the present route : " The path leads quite upright,
but twisted in the manner of a snail's shell, with
perpetual windings and short bendings to the right
and left."*   This was the state in which it existed
when visited by Scheuchzer in the year 1705.   From
his plate as well as his description, it appears that,
in some part of the ascent, travellers had then to pass
from cliff to cliff on stages or wooden bridges, supported by chains.†

It is no wonder that, in those days the passengers
were sometimes in the habit of covering their heads

* Ascendit iter rectà in altum, in modum fere cochleæ, habens
perpetuas ambages et flexuras parvas ad lævum et dextram.

† Per anfractuosos quidem petris ipsis passim incisos, trabeculis
ligneis veluti ponticulis atque muris suffultos mæandros.

with a veil to prevent giddiness ;* at present there is not only no danger, but no aspect of danger in the whole tract.

The following is the history of the Gemmisteig, as we now see it. In the year 1686, the local authorities of the town of Leuk, leased the path to the Commune of Leukbad, for the term of twenty-five years, on the condition that the latter were to keep it in repair, and pay one moiety of the actual toll levied on it, to the municipality of Leuk. When this lease expired in 1711, it was found that the path was in great disrepair, and, in consequence, the Leukites obtained from the government of the Vallais, leave to double the toll, with a view to its restoration. This, however, does not seem to have been set about before the year 1736, when the tolls of the path were once more mortgaged to a company, and now for a period of eighty years, on condition that the path should be effectually and permanently restored. The work was forthwith taken in hand, under the direction of an engineer from the Tyrol, and, after five years' labour, was finally completed and opened in the year 1741. At the expiration of

---

* " Est adeo præruptus, ut accolæ et aliarum nationum homines profunditatem non assueti, eum ascendentes et magis etiam descendentes, oculos proper vertiginem capitis velare cogantur."— *Itinera*, 315. Munster, a much older authority, expresses his own feelings, on the occasion of ascending it, in a still more striking way : " Ich weiss wohl, da ich aus dem Bad auf dem Berg stieg, den zu besichtigen, zitterten mir meine Bein und Herz."— *Cosmographie*.

the lease in 1824, the tolls were once more sold by the town of Leuk, and this time in perpetuity; with the sole conditions that the path should not be allowed to pass into the hands of foreigners, and that, if put up for sale, the municipality should have the first offer. It is a mistake that this passage was ever part-property of the canton of Berne, as is commonly stated.*

The base of the Gemmi-steep has a considerable slope formed of the debris of the rocks above, and where this joins the valley there is a small wood of firs, planted no doubt, as is usual in such situations, to guard against the fall of avalanches. A little further on at the side of the path there are several huts and pens, evidently intended for cattle and sheep, and which we thought must be conveniences for holding the animals during a fair. They are, however, for the purpose of separating the stock of the different proprietors, when passing to and from the pastures of the Gemmi, in the beginning and end of summer. The path to the Baths leads all the way through meadows, and may be a mile and a half in length.

We arrived at the Baths of Leuk (Leukbad or Leukerbad) at half-past five, and took up our quarters at the Hotel des Alpes, a splendid new establishment, containing a hundred beds, and having a large bath-house attached to it. We joined the table d'hote at six. The company was not numerous,

* Les Sources Thermales de Loëche, par J. H. Grillet, Sion, 1845.

not more than a dozen, and they seemed to be all Germans or Swiss. Among the number was Dr. Grillet of Sion, one of the physicians in attendance during the season, whose acquaintance I was fortunate in making. From him, and from his friend Mr. Majthia, the intelligent superintendent of the Baths attached to the hotel, I obtained much information respecting the place, the waters, and their mode of administration. The small number of guests was accounted for partly by the bath season being just about to close, and partly by the general badness of the season, as to visitors, throughout Switzerland. Here, as everywhere else, we had great lamentations over the latter clause of the explanation. Having arranged our plans for to-morrow, which comprehended the examination of Leukbad and its vicinity, and the subsequent journey to Vispach, we willingly followed the rule of the baths and retired at an early hour to our rooms. The evening was very fine, but the air was cool : the thermometer in the air at eight being only 55°. Our windows looked out immediately on the southern base of the Rinderhorn, and on the vertical mountain range which join it on the east, and which is here quite close to us. It is from the glaciers and snows of these mountains that the river Dala which traverses the village near the hotel, takes its precipitous origin.

CHAPTER XXI.

THE DALALADDERS—DEFENCE OF LEUKERBAD FROM AVALANCHES
—THE TOWN—THE HOT SPRINGS—THE BATHS AND MODE OF
BATHING—ESTIMATE OF THE VALUE OF HOT AND COLD BATH-
ING—SUGGESTION OF A LEUKBAD AT BATH—CLIMATE OF
LEUKBAD—GUIDES OF LEUK—THE CATHOLIC CLERGY—NEW
ROAD TO LEUK—VIEW FROM THE TORRENT HORN—VALLEY OF
THE RHONE—LEUK—TOURTMAN AND ITS CASCADE—VISPACH
—ITS CHURCHES—CHAMOIS.

August 28.—A lovely morning. Thermometer
at six, 50°. As soon as we were ready we proceeded, in company with Mr. Majthia, to inspect
the baths, and to take a walk to the *Delaleitern*, a
series of ladders which enable the inhabitants of
Albinen, a village on the top of the eastern cliff, to
communicate with the valley of Leuk. We reached
the ladders in about three quarters of an hour, our
walk leading us at first through meadows, and then
through a fir-wood running along the base of the
cliff to the south, and extending quite down to the
banks of the Dala. The Delaleitern consist of a
series of rough wooden ladders, much like those in
common use in England, placed, one above another,
along the face of an almost vertical cliff. They
are altogether eight in number, containing, on an
average, twelve steps rather wide apart. They are

not in a continuous line, each being attached by its own wooden fixings to the rock, according as the fissures and ledges of the cliff indicate the most convenient and safest direction. We scrambled up the first two which are shorter than the others. They are in no other respects curious, except in the oddity of the contrivance and the seeming hazardousness of the transit. These ladders are in habitual use, by night and day, and the travellers on them often carry large burthens. Accidents are extremely rare, although the least slip must prove fatal.

In going and returning through the meadows close to the village, we passed a nice promenade laid out with seats, for the use of the visitors; and our friendly guide pointed out to us the site of the stony embankment which has been erected to defend the place against the avalanches from the mountains which so closely overlook it from the east. This embankment had long existed in a very imperfect state; but it has been so enlarged and strengthened since the year 1830, as to be now supposed effective against the heaviest falls. It is 690 feet long, and presents a sloping front towards the mountain, seventeen feet high.

It is not without reason that this precaution has been taken, as the village and the baths have been repeatedly invaded, and more than once almost entirely destroyed by these terrible visitors. The most memorable of these falls are those of 1518 and 1719, in both of which all the baths and nearly the whole village were destroyed, with the loss of sixty-one persons on the former, and of fifty-one on the latter occasion. Some of the baths and houses were also destroyed twice between 1518 and the end of the century; likewise in 1720, 1756, and 1767. Since this latter date no serious accident has occurred, owing to the ramparts of defence subsequently erected. In the report of the disaster of 1719, drawn up by an eyewitness, M. Matter, of Leuk, it is stated that four of the inhabitants were carried by *the wind* of the avalanches, through the air, to the meadows lying some distance below the village, where their bodies were found three days after.

The small town or village of Leukbad or Leukerbad, so called to distinguish it from the town of Leuk, at the mouth of the valley, is a wretched place as to its architecture and streets, consisting (with the exception of its hotels) of a set of ill-shapen, blackish, wooden houses or huts, crowded one upon another, without plan or order, and with scarcely a single private dwelling which a gentleman could inhabit. The exceptions mentioned, the hotels, present a striking contrast to their neighbours, almost all of them being very large buildings of stone, containing from fifty to one hundred beds, and in the season having a proportioned number of guests at their tables d'hotes. There are no less than seven of these large establishments.

The hot springs which give to Leukerbad all its

celebrity are more than twenty in number, and all rise either in the village or its immediate vicinity. By far the most considerable in point of size, surpassing, indeed, all the others put together, is the Lorenzquelle, which issues as a fountain in the small market-place. It is of the invariable temperature of 124° Fahr., and is the warmest. Another of the springs is 120°; another 115°; and some of the smaller ones in the vicinity of the village (no doubt cooled in their transit) are only 99° and 94°. They are perennial and all of the same chemical composition. The water is colourless and tasteless, contains a moderate proportion of sulphate of lime, a little sulphate of magnesia, and traces of potass, soda, silica, and iron. In fact, but for its heat, it might be regarded as a good drinking water, only rather hard; and it is far from proved that, as a medium for baths, it possesses any advantages over common spring water.

The following are the principal bathing establishments: the Old Bath; the Werra Bath; the Zurich Bath; the Bath of the Hotel des Alpes; the Poor Bath; and a grand new Bath now building. Altogether there are eighteen or twenty large public baths, varying in size from 8 feet by 11, to 18 by 30, and capable of containing each from 15 to 35 persons; there are also numerous smaller baths, capable of holding from four to six. They are all old-fashioned, without any ornament, extremely dingy, and, though not dirty, certainly dirty-looking; in a word, much as they were a

hundred years since, and certainly not very inviting
to a stranger. They are little more than three feet in
depth, so that the bathers must seat themselves,
which they generally do, when they wish to have
the whole body covered by the water. All the baths
are emptied and filled every day. The water is
lowered in its temperature by the addition of cooled
water, but as the taps are at the command of the
bathers, the actual temperature employed varies
considerably. In four different baths in which there
were bathers, I found the temperature to be, respectively, 95°, 96°, 98°, 99°.

In making use of the baths, the usual course
followed is to go into the water at four or five o'clock
in the morning, to remain in it from one or two to
five hours, and to go into it a second time in the
afternoon, and remain from one to three hours;
making the daily stay in the bath from two to eight
hours. The bathers undress and dress in heated
rooms adjoining the baths, and always retire to a
warm bed in their hotel, for half an hour or an hour,
after bathing. They are clothed in very long dressing
gowns of flannel or thick linen, reaching from the
throat to the feet. Thus dressed, both sexes occupy
the same bath. Each person is provided with a
small floating table, with a small basket for holding
the handkerchief, snuff, books, &c., also for eating
off, playing on, &c. At the time of our visit, none
of the baths contained more than ten or twelve
persons ; but we saw and heard enough to enable us
to judge of the strange scene they must present

when they are quite full : as it was, there seemed great sociality and mirth among the company.

The ordinary period of a course of bathing, or *cure*, as it is called, is twenty-five days, and for this the patient pays a napoleon ; a single bath costs a franc.   Two or more seasons are often deemed requisite for a complete cure.   The water is used internally as well as externally, sometimes in conjunction with the bath, or sometimes by itself.   A course of this kind is only half as long as that of the bath, viz., about twelve or fifteen days, and consists of from two to ten glasses, taken in the morning, fasting, with an interval of ten or fifteen minutes between each two.

The baths are employed for many chronic diseases, but their greatest reputation is in cutaneous diseases, scrofula, chronic rheumatism, and indolent gout. Of their great efficacy in many such cases, as well as in others of a different description, we have sufficient proof in actual experience ; and this is a result that might be fairly expected from so powerful an agency as hot water, when applied in the manner it is applied here.   Immersion in a fluid of a temperature approaching or exceeding that of the human blood, for a fourth or third part of every twenty-four hours, during the space of a month or two, *must* produce some important modification in the actual condition of the animal functions ; and it would be strange if this modification were not sometimes beneficial as well as sometimes injurious.   It could be easily shown, on physiological grounds, how this should be so ; as it is known by actual experiment to be so.

Employed in this manner, hot water, like cold water as used by the hydropathists, is a very powerful agent both for good and ill; its application, therefore, requires great consideration and caution ; but I am convinced that, with such consideration and caution, it, as well as the cold water-cure, may be, and is, productive of most excellent results. The mode of employing the ordinary cold and warm bath in England, that is, their very brief and occasional use, is unquestionably advantageous both in preserving and restoring health ; but it is incapable of producing those great and permanent effects, which may be wrought by the prolonged and, as it were, continuous use of water, whether hot or cold.

In proportion as the natural or hygienic mode of treating chronic diseases makes progress——that is, the mode of treating them by such general means as influence, in a natural way, the whole animal system and not a part of it only——in other words, in proportion as an enlarged, comprehensive, and really scientific method takes the place of the present narrow, exclusive, and empirical medicinal method, so will the employment of such general agents as air, exercise, friction, water, &c., attain an increasing estimation in the minds of the medical profession. The admirable virtues of cold water, when systematically applied, have been already sufficiently proved, even in the rude and ignorant attempts of the unscientific men who, for the most part, have hitherto prescribed it ; and I am disposed to believe that a somewhat similar development of the powers of hot water, only waits for the advent of some daring innovator like the inventor of hydropathy. And when the time arrives for the legitimate members of the medical profession to take both methods out of the grasp of their primitive energetic but unscientific professors, and apply them, without charlatanry or empiricism, on philosophical principles, we shall then find that practical medicine has therein made a most important and substantial advance.

As the waters of our own city of BATH are in many respects similar to those of Leukerbad, I would call the attention of the physicians of the former to what has been accomplished by the prolonged diurnal bathing in the latter place. If they will not make a trial of the practice on scientific grounds, I expect that they will find it set on foot by some speculator from motives of mere personal interest. I believe that a grand success awaits the fortunate projector, who has the foresight or the boldness to establish a LEUKERBAD-BATH at Bath.

I by no means think that effects equally beneficial and extensive as those that result from the systematic use of cold water, will ever signalize the employment of the hot bath, as I deem it incapable of producing such effects ; but when we consider the admirable results of its application in certain cases, more especially in inveterate cutaneous diseases and in some forms of gout and rheumatism, in which cold water is less admissible, and when we regard, moreover, the in-fluence of fashion in magnifying mundane things, I should not be surprised if such an establishment as that now indicated might be found to be a rather formidable rival of the grand temples of the water gods of Malvern.

Bath would have one great advantage over Leuk, inasmuch as its *season* might last the whole year through, instead of two or three months as at the latter place, whose rigid climate precludes all access to it during nearly eight months out of the twelve. This extreme severity of the winter season at Leuk, is accounted for partly by its great elevation above the sea (about 4600 English feet), but principally by its singular local position, which may be truly repre-sented as a basin, like that of Glarus, dug out of the very centre of a ridge of snowy mountains, and with walls literally vertical on every side, as the twisting of the valley renders the opening to the south the same in effect, and indeed also in appearance, as if the gigantic girdle of stone circled it on every side. If ever there was a spot which answered to the descrip-tion of the happy valley of Rasselas, in regard to mere topographical configuration, it was surely this; and if the inhabitants could only retain their de-lightful summer climate all the year round, they need have small cause for envying the dwellers in the Abyssinian paradise. But the Leukerbadische winter is terrible, even without the avalanches. It begins in October, and lasts till May, and for seven months the village and valley are buried in snow often to the depth of from four to six feet. It sometimes snows for a week or more without cessation; in 1843-4 it snowed for thirteen days uninterruptedly. The thermometer often falls to 10° or 11° Fahr. below zero, and for months the inhabitants are almost confined to their houses. A curious illustration of the extreme cold is the fact that the women here, such of them at least as go out of doors, are in the habit, during winter, of wearing that habiliment which is commonly supposed to be peculiar to the other sex, and is regarded as the representative of masculine authority. It is commonly supposed by strangers that it is only the female frequenters of the Dala ladders that wear this garment; but this is a mistake. The only thing at Leukbad that can withstand the cold are the springs; and it must be curious to witness the phenomenon they present in winter, of a smoking streamlet running through the fields of snow, as it is said to do, for an extent of 800 feet.

The season and the scene, however, were, at the period of our visit very different indeed; as nothing could exceed the fineness of the warm and sunny day when we left the baths, or the romantic beauty of the Dala vale through which we passed in our way to Leuk. We were all now walkers; and as the road was excellent and, with one short exception, all down hill, our progress was both easy and rapid. We left

14

Leukbad about half-past ten, and arrived at Leuk about half-past twelve or one.

Our guide, or rather porter—for no guide was necessary on so plain a route—was a good-tempered and simple man, who to his present office added the occupations of shoemaker in the village and chorister in the village church.   He spoke most highly of the village priest, as a good man who attended zealously on his flock out of church as well as in church, and bestowed on the necessitous his worldly advice and assistance as well as his spiritual consolations. I was the more pleased to hear this, as there is, certainly, at present a considerable feeling against the clergy in the Catholic cantons.   The impression is widely felt and avowed, that the priesthood think and act as if they had an interest different from that of the state and the people at large.   They are believed still to possess, in a great degree, that desire for power which has always been characteristic of the church, and they are accused of being opposed to the education of the people, as leading directly to the diminution or destruction of this power.   The most intelligent and best-informed persons I conversed with in the Vallais were of this opinion, and they evidently regarded the evil as one not only that must be repressed, but that was now in progress of being repressed.   The history of the late Sunderbund war seems to have opened the eyes of the people to this feature in the character of the priesthood, much more than anything that had taken place previously. This war is generally believed to have been suggested and fostered and promoted in every way by the Catholic clergy, and mainly, if not solely, because the measures of the liberal party in the country were thought to tend to the advance of secular education and the greater enlightenment of the people generally. The defeat of the party of the Sunderbund and consequent triumph of the radical or liberal party generally, seemed to be regarded by the laymen of the very cantons which had constituted the league, as a positive good instead of an evil. The war was most unpopular; and the priests, as the alleged prime movers in it, naturally shared the unpopularity.

The guides at Leukbad, and I believe generally throughout the canton Vallais, are an organized body, and can only act in due routine. We paid our guide's fee to the commissioner before starting (3 fr.), the conditional Trinkgeld only being as usual left for private adjustment. The money is funded for the benefit and convenience of the contributors, being forthcoming on demand, with the exception of a small per-centage for administration. There are no less than ninety guides enrolled in the valley of Leuk.

Crossing the river Dala as it passes through the village of Leukbad, we continued on its right bank the greater part of the way, only crossing over to the left within a couple of miles of Leuk. For about half the distance from the baths, there is a capital new carriage-road, and men are employed in completing the remainder to Leuk. This road has been a good many years in hand, and is likely to be several more, as the number of workmen employed on it is inconsiderable. When completed, it will be a very fine road and of great service to the baths. In several places it has been necessary to blast the cliff to make room for it; and where the Dala is crossed lower down, a very lofty and handsome bridge has been erected.

The general character of this valley is that of a grand ravine bounded by two precipices of almost vertical rock, but leaving sufficient space between for the growth of trees and shrubs, for a small meadow here and there, and for the windings of the furious Dala. Though bold, it is at the same time rich and beautiful; and these qualities seem to be enhanced by the charming prospects around and above it. From the brow of the cliff on our left hand, there extended far upwards to the base of the distant mountains, one of those green Alpine slopes known by the name of Alps, which seemed to us more than usually rich and brilliant. Here and there amid the green pastures, several villages, now bright in the sunshine, looked smiling down upon us, and among others Albinen, formerly mentioned, with its smart church and glittering spire. It is to the north-east of this village that the Galmhorn or Torrenthorn lies, a mountain about 9500 English feet in height, and much frequented by the visitors at the Leuk baths, on account of the magnificent prospect it commands. Our friends at the baths were strong in their recommendations to visit it, assuring us, one and all, that there were few if any views in Switzerland superior to ·that which it presents. Since then, I have read Engelhardt's account of the scene; and from his statement I am disposed to believe that the report of our friends at the baths, who from local predilections might very naturally be somewhat prejudiced in its favour, was, if anything, below the truth. We were the more ready to submit to the hard requirements of our Holiday that we should not make any unnecessary delay, by the fact that this scene is not even mentioned in our Guidebooks as a spot to be visited on account of its fine views. Engelhardt calls this panorama " a magical scene, of the wonders of which the view from the Gemmi gives us a foretaste not to be despised."*.... " For the lover of Nature, a joy

* The following is a list of the mountains said to be seen from the Torrenthorn, and which are all minutely described in the ' Naturschilderungen.' To the east and south-east, the Fletchhorn, Vortelhorn, Monte Leone, the Dom, Rothhorn, Legerhorn, Taeschhorn, Rimischhorn, Strahlhorn. To the south, the Weisshorn, Brunneckhorn, Schwartzhorn, Saasgrat and Balfrein. Owing to the interposition of the Weisshorn, Monte Rosa itself cannot be seen, but its neighbour the Breithorn can; and also, further west, the Matterhorn, Dent Blanche, Blauzahn, Bejui, Optemma. Still further to the west is the Combin, and quite on the extreme west Mont Blanc. Coming thence round by the north, we have in order the Buet, Dent de Midi, Moevran, Diablerets, Sanetsch, Rawyl, Schwartzhorn, Lammerhorn and Windstrubel. In the north-east we have, near us, the Bietschhorn and Nesthorn; and,

unspeakable; for the topographer, a very treasure of trigonometrical bearings." Let no traveller then— no Holiday traveller even—commit the mistake we made in not visiting the Galm or Torrenthorn. It is a very practicable undertaking, and easily within the compass of a day's ride or walk from Leukbad. The actual height of the mountain is, as above stated, only about 9500 feet above the sea, that is, about 4800 above the baths; and, with the exception of the last two miles, the whole journey can be made on horseback, if preferred.

After a delightful walk of some two hours we arrived at Leuk—a very old and wretched-look- ing town, but beautifully situated on a small hill overlooking the Rhone, and commanding a fine view of the Rhonethal both up and down. With the exception of the church, an old castle, and one or two houses, the whole place consists of squalid wooden buildings more like huts than houses. The population is about a thousand. The church is a large building, richly ornamented interiorly with imagery and paintings. Like all the churches in this country, it is well pewed, or rather well benched, like the Protestant churches in England.

The view down the valley of the Rhone from the hill above Leuk is fine. The valley is much wider

far off, the Breithorn (of the Oberland), Grosshorn, and two others, supposed to be the Jungfrau and Finsteraarhorn. Dr. Grillet, in his Topographical Account of the Baths of Leuk, gives a panoramic view of the same magnificent scene, in which are delineated and named no fewer than eighty-four mountain peaks.

and more extensive than any of those already seen. Its boundaries on either side are formed by a continuous series of mountains abutting on the valley with rounded fronts adjoining each other. These, as we looked along the valley to the south-west, shone out distinct and bright in the sun near at hand, but gradually grew fainter and bluer in the distance, until finally lost, and as it were cut off by a loftier snowy range, which seemed to cross them in the far horizon. As far as we could see it, the channel of the Rhone presented the usual aspect of a mountain torrent in a level country, the stream itself occupying only a small line in the midst of a great extent of bare stony mounds and ravaged plains on either hand. The name by which the river is here designated by the common people is *Rotto;* the more instructed call it *Rhoné*, accenting the last syllable.

We stopped at the *Sun* in Leuk, which we found to be a very tolerable inn for such a place, with a clean and obliging landlady and moderate charges. We here engaged a one-horse char for Vispach, for which we paid nine francs. Immediately below the town we crossed the Rhone by a covered wooden bridge, and pursued our journey by the famous Simplon road, close along its left bank. This journey is unpicturesque and monotonous, as well on account of the flatness and straightness of the road as from the great sameness of the bounding mountains, and the coarse marshy or bare stony aspect of the banks

of the river.   The mountains on either side consist
of huge, bluff, roundish rocks, either entirely bare
or sprinkled here and there with a scanty crop of
firs or little patches of grass.   The boundary on the
left bank is, however, much greener, better wooded,
and richer than the other ; and in some places the
slope at the base is sufficiently gentle and wide to
allow room for a small farm.

While we were hesitating whether we should stop
to see the cascade behind the roadside village of
Turtmann, our horse fortunately decided the point
by running the shafts of the carriage right against
a wall, and disabling the vehicle by sundry fractures.
While it, or another, was preparing for us, we set
out to visit the cascade, which is not more than
half a mile off the road.   In crossing the village,
we were taken in hand by a volunteer guide, who
was evidently a half-witted cretin.   We could have
easily found our way by ourselves, but we followed
him and soon reached the cascade.   It is a very
splendid fall, fully a hundred feet high, and with a
body of water greater than the Reichenbach.   It
has one peculiarity which is very striking, but which
is not easily described in words.   There appears to
be one fall within another, or two strata of water,
the one below being partially inclosed by the one
above.   The inner or lower portion, which is the
main body of the stream, consists of a large well-
defined mass of broken or white frothy water ; the
upper, of a thin, glassy, perfectly transparent film or

thin expanse, wrapping round the other as it were, but allowing the whole of it to be seen through the covering. This singular appearance only exists at the very point where the stream shoots over the rock, the two strands of the fall uniting into one frothy mass immediately below : it is probably produced by a portion of the water being projected upwards from a sort of shelving basin in the rock which forms the lip of the precipice. This stream, the Turtmannbach, originates in the glacier which bounds the west side of the Weisshorn; but as it has a course of some extent through the intermediate valley, it had lost a good deal of the characteristic coldness of a stream so originating : I found its temperature to be here as much as 40°.

On returning to the village we found another char prepared for us, and proceeded on our journey. We arrived at Vispach at half-past five, and took up our abode at the *Weisses Pferd*, or Hôtel de la Poste, a small but tolerably good inn, and certainly the best in the town. While dinner was preparing, I went out to look at the town, and was agreeably surprised to find it much superior to what I had expected. Compared with the places we had hitherto seen in the Vallais, it is quite magnificent, with its numerous large houses of stone, its open streets and its splendid churches ; and, indeed, it is the only respectable-looking place we had seen since leaving Thun. It is beautifully situated in the very gorge of the valley of the Visp, the larger part of it on a

14 §

promontory or projecting mound on the right bank of the river which half-encircles it on the south and west.   A part of the town lies lower, insomuch as to require being defended by artificial works against the inroads of the Visp.   It contains some very good houses and none of wood; among the larger houses there are a few evidently very old. I saw some with the inscribed date of 1600; and one is pointed out which is known to have been inhabited by a certain Countess Blandra in the early part of the fourteenth century.

The whole aspect of the place corresponds with its ancient history, when it was the fashionable residence of the gentry of the upper part of the Canton Vallais.   There are two very handsome churches in the town, the Dreikönigskirche and St. Martins-kirche, both situated on the high mound overlooking the river. The last, which has only been built about a hundred and fifty years, has a light and handsome tower of considerable elevation. I visited them both. They are highly ornamented with gorgeous altar-ornaments, shrines, and pictures.   In one of them I found, down in an underground chapel, where there is a large collection of skulls, a poor half-crazy man, a sort of cretin, praying by himself in the twilight.   I had the curiosity to ask him what he prayed for, and received the significant reply that he prayed for himself and also for those good people who gave him something—a reply which surely merited the few batzen he received.

There is no kind of manufactory in Vispach ; but I was assured that its prosperity is reviving, as seemed, indeed, to be indicated by a certain bustle I saw in the streets, and the aspect of more than one house under repair.

We made a very tolerable dinner at the White Horse, chiefly off roasted chamois dressed with apples. These animals are said to be still very common on the mountains in this neighbourhood, and are, as usual, much sought after by sportsmen. The sport, however, is rather an expensive one, as every Jäger has to pay from 25 to 30 Swiss francs for a licence to shoot Gemsen ; and it is reckoned a great feat to shoot as many as ten in one season.

Before going to bed we, as usual, made arrangements for our journey to-morrow along the valley of the Visp to Zermatt at the foot of the Matterhorn. On account of the distance, about thirty miles, I was persuaded to ride ; but my companions preferred walking. Besides the horse and his leader, we engaged a stout guide for the carriage of some of the knapsacks. The charge for the horse was nine francs per day ; the same sum being charged for the second day, or day of return, whether the traveller uses the horse or not. Our guide's pay was at the usual rate of six francs per day.

CHAPTER XXII.

August 29.——We started from Vispach at half-past six. The path leads close along the right bank of the Visp until we reach Neubruck, about three or four miles above Vispach, when we cross it by a good bridge of stone, having a little oratory midway on one of the parapets. We then tracked the river on its left bank, as we had before done on its right. About two miles beyond Neubruck we reached the large village of Stalden, beautifully situated on an eminence overlooking the junction of the two branches of the Visp—the eastern branch from the valley of Saas, and the western branch whose course we were about to follow. These two branches of the Visp both originate in the glaciers of the group of Alps of which Monte Rosa is the centre, the one on the north-east, the other on the north-west: they are separated during their course, until they meet here, by the vast mountain ridge which arising from the north side of Monte Rosa, runs directly north, and here terminates abruptly in front of the village of Stalden. This village consists of a good many dirty-looking wooden houses crowded together, but, as usual, has a very neat church. Though an open locality, it was not free from cretins. I went into a house to see one who was sick in bed. A short way above the village we also met with three of these on the road, two boys and a girl, about the ages probably of five, six, and eight. The girl could speak, but the two boys were evidently deaf and dumb. While engaged in trying to converse with these poor creatures, two young women came up on their way to Stalden, and seemed not a little amused at the imbecility of the poor creatures. One of the girls was, however, herself diseased, having an enlarged and ulcerated wrist-joint, evidently of a scrofulous character.

At Stalden the path turned a little away from the river side, but soon came close to it again, and, a mile or two further on, crossed to the right bank. After continuing on this side for two or three miles, we again crossed to the left bank about a mile before we reached the village of St. Nicolas, which we did at eleven o'clock.

Between Stalden and St. Nicolas we passed several waterfalls; three on the left bank, the Emdbach, the Augstportbach, and the Jungbach; and one on the other side nearly opposite the Jungbach, called the Riedbach. The last two flow directly from glaciers of the same name, namely, the Jung-

gletcher and the Riedgletcher. This last-named glacier lies immediately above the village of Gränchen,
which is very conspicuous from the other side of
the valley, and which is distinguished as the birthplace of Thomas Plater, one of the greatest scholars
of the sixteenth century, and father of Dr. Felix
Plater, the celebrated physician, professor of medicine at Basel. Peter, the father, was originally a
goatherd and cowherd in this valley ; afterwards he
established himself at Basel, first as a ropemaker,
then as a printer, then as a teacher of Greek and
Hebrew, and finally he became Professor and Rector
of the Gymnasium in the same city.

The valley of the Visp from Vispach to St. Nicolas
is like that of the Dala, or of the Aar from Imgrund
to the Handeck, a narrow ravine, with precipitous
sides, with a furious torrent in its bottom, and with
a footpath now climbing high on the breast of the
bounding mountain, now descending to the very edge
of the stream. It is, however, much more like the
valley of the Dala than that of the Aar, inasmuch as
it is wider than the latter, and fully as rich as the
former if not richer. As far as Stalden, indeed, the
banks are covered, in many places, with vineyards ;
and at Stalden the footpath is actually overhung
with the vines suspended on the high trellis-work.
The whole valley is also finely wooded, except on the
upper portion of the mountain barriers, which are
frequently too steep and bare to admit of vegetation
of any kind. The pathway is, for a mule-path, very

good; but in many places it passes along the brink of frightful and dangerous precipices——dangerous because the fall of the horse would, in such places, ensure the destruction of the rider. The views in the neighbourhood of Stalden are peculiarly fine, especially that which presents to us the northern front of the mountain promontory at whose foot the two rivers meet. This promontory is the base of the snowy Balfrein which we had seen so well from the Gemmi, and which we had also seen from Vispach: in this last situation it is often supposed to be Monte Rosa. From Stalden, all along, except when prevented by the cliffs immediately near us, we had a fine view before us of the Weisshorn and its two subordinate peaks the Bruneckhorn and Schwartzhorn. Here also the mountain boundaries of the valley grow bolder and loftier and more picturesque as we advance. The road, however, with the exception of a few short bits, was nowhere very steep, although the acclivity, as shown by the unbroken rapidity of the river, was continuous.

During the whole of this day's journey we were struck with the profusion of flowers, and I may also say fruits——as our path may be said to have been continuously bordered by beds of wild strawberries and rows or rather thickets of raspberries and bar-berries. The latter were, indeed, so plentiful that the whole valley was, as it were, painted with their beautiful bright yellowish-red berries. There was also a great supply of a species of wild currant, showing a beautiful contrast between its glossy black fruit and its rich green leaves.   In the neighbourhood of the villages there was also a good show of walnut and other fruit trees. From the vineyards at and below Stalden, the natives make no less than five kinds of wine, some of which are said to be peculiar to the locality.

The village of St. Nicolas is finely situated on a rich shelf of ground formed by the gentle bending backwards of the base of the mountain, and sloping gradually down to the bank of the river : it consists chiefly of poor wooden houses, but it has a large church.

Having been recommended by our friends at Vispach to make use of the Curé's house as our inn, we immediately proceeded thither, and on pulling a tiny bell at the gate (the first I had seen in the country) we were admitted by the master himself, and at once shown up stairs. After apologising for taking the liberty, we propounded our wants——rest and a breakfast——and had promise of immediate gratification ; and, in fact, the good father, dressed as he was in his long priestly coat, set about providing all we wanted with his own hands——laying the tablecloth and dishes, grinding the coffee, and, in a word, performing all the duties belonging to the offices of cook and footman.   He said his man-servant was away engaged at his farm work ; but it was evident that his services could be well dispensed with, as an excellent breakfast of coffee, milk, eggs, butter, honey, cheese, preserved plums, &c., was provided and nearly finished before the man made his appearance.

We were, of course, reluctant to be thus waited on by a person of our host's profession, and made many apologies ; but the good man soon convinced us that they were unnecessary, by the unaffected readiness and simplicity with which he served us. He seemed to act as if his present proceedings were a necessary consequence of his social position in this locality; yet in doing what he seemed to feel to be his duty he betrayed not the slightest evidence that the duty was not perfectly agreeable to him; nay, more, it seemed to me that while he was performing all the functions of a servant, he still preserved the bearing of a gentleman. There was no symptom either of real pride affecting humility from vanity, or of a real subserviency originating in a base nature and practised for selfish ends. Everything with our good host seemed natural, simple, and true. Without pretending to believe that he was acting from religious motives, I confess that in contemplating all his proceedings, from first to last, I could not help reverting mentally to that equality of the human brotherhood, which was both professed and practised by the founders of the religion of which he was a minister.

When the time for our departure came, not knowing exactly how I should remunerate our host for the expenditure of his goods, I emptied my purse in my hand, and begged he would oblige me by taking what he pleased. Without the slightest coyness or hesitation, he at once turned over the various pieces, and selecting three French francs from among them, gave me to understand that this was to be the payment. This sum being less than we should have paid at a common inn, I remonstrated, and pressed him to take more. I urged him to accept merely a five-franc piece if he would take no more, but he steadily refused. I then begged he would allow me to give him something for the poor or sick of his flock; he assented, and betaking himself once more to the chaos of Swiss money in my hand, after some search he picked out the smallest piece of silver money he could find, which seemed to be half-a-franc; and I could not prevail on him to accept anything more.

This conduct of our host, and all that had preceded this, excited more than usual interest, and I entered more fully into conversation with the honest priest. Being struck with his bad German and worse French, I asked after his nativities, and learnt that he was a foreigner like myself in these regions, one of the exiled sons of Poland, Johann Szulski by name. He had wandered from his country when quite a boy, and had spent nearly all his life since in Switzerland. He was formerly curé of the parish of Randa, further up the valley, and had been twenty years in his present parish.

We went with the curé to his church, and saw all its finery, public and private. The church is highly ornamented with the usual gilding and doll-work of the altar, shrines, &c.; and in the vestry we were shown sundry fine vestments and vessels, and a few relics. Among the rest was one of some value, both as to its intrinsic sacred qualities and its jewellery merits; but it was to us more curious from its history. It was presented to this church about the time of the Reformation, by a certain bishop who had embraced the new doctrines, and to whom, therefore, it was no longer of any use. The holy man, however, seems to have had some doubts either as to the stability of his own faith, or of the new order of things generally; as he made his present conditionally with the power of resuming it, if he should return to his old ways. As the relic is still here, it is to be presumed that the cautious bishop never did return to his original faith, or, if he did, that he had learned, in the new school, to have some doubts of the virtues of a dead man's toe.

Our friend Johann is what we would call the rector of St. Nicolas, having two curates under him to assist in the services of the mother church and some neighbouring chapels. He is not paid by direct tithes, but by a forced commutation on the property of the parish. The parishioners here appear to have the right of selecting their own pastor, subject to the approval of the bishop at Sion; but different parishes have different regulations in this respect. He has a large house, with a good many beds scattered about different parts of it for the accommodation of travellers as well as friends. Some

of the rooms are also appropriated to still more secular
uses, as we saw a large heap of thrashed wheat in one.

We remained full two hours at St. Nicolas, and
then proceeded on our journey. A very short way
above the village we again crossed the river, and
thenceforth kept on its right bank until we reached
the vicinity of Zermatt. The bridge by which we
now crossed, and all those we had seen since leaving
Neubruck, seem of a formation peculiar to this
valley; at least I had not noticed it elsewhere.
The mode of construction is as follows : in the first
place, a number of large fir trees, rough as cut down,
are laid side by side on the rock on each bank; their
smaller ends projecting towards each other across
the stream, the larger resting on the shore and
weighted with large blocks of stone. Layer upon
layer is thus laid, each succeeding one projecting a
certain way beyond that immediately below it, and
the other shore-pointing extremity being attached
to the layer immediately under it by large wooden
pegs. A sort of approximating arch is thus formed,
and when it has been projected as far on either side
as is requisite, a final layer of the longest trees is
laid across, so as to fill up the remaining space from
side to side. These latter are attached to each other
by means of cross-beams fixed to them beneath.

Above St. Nicolas the same general character of
the valley continues ; but there is, on the whole, a
gradual but very slight decrease in its width, and an
equally gradual increase in the loftiness and wildness

of its mountain boundaries.   About a mile above
St. Nicolas, there is on the same side a small village called Schwidern, the only inhabited place we
observed on the left bank, the great steepness of the
mountain wall, and its close approximation everywhere to the river, presenting alike cultivation and
residence.   A little beyond this hamlet there are
two waterfalls, the one named Blabach, the other the
Dumibach; the former flowing from the Barrglet-
cher, the latter from the Brunneckhorn.   This last
seemed to us nearly as large as the Reichenbach at
Meyringen; and, like it, it consists of a series of
falls, the first and largest being high up near the
top of the mountain and overshooting, the rest lower
down and forming a continuous foamy tract along
the face of the cliff.   The afternoon was extremely
hot, the sky being without a cloud, and the air
without a breath of wind.   We were, therefore, glad
after a couple of hours, to take advantage of the
shade of a fir wood (the Lerchenwald) which we
were passing through, to rest ourselves for an hour
or so on the grass.   At the southern border of this
forest, we met first with one, and after a short time,
with a second torrent, the beds of which were filled
with enormous blocks of stone, through which the
white glacier water rushed furiously down to join the
Visp.   The first of these streams was so swollen by
the melting of the snows, this hot day, that we had
some trouble in crossing it.   They came from the

Grabengletcher which here descended from the
Grabenhorn towards the valley.

We had now reached the parish of Randa, an open
space of some extent, with a handsome church and
village of considerable size, famous for its misfortunes
through the fall of avalanches. The cause of its misfortunes in this way, or rather the medium through
which they were produced, was obvious.   Hitherto,
as we had advanced along the valley, the mountain
barrier opposite to us had been one continuous vertical
wall of enormous height.   Occasionally, as our path
receded eastward from the river, we could see the
snowy peaks far beyond and above the cliff ; but we
had seen no deep gap in it capable of forming the
pathway of an avalanche from the snowy regions
above.   Here, however, nearly opposite the church
of Randa such a gap existed, and half-way down it
we saw projecting the abrupt extremity of a huge
glacier pouring out its furious and milky torrent to
the Visp.   This is the Biesgletcher, a lappet or
tongue of that huge field of ice and snow which
reaches upwards, through a continuous slope of many
miles, to the ridge which joins the Weisshorn with
the Brunneckhorn, and where the glaciers from
both these peaks unite.   Although the village of
Randa lies at the opposite side of a wide valley, and
consequently at a very considerable distance from
the base of the cliff down which the glacier projects
——a mile at least, sad experience has proved that

it is by no means beyond the reach of the tremendous projectiles which have from time to time been discharged from this gigantic shoot. The last great accident of this kind occurred in the year 1819, and was attended by some peculiar phenomena.

Both on the present occasion and on my return I made inquiries respecting this particular fall; and I had also the advantage of receiving a precise account of it from the good pastor of St. Nicolas, who was curé of Randa at the time of its occurrence. The fall took place about five o'clock on the morning of the 27th of December, at a time when, fortunately, all the inhabitants of the village, except about twenty, were gone to Zermatt to assist at the Christmas festivities. The priest was awakened by a sudden shock and tremendous noise, his bed being thrown up as with an earthquake. His first impulse was to get out of his house or to hide himself in the cellar; but he remained in his room until the shock was past, when he went out to look after his flock. He says there was a tremendous rush of wind *succeeding* the first shock and noise, and evidently coming from the side of the valley *opposite* to that down which the avalanche had fallen. This wind was, no doubt, occasioned by the rebound of the air compressed against the opposite mountain. Szulski thinks that it was this blast of wind from the eastern mountain that did most damage by unroofing and otherwise injuring the houses.

The body of the snow and ice that fell took a

direction to the north of the village, and none of
the continuous mass reached it; but the whole village was strewed with loose snow and small fragments of ice, in some places to the depth of several
feet; and all the fields around, when the snow
melted, were found covered with fragments of rock
and stones as big as a man's head. The pastor's
glebe, which lay on the side of the village furthest
from the fall, was so covered with these projectiles,
that he had no hay the following summer, and it
was a long and expensive task to get his fields
cleared of the rubbish. One hundred and eighteen
houses, including barns and stables, were more or
less destroyed; all the chimneys thrown down,
and the greater part of the houses quite un-
roofed. Two persons were killed, and a few more
wounded. A wooden hut in which there were
two women, was carried more than a hundred yards
from its original site, the women remaining unhurt.
All the hay of the village was scattered over the
woods and up the mountain. Well and truly, then,
might the good pastor Johann sum up his recol-
lections of the event in the emphatic words: " In
summâ, maxima miseria Randæ fuit."

The mass of ice and snow, which was of enormous
depth, blocked up the river entirely for ten days,
and was gradually converting the whole of the
upper valley into a lake, when at last, just as the
water had reached the level of the top of the obstructing mass, it forced its way beneath, and emptied

itself; but the snow was not all melted till the second summer. The avalanche was evidently a portion of the Weisshorngletcher, which had become disrupted from some cause, probably at a great height, and it no doubt brought with it from its bed in the mountains many of the rocky masses (its moraine) which were found intermixed with the ice. A similar accident occurred in the year 1737, in April, and destroyed, it is said, 140 houses.

I have already noticed the glacier torrents which we passed on our way to Randa. Shortly after leaving it we passed some more descending from the Wildgletcher, near the village of Inderwild. They were less than the former, although, like the latter, we found them on the present occasion much larger than when we crossed them two days afterwards on our return.

This varying and as it were intermitting size of the glacier streams, is peculiar to all the Alpine torrents, great and small, during the summer; but, for obvious reasons, more markedly so in the greater than in the smaller. The general rationale of the variations is very obvious, but their periods and degrees, in individual cases, depend on numerous contingencies. As a general rule it may be stated, that the snow rivers are lowest in the morning and highest in the evening or early part of the night. As the sun begins to make an impression on the snowy and icy masses, there is necessarily a proportional and progressive increase of the flow of water

15

from them; but the rapidity of this increase, as well as its amount, and the period of its maximum intensity, will depend on the season, the state of the weather, the length of the day, the locality and special conditions of the glaciers, &c.   In the instance now before us, the numerous torrents crossing our path are said to remain comparatively small until eleven or even twelve o'clock, and then begin to increase rapidly all the afternoon.   Our own observation is in accordance with this statement.   We crossed the Lerchenwald, or Grabengletcher stream, on our way to Zermatt, about half-past three P.M., and found it, as I have stated, full to overflowing—in fact, a large stream dashing furiously and with a loud noise over and through its rugged bed of huge boulders and rocky fragments. On the second day afterwards, we crossed the same spot between seven and eight in the morning, and found the stony bed almost dry.   So changed was the spot that one of my companions who had walked on before me was not aware that he had passed it, and inquired when we should reach the stream that had occasioned us some trouble two days previously in getting across it.

Beyond Randa the valley becomes gradually narrower and more rugged.   For some time we had seen, high over the mass of mountain that formed the immediate boundaries of our path, several of the peaks of the group of Monte Rosa, the Breithorn, the lesser Mont Cervin, &c.; and as we pushed

on through the narrow defile by the side of the torrent, all at once on turning an angle in the path,
the Matterhorn itself burst upon our view, straight
before us, almost close to us, shooting up into the
sky its gigantic yet slender pyramid of snow, in-
tensely bright in the sunshine which had long left
us and all the valleys at its feet.   It is impossible
to overrate the grandeur and beauty and picturesqueness of this magnificent peak, which is unquestionably the most extraordinary we saw in the Alps,
and that which, when first seen, most excites the
feelings of surprise and wonder.   It is unlike any
of the other Mountain Peaks or Horns, and therefore strikes and fixes the attention, as well from its
strange singularity as its grand intrinsic features.
It is so very different from what we have been
accustomed to find in natural scenery, that among
the ideas that crowd the mind in first contemplating
it, those of Art and The Artificial come with the
rest; and I am not sure if even that of oddness is
entirely excluded; but all such commoner notions
are speedily extinguished or absorbed in the grand
and solemn impressions left by its majestic size
and its aerial elevation.   The special peculiarities
which immediately distinguish it from other peaks,
are its perfect isolation and marvellous slenderness
in relation to its height.   From a comparatively flat
or level base, and with scarcely any previous grada-
tion towards a rise or break in the outline of the
mountain ridge, it suddenly shoots up into the sky

with all the abruptness of an obelisk, in the form of a
thin cone or pyramid, or a pyramidal pillar of snow

—rising 3700
feet above a
base which is
itself 11,000
feet above the
sea.

Although we
were now close
to the village
of Zermatt, we
had to cross
the rocky gulf
of the river
thrice before

reaching it—first to the right and then back again to
the left bank.   We reached the village exactly at six
o'clock, and found the inn unoccupied except by one
traveller, an Englishman, who had just arrived from
the Italian side by the pass of St. Theodule.

The village of Zermatt is, like all the others in
the valley of the Visp, except Vispach itself, a
crowded assemblage of dark, dirty-looking wooden
houses, with the usual exception of the church, which
is neat, even handsome, both externally and internally.   The inn is also of wood, but it is new and
of considerable size, having a large eating-room and
half-a-dozen or more bedrooms on two floors.   The
landlord, Herr Lauber, is usually called a Doctor,

but he himself disclaims any higher title than that of a bone-setter. He has never been medically educated. His wife is a neat, handy, and kind person; and although the *cuisine* is not of the first style, it is decidedly better than might be expected in a situation so wild and remote. Taking the whole of the accommodations into account, the traveller may consider himself fortunate in being able to obtain them: and if he can command the time, he will find a few days' residence at Madame Lauber's by no means disagreeable.

The day had been throughout extremely hot. Our course having been directly south, we had scarcely any shelter from the sun, whose rays seemed to be concentrated in the depth of the valley. As on former journeys, we had here also the striking contrast of almost a tropical temperature, and the richest display of summer vegetation, at the base of and overlooked by peaks of eternal snow. And we had an analogous contrast on a smaller scale, nearer at hand, that namely between the same high temperature of the air and corresponding luxury of vegetable life, and the wild, cold, and wintry-like torrent, which was for ever dashing along and roaring by our side. The temperature of the river was only 37°, while that of the air in the shadiest spots, during the middle of the day, was more than double. Towards evening, however, when the immediate influence of the sun was withdrawn, the air speedily became cool, and at eight o'clock at Zermatt was only 55°.

CHAPTER XXIII.

August 30.——When I rose at half-past five, the
valley of Zermatt was still in comparative shade, as
were the whole of the mountain masses forming its
immediate boundaries ; but right in front of our
windows was the glorious Matterhorn, towering
from the dim landscape, like a cone of fire, in the
blue sky.   It and it alone had as yet caught the
rays of the unseen sun, and standing out as it did
in such abrupt and singular isolation, it seemed for
a moment to convey the impression as if its brilliancy, like its snows, was part and parcel of itself.
But this exclusive glory, as far as it was one of
light, soon came to an end : the line of illumination
gradually descended lower and lower ; the fiery hue
became whiter and whiter ; and while our eyes were
still fixed on the peak, its base and the wide-spread

snowy ridges on which it rested, had all assumed an equal brightness with itself.

Our plan for the day was to visit the Riffelberg, in order to obtain a more complete view of the snowy realms which we knew extended around us on all sides, though the greater portion of them was now hid from us by the flanks of the mountains which immediately surrounded our valley. We retained the services of the guide who had yesterday accompanied us from Vispach, and who professed to be acquainted with the route and what it led to. We took with us also a young man of Zermatt, a friend of our guide, whose local knowledge of the country was still more precise. As we were given to understand that we had plenty of time for accomplishing our task, we breakfasted at leisure, and did not set out on our expedition till seven o'clock. The morning was delightful, the sky without a cloud, and the air agreeably cool. At half-past five the thermometer had been only 45°, and though the air was now much warmer, it still indicated the high elevation of Zermatt, which, according to Keller, is considerably more than 4000 English feet above the sea. We were now all walkers.

Our route lay directly south, at first along the left bank of the Visp, but this we crossed immediately above the village, and then left it on our right. On crossing the river we passed through a small hamlet called Wiegelmatten, and also crossed a good-sized stream rushing on to join the Visp.

This is the Findelbach or stream of the Findelgletcher, part of the ice-sea of Monte Rosa : it flows along the northern base of the hill we were about to climb, the Riffelberg. For a short time we proceeded along level ground at the base of the mountains, but the ascent soon became very steep, and so continued nearly through the whole journey. Our path, which was often very imperfectly indicated, lay for a considerable space through woods, opening at times into bare pasture land, at times winding along slaty cliffs. Forsaking at last the region of trees, we entered on a coarse moorland-tract, which finally terminated in a region like that we had crossed at Swarenbach on the Gemmi, where the entire surface consisted of loose slaty blocks with scarcely a trace of vegetation, except a few scattered plants of the beautiful dwarf gentian.

Along our whole tract the Matterhorn continued visible on our right hand, and as we reached a higher level, the snowy peaks and ridges with which it is connected on either hand become gradually more and more conspicuous ; but the rise of the mountain we were ascending hid from us almost entirely all that lay beyond it to the south, as well as to the east and north, until we had got nearly to its very top. This we at last reached ; or rather we reached a point which our guides would have fain persuaded us was the usual goal of the visitors of the Riffelberg. It was the extreme southern point of this mountain, the verge of a cliff immediately overhanging the glacier valley which divides it from the ridge of the Monte Rosa chain of mountains. Although affording a splendid view of these, it was clear even to a stranger that the spot was not the best that could be obtained. We were, in fact, in a narrow valley, open indeed to the south, but bounded closely on the east and west by two hills of considerable height. That on the right was extremely steep, and ending in a peak. This was the Riffelhorn, which sometimes gives its name to the whole mountain. The eminence to the east was of much easier ascent, and also appeared to us higher, and therefore likely to afford the best prospect : we accordingly determined to ascend it : its summit must be upwards of 3000 English feet above Zermatt.

This hill is known by the name of the Rothe Kumm. Its elevation above the valley at the foot of the Riffelhorn may be judged of by its taking us an hour and twenty minutes to ascend, or say an hour, exclusive of restings by the way. With the exception of two or three mound-like ridges or terraces at the base, and which showed a scanty covering here and there of coarse grass, the whole surface of this hill was literally a continuous mass of loose blocks of slate, dry and clean as if newly quarried, with scarcely a particle of intervening mould or even decayed rock, and without a trace of vegetation, except here and there a patch of lichens, and, at yet rarer intervals, the blue eye of the gentian. We reached the summit of the Rothe Kumm

15 §

a little after eleven o'clock. Well had we judged that
the view from its base was not all that we ought to
see from the Riffelberg; and well would the labour
of ascending it, had it been ten times greater than it
was, have been repaid by even a momentary glimpse
of the scene which now presented itself from its top.

Let the reader conceive himself placed as on a
"specular mount" or watch-tower, on the top of
an isolated hill, at the hour of noon, and beneath a
sky without a cloud. On looking round, he finds
himself in the centre of a circle of mountains among
the loftiest in the world, sloping ruggedly upwards,
mound upon mound, terrace upon terrace, from the
glacier valleys at his feet, and filling the blue horizon
with a vast unbroken barrier of snow, crowned everywhere with a continuous ridge of jagged summits,
and shooting up at intervals far above the general
level, into gigantic crags and domes and solitary
peaks—all bright in the brightest sunshine, and
dazzling almost as sunshine itself. High as it seems
on looking down on the valley, the station of the spectator does not reach half-way to the level of the
fields of ice and snow which surround it, and from
whence the ridge of mountains springs.

The diameter of this circle of mountains measured from their summits, may probably vary from
ten to fifteen or twenty miles; consequently the
distance of the individual peaks from the spectator
——making allowance for his non-centrical position
and the irregularity of the circumferential line——

Plate II.

might vary from five to ten or fifteen miles. The sublimity of the whole circle may be judged of from the
elevation of some of the individual masses composing
it, above the sea, and above the valleys at their base.
Thus, nearest to us of all, and most conspicuous from
its colossal bulk, we have on the south-east the
Monte Rosa, 15,100 feet above the sea, or from 7000
to 8000 feet above the Riffelberg; on the south-west
the Matterhorn, 14,700 feet above the sea; on the
east the Cima de Jassi, probably 14,500; on the
west the Dent Blanche, full 14,000; to the north,
eastward, the Dom, 14,500, and westward the Weisshorn, 14,800.

When I represent the spectator on the Riffelberg
as in the centre of a circle of snowy Alps, I do not,
of course, mean either that the mountains composing
the circumference are ranged in the exact mathematical relations of the points composing a circle,
or that the Riffelberg is the exact mathematical
centre; but I speak rigidly when I say that, for a
scene in nature, the circle is astonishingly complete,
and vastly more so than the examination of the relative positions and distances of the individual mountains on the map would lead us to believe. The
fact is, that though the loftier peaks, taken singly,
make no nearer an approach toward the constitution of a circle, than in being placed, as the phrase
is, all round the compass, so that the eye can turn
in no direction without seeing some of them: still
the lower masses (all snowy) uniting these, being

continuous, and all of them, whether near or far off, extending their snowy slopes and glaciers to the very borders of the enormous hollow in the centre of which the isolated Riffelberg rises,* the *effect* is nearly the same as if the peaks were themselves in the exact circular line, or rather it is greatly finer from the irregularity; while, literally and strictly speaking, the circle is to the eye of the spectator quite complete. Not only is the broad circular line of snow and ice fields which surround the spectator complete, but the points in its nearer border are nearly equidistant from him, although the more prominent points, the peaks that rise from it, may occupy a nearer or more remote place in this field.†

It is, of course, the peaks that mainly attract attention, and it is as much by their great number and by their variety of form, as by their enormous height, that the mind is spellbound in contemplating them. Ten times, at least, and probably more, did I make my guides name to me peak after peak in

---

* With the exception, of course, of the mountains of the Oberland.

† Let any one who may doubt the virtual circularity to the eye and the feelings, of these chains of mountains as seen from the Riffelberg, go (to compare small things with great) into the centre of the Green Park in a dark evening, after the lamps are lighted, and he will understand what I mean. Although the park is much more like a triangle than a circle, the line of lamps surrounding it has to the eye a circular effect, the perception being too much impressed by the dazzling objects surrounding the focus of vision to notice the varying lengths of the different radii.

the glorious circle; and with the view of impressing their names and places on my mind, I covered my note-book with diagrams and with many lists of names in succession, to test the accuracy of our nomenclators. I drew rude pictures of the ship-man's card, and placed the names of the points of the compass within my circles, and the names of the mountains without, according as they seemed to me to bear. On returning to Zermatt, I sent for another guide, who was said to be the best informed in the place, and went over my notes with him. Finally, since my return home, I have compared my own memoranda with the maps of Keller, Engelhardt, and Professor Forbes; and the following, I think, is a tolerably accurate list of the loftier and more conspicuous peaks and summits which constitute the grand points of this truly magical circle.

Beginning at the east and turning round by the south, we have, first, the grand group of Monte Rosa filling the whole horizon to the east and south-east, and partially to the south, and consisting of the following summits and peaks, in order: The Cima di Jassi; the Weissthor; the Greater or true Monte Rosa; the Lesser Monte Rosa or Rosenhorn (called also by my guides, Silberbasch); the Lyskamm with its two peaks, Castor and Pollux; the huge Breithorn. Proceeding onwards towards the west, we have, still in the south, the Lesser Matterhorn or Lesser Mont Cervin, and, filling up the whole south-western horizon, the Col of St. Theodule and the Furgengrat, terminating in the greater Matterhorn on the west. Succeeding this, in order, and with it filling up the western horizon, come the Höhwenghorn (near it); the Dent Blanche, nearly in the same direction, but far beyond; the Moming or Ebihorn; and then, crowding one upon another in the north-west and north, we have the Gabelhörner (numerous peaks); the Trifthorn; the Rothhorn; the Schallenhorn: and finally, coming near the north point, the lofty Weisshorn and the Bruneckhorn. Directly south, much beyond these, and altogether out of the line of our inner or home circle, two or three vast peaks of snow rise in the far horizon, filling up the small gap in our immediate circle left by the valley of the Visp between the Weisshorn on its western, and the huge Dom on its eastern side. These were believed by our guides to be the Aletschorn, Bietschhorn, and Jungfrau; but it is stated by Engelhardt that the third mountain seen in this direction is the Nesthorn, not the Jungfrau. Be this as it may, the mountains seen by us in this point——though at an immense distance——were just as distinctly visible as those near to us, and filled up exactly the only gap left in the snowy girdle that surrounded us. Turning to the east, we have, finally, the complement of our circle constituted by the series of peaks which surmount the ridge of mountains that divide the valleys of Saas and St. Nicolas, and which showed themselves to us in the following order : the Dom, the Taeschorn, the Alp Hübel,* the Mittagshorn, the Rimischihorn. To this last join on the several peaks of the Strahlhorn, which, in their turn touch the Cima di Jassi, with which we began our enumeration.

I ought to mention, that had I not fortunately been able to correct my bearings by the sun, I should probably have been led into enormous mistakes by my compass, as I found it pointing almost west in place of south at noon ! I therefore put its indications aside, and took my bearings from the sun.†

The Diagram on the next page will convey a clearer idea of the bearing and relative position of the mountains constituting the panorama of the Riffelberg than any verbal description, however accurate or minute.

Every mountain and peak here indicated, was equally visible, if not at the same moment, at least from the same spot, and requiring only the turning of the head and body to enable the eye to sweep the horizon : all, save one, the Strahlhorn. The view of this from the summit of the Rothe Kumm was partially intercepted by the other hill or hills on the eastern side of the Riffelberg, called by our guides the Görnergrad and Stockspitz. Before we could see the Strahlhorn peaks we were obliged to go a little further north, as I did on my return.

* This name given to one of the peaks by our guides I do not find in any map.

† I see that Professor Forbes experienced a similar deviation on the same hill, though not exactly on the same part of it : he took his bearings on the Riffelhorn itself.

A. The Riffelberg.	12. Gabelhörner.
1. Monte Rosa.	13. Schallenhorn.
2. Lyskamm.	14. Weisshorn.
3. Castor and Pollux.	15. Bietschhorn and Nesthorn.
4. Breithorn.	16. Oberland Alps.
5. Lesser Matterhorn.	17. Grabenhorn.
6. Col of St. Theodule.	18. Dom.
7. Furgengrad.	19. Mittagahorn.
8. Matterhorn or Mont Cervin.	20. Rimischihorn.
9. Höhwenghorn.	21. Strahlhörner.
10. Dent Blanche.	22. Cima di Jassi.
11. Moming, or Ebihorn.	23. Weissthor & east range of the Rosa.

Being unwilling to leave even this small break in our snowy circle, I was anxious to ascend the intervening hill, although it would have taken an hour or hour and half to reach its top; but I was ultimately deterred by the reluctance both of my guides and my companions; and so I did not go.

But I would strongly advise all visitors of the
Riffelberg to ascend this hill as well as the Rothe
Kumm, or, at least, to ascend *it*, if my conjecture
is correct that it presents precisely the same view
as the latter, with the addition of the Strahlhorn at
the same time. It is a natural feeling to be the
more anxious for attaining completeness in any aim
or object, the nearer we approach this completeness
or perfection : and this was my case on the present
occasion, although what I had attained was to me
satisfactory beyond all previous expectation or hope,
and productive of an amount of gratification which
seemed scarcely surpassable.

In looking back to this gratification, and attempting to analyse it, I would say that it was com-
pounded of many elements—all, no doubt, more or
less allied, though some of them seeming of opposite,
if not contradictory qualities : assuredly the forms
or modes of the enjoyment varied greatly from time
to time. I can but ill describe what I felt, but I
know I felt vividly and strongly. There was considerable excitement, but only of that kind which
arises from the calmer and graver emotions. Though
beautiful almost beyond conception, the scene was
no less solemn.

Sitting there, up in mid-heaven as it were, on
the smooth, warm ledge of our rock ; in one of the
sunniest noons of a summer day ; amid air cooled
by the elevation and the perfect exposure to the
most delicious temperature ; under a sky of the

richest blue, and either cloudless or only here and
there gemmed with those aerial and sunbright
cloudlets which but enhance its depth; with the
whole field of vision, from the valley at our feet to
the horizon, filled with majestic shapes of every
variety of form, and of a purity and brilliancy of
whiteness which left all common whiteness dull;——
we seemed to feel as if there could be no other
mental mood but that of an exquisite yet cheerful
serenity——a sort of delicious abstraction, or absorption of our powers, in one grand, vague, yet most
luxurious perception of Beauty and Loveliness.

At another time——nay, it would almost seem at
the same time, so rapid was the alternation from
mood to mood——the immeasurable vastness and majesty of the scene, the gigantic bulk of the individual mountains, the peaks towering so far beyond
the level of our daily earth as to seem more belonging to the sky than to it, our own elevated and
isolated station hemmed in on every side by un-
trodden wastes and impassable walls of snow, and,
above all, the utter silence, and the absence of every
indication of life and living things——suggesting the
thought that the foot of man had never trodden,
and never would tread there : these and other analogous ideas would excite a tone of mind entirely
different——solemn, awful, melancholy.

Then would intervene thoughts and ideas still
more fantastical and visionary; the reason, while
recognising their unreality, submitting without a

struggle to their domination. Among these fancies there was one which haunted me for a space, and which, no doubt, was excited, though quite unconsciously at the time, by the suggestive forms of some of the mountains, as well as by the immobility and silence of everything connected with them. It was that of being environed and guarded, and as it were imprisoned, in an awful circle of Titanic Sphynxes, planted there from all time, in the dreadful silence of some mysterious watch. There they seemed to sit on their icy pedestals, side by side, in death-like repose, looking down on you with their fixed and melancholy eyes, breathing over the senses a sort of magnetic stupor, and chaining soul and body to the spot by an irresistible fascination.

Although the scene here attempted to be described needs no extraneous aid to enhance its qualities, I can hardly doubt that, in my own particular case, the impression made on the mind was in reality strengthened by surprise. I had had no distinct notice or indication of what I was to see from the Riffelberg. I had never heard the view named except by Dr. Hasse, and he had merely, in our hurried interview, advised us to visit it as something extremely well worth seeing, but without entering into any particulars : no one else who had seen it had mentioned it to me ; I had read no account of it except that in our Guidebook, and this conveys no just idea of the thing : even our partial views of this morning, and while ascending the mountain itself, had in no manner prepared me for the overwhelming splendour of the sight which burst upon us on reaching the summit of the Rothe Kumm. I said at the time, and I still feel disposed to believe, that the whole earth has but few scenes that can excel it in grandeur, in beauty, and in wonderfulness of every kind. I thought then, and I here repeat my opinion in cool blood, that had I been brought hither blindfolded from London, had had my eyes opened but for a single hour on this astonishing panorama, and had been led back in darkness as I came, I should have considered the journey, with all its privations, well repaid by what I saw.

There have been other visitors of the Riffelberg who seem to have been even more moved by the wonders it displays than we were. Our feelings as well as our imaginations were, no doubt, livelily impressed, and we were, like Hamlet, somewhat troubled

" With thoughts beyond the reaches of our souls;"

but this was coming far short of M. Desor, who ascended this " specular mount" in 1839, in company with MM. Agassiz and Studer. In his case, the wonderful vision would appear to have had no less an effect than that of abolishing some of the most besetting weaknesses of humanity, and transmuting him——for the time at least——into a pattern of moral goodness and christian charity, as may be seen by the subjoined extract from his narrative.*

* " L'individualité tout entière s'efface, en quelque sort,

On leaving the Rothe Kumm to return to Zermatt, our party separated; my two companions preferring to return by the way they came, I choosing to make a bend to the north-east, in order that I might see the Strahlhorn face to face, as well as the Findelgletcher, lying between that mountain and the Riffelberg. So we parted company on the top of the Rothe Kumm—my young friends taking with them *the Goats*, I *the Guides* with me.

This division of attendants needs some explanation; and what I have to give will not afford much novelty to Alpine travellers. In the earlier half of our journey to the top of the Riffelberg, we encountered, in passing a patch of mountain pasture, a small flock of goats—five or six in number—which immediately joined our party, and kept close company with us, through the rest of our route, in spite of much remonstrance on our part. After repeated attempts to dismiss them, we were at last forced to admit their society, which was certainly of the closest kind. They intermixed themselves with their new biped friends in the most familiar fashion, pressing

devant ce monde nouveau que vous admirez pour la première fois; et avec elle disparaissent pour un instant tous les calculs, toutes les vanités, toutes les ambitions, tous les froissemens qui accompagnent la vie de tous les jours. Une profonde impression est produite sur vous, et vous vous y abandonnez entièrement. Rien d'égoïste ne saurait alors trouver place dans votre âme. Mon ennemi mortel se serait présenté devant moi : je lui eusse tendu la main sans contrainte, et j'en eusse été heureux."—Journal d'u Course faite aux Glaciers du Mont-Rose, par E. Desor; Bibliothèque de Genève, 1840.

upon our heels and hands, and leaving nothing undone to attract attention and consideration. When we stopped they stopped, when we moved they moved, and whatever vagaries we committed they did the same.

It was really almost pathetic as well as ludicrous, to see the poor beasts gratuitously scrambling up rocks and banks which we might be climbing to get a better prospect, or going far out of their way, if they had one, certainly out of good pasture-ground, in order to bear us company in the pursuit of objects which in no way concerned them personally. When a tempting bit of grass came in their way on the side of the path, or in the crevice of a rock, no doubt they would crop it in passing; but no pasture, however tempting, would really stop them, much less seduce them to the right or left : still on they went, with us, before us, behind us, amidst us, dodging us, nudging us, with all the gravity of the caprine nature, and with a determination of zeal which could only be explained by the spurring on of some great desire hoping for gratification. Even when we had entirely left the region of vegetation, and had to clamber up the stony slopes of the Rothe Kumm, our poor friends never left us for a moment, but scrambled with us—much indeed to our envy on account of their superior agility—and rested not until they rested beside us on the very summit. They sat patiently there all the time we did, and then attended my young friends a good way beyond the spot where we had first encountered them.

The secret of all this marvellous zeal and ostensible affection on the part of the goats, lies in their *fondness for salt*, a delicacy which their experience has told them is only to be found in the society of the human animal, and to gratify their love for which no trouble is thought by them too great. This love, however, although a natural instinct in the goat as well as many other animals, is, I fear, rather a sophistication in the extent to which it is carried by them in their domestic state, a sort of saline dram-drinking which perhaps ought no more to be encouraged than the cravings of our gin-drinkers. Their wild cousins, the Gemsen or Chamois, have the same taste for things saline, but they can only indulge it in that more limited degree and unconcentrated form in which Nature presents most of her products to her children.

Scheuchzer tells us that there are certain spots in the Alps, known by different local names, as *Gläck, Läckinen, Sulzen,* which these animals are known to frequent in great numbers, for the purpose of *licking* certain rocks having, or supposed to have, a saline impregnation. For this purpose they are said to travel very great distances, returning to their original haunts after satisfying their longings. The hunters who know these localities do not fail to take advantage of these gatherings, although their prey are said to become emaciated during the prevalence of the saturnalia.*

* Itinera, pp. 155-79.

The analogous SALT-LICKS of America, frequented
by the deer and other wild animals of that country,
are well known; and it will not fail to strike the
philologist that the name as well as the thing, has
probably the same original, through the metamor-
phoses of the Anglo-Saxon: *lecken* is still the German
verb for *to lick*.

In descending the Rothe Kumm, as in ascending
it, we encountered many patches of snow lying in
its hollows, and were not sorry to be able to fill our
alpine cups at the pools into which they were visibly
melting in the sun : for though the air was deliciously cool, the reflected heat of the sun in sheltered
places was very great.   On the summit of the Rothe
Kumm, however, the thermometer in the shade—
that is, in a hollow under a huge fragment of
rock—was only 54° at noon.

A very little deviation to the north-east brought
us in sight of the Findelgletcher, which is merely
a lappet or tongue of the huge ice-sea of Monte
Rosa, which at its lower margin girds the Riffelberg
all round except on the north.   The main body of this
sea lay immediately before us as we sat on the Rothe
Kumm ; and its feeding rivers, solid and silent as
itself, were seen pouring down, in every direction,
from the base of all the snowy peaks around and
from the vast gulfs between them ; the grand primary
feeder being traceable far upwards to the south-east,
till it disappeared on the horizon, in the direction of
the unseen Monte Moro.

The union of these numerous glaciers in one, and the composite structure thence resulting, was admirably seen in that portion of the icy mass lying close under us to the south-east and south, and occupying the whole space between us and the base of Monte Rosa. This portion is what is strictly named the Görnergletcher, and which is here seen taking that majestic sweep round the southern base of the Riffelberg which will soon lead it to its terminus in the valley of the Visp. Along the whole expanse of this glacier, as far as it can be traced towards either extremity, those continuous ridges of rocky fragments, termed *medial moraines,** three or four in number, are seen braiding the bright surface with their dark longitudinal bands in a very striking and beautiful manner,—all running parallel to each other, but in those easy and gently-waving lines which nature loves. These bands, produced as they really are by the motion of the glaciers, and accurately indicating to the physical inquirer the true line of their progress, excite in the mind of the ordinary spectator the same idea from mere visual analogy, by recalling the appearance of those longitudinal streaks one often sees in rivers, produced sometimes by currents, sometimes by the admixture of streams of different colours, and occasionally by other accidental changes on the surface from more temporary causes. A very good idea of this beautiful

* For some account of the mode of formation of these, see Chapter XXVIII.

16

appearance will be conveyed by Plate I, which attempts to represent the vast and magnificent bulk of Monte Rosa gradually rising up from the level of this splendid glacier.

In one part near the centre of this glacier, and directly opposite the Rothe Kumm, there was also visible at the period of our visit a small lake contained in the solid ice itself, its water of the most beautiful transparent green colour, and its surface bright and unruffled as a mirror : as if in accordance with the other marvels of the scene of which it formed a part, it was a lake to wonder at; its banks and walls and bottom, in place of rocks and earth, seeming to be formed of the most beautiful transparent sea-green crystal. It is, I think, termed by some the Görnersee or Görner Lake; but owing to its small extent it is merely indicated in the Plate.

In dwelling so long on the features of this locality, it seems hardly just to the grandest of them all, MONTE ROSA, not to devote a few words exclusively to it. Like Mont Blanc and the Jungfrau, its very vastness, or rather its concentrated massiveness unbroken by peaks of proportionate size, makes it seem less lofty than it really is ; and its immediate union on either side with a range of sharper snowy summits approaching its own elevation, tends still further to prevent a just appreciation of its true character at the first glance. But, as in the case of all things great in themselves, further contemplation speedily makes amends for the momentary wrong, and bids this majestic mountain assume its true place in the mind and memory of the spectator, as the sublimest and most impressive of all the objects of this incomparable scene.

My descent from the Riffelberg was by a path entirely different from that by which I had ascended; or rather it was by a new route without any path at all, and fronting the old track as with the convexity of a semicircle. I took at first a sweep to the north and then to the west, my object being to reach the abutment of the Görnergletcher in its valley on the west side of the mountain. The walk was delightful, being, throughout, on a sort of smooth down, covered with a thin coat of green-sward, without any trees, and with only a sharp ledge of rock shooting up here and there, or a large erratic boulder, imbedded in the turf, at remote intervals. The descent was, in many places, very steep, and my shoes having become very slippery with the grass, I got a good many falls on the turf; but I was as yet too much excited by the spectacle of the last two hours to care for them or even to feel them. I was almost in the happy condition of a drunken man, as to insensibility to injury. I felt my bruises, however, a little when I got up *sobered* next morning.

When we had got over three quarters of our journey, we came to one of those sunny summer villages of the alpine cowkeepers, which it is so delightful to encounter in a hot day on the moun-

tains, and where the warm and honest welcome and
the homely fare seem to be in exact accordance
with the wild and simple nature which surrounds
you, and with your own more natural and as it were
desophisticated wants.   What a charming appetite
you feel both for food and drink—and what capital
food is set before you !   Can anything exceed the
luxury of sitting down there on the stone bench at
the door, or on the green turf in the sun, and
quenching your thirst from the wooden bowl overflowing with the milk that has been cooling in the
shade since sunrise ?   Can aught surpass the butter
in its freshness, or the cheese in its newness ?   Is
not even the black peat-like mass called bread, the
relics of last year's general bake, within the grasp
of the masticating process, and amenable to the
Digestive Powers that be ?

The satisfaction of myself and of my guides with
the hospitality of our good milkwoman on the
present occasion, was not a little enhanced by the
charming cheerfulness of her manner and her unaffected conversation.   She was, moreover, better-
looking than usual ; and had the rare beauty for a
Swisswoman, of excellent teeth.   I cannot account
for the great defect of good teeth among the women
in Switzerland, but it is almost universal ; the teeth
being not simply discoloured or partially decayed,
but actually lost and gone, and often to a great
extent, even in young persons.   In many cases the
missing teeth I found had been extracted *vi et armis,*

and therefore I infer that the ladies of the Alps are not over-patient (under toothache), or that their doctors are zealous over much.

The summer chalet of our hostess was planted on a small flat terrace on the mountain side, looking right at the Matterhorn and the sun, and overlooking a bright green valley far below, with a wide level meadow in the centre. Half-way on to this meadow the huge head of the Görnergletcher was seen to advance, from a chasm of dark rocks crowned with firs; and a little below it we had a glimpse of the white Visp rushing along between its banks of green.

On approaching the borders of the glacier, its immense height and depth were at once visible, though this was not discoverable as we looked down upon it from the mountain : it projected into the green valley like a vast promontory or mound of ice, and formed a striking contrast in its wild wintry aspect with the smiling pasture land upon which it had intruded. It was closely bounded on its sides and front by a *moraine* of rocky fragments and earth, about ten or twelve feet high and nearly of the same width, which, from its accurate adjustment to the outline of the mass, and from its artificial look generally, suggested the idea of a pigmy barrier raised by some Alpine Mrs. Partington to arrest the giant's progress. This progress, though of course not directly visible, was strikingly indicated by the surface of that portion of the meadow imme-

diately bounding it, which was turned up and twisted
and rolled upon itself in huge folds, evidently quite
fresh, just as we see the earthy swaths of green-
sward turned aside by the plough, or the turf of a
common, contorted and rising in rolls before the
turf-cutter's spade. Our Zermatt guide informed
me that the advance of the glacier had been regular
since he had known it, and at the average rate of
about four yards annually.

The width of the glacier at its extremity appeared
to me to be only about three hundred yards, its mass
being compressed into this narrow space by the rocks
on either side. About midway in its width, and
where it rested on the earth, the cliff-like front of
the huge mass was perforated, and, as it seemed,
also supported, by an enormous arch of translucent
ice of a beautiful blue colour, from beneath which
the furious Visp, already a full-grown river, was
rushing and roaring over its rocky bed in one mass
of foam. The arch was nearly regular in its outline, but was low for its great width; and at its
sides it had the rudiments or fragments of some
smaller arches less accurately defined. The mass
of water issuing from it was enormous, and as well
from its depth and width as from its force, could
not possibly be forded by man or beast. It was
extremely cold to the touch, and exhibited by the
thermometer a temperature just one degree above
freezing, viz. 33°. In the morning I had tried its
temperature at Zermatt about three or four miles

below, and found it one degree higher, viz. 34°; and yesterday I had found it between Zermatt and St. Nicolas to be four degrees higher, viz. 37°.

In descending the mountain we had seen the sun gradually coming nearer the snowy peaks in our front, and when I left the glacier the whole valley was in shade, and the air began to feel rather cool. Immediately below the glacier we crossed the Visp by a bridge, and pursued our course to Zermatt along its left bank. In our way we also crossed the Zmutt-bach, a large stream coming from the glacier of Zmutt at the base of the Matterhorn, and joining the Visp not more than a mile from its source. When about half-way to the village, I met advancing up the valley on foot, the venerable Moritz Engelhardt, the celebrated Alpine traveller, and author of the minutest account that exists of the topography of this district, as well as of the best views we possess of some of its grandest scenery. Although now at an advanced age, he had once more come into Switzerland to refresh his memory of the grand scenes he had visited so often, and which he loved so much. He was now proceeding to inspect the glacier which we had just left. It is to his pencil the reader is chiefly indebted for the views of the grand chain of Monte Rosa and the Matterhorn illustrating the present work.

We reached Zermatt about five o'clock; and, not-withstanding the good day's work already done, I was still so inspirited by the excitement of what

I had seen, that I was not merely altogether unconscious of fatigue, but really felt as if I could have
started at once on a second journey with the utmost
alacrity.   It was no great novelty to a physician to
witness an augmentation of nervous energy and muscular force from mental causes, precisely similar to
that which attends the primary stage of inebriety from
strong drink ; but I hardly recollect to have experienced this, in my own person, to such a degree as
at present, since boyhood.   In such a mood it was
perhaps as well that my bibbings were not of the
vinous sort, otherwise a very little of the artificial
added to the natural excitement, might have led to
even more fantastical imaginations than those of the
Rothe Kumm above commemorated.   As it was,
however, thanks to Madame Lauber's roast beef and
the crystal springs of Zermatt, we were all soon
sobered into the grave realities of a good dinner,
followed in due time by a traveller's sleep, equally
good and no less enjoyed.

CHAPTER XXIV.

August 31.——Another clear and cloudless dawn :
our first look from the window greeted, as yesterday,
by the glorious Matterhorn, gleaming up in the blue
sky in its morning robe of fire, and telling the
dwellers of the valley of the approach of a bright
sun yet unrisen to them. Its reflected light had
reached us, but none of its heat ; the thermometer
in the open air standing at half-past five at 43°.

Having settled our accounts with good Madame
Lauber and taken our coffee, we set out at a quarter
to seven, on our return to Vispach ; I and one of
my companions being the walkers to-day, the other
taking a horse, on account of a slight sprain incurred
in the journey of yesterday.

As we returned by the same path (there is no
other), passed over the same ground, and through
the same scenes, there is little to tell of this day's
journey. It must not, however, be supposed that it

16 §

afforded little to enjoy.   Amid scenes so beautiful, so rich, so picturesque, so grand, and varying with every turn in the path, and with every rise and fall in the ground over which it led, many repetitions of a journey precisely the same would fail to make it monotonous or tiresome; much less, then, would a first repetition, as ours was, fail to do so, more especially when it is considered how very different the same landscape appears when viewed in opposite directions. On this account, I am not sure that we did not enjoy this day's journey fully as much as when we ascended the valley two days before. The views were different, though the things viewed were the same ; and our improved knowledge of them only made us see fresh charms in beauties which were too rich to be easily exhausted.   For myself, I must confess, also, that I was in even a more enjoyable mood than when I ascended the valley.   The excitement of yesterday, not yet quite gone off, lent its help to sharpen the perceptive powers; while the great difference between the two classes of objects offered to the eye, then and now, prevented any of that depreciatory influence which direct rivalry necessarily occasions.

For some time after leaving Zermatt, we cast many a lingering look behind to the Matterhorn, now shining in all the whiteness of full sunshine ; but on turning the same angle of the cliff which had first revealed it to us on our way up, we lost sight of it at once and entirely.   We still saw the Breithorn, and some of the other peaks more to the east;

but the great snowy girdle of the Riffelberg had disappeared as completely as if we were a hundred miles distant.

It may seem strange to those who have not visited Switzerland, that one can so completely lose sight of the loftiest mountains while yet in their very vicinity; or that the ascent of a mountain comparatively so low as the Rigi, the Torrent, or the Riffel, should at once reveal scenes so wonderfully different from those seen from the valleys at their feet. A little reflection, however, and reference to what may be regarded as the uniform configuration of the Swiss valleys, viz. their extreme depth and narrow ravine-like character, will explain the fact at once. The steepness of the immediate boundaries of the valleys—a steepness which it is hardly an exaggeration to call vertical—and their close approximation below, necessarily exclude from the sight of the traveller at their base everything but the sky, and the peaks which rise from or very near to the lateral barriers; or such mountains as may rise in the distance in the direction of their own longitudinal course. When, however, you get fairly out of and above the valleys, all the peaks that are higher than yourself, generally speaking, become immediately visible. It is then that the prospect becomes truly Alpine, and assumes its grandest and most sublime character; the zest of surprise and novelty being, in most cases, added to all its intrinsic wonders.

In reflecting on the effect on the mind of scenes of this kind, I am disposed to believe that, when, as in the instance witnessed yesterday, the objects are seen in a circular form, or all round the horizon, their effect will be much greater than if placed linearly or in one direction; also, that the degree of impressiveness will vary according to the distance of the mountains, whether disposed linearly or circularly; the effect being lessened alike by great proximity or great remoteness. What, I think, helps to give to the Riffelberg view its matchless character, is the happy medium distance at which its panorama is disposed. It is in this respect, I think, as formerly stated, that the view from the Rigi is defective, and on the same account, I expect that the view from the Torrenthorn, grand and magnificent as it must be, will prove inferior to that from the Riffelberg, the circle of mountains being so much more remote in the former case.

In tracing the course of the Swiss valleys by the ordinary track along the banks of the torrents in their depths, although, as just stated, the loftiest mountains placed laterally, are commonly shut entirely from view by the cliffs on either hand, it almost always happens that the prospect, at the extremity of the view, up or down, is closed by some grand snowy ridge or peak, shooting up into the sky from the deep gap in the mountains formed by the ravine. This appearance is often very striking. The huge mass seen at a distance along the vista of the valley, seems as if it closed up all passage in that direction as with a wall of snow; while the contrast of its dazzling whiteness——first with the blue sky above it, and then with the two dark mountain masses that seem to abut against it on either hand, gives it a character of wildness and picturesqueness quite peculiar. We had this fine feature in our landscape almost all the way as we ascended the valley of the Visp, the bounding barrier of snow being supplied, during the earlier part of our journey, by the Balfrein and the Weisshorn; and during the latter part, by the Breithorn and the lesser Matterhorn. We now had it again in descending in the opposite direction: the vista being closed up to the north, by the peaks of the Bietschorn and others of the more distant chain of the Oberland. We had noticed the same thing previously, as in the Reichenbach valley with the Wetterhorn for the culminating boundary, and in the valley of Lauterbrunnen shut up and dominated by the Jungfrau.

Partly, perhaps, from our now having the sun nearly behind us while it shone brightly on the mountain barrier on our left, the cliffs on the other side of the Visp appeared to us much grander and also more beautiful than when we were ascending the valley. In many places they were of enormous height, and often quite vertical, altogether too steep to afford footing for trees. At other times, however, and more frequently, they were beautifully but sparingly shaded with long rows of firs up to the very

top, the trees finding a footing in the exposed lines
of stratification, and following the course of these
exactly, whichever way they turned or twisted, often
in a fantastical but always in a beautiful manner.

As we passed the small villages and hamlets we
found everybody busy at work, as usual, either cutting
or carrying their endless crop of hay or digging their
sloping fields with their huge hoe. This hoe, which
I first saw in the Zermatt valley, is of a very peculiar
construction, which has, no doubt, been excogitated
by the special requirements of the land.   Its handle
is very short, and its head or metallic cutting part
very large, quite as large as one of our smaller
spades, but of a more pointed triangular shape; it
is fixed on the handle at an acute angle of not more,
perhaps, than 20° or 25°.   This hoe stands the
labourers in place of both plough and spade, and
is, no doubt, better suited to the steep fields than
either.   Digging downwards, from the upper end of
the field, with their face to the hill and their back to
the valley, they make great progress in their crab-
like course, and seem to turn up the soil very effectually and to a considerable depth.

We reached the hospitable mansion of our good
Johann Sczulski of St. Nicolas, about eleven o'clock,
and again had the benefit of his friendly ministrations
at our plentiful and luxurious breakfast.   On this
occasion we met like old friends, and what with
German and what with Latin, I contrived to obtain
much interesting information from the worthy and

kind-hearted pastor. It was on this occasion he gave me the minuter details of the fall of the avalanche at Randa, already noticed, of which he had prepared at my request a short account in Latin. I found his narrative quite in accordance with the information I had obtained at the village of Randa from an old man who had also witnessed the fall. In taking leave of the good priest, which I did not do without very friendly feelings, I could not prevail upon him to accept more than a five-franc piece for all the trouble we had put him to, and for the free expenditure of his worldly substance on five hungry men ——for the guides were his guests as well as we. In final reply to my offers of service to himself, if ever an opportunity should occur, the good man, showing the same kindly nature as in everything else, recommended to my sympathy any of his unhappy countrymen who might cross my path in their exile. And so we took our leave of St. Nicolas and its simple-minded and gentle priest.

We were all again on foot, as my companion's horse had cast a shoe on the journey, and all the resources of the parish could not supply another. It was now past one, and the sun extremely fierce; but fortunately our course was directly north and the heat was not felt oppressive.

About a mile below St. Nicolas, on the same side of the river, and again about four miles further down the valley, we saw two of those frail memorials which are usually raised in Switzerland on the spot where an avalanche has fallen with fatal results. The first of these commemorated the death of three men in February, 1844, by an avalanche from the Jungberg; the second, that of two men from a similar cause in March of the present year 1848. In this latter case the fall was stated to be unusual (ungewohnter), but whether from its locality or date I know not. These inscriptions are in rude German verse, and painted on wooden boards erected close to the path. They invoke prayers for the souls of the slain, and remind the reader of the necessity of taking care of his own amid the uncertainties of life.

About a league below St. Nicolas we had now a much better view of the church of Emb (Emb-kirche) in its singular niche on the top of the opposite cliff, than we had in our way up. The cliff is extremely high, full a thousand feet at least, and is perfectly vertical and bare to within a third of its base, when it projects a little outwards. On its top a little hollow is, as it were, scooped out and sloped backwards with a gentle inclination. In this hollow the little church is placed, apparently close to the edge of the precipice, but amid rich green meadows and trees which climb the slope behind it, and rise up in beautiful relief on the blue sky beyond. At one side of the church there is a waterfall, shooting from the edge of the cliff: it was now slim and slender like a miniature Staubach, but is said to be sometimes of very considerable size.

There is no apparent access to this aerial village

from the valley below, but our guide told us there
is a path, though rough and difficult. It is, however, now scarcely used, as the bridge which led
across the river has been for a considerable time
destroyed. This Emb is a parish, and stretches a
good way beyond the brow of the hill which here
bounds our horizon. With safer ground to build
on, it seems singular that the inhabitants should
have erected their church in so fearful a position,
which, one would think, must keep every mother in
the village in perpetual terror for the necks of her
children. But it would almost seem, from the
singular position of many of the churches among the
Alps, that the godly men of the old times preferred
a picturesque to a convenient or safe locality. The
greater probability, however, is, that it was the
protecting vicinity of some chieftain's castle, now
vanished from the spot, that determined the site of
such churches.

We reached Vispach at five o'clock ; ten hours
and a quarter from the time we left Zermatt, eight
hours and a quarter being spent in walking and
two in resting at St. Nicolas. Reckoning from the
pace at which we walked, I should calculate the
distance between the two places at about twenty-
seven or twenty-eight miles. Being, with a very
trifling exception, all down-hill, the walk was extremely pleasant and was in no way too much even
for the senior pedestrian. We dined as before at
the White Horse, and had, among other delicacies,

some more Gemse. Among these delicacies, however, both here and at Zermatt, and indeed all along
our course since leaving Thun, we had seen none
of our favorite Forellen or trout. Upon inquiring
the reason, I found it satisfactorily explained by a
trait in the natural history of these animals which is
well known to the inhabitants of this district, and
is no doubt observable in others similarly circumstanced. We had no trout presented to us because
there were now none to present, they having all at
this season (the end of August) deserted the snow-
water torrents to take up their abode in the lakes
into which these empty themselves. For the following particulars respecting the proceedings of
the Forellen of the Visp I am indebted to Mr.
Engelhardt.

So soon as the glaciers and snow begin to melt
in the spring, and the river assumes the troubled
and milky character of a true *Gletcherstrom,* which
is usually about March, the trout forsake it in a
body and proceed down the Rhone to the lake of
Geneva, where they remain the whole summer.
Advantage is taken of this migration by the inhabitants on the banks of the Rhone; and a very
active and successful fishery is carried on during
the period of transit, the larger trouts being salted
for winter use. In the end of autumn, when the
glaciers have ceased to melt and the river reassumes
its wintry clearness, the Forellen once more leave
the lake, ascend the Rhone, and find their way into

the Visp——and of course the other lateral streams also——where they spawn. During the period of their immigration or return, the inhabitants are prohibited from fishing.

After dinner I called on one of the medical gentlemen of the town, to whom I had been introduced at my former visit. Besides communicating to me some interesting information respecting the diseases of the place, he kindly took me to see a cretin patient which he assured me was the only one in the town. It was a boy, 13 years of age, the son of very respectable and healthy parents, and the only one affected out of a family of several children. He is a heavy lumpish idiot, nearly deaf and quite dumb. He can drag himself about the room on his knees, but cannot stand or walk. His head is large and angular and of irregular shape, but his forehead is of fair size and not stunted as is so commonly the case in common idiots. He amuses himself with little playthings like a child of two years old, placing the pieces in lines and figures, and so forth. He manifests a certain degree of affection towards his mother and his brothers and sisters. He was exhibited to me without the least reserve, and his own mother spoke of his condition and doings with apparent unconcern, if not with positive levity.

The surgeon assured me that there was a marked decrease in the number of cretins in the district during his own time. He, however, admitted that

they were still to be found in a greater or less proportion in all the deep lateral valleys, as well as in
the great valley of the Rhone itself.

Our journey of to-morrow was to be along the
valley of the Rhone as far as St. Maurice, and was
to be performed throughout in carriages. We covenanted with our host to convey us to Sion with
the same pair of horses and driver——a distance of
about thirty miles——for 25 francs and Trinkgeld.
Although we found this to answer tolerably well,
our journey would have been quicker, and nearly as
cheap, had we posted it, as we did the rest of the
journey beyond Sion. We might have changed
horses at Turtmann and Sierre, without losing the
time we expended at the same places in resting and
feeding our single pair.

CHAPTER XXV.

September 1.—Last evening as we approached the end of our journey we had seen the clouds collecting on the mountains beyond the Rhone, and were therefore prepared for an interruption of that model weather which we had so long enjoyed. We had made arrangements for being called at four, intending to start at five, but not being called at all, our late pedestrian feats made us sleep till past five, and we did not set out on our journey till a quarter to seven. There had been rain in the night, and all the mountains had still on their robe of mist; but the morning was now fair though dull, and the air much warmer than we had found it in the morning for some days past,—the thermometer at six being as high as 60°. The weather continued fine until we passed Turtmann, when rain came on and lasted until we reached midway between Sion and Martigny—that is, until about two o'clock.

It was fortunate for us that we were now on

ground which was but of comparatively little interest to the wayfarer.   The valley of the Rhone is
certainly fine; but from its great size, its boundaries, generally speaking, do not admit of that
close examination from the road-traveller which is
requisite for the disclosure of individual beauties;
while the mountain ranges, on either side, are,
for the most part, of a somewhat monotonous
character.   To enjoy the beauties of the Great
Rhone-valley one must leave the main road and go
at least close to the mountain-foot; or, rather, one
should penetrate into the lateral valleys and ravines
which open into it.   Some of these are said to be
very fine; and judging from the two explored by
us, I have no manner of doubt that they are so.

After passing Leuk, the valley becomes much
wider, and continues so most of the way to Martigny.
Its general character becomes also less wild and
richer; and for a considerable distance, in the vicinity of Siders and Sion, there is space for extensive
cultivation between its two mountain boundaries.
Beyond Sion, half-way to Martigny, the low
lands are more subject to the overflowing of the
river, and the soil is here coarse and marshy.   We
crossed the Rhone a little before reaching Siders,
and continued on its right bank until we reached
Riddes, about eight or ten miles from Martigny;
here we recrossed the river and continued on its left
bank all the way to Saint Maurice.

We stopped for an hour at Siders or Sierre, and

had breakfast at the Soleil, which is an excellent inn, with a most attentive and civil landlady. We stopped again at Sion, where I paid my promised visit to Dr. Grillet, the physician, whom I had met at the baths of Leuk. I found him in full uniform, the militia to which he was attached as surgeon being then called out on duty, and stationed in this old city. Dr. Grillet was kind enough to take me to the hospital, in the inspection of which I met with great courtesy from the Abbé, its superintendent.

My chief object in visiting the hospital was to see the cretins; this being, as far as I know, the only public establishment in Switzerland into which these poor creatures are admitted. The ward for the cretins is a separate building in the garden and is of small extent. There were only eight patients in it, five females and three males. Three of the women were old and of average size; two of them, one thirty, the other nineteen, were not taller than children of five or six, if so tall. Some could speak, some could hear but could not speak. In all the skull was misshapen; the site of the anterior lobes being either very flat or the skull very narrow in this region: the head, however, was of an average size, and in some large. The dwarf of thirty could just only walk or rather waddle. The general health of all of them was good, as far as regards appetite, nutrition, &c. Dr. Grillet and the Abbé assured me that the disease was greatly diminished throughout the country, and was still diminishing; the number of cases now admitted into the hospital being much fewer than formerly. According to Dr. Grillet, there is not at this time a single cretin in the city of Sion, except in the hospital. The great diminution of the disease both Dr. Grillet and the Abbé attributed to the gradual improvement of the sanitary condition of the district, as well as of the people, especially in regard to the greater cleanliness of the houses and persons, and to the freer use of fresh air. They both contemplated its final extinction as an event that was certain, though not very immediate. Besides the individuals in the cretin ward, I saw several other semi-cretins going about the passages of the hospital, ugly little men and women, with merry, childish manners, but with an old look. They could speak and do some work, and were, in fact, employed about the duties of the hospital. It did not appear that any steps were taken in the establishment for the mental improvement of the cretins. They are well cared for as to their health and comfort, but nothing more. Dr. Grillet informed me that a very elaborate statistical report on the state of cretinism throughout the country had recently been called for by the government, and drawn up by the members of the medical profession. It is to be hoped that this highly interesting document will ere long be made public.

We took post-horses at Sion, changing them twice between it and St. Maurice, viz. at St. Pierre and Martigny, paying for each stage ten francs and drink-money. We reached St. Maurice just as it began to grow dark in the valleys. In our way from Martigny to St. Maurice we stopped for a few minutes to observe, first, the singular torrent of the Trient dashing out from a narrow chasm in the cliff, something in the style of the Tamingenbach at Pfeffers; and then, to admire the fine cascade of Sallanches, called the Pissevache. Though having a less body of water than that we had last seen, the Turtmannbach-fall, it is much loftier than this, and has a more elegant character altogether. Further on we passed the remains of the singular Mud-torrent which in August 1835 descended from the Dent de Midi and overran the valley in a continuous stream, 300 or 400 yards in width. It is now covered with coarse grass, and only betrays its origin by the inequalities of its surface and the cuttings for the road through its mass.

Here the Dent de Midi came in view close on our left hand, and its magnificent peak was revealed to us while the setting sun was yet red upon it. It reminded us of the Matterhorn by its general outline and its isolated relation to the mountains at its base; but it is in every way inferior to that matchless peak. It is 4000 feet lower than the Matterhorn, and its shaft and peak look stunted—what is vulgarly called *stuggy*—when compared with the slender and elegant proportions of the other.

17

We put up at the *Union* at St. Maurice, and found it an excellent hotel in all respects. We had a good table-d'hôte dinner, or supper, at eight o'clock, and clean and comfortable bedrooms. Our plan for the following day was to proceed with the Diligence in the morning to Villeneuve, and there join the steamboat for Geneva.

As the only remaining portion of our contemplated journey in Switzerland was the tour of Mont Blanc, had we been properly prepared for it we would have remained at Martigny and entered at once upon it, either proceeding by the pass of St. Bernard or by Chamouni. But, unfortunately, we had omitted to provide ourselves in London with a Piedmontese passport, and we had no alternative but to proceed to Geneva to obtain one. This added a day to the Holiday, but the extension could hardly be regretted, as it supplied us with the opportunity of seeing the country between St. Maurice and Villeneuve, and, what was more, of sailing from one end of the Leman lake to the other, in one of the loveliest days of this delightful season.

September 2.——The rain and clouds of yesterday had quite disappeared, and what I have called our model weather was restored. The Diligence started between seven and eight, and we were fortunate enough to secure outside places. For the mere road-traveller the top of the Diligence is the very best situation for obtaining a view of a country in a rapid

transit through it; as you are raised above the walls
and hedges on either side, and can take an unobstructed view of objects both before and behind you.
You have the benefit also of being near the coachman,
who can always give the names of the remarkable
things that present themselves in your progress ;——
to say nothing of the pleasure derived from the
consciousness of having a sort of commanding
position, and the comfort of a free breeze in the
warmest weather.

The Rhone at St. Maurice is compressed into a
deep but narrow stream by the projecting base of
the mountains on either side; its muddy waters, of
a dirty white colour, reminding the English traveller
of his own sweet Thames at London bridge. Immediately on leaving the town, we cross the river
by an ancient bridge, and come at once into the
Canton Vaud, which stretches from hence round
the eastern end of the lake of Geneva, and along
the whole of its northern shores. The road to Villeneuve follows the line of the Rhone all the way,
but at some distance from it, on its right bank.
The country is extremely rich and beautiful; well-
wooded and cultivated; crowded with villages and
farmhouses, and forming a striking contrast, as
everybody has remarked, with that part of the
valley of the Rhone which belongs to the Canton
Vallais. The most striking object in the landscape
was the Dent de Midi, which towered behind us in
the southern horizon through the whole of our

journey by land, and during the greater part of our voyage on the lake.

We reached Villeneuve before noon, and finding the steamer waiting our arrival, went immediately on board. The vessel was large and well fitted in every way, and there were already many passengers on board. She stopped at all the places of any note along the northern shore, Vevay, Ouchy (or Lausanne), Morges, Rolle, Nyon, Coppet; and reached Geneva, a distance of between fifty and sixty miles, at half-past six. The weather was superb; and for a mere pleasure voyage over one of the finest pieces of water, bounded by a rich and cultivated shore, and with magnificent mountains in the distance, nothing could be more delightful.

The great extent of the lake of Geneva gives it quite the character of a sea; and the brightness of the sun and sky on the present occasion, and the exquisite blueness and purity of the water, reminded me of the Atlantic when slumbering in a calm around the beautiful islands of our own West Indies. There was, however, a want of that exquisite combination of grandeur and beauty close at hand, which renders the lake of the Four Cantons so impressive. Lake Leman is too large to be grasped in the same landscape with its shores; or rather its immediate shores are too tame, and the grand features of scenery visible from it, too remote, to constitute that sort of individualized home-picture which it is always so delightful to contemplate.

It must not be imagined, however, that the views from the lake, whether near or remote, are not beautiful in a high degree. The country all along the northern shore, for the whole fifty miles of our voyage, presents the perfection of a quiet and rich rural landscape. The land slopes gently upwards from the water; the green fields are chequered by a profusion of irregular hedgerows and orchards, and speckled throughout with cheerful-looking villages and white farmhouses beside their clumps of trees. It closely resembles some of those exquisite landscapes of England, often seen in the vicinity of our towns, where the country though richly agricultural is yet very populous.——And then for the distant landscape : The long blue range of the Jura to the north-west and west ; the loftier line of peaks which divide the Pays de Vaud on the east, from the cantons of Berne and the Vallais, including the picturesque Diablerets and the Oldenhorn, both upwards of 10,000 feet above the sea ; the Dent de Morcle and the yet loftier and more picturesque Dent de Midi (10,500 feet above the sea) in the south-east ; the Alps of Savoy to the south, and, far beyond them and above all, the snowy vision of Mont Blanc mingling with the clouds in the horizon, full fifty miles distant :——all these, seen in succession as you look round the horizon, constitute a series of pictures which can never tire, and to which I seem to have done but scanty justice in coupling them with even a single depreciatory word. To the admirers of water-views or sea-views more especially, and, yet more, to that large class of men in whose minds all the delights of sailing are associated with a fine expanse of water, the lake of Geneva must present beauties hardly to be surpassed.

Independently of its natural attractions, also, this lake possesses much interest from the great men with whose names its waters and its shores are knit in the memories of all, and from the immortal works which have had their birth amongst them, or taken them for their theme.   To the old names of

" Rousseau, Voltaire, our Gibbon, and De Stael,"

must now be added that of the poet who has thus associated them.   Lord Byron spent a considerable portion of the year 1816 on the banks of this lake, and composed some of his finest poetry during his residence, viz. the Third Canto of Childe Harold, The Dream, Darkness, and the Prisoner of Chillon. The first three were written at Diodati, on the southern shore of the lake near Geneva; the last at the small town of Ouchy, on the occasion of his being detained there a couple of days, along with Shelley, by stress of weather, when on a boating expedition.   We landed some of our passengers at this place, and saw the small inn where the poem was composed.   This was interesting; but some of the natural scenery was rather disenchanting.   For instance, I found some difficulty in realizing in the plain, old, humdrum-looking house of Chillon, what had once taken so strong a hold of the imagination as the abode of the " Prisoner." In attempting also to evoke the old memory of the "small green isle, scarce broader than his dungeon floor," which cheered and saddened at once the heart of the Bonnivard of the poem, I was not a little baulked by the artificial and *natty* look which has been given to it by inclosing it with a high white wall. The " three tall trees" growing within this tiny inclosure, reminds one too much of a painted flower-pot with its geraniums, to permit the idea of the " little isle" to take a poetical hold of the fancy.

Vevay, Clarens, and Meillerie were better; as the obviously great beauty of the two former, and the remoteness of the other, left the old visions of Jean Jacques undisturbed. Lausanne looks beautiful from the lake, with its splendid church and fine large houses scattered over and crowning the slope of the hill. It naturally possesses especial interest for the English traveller, as the abode of the author of the ' Decline and Fall,' although the antiquary will find no other local memorial of him but the hotel which bears his name, and which now stands on what was his garden. We cannot see Ferney from the shores of the lake; but it and Les Délices, both close to Geneva, will be always joined with the name of the wonderful man who so long lived there. The castle of Coppet, too, close to the small town of the same name, where we took up some passengers for Geneva, though illustrated by genius of an in-

ferior stamp, will have an interest to many as
the abode and final resting-place of the author of
' Corinne' and ' De l'Allemagne.'

> " Leman, these names are worthy of thy shore,
> Thy shore of names like these !"

The body of passengers on board the steamer was
made up of many elements, but the great majority
seemed, like ourselves, more occupied with pleasure
than business.   A considerable proportion consisted
of inhabitants of the immediate districts ; the residue
being foreigners, and principally English.   Of these
last I think we landed some and received some at
every halting-place.

There was nothing novel or strange in the economical arrangements or the proceedings on board.
We had, of course, no lack of good fare below, and
we had plenty of Swiss and French newspapers on
deck.   There were English papers also—more especially the ubiquitous " Galignani" and the omni-
scient " Times."   But I cannot say they were much
read, though eagerly looked for, here as elsewhere.

It is marvellous how politics and quidnuncism
lower in interest and value amid the active labours
of a tour, and in the presence of great Nature.
The mind is not simply preoccupied ; its faculties
accustomed to the permanently Grand and Beautiful,
are no longer in harmony with such things.   I will
not say that the more cordial affections are also
likely to be weakened under such circumstances ;

but I think it might be a fair question in the schools of Love, whether it would not be more politic in the interested parties, to advise a hesitating gallant rather to travel in Holland than in Switzerland.

As usual, we had a band of music on board, levying contributions on the pockets—some might perhaps say on the ears—of the passengers : and we had, also, for a time, two more interesting supernumerary performers, one in the person of a very handsome but very rakish-looking Spaniard, who sang to us several airs with much power and skill. This being Saturday, he told us that he was on his way to the other or Catholic side of the lake, where he could still exercise his art on the morrow.

On landing at Geneva, we put up at the Couronne, a splendid hotel on the Quay, facing the lake, and which we found, both at present and on a subsequent visit, a very comfortable residence. We had an excellent table-d'hôte dinner soon after our arrival, at which some twenty or thirty sat down. On occasions of this kind, and still more, perhaps, in the German than the Swiss inns, we had often admired the indefatigable zeal of some one of our opposite neighbours, who, *audax omnia perpeti,* would let nothing that the waiter presented pass him. On the present field of action we were still more astounded at the marvels performed by two or three little folks near us, mere infants of three or four years old, whose most loving father literally

17 §

loaded their plates with part of the contents of every dish in succession, and which they did their best to dispose of in the usual manner. Whether the good man proceeded on mercantile considerations, thinking that he ought to have for his money money's worth, I know not; but if he did so, he certainly seemed not to have miscalculated either the practicability or the safety of his speculation ; for we saw all concerned in it, alive and merry, next morning.

Geneva is a fine town with many good houses, and two or three handsome streets. The quays fronting the lake and the ranges of buildings on either side of the bridge across the Rhone are splendid. The shops remind one of London; and the bustle in the principal thoroughfares bespeaks a much greater commercial activity than we had yet seen in Switzerland.

Next to the lake, the most beautiful thing about Geneva is the Rhone which is seen pouring its broad, blue stream of exquisite purity, so rapidly yet so silently beneath the flat, low bridge which brings the spectator almost on a level with its surface. One can hardly tire in looking down into its clear waters and watching their unceasing, resistless, yet undisturbed and quiet flow, like the determination of a great will. And how unlike the impure and turbulent stream we saw but yesterday struggling between the rocks of St. Maurice ! It reminds us of one of Dante's spirits just escaping from its penal purification: Lake Leman is truly *Il Purgatorio* of the Rhone :

> "———— dalla santissim' onda
> Rifatto sì, come piante novelle
> Rinnovellate di novella fronda
> Puro e disposto a salire alle stelle."

On a small island in the midst of the stream, or rather at the extremity of the lake, accessible from the bridge just mentioned, there is a bronze statue of Rousseau. The site is beautiful, the whole of the little island being converted into a promenade shaded with trees. The face of the figure is turned in the direction of the town, as if looking towards the Hôtel de Ville, where the author's famous *Emile* was burnt by the hands of the hangman in the year 1762, in obedience to the order of the Council of Geneva. Some fifty years after his death, "the whirligig of time (as usual) bringing about its revenges," the council and citizens of the same town erected this statue in his honour; and his fame and glory are now regarded as part and parcel of that of his native city.

CHAPTER XXVI.

September 3.——Having obtained our passport for
the territories of his Sardinian Majesty, we determined on proceeding at once on our journey to Mont
Blanc. We accordingly agreed with a voiturier to
take us to Sallanches, paying for the whole journey,
in a neat open caleche with a pair of horses——32
francs and Trinkgeld, or, as the gratuity was now
called, *à bonnes mains*. We had once more come in
contact with our heavy baggage at Geneva; but we
again left it behind us at the Couronne, taking with
us only our knapsacks and such a diminished stock
as would last us for a week, which we reckoned on
being the extent of our absence from Geneva.

We set out at eleven for Sallanches. In half an
hour, or little more, we had crossed the frontiers
of the small canton of Geneva; and at the village
of Annemasse, a little beyond, our passports were
inspected by the Sardinian authorities. Our course
lay south-east along the right bank of the Arve,
but, for some time, at a considerable distance from

it. About seven miles from Geneva we crossed a river of considerable size; the Menoge, one of the tributaries of the Arve which here runs in a deep valley. On ascending the hill on the other side we came upon pretty flat but open and high ground, overlooking the Arve which was now close to us, and commanding extensive views on every side. The range of the Jura lay behind us, gradually lessening to the view; and the lofty ridge of mountains which had filled up our horizon to the south-east all the way from Geneva, was now developing itself into distincter masses and peaks close before us. The Arve lay below us, presenting the usual signs of an Alpine torrent when freed from its close boundaries of cliff and mountain, a turbid, white stream only half-filling its dry stony bed and, here and there, showing traces of wider incursions into the ill-defended fields on either side. The land was apparently well cultivated, and the country everywhere bore the aspect of a prosperous agricultural district. Its champaign and comparatively tame character, reminded us of some parts of England, and yet more of Scotland, where we more frequently see a wide extent of cultivated country, like this, bounded by ridges of moderately high mountains in the distance.

Having passed through two or three small villages, and near the ruins of the antient castle of Faucigny, we came at length close to the base of loftiest of the mountains we had been all the day approaching. This is the Mole, rising 6140 English feet above the sea. Directly opposite, and at no great distance, stands Mont Brezon, nearly as high. The river Arve issues from between them into the open country, from the valley formed by their prolongation to the south-east. A little way within the mouth of this valley stands Bonneville, close to the river on its right bank. This we reached between one and two o'clock. Bonneville is prettily situated on a bend of the river and has a fine view of the mountains which closely bound it on either side ; but its low position amid the flat grounds subject to the inundations of the Arve, renders it obnoxious to malarious fevers. It is a neat little town, containing probably 2000 inhabitants, with a fine large church, an hospital, and a small town house, indicating its rank as the chief town of the province.

While our horses were resting, I introduced myself to one of my medical brethren, whom I found to be a well-informed man, and who kindly gave me some interesting details respecting the district. Intermitting fever is extremely prevalent here. Cretinism is known to exist only in one village in the district, which lies in the mouth of one of the lateral ravines which open into the great valley of the Arve. In my return through Bonneville, I saw two of these cretins. They had come from their village to the town ; and though they could not speak intelligibly, they had sense enough to display their begging skill to the passengers in the Diligence. They were not quite dwarfs, but they were feeble and stunted, with ill-shapen heads.

Crossing the river by a handsome stone bridge at Bonneville, we continued our journey along the left bank of the Arve, close to the base of the Brezon. The portion of this fine mountain ridge seen by us from the road is not very lofty, nor is the slope extremely steep. It is, indeed, too steep for cultivation, but it is richly clothed with bushes and dwarf trees to the very top. The mountain bounding the valley on the other side is both loftier and steeper, and consequently more rocky and bare of trees. The space between is everywhere well cultivated and well wooded. The road is throughout shaded with fruit trees of all sorts, apples, cherries, walnuts, chesnuts, &c., and passes through many small hamlets having all the appearance of prosperity and comfort.

As we approached the small town of Cluses, about ten or twelve miles from Bonneville, the mountains opposite to us, which had been gradually becoming more sloping and green, took at once a circular sweep westward to unite with the ridge on our right hand, so as apparently to close up further progress in that direction. This sweep, however, had none of that rugged grandeur which we had so often seen in the terminal boundaries of the Swiss valleys. On the contrary, the mountains composing it were better wooded and less precipitous, and cultivated a considerable way up their flanks; and here and there, as if still further to enhance the gentle beauty of the scene, small promontories crowned with trees were seen projecting from the green slopes and rounded knolls, variegated with hedges and corn-fields rising up in their front. While we seemed to be advancing directly onward towards the centre of this charming amphitheatre, and were wondering how we were to cross the mountains in its back-ground, all at once we found the Arve again close before us in the midst of Cluses; when, crossing the bridge, and then turning suddenly to the south, at right angles to our former track, we in an instant lost sight of our bright and beautiful valley amid the gloom of a narrow ravine of perpendicular rock, into which we had so unexpectedly entered. This sudden change of direction in the road, and the as sudden and great change in the character of the scenery bounding it, is very striking; and I hardly know which of the two surprises is the greatest, in coming, as we now did, from the valley to the gloomy ravine, or from the ravine to the valley, as we did on our return. The passage is here so narrow that there is little more space than what is required for the river and the road, and all that the traveller sees at first, on entering it, are the rugged cliffs on either hand and the strip of blue sky above them.

The small town of Cluses which is built partly in the mouth of the gorge and partly in the open plain outside, is a busy-looking place indicating the com-mercial pursuits of its people who, as well as the inhabitants of the villages in the neighbourhood, are principally occupied in watch-making, or rather in some of the preliminary operations of watch-making. The freshness of many of its houses, and the unfinished condition of others, show, at once, that it has been a sufferer from fire; and the greater neatness, smartness, and size of the new erections, and their greater distance from one another, show at the same time that such fires, however deplorable at the period of occurrence, are really in the long run blessings, not curses, to many towns. Formerly at Tusis and Altorf, now at Cluses and afterwards at Sallanches, we were particularly struck with this fact; and could not help remarking, then as now, how strikingly analogous in their results, as educing good from evil, are most of the great catastrophes occurring in the world, whether in physical nature, in the economy of man's external life, or in the province of mind. Assuredly in Switzerland, Fire has more than vindicated its ancient honours as a purifier: it has been the grand sanitary reformer and improver. It is in this sense as in so many others that Time, in Lord Bacon's phrase, is the Great Innovator.

The change in the scenery which had taken place so abruptly, continues, in a modified degree, all the way until we approach Saint Martins and Sallanches. The rent-like steepness and narrowness of the cliffs, to be sure, soon ceases on leaving Cluses; but the valley remains comparatively narrow throughout, and its boundary on our left hand, that is, on the right bank of the river, shows itself, the greater part of the way, as a lofty bare ridge of upright rock. The road continues close to the base of this the whole way. On the other side of the valley the mountains are still grander and higher; and at one point, as we approach the small cascade of Nant d'Arpenatz (which is very beautiful, and exactly resembles the Staubach in being metamorphosed into spray in midfall), rise up in a singularly fantastic congeries of peaks crowded one upon another. In these, as well as some that now made their appearance over the brow of the cliff on our left hand, we recognised that peculiar configuration which the calcareous rocks assume in this district, and which receives its full development and most striking manifestation in the *Aiguilles* of Mont Blanc.

The peaks now rising on our left hand, were the most northern of the Aiguilles de Varens, which are seen in all their extent at Sallanches, and which form so striking a feature in the landscape as viewed from the valley of Montjoie. On the present occasion, they presented themselves to us in a singular point of view. It was within less than an hour of sunset, and the valley where we were travelling and its immediate boundaries on our left hand, had been for some time entirely in the shade, the sun being hidden by the mountains on the other side. On arriving, however, at a portion of our own boundary which was somewhat lower than the rest, all at once the peaks of the Varens disclosed themselves over it, shining in the sun with the most startling brilliancy. Though high above us they yet seemed close at hand; and the contrast which their fiery brightness and their sharp outlines formed with the sombre cliffs below them and the clear blue sky beyond them, was exceedingly picturesque. Their colour, too, was very extraordinary. I have called it fiery, and this not merely from its vividness, but from its peculiar tint; though this epithet does not accurately represent what we saw. In my notes, written at Sallanches, I have said that the colour when the peaks were first seen by us was a greenish-yellow, and this gradually changed into a bright brick-dust or ochrey colour as the evening advanced. The effect was, of course, much heightened by the grandeur, as well as the singular configuration and other physical qualities of the objects. The peaks or rather pinnacles are composed of rock perfectly bare, with all its outlines sharp and definite, and shoot up into the sky with the slenderness of an obelisk, to the height of 7600 feet above the sea. The natural tint of the rock is a sort of a pale salmon colour; and the singular hues which I have mentioned seem to be a combination of this with that soft yellow which characterises fading sun-light.

We were now within a short distance of our journey's end, and as we suddenly swept round the angle of the rock that still hid St. Martins from us, and turned our horses' heads across its bridge towards Sallanches, a prospect still more glorious burst upon us——nothing less than the mighty Mont Blanc itself, towering to the sky in our very front, and in that crisis of its beauty, too, of which every one has heard so much, when

> " The rose-tints which summer twilight leaves
>   Upon the lofty glacier's virgin snow,"

were yet in their full brilliancy. We were fortunate in the moment of our arrival, as, a quarter of an hour later, we should have lost this most beautiful display of colour. It was even now only visible on the very summits, and speedily disappeared entirely, leaving the whole enormous mass, of the same pure white, shining with a subdued brightness in the clear twilight sky.

We put up in Sallanches at the Bellevue, where we found good enough accommodation both as to food and lodging. It is a new house, like all the rest of the town indeed; the whole place having been reduced to ashes by an accidental fire eight years before. In consequence of this the town has risen up in a shape much superior to the old. The houses are all built of stone, are large and airy and nearly all separate from one another. Only one of the original fabrics seems to have escaped destruction. It is now distinguished by an inscription recording the fact; and serves, like certain establishments in the country, as a fixed time-mark to indicate the progress that has been made by its fellows in the march of improvement.

CHAPTER XXVII.

September 4.——The object of our present journey being to make the tour of Mont Blanc, we had two obvious routes before us; one by Chamouni, Martigny, and Mount St. Bernard, and so round by its north-eastern flank to our present starting-place; the other, taking precisely the same line, but in a reverse direction. We preferred the latter, from a notion that the views were better; though, after making the journey, I am not sure of its superiority in this respect.

We had arranged over-night to make the village of St. Gervais our first halting-place; and as there was a good carriage-road as far as the Baths below it, we took a car thither, for which we paid six francs. We were up betimes in order that we might see Mont Blanc at sunrise. The morning was beautifully clear, Mont Blanc and every peak within sight being without a cloud, though the level of the Arve, above and below us, was covered with a low mist. The air was rather cold, the thermometer being 48°. The mighty mountain was now, in the dawn, just as we had seen it in the twilight; a seemingly-solid mass of the purest snow, crossing and entirely shutting up the vista of our valley to the south-east, and rising up into the sky beyond like an enormous roof with the sloping side towards us. The eye, fixed on the huge central bulk, hardly notices the mountains on either side, or such of its own pinnacles as are seen from hence; no sharp angles or sudden contortions disturb the great lines of its contour; and not a single uncovered cliff breaks the broad whiteness of its surface. I am not sure that this severe simplicity of character does not produce a disappointing effect at first— the eye seeming to desiderate something more picturesque, something to excite a quicker and more facile wonder; but in the end it adds greatly to the sublime and awful impression which its uncomprehended vastness makes upon the mind.

As the day began to dawn, the eastern horizon became beautifully streaked with level lines of bright clouds, and I kept watching the summit of Mont Blanc in hopes of seeing it illumined by the first rays of the sun; but I was disappointed. Though still clear from every vestige of cloud, it exhibited no trace of that partial splendour of illumination which we had seen so strikingly on the Matterhorn and other snowy peaks, at sunrise; and even when the sun had risen to us, there was no other change in the snowy mass but a simple increase in its whiteness.

Although aware of our position to the west and north of Mont Blanc, I had still fancied that some portion of its vast range would be found to have such a direction relatively both to the rising sun and to ourselves, as to admit of the illumination I was looking for. I was so convinced of this at the time, and even afterwards, that I concluded that, although on my watch a good while before five o'clock, I was nevertheless too late, and had not made sufficient allowance for the loftiness of a height which must see the sun long before all its fellows of the sky. But it is now clear enough that my expectations had no better foundation than a mistake both in my geography and topography; as was, indeed, demonstrated only forty-eight hours afterwards, when being placed exactly opposite on the other side of Mont Blanc, we saw the desiderated illumination in all its splendour, at a much later hour than that at which I was now looking for it.

In reference to the observation just made, that the risen sun worked no other change in the appearance of the snow but "a simple increase in its whiteness," I may here briefly record a remark that often suggested itself to me while watching the snowy Alps during the many bright days of our journey. With exception of the peculiarities of the reflected light on these at sunrise and sunset, as noticed, for instance, in the cases of the Tödi and Matterhorn and now on Mont Blanc; and of their partial and transient obscuration by the shadows of distant clouds between them and the sun, as in the case of the Weisshorn seen from the Gemmi; the effect of the brightest sunshine upon them, as contrasted with that of mere diffused light, was both different in kind and less in degree than I had expected. Nothing, to be sure, could exceed the brilliancy of the whiteness exhibited by them in the sunlight; but, generally speaking, it was still mere whiteness, and had little of that glitter or glare or flame-like splendour which we are accustomed to see produced by sunshine on other objects.

In looking at a mountain not covered with snow, whether its surface be of rock, heath, turf, or be overgrown with trees or brushwood, we see at once whether it is in sunshine or shade, not merely from the variation, but the varying intensity of its colours; but this is hardly the case with snowy mountains, or at least, with such as are completely covered with snow: they may show more white or less white, but there is little or no special change in the kind of coloration. It is, no doubt, from the constant presence on ordinary snowless mountains, of objects causing shadows and capable, at the same time, of reflecting and refracting the rays of light, in very different degress, that we are never at a loss in looking at them, to say whether they are directly illuminated by the sun or not.

We left Sallanches a little before six, our road lying along the left bank of the Arve, on a flat, close under the base of the mountain, which was now become only moderately steep, and admitting of cultivation some way up its slopes. The Forclaz was in our front as we advanced, and directly between us and Mont Blanc; but although 5700 feet above the sea, it not only interposed no obstacle to the view of the mountain behind it, but seemed in itself only a hill of very inconsiderable height. As we approached its base, however, which we did a few miles after leaving Sallanches, its proximity to our path excluded all further sight of Mont Blanc, although nearly triple its own elevation.

Having crossed the Bonnant, or, as it is named, Bonn Nant, in two distinct words, and according to the German or English pronunciation of the syllables, we turned from our path at right angles along its course, and soon reached the baths of St. Gervais in the depth of the ravine. This establishment consists of a single house of great size, containing no fewer than one hundred and twenty beds. As we had so hard a day's work before us, we did not delay to visit the establishment, nor even to view the cataract formed by the river only a short way behind the house. The water is slightly sulphureous and saline. Having lost the note I made of it at the time, I cannot state more precisely its temperature; but I see that Professor Forbes, whose accuracy is unquestionable, makes it to vary from

18

104° to 106°: it is remarkable that Mr. Bakewell makes it only 94°—98°.

The position of the bath-house is beautifully picturesque, in the depth of a narrow valley richly wooded, and commanding one fine view, that of the peaks of the Varens on the other side of the Arve; but it is much too confined, both in its air and in its walks, to afford a very desirable residence for the invalid.   Having a wish to examine this establishment more at leisure, I was desirous of coming on here the preceding evening and to sleep here; but was fortunately out-voted by my companions.   It would have been a great mistake had we done so, as we should have thus entirely lost the grand views which we had of Mont Blanc, both in the twilight and the dawn: and as there are good inns at Sallanches, and also at St. Martin's, I strongly recommend it to all travellers to do as we did, and not as I wished to do.

Having dismissed our voiturier, and procured a man at the baths to carry our knapsacks, we proceeded at once to climb the hill to the village of St. Gervais, which lies immediately above the baths. The ascent is all the way through a thick wood and is very steep.   It took us three quarters of an hour to reach the village; and we were detained an hour longer waiting for a guide and his mule, which last was again required by my companion, who had not yet recovered from his accident on the Riffelberg.

St. Gervais is a beautiful village, beautifully

situated, with a fine large church well decorated within, and charmingly set off externally by one of those pretty and cheerful-looking spires covered with bright tin, which we had so much admired in the Grisons country, and which we were glad to meet again in Savoy. To reach it we had to pass through fields of rich pasture, surrounded by hedge-rows full of wild flowers, and interspersed with little orchards of chestnut, walnut, and other trees, all loaded with fruit. As we sat by the wayside waiting for our mule, and basking in the warm sun amid all this luxuriance of life and beauty, we could hardly believe, for a moment, that we were so nigh the region of frost and snow and eternal barrenness. But this is only one of the many realities in this wonderful land, which not merely equal but surpass the fancies of the poet : what Tasso imagined in his Armida's island, and set down as being possible in nature through enchantment only ("cotanto puote sovra natura arte d'incanto"), may be said to be literally true in Switzerland :

> "———— Là di nevi e di pruine
> Sparsa ogni strada : ivi ha poi fiori ed erba :
> Presso al canuto mento il verde crine
> Frondeggia, e'l ghiaccio fede ai gigli serba,
> Ed a le rose tenere."

We left the village at nine, and proceeded on our way, directly south, along the valley of the Bonnant or Montjoie, keeping all the way on the right bank of the river, or, at least, till we had reached Nant

Bourant. The valley preserves for eight or ten miles the same rich character with which it commences at St. Gervais, being in most places of sufficient width to admit of a considerable extent of level pasture ground, and the slope of the bounding mountains on either side being not too steep to allow the cultivation to be carried some way up their base. Indeed, this cultivation in many situations seemed hardly to stop, until it was fairly checked either by a perpendicular cliff, or by the near presence of a glacier. But it was only on our left-hand side of the valley where the last-named obstacle occurred. Here, during the greater part of our journey, whenever the path took us some distance from the mountain base, we could always see above our heads the snowy ridge which forms the southern prolongation of Mont Blanc ; and in several places we came very near the terminal lappets of the glaciers, which it sends down towards the valley. These are the glaciers of Bionassay, Miage, La Frasse, and Tre-la-tête.

The mountains on the other side of the valley had no snow, but they are very lofty, and almost all terminate in steep, rugged cliffs or peaks of naked rock, sometimes extremely picturesque. The highest of these is Montjoli, behind Nant Bourant, which sends a lofty ridge along the edge of the valley to the north : it is 9600 English feet above the sea.

Although, on account of the great heat of the day, the walk was a warm one, it was not at all difficult, at least in the earlier part of the day ; the road being good and by no means steep : in fact, there is a tolerable carriage road as far as Contamines. The path continues close to the Bonn Nant almost the whole way, and the river preserves throughout the headlong and turbulent course, and turbid aspect and low temperature characteristic of all the snowy torrents of the Alps. Between St. Gervais and Contamines, we crossed two considerable torrents hastening to join the main river—one from the glacier of Bionassay, the other from that of the Miage. I found their temperature 41°, that of the main river being higher by 4°.

About two or three miles from Contamines there are three small oratories erected, close by the road side, two of them containing small figures of Christ and the Virgin. On these the following inscription greets the wayfarer in good clear print : " Monsieur Louis Rendu accorde l'Indulgence de 40 jours à Quiconque recitera un Pater Noster et un Ave Marie devant cet Oratoire." This is certainly a very civil thing of M. Rendu ; but, as far as I could learn, his civility does not seem to be much appreciated by those who have the best opportunities of profiting by it. I conversed with several of the country people on the subject, and found some careless, some doubtful, and some openly sceptical and recusant. One young man said he had not yet found time to go and say the required prayers. A man and his wife, busy in their hayfield near at hand, seemed to regard the thing as a capital joke, when I asked them if they took advantage of their vicinity to the Oratory, to make so profitable a bargain for their peccadilloes. A third cottager, an old man of a graver stamp, treated the subject more seriously, and in a way not at all complimentary to Monsieur Rendu. He said that it was, to say the least, an absurdity to think that any man, be he who he may, priest, bishop, or pope, could pardon the sins of another man. He told me that these oratories have been erected at the expense of individuals of the neighbourhood, either before death or in terms of their last will, as means of atonement for their own offences.

M. Rendu is, I believe, the bishop of Annecy, bishop of the diocese, and is, in spite of these puerilities, known to be a man of science. It spoke little for the knowledge or curiosity of the people of the district, that few of them seemed to know who this M. Rendu was, or where he lived.

We reached Contamines between eleven and twelve, and found the means of making a tolerable breakfast, though the inn is somewhat homely. This small village is situated amid rich and open fields, where the valley still remains of considerable width; it contains a handsome church. We rested here about an hour, partly for the purpose of having some provisions cooked for our dinner on the mountains, as we did not intend to stop again until we arrived either at Chapiu or Motet,—and we had a long journey to either.

Shortly after leaving Contamines, the valley contracts rather suddenly, the cliffs on either side cooping up the river in a narrow rocky channel and forcing the path, now reduced to an indifferent mule track, up over a steep and bare rock at a considerable height above the stream. The ravine and the bounding cliffs are here clothed with trees, and the river pursues its precipitous course, rather heard than seen, in its deep rocky bed. This wild forest scene continued until we reached the open valley where the little village and inn of Nant Bourant are planted. A short way below this, the Nant forms two very picturesque cataracts deep in the recesses of its rocky channel, and not discoverable without some difficulty. They are near the spot where the road crosses the river, which it does on a lofty stone bridge.

At Nant Bourant, the scene changes once more, the valley becoming more open, but now quite shorn of the rich vegetation and foliage which distinguish its lower portions: the pasture-fields grow coarser as we advance, and soon terminate in that barren moorland which marks the more elevated valleys of the Alps. We were now on the left bank of the Bonn Nant, and soon reached the cul-de-sac or basin from the semicircular walls of which, or rather from the snows on their top, it takes its rise. It is on the top of the cliff constituting the south-west corner of this basin, that the Col de Bonhomme is situated, and it was up the steep breast of this cliff that we had to toil, by one of the usual zig-zag paths, to reach it.   Near the top we passed several patches of snow in the hollows of the cliff, from which one of the primary branches of the Nant was flowing.   I was at first surprised to find the water issuing from beneath the snow ten degrees above the freezing point; but this was explained as we advanced by the fact of the stream, which was shallow, having run some distance in the open air previously to entering its channel beneath the snow; it had originated in a mass a good way further up.

On reaching the top of the ascent, we turned to the left hand under the base of the cliff constituting the eastern boundary of the Col de Bonhomme, and proceeded eastward in the direction of the Col de Fours, over a most rugged track consisting of huge fragments of slaty rock loosely piled on one another, without soil or vegetation, such as has been already noticed in other parts of our journey.   So soon as we had attained the summit of the Pass, a splendid view of the Tarentaise and Alps of Savoy to the south and south-east, burst upon our sight, and became still more magnificent as our path led us higher along the brow of the cliff.   The whole field of vision before us, from the base of the rocks on which we were to the distant horizon, was filled, and, as it were crowded, by one continuous series of mountain ridges and peaks, shooting up and cross-ing each other in all directions, in the strangest and wildest yet most beautiful confusion.   These mountains had not the lofty grandeur of the Swiss Alps, being spread out even on a lower level than our own; but there was something inexpressibly fine in the appearance they now presented. There seemed not to be one spot of level ground in the vast expanse; and we had no other indication of the valleys that divided the successive ridges from one another, but the dark shadows interposed between the brighter peaks that kept the sunshine from them. The sun, now half-way down the sky, shed over the whole that brilliant yet mellow and misty kind of light which is so beautiful a feature in the evening landscape, and which communicates to it an expression of such profound and impressive repose.*

In the extreme south, basking, as it were, in the flood of yellow light pouring on it from the south-west, and beautifully relieved against the bright sky beyond, a long ridge of loftier mountains bounded the horizon. This ridge was marked by a peculiarity which may enable others better acquainted with the country to recognise and identify it : about its centre there was a huge abrupt gap running half-way down its mass, with vertical sides and a circular

* These sunny evening scenes, when the view is not merely extensive, but also undisturbed by movements or action of any kind, vital or physical, do not simply convey the expression of repose in themselves, but extend it to the mind of the spectator, and superadd feelings of tenderness and melancholy. Wordsworth tells us "of the setting sun's pathetic light;" and I have always felt how true to nature is that trait in Crabbe's admirable picture

18 §

base, its edges looking to us as sharp and definite as if they had been cut by art.

In the south-eastern horizon, the sea of peaks was overtopped by a range of yet grander mountains covered with snow, which became more conspicuous as we advanced towards the Col de Fours; and in climbing this we saw also many other snowy peaks still loftier, and some of them at an enormous distance. Among these distant peaks we were particularly struck with one which, from its symmetry and general beauty, reminded us of the Wetterhorn as seen from the valley of the Reichenbach. This mountain, although named differently by our guide, is no doubt the Aiguille de Vanoise, which Professor Forbes justly calls " one of the most elegant moun-

of Melancholy Madness, which places the miserable Sir Eustace amid scenes like these—scenes of beauty not of horror:

> " Upon that boundless plain below,
>   The setting sun's last rays were shed,
> And gave a mild and sober glow,
>   Where all were still, asleep, or dead ;
> Vast ruins in the midst were spread,
>   Pillars and pediments sublime,
> Where the gray moss had formed a bed,
>   And clothed the crumbling spoils of time.
> There was I fixed, I know not how,
>   Condemned for untold years to stay :
> Yet years were not ; one dreadful *Now*
>   Endured no change of night or day ;
> The same mild evening's sleeping ray
>   Shone softly solemn and serene ;
> And all that time I gazed away,
>   The setting sun's sad rays were seen."

tains in the Alps." The same authority tells us
that the snowy mountains here seen by us, are
those of the Upper Isère, and extend towards Mont
Cenis. Our guide pointed out one of them as
Mont Cenis itself; but I am unable to say if he
was right in doing so.

The whole of this scene was so charming, and
moreover so different from anything we had yet
seen, that we were disposed to make our halt longer
than was requisite, either for our refreshment or
rest : and it was not without good reason, as we
afterwards found, that our guide hinted to us more
than once, that we were yet a long way from Motet.
The increasing coolness of the air began also to
warn us that the evening was coming on, though it
had little claim to be very warm even at an earlier
hour, at our present elevation, which was full 8000
feet above the sea. During our dinner-time, from
half-past five to six, the air in the shade was 49,°
and the temperature of a little rill from the cliffs
above was 42°.

We had a full hour's scramble across a rocky
track like that recently passed, before we came to
the Cime de Fours, and then we had a still more
painful one up the steep brow of this to the Col
which separates it from the snowy ridge on our left
hand. The whole of the tract we were now climbing,
was evidently but recently freed from its covering
of snow, as the soil was yet wet and loose, and our
path was bounded on both sides by patches still

remaining undissolved. In crossing one of these, just as we surmounted the Col and were beginning to descend the mountain on the other side, our mule lost its footing and tumbled over and over on the hard slope of snow. Fortunately she had no rider at the time, and received or inflicted no further damage than the disorganization of some little matters in the knapsacks she was carrying. The Col de Fours is about 9000 English feet above the sea. It is seldom seen by travellers so free from snow as we found it on the present occasion; one advantage of making the transit later in the season than usual.

So soon as we had crossed the Col we lost sight of the sun, and though, in descending, we had for a short time a beautiful vision of the new moon——looking as if perched, with her horns upwards, on the very pinnacle of the Cime at our backs, reminding us of the pictures of Diana——she also speedily disappeared, and was seen no more that night. We then began to perceive that it would be quite dark long before we reached our destination. Indeed, it may be said to have been as dark as it was likely to become in this fine summer night, before we reached the bottom of the mountain, the descent of which was troublesome, as well from its great steepness as from the loose and slippery nature of its surface. But the tract of country at its base was more troublesome still, being a succession of steep banks, and streams and bogs, and rough moorland full of ruts and stones, which it was far from an easy task to get through in the dark; nor was it accomplished, on my part, without manifold plunges into pools and bogs, and more than one fall on the slippery turf. Our guide, too, though a sharp fellow and well acquainted with the country, lost his way more than once, and we had thus to traverse a good deal more ground than would have been otherwise necessary.

At last, however, we escaped from our trackless wilderness and got upon the regular mule-path from Chapiu to Motet; and keeping this for the better part of an hour, we at length arrived at our journey's end, but not before half-past nine, nor until we were all sick enough of our involuntary explorations of Alpine scenery in the dark.

Although our present experience sufficed to convince us how impossible it would have been to escape from our difficulties without a guide, if we had even eschewed positive danger; it would not be quite fair to conceal that we were far from unhappy in our vagaries. The fact is, we had implicit confidence in our guide; and being thus freed from fears of ultimate safety, were not prevented from taking all the enjoyment out of our position, which it was capable of affording. It was a beautiful star-light night, and there was the light of a young moon on the mountains, though none of it descended to our level; the air was also perfectly calm, and not at all chilly to men in active exercise like us. Under such circumstances our little difficulties and accidents were more frequently the source of mirth than otherwise, and, once over, were regarded rather as a pleasing variety in a prosperous tour. Had we had no guide, however, the picture would have been quite reversed; and therefore it is that I warn all travellers who run any chance of being benighted in these regions, not to cross the Col de Bonhomme or the Col de Fours without one.

Our expectations as to accommodations at Motet had been very moderate; but I confess I was still somewhat disappointed on being told that the miserable hut at which our guide drew up, was to be our resting-place for the night. We soon found, however, that the outside was the best part of the establishment. It was clear that no travellers were expected at the hostelry at this late hour, as the door was barred and neither light nor sound was discoverable. After a time we were admitted by an old woman, who turned out to be the mistress of the house, and who received us graciously enough, but with the rather discouraging announcement that all her beds were full! As this was the only house in the place, we had no alternative but to enter and make the best of what had befallen us.

The little low place inside the door appearing to us on entering to be only an anteroom or kitchen, we at once proceeded onwards, candle in hand, to another fronting us, when we found ourselves in the very penetralia of the mansion, in the middle of a bedroom, surrounded by three curtainless beds with sundry occupants. On retreating we found, on explanation, that these two chambers constituted the whole house, and that all the spare beds were pre-engaged by earlier travellers. What was to be done? The occupants of one of the beds were two young chamois hunters, that of the other was a young damsel on her way to Cormayeur; and the third bed was the landlady's own, out of which she had just risen to let us in.

The chamois hunters very politely offered to resign their rights in favour of my companions, and the landlady her's to me. My young friends, however, gave the preference to a small hayloft over head, and as the hunters consequently resumed their station, it remained to be determined who should be the occupant of the remaining bed. My walk of thirty and more miles made me very ungallantly accept the good woman's urgent proposal to take her bed; and, having fortified myself against attacks from the domestic *Raubvögeln* (which its acceptance too probably involved), by completely dressing instead of undressing myself, I took up my position in my own corner, and soon forgot my companions and myself. When I awoke in the morning, the hunters and the damsel were gone. My young friends, I found, after some difficulties with the Raubvögeln aforesaid, had contrived, as well as myself, to get an excellent night's rest. Where our guide slept, I know not; but as he was not only an old guide but an old soldier to boot, I doubt not he was as successful as his *clientèle*.

CHAPTER XXVIII.

VALLEY OF BONNEVAL — ASCENT OF THE COL DE LA SEIGNE — VIEWS FROM IT — MONT BLANC — THE ALLEE BLANCHE — GLACIER OF THE MIAGE — THE LAKE OF COMBAL — THE RIVER DOIRA — GLACIER OF THE BRENVA — FORMATION AND MOTION OF GLACIERS — THEIR MORAINES — VAL FERRET — CORMAYEUR — GLACIER - WATER — CAUSES OF ITS PECULIARITIES — TOWN OF CORMAYEUR — AN ELIGIBLE RESIDENCE.

September 5.——The sun was high in the heavens and had for some time lighted up the depths of the valley, before we left our night's quarters. It was, in fact, eight o'clock ere we were fairly on our road to Cormayeur. The valley of Bonneval, in the north-eastern part of which Motet stands, is a wild Alpine scene surrounded on all sides by steep and lofty mountains, and itself too elevated to admit of any other than a stunted vegetation. The lofty Cime de Fours now shone clear in the sun behind us, and we had a glimpse of the rugged region at its base, the scene of last evening's scramble. In looking back to that little adventure, and to the course of the journey preceding it, I am here led to remark that the traveller who does not leave St. Gervais at least a couple of hours earlier than we did, should make Chapiu and not Motet the termination of his day's labours. This will allow a fairer distribution of the work, as the walk to Cormayeur is not a toilsome one; and it can hardly be that the accommodations at Chapiu are not better than those at Motet.

Immediately on leaving Motet the ascent to the Col de la Seigne may be said to begin, and it continues steep, but not extremely steep, the whole way to the top.   The day was bright and beautiful as usual, though the air felt cold until we got into the valley on the other side.   Our path up the mountain retained throughout the same character of roughness and comparative barrenness which had marked our track ever since we left the meadows above Nant Bourant.   We had, however, a fine wild view of the mountains behind us, whenever we stopped to look back or rest; and on either side we had steep and lofty barriers of rock, showing here and there huge masses of snow in their hollows. Directly in front we had nothing but the bare moor-like face of the pass, and the bright blue sky over the Col in which it terminated.   When we reached this, however, which we did about ten o'clock, we came at once upon one of those glorious views—always new, always different—which greet the climber of every Alpine pass at last, and repay in moments the labour of hours spent in attaining it.

Although the Col de la Seigne is about 8000 English feet above the sea, yet being, like all passes, bounded on either side by loftier mountains, the views from it are restricted to two main directions principally.   In these directions, however, they are very fine.

On our right hand, towards the south-east and east we had an extensive and splendid prospect over the mountains of Piedmont and over a portion of those in Savoy which we had seen yesterday from the Col de Fours; and directly before us and below us stretching lengthwise to a great distance on the north-east, lay the deep valley of the Allée Blanche, with its mighty barriers on either side. On the left-hand or north-western side, this barrier consists entirely of the bare rocky basis of Mont Blanc, rising up all along from the depth of the valley, like a sheer rampart, crowned at intervals with sharp peaks and pinnacles, and bearing, as a wall bears a roof, the snowy wilderness that stretches upwards to its summits in the sky. The face of the mountain immediately bounding the valley is much too precipitous to retain the snow, and looks even darker than it really is, from contrast with the dazzling brightness overhead. The range of mountains that bound the right-hand, or north-eastern side, the Cramond, &c., although magnificent and of the full height of 9000 English feet above the sea, look quite dwarfish in the presence of their neighbours.

The descent from the Col de la Seigne is not very steep, and we soon reached the gentler slope of the valley, which we continued to trace in almost the same direction during the whole day. For many miles it retained the coarseness of vegetation and comparative barrenness characteristic of the highest Alpine ravines, but as we lowered our level it gradually assumed a gentler and richer aspect, and eventually presented to us many spots of great vegetable luxuriance as well as beauty.

The Col de la Seigne, like every Alpine pass, is the bounding terminus, or rather source, of two watersheds draining the valleys on the opposite sides, and running in opposite directions. In the earlier part of our journey in Switzerland all the streams we met with, whatever their direction, found their way into the Rhine and eventually into the Northern Ocean. Since we crossed the chain of the Oberland, we had found them all seeking the Rhone, to end with it in the Western Mediterranean. Now, for the first time, we found in the stream we saw springing from the patches of snow that filled the hollows of the Col as we descended, a tributary of the Po and the Adriatic. By the banks of this stream, the Dora or Doira, lay our course all to day, and part of to-morrow. Fed as it was by a continuous tract of snow on the mountains above, and by the huge glaciers of Mont Blanc, which one after another descend to its very side, it speedily becomes a rapid and tumultuous torrent ; and when we left it, next day, at the city of Aosta it had grown into a splendid river.

For many miles as we descended the valley there was not a trace of human habitation, except two or three rude Sennhütte or chalets for collecting the produce of the cows which were scattered over the pastures on the base of the mountains. One of these flocks consisted of a hundred cattle, all under the charge of a single lad, who presented, in his red jacket and peaked hat, a token that we had now got on the Italian side of the Alps. As we advanced we came closer and closer to the base of Mont Blanc, which is in many places literally a perpendicular cliff, and of truly enormous height. In one spot, where the cliff is the loftiest, the rock assumes so strongly an architectural appearance that you seem to see before you the front elevation of a gigantic gothic building with its formal overhanging pediment, surmounted and guarded on either side by figures of like proportions. Some of these seeming figures are the aiguilles or peaks which showed so strikingly as seen in profile from the Col de la Seigne, but which now, in a front view, looked like mere projections from the cliff, though themselves of enormous height; the vastly greater height of the mountain above them and against which they lay, making them dwindle into comparative insignificance.

Next to the view of Mont Blanc itself, the most striking objects in this day's journey—and indeed among the most striking in the whole Alps—are the vast glaciers which descend from the mighty mountain into the valley of the Allée Blanche. These glaciers show themselves in almost a continuous series on our left hand, as we pass along the valley, peeping out or shooting forth from every gap in the battlements of the sheer cliff which forms its immediate boundary. But by far the most conspicuous are those of the MIAGE and the BRENVA, which, as well from their enormous bulk as from their peculiar configuration, course, and other physical relations, entirely arrest the attention of the traveller.

The first of these come to is the Miage, lying nearly midway between the Col de la Seigne and Entrêves at the top of the valley of Aosta. The appearance presented to us by this glacier, when we first came in sight of it on descending the Allée Blanche, was precisely that of a gigantic railway embankment, shooting out from a hollow in the face of the cliff constituting the base of Mont Blanc, and stretching slantingly across the valley, as if to render it passable in mid air. The side of the glacier turned towards us was so completely covered with moraine from top to bottom, that nothing was seen but a rocky or earthy surface; and the impression of the artificial character was remarkably strengthened by the raw, recent appearance of the materials, and by their disposition in vertical ridges and furrows indicative of their successive descent from above downwards. The outlines of the mass were as sharp and symmetrical and its direction as straight as any embankment designed by the engineer or built up by the labourer's barrow : although its dimensions, doubtless, were somewhat more in harmony with the doings of Titans than of "Navvies." Crowning the top of the huge mound, like a bright wall rising above and running along its black edge, the backbone of the glacier was seen glittering in the sun; and a fanciful eye might have likened it, in its relative position at least, to the railway "train" as we sometimes see it sweeping along its lofty path, relieved against the sky beyond. The ridge of glacier, seen from our position, looked as if it were a wall of ice built up upon a seemingly-solid mass of earth, instead of the latter being merely a thin layer of rocky fragments which it had itself transported from the regions above and here thrown off from its edge as a *lateral moraine.*

At first sight, the glacier appears to abut against the opposite boundary of the valley so as to obstruct all further progress; and this notion seems confirmed by the obvious fact that the river has been actually obstructed by it and dammed up into a lake of some extent (termed the Lake of Combal) around the borders of which the pathway is forced to turn aside;——but on advancing forwards it is found that though the moraine has been actually thrust against the cliff, and thus formed a high embankment for the waters of the artificial lake, the glacier itself, for some unseen cause, has stopped short in its original course and turned off down the valley in a direction parallel with the cliff, between which and its own hill of moraine it has left a deep and narrow ravine through which the river struggles. In this its new direction the glacier has stretched several miles, if we may judge from the length of time—about an hour—it took us to reach its extremity.   To be sure, the path was very rugged and difficult, being, for the most part, on the slope of the moraine itself, and consequently made circuitous by fixed rocky fragments too large to cross, by blocks recently fallen on it, and by being frequently broken up by small streams pouring down the slope from the meltings of the glacier overhead.

Where the transverse ridge of the moraine forms the embankment of the Combal lake, an artificial sluice has been constructed, with the view of ensuring a more regulated discharge of the water; and here it was that we crossed the stream, thenceforward keeping on its left bank until we had entirely passed the glacier.   The final terminus of this looks down the valley towards the north-east, and is divided into two arms which project to a great distance beyond the central moraine, which has here actually stopped the advance of its own glacier and split in two the very stream which formed it.   Before this division, the glacier looked to us full a mile in width.   All along the ravine formed by the moraine of the Miage and the base of the Cramond, the course of the Doira is very precipitous; and as the whole of its bed here consists either of ledges of natural rock or of the rocky fragments of the moraine, its progress is marked by vast turbulence, foam, and noise.

On escaping from this squalid gorge and turning a little in front of the southern arm of the glacier, we crossed again to the right bank of the Doira, and came once more upon a green and wooded hill formed by a spur of the mountain on our right, and from which we had a fine view of the glacier now fronting us.   On this small promontory there are two or three huts, one of which bears the signal of a hostelry; and here we stopped a short time and partook of some milk while resting on the turf.   Immediately beyond this we entered upon a beautiful meadow nearly a mile in length, perfectly flat and now overgrown with autumn crocuses in full bloom.   This is termed the Val Veni. At its lower extremity we had some difficulty in getting upon the high ground again, owing to the overflowing of the river, but when we did so, we entered on an elevated path which conducted us through a pine forest covering the whole base of the mountain for some distance.

All along this part of our path, we had directly before us the magnificent glacier of the BRENVA, which, issuing from the eastern ridge of the summit of Mont Blanc, shoots across the valley precisely as that of the Miage, from which it is distant about three miles.   Like the Miage, the Brenva turns its course somewhat down the valley on escaping from the steep cliff, but not so much as to prevent it from crossing the valley as the other does.   Nay more, the Brenva, uninfluenced by its moraine, crosses the valley entirely and abuts boldly against the base of the cliff on the other side, so as to fill up the entire space occupied by the river and the pathway. The latter is forced up along the spurs of the mountain through the forest; the former finds its way beneath the glacier, not being again visible until it is seen rushing from under its lower border into the green meadows of the valley of Entrêves. The portion of the glacier which abuts against the cliff and also that which crosses the valley, presents the more common aspect of a rough hummocky surface; higher up, where it descends more steeply from Mont Blanc, it exhibits the bold pinnacled structure in a striking degree. Along its lower or eastern border, which may be said to constitute the upper or western boundary of the Val d'Entrêves, the lateral moraine is rather narrow, and looked more narrow than it is, from the position from which we viewed it: and the glacier, consequently, seemed to rise sheer up at once from the valley like a gigantic wall, at the base of which green meadows were spread out and, at a very short distance, numerous corn-fields thickly dotted with shocks of the recently cut corn.

In looking directly down from our pathway upon the Brenva, as well as on the Miage, the great icy mass looks as if it were *encased* by its moraine on either side, no part of the glacier being then visible but its upper surface. On the moraine which bounds them on the west, more especially the moraine of the Brenva, which rises opposite to the pine-forest on the mountain base, there has grown up an extensive

19

wood of scattered pines reaching nearly to its summit, and consisting of trees of such size as to indicate a growth of many years. These trees have been evidently chance-sown by the winds,——and afford another beautiful illustration of how Nature seeks to repair her own injuries.

The eastern extremity of the Brenva glacier abuts closely against the bare cliff without any intervening moraine, in part of the line of junction at least, but lies flat and without any sign of being forced upwards along the face of the rock ; the *vis a tergo* or impelling power appearing at present to take the line of direction of the valley of Entrêves, viz. to the north-east. On former occasions, however, the line of force seems to have been more direct, as the end of the glacier, instead of occupying its present low position where it adjoins the rock, has been known to climb the cliff to a great height. It appears from the documents given by Professor Forbes, in his book on the Alps, that it actually reached, in the year 1818, an elevation of 300 feet above its present level, ascending to the vicinity of a little chapel now standing high up on the brow of the cliff, and shattering it so as to render it necessary to take it down. It was in this year that Captain Basil Hall made a tour of Mont Blanc, and in describing the Brenva he notices the fact of this singular rise of its extremity : he says——" So complete a barricade was formed by the glacier, at one place, that we found some difficulty in getting past ; for though the road, purposely contrived to be out of the reach of such accidents, had been carried forty or fifty feet in perpendicular height above the bottom of the valley, it was all rubbed away by the glacier having slowly climbed up to it."*

Nothing can give the traveller a more practical and impressive illustration of the wonderful movements and progressive advance of glaciers, than the phenomena which these two magnificent examples force upon his attention. Here, assuredly, he that runs may read; it being just as obvious what has taken place here, as where the traveller is driven from his accustomed path by the overflowing of a river, or the rising of the tide on the sea shore. It is clear enough to any passenger through the Allée Blanche and Val Veni, that the present is not the original state of things, and that there must have been a time when the Doira pursued its way undisturbed along the centre of the valley, before it was thrust from its course, or bridged over by these rivers of ice flowing from the dismal ocean on the summits of Mont Blanc. When this epoch was, however, no memory exists; but that it is within a space of time not inconceivably remote, seems evident from the phenomena presented by the moraines, which may be regarded as a sort of permanent chronological index, pointing out the action of the still-renewed, still-perishing glaciers which deposited them.

* Patchwork, vol. i, p. 108.

That glaciers have a continuous motion from their source, down the slopes of the mountains on which they are found, although this is too slow to be obvious to the eye, is a fact that cannot escape the notice of any one who investigates their ordinary appearances, and is demonstrable by irrefragable evidence. Although in many cases they seem to recede, year by year, to an extent measurable annually or in a period of a very few years, as in the case of the Grindelwald and Görner glaciers formerly mentioned; and although their terminal extremities actually do often recede in relation to the material objects against which they abut, it is well known that this retrocession is only apparent as regards the total mass of the glacier. In all cases it is demonstrable that the great body or stream of ice is continuously progressive, any one point of it being, each year, further from its origin, and nearer the valley below, than in the preceding year; the seeming retrocession depending entirely on this, that the amount of decay of the terminal extremity, from melting, exceeds the extent of progress of the whole mass. This is the case, at present, with the glaciers of Grindelwald; and, it is said, with the glaciers of the Bernese Oberland generally. On the contrary, as we have seen, the Görner glacier in the valley of Zermatt, and the Brenva now before us, are encroaching every year, more and more upon their respective meadows, ploughing up the greensward before them, and overturning trees and houses with their irresistible but slow advance. But that the progress of the mass is equally real in the one case as in the other, admits of no question.

Each of these glaciers—and we may say every glacier in the Alps—discharges annually at its terminus, under the name of *moraine*, a portion of the load of solid rock and comminuted cliff which it has conveyed from the mountains above, and which it has never ceased, for a day, to bear onwards on its back, though it may have been many years—nay centuries—since it first received its burthen! Of the ordinary evidence proving this fact of the motion of glaciers, the most striking and unquestionable point is the well-ascertained advance of certain of these large masses of rock, well known by their size, shape and other peculiarities, to the people of the locality. Masses of this kind have been for the whole of a life the familiar acquaintance of the guides accustomed to visit the glaciers, who can point out the advance they have made beyond some fixed landmark since their earlier acquaintance.

It is only, however, of late years that the phenomena of glacier-motion has been thoroughly investigated and reduced to mathematical certainty. And it is to our countryman, Professor Forbes of Edinburgh, that the scientific world is mainly indebted for this great advance in our positive knowledge. A full and most interesting account of Professor Forbes's proceedings in settling this important point, is given in his classical work on the Alps—a work which of all that have been written on this inexhaustible theme, can alone bear comparison with that of Saussure. From Professor Forbes's observations on the glaciers on the other side of Mont Blanc, at Chamouni, it appears that their progress is continuous day and night, summer and winter, but varying in varying circumstances. For instance, the motion is less in winter than in summer; less by night than by day; and less at the sides of the glacier than in the centre. The motion at the side was found in summer to be about seventeen inches, and in the centre about twenty-seven inches, in the twenty-four hours; and during the winter it had decreased to about thirteen inches. In the course of three months the glacier had advanced 103 feet. The annual average progress of the glacier of the *Mer de Glace*, during the different seasons, may thus be set down in round numbers, as about 500 feet; or one mile in ten years. As some of the glaciers in Switzerland are calculated to be twenty miles in length, it thus appears that it would require no less than two centuries before that portion now constituting the upper extremity of the glacier, could reach the terminal moraine in the valley; and yet, during the whole of this period, there would not be one single moment in which the vast mass was not actually advancing!

Many theories have been proposed to account for this singular motion in glaciers, but the only one that seems capable of coping with all the difficulties of the problem is that of Professor Forbes, who considers the glacier mass in the light of a partially fluid or at least of a ductile mass, which flows down the acclivity of a mountain just as a mass of semifluid pitch or mortar would do. He shows that the seeming solidity of the ice of which glaciers consist, affords no sufficient objection to this theory.

The mode of formation of glaciers has been clearly pointed out by many observers. It takes place exclusively in the higher regions, at the line of perpetual snow; the glaciers receiving no accession whatever from the snow that falls upon them lower down——this being melted as completely by the summer heat as it is on the earth at the same elevation. The glacier is fed at its upper extremity by constant additions of its own material which is thus formed : " The summer's thaw percolates the snow to a great depth with water, the frost of the succeeding winter penetrates far enough to freeze it, at least to the thickness of one year's fall, or by being repeated, in one or two more years consolidating it more effectually." (Forbes, p. 31.) The new ice thus formed unites with that with which it lies in contact, each new addition taking the place of that which is moving perpetually away.

When we once understand the facts of the formation and perpetual progress of glaciers, the phenomena of *moraines*, or those vast and constantly augmenting accumulations of rocks and earth which they discharge at their borders and terminal extremities, become readily explicable. The agency of frost acting on water that has percolated rocky masses, is known to all who have noticed what takes place in a common quarry when a severe frost has succeeded rain or a thaw; the water frozen in the chinks which it has penetrated, rending the rocky masses asunder just as we see it rending our water-pipes asunder, and on the same principle. This is a process which is perpetually taking place in all those regions of the Alps where glaciers exist. The water from the snow melted by the summer sun penetrates into the fissures of the subjacent cliffs, and when congealed by the frosts of the succeeding winter, rends them asunder with a force that is irresistible. The masses thus separated, varying in size from that of a mere superficial scale to fragments of scores or hundreds of tons in weight, are precipitated from the cliffs in enormous quantity, and strew the valleys through the whole of Switzerland with their ruins. Where the valleys or steeps at the base of these cliffs are occupied by glaciers, the fragments are of course deposited on their surface, and resting there, they are carried along by their slow but unceasing motion, and eventually deposited at their extremity or sides, according to their original position on the mass. Each glacier as it moves along has thus a sort of coating, or rather sprinkling of slaty rubbish and rocky fragments over it, which are more or less thickly sown according to the nature and relative position of the cliffs bounding it. In general these fragments are distributed quite irregularly over the surface of the glacier, and, when seen at a distance, often give it a dark or somewhat dirty look. Along the border of the glacier, however, the fragments, as might be expected, are much more copious, and, being constantly thrown off by the process of melting, by the occasional rising and falling of the ice-stream, and by the simple advance of the portions on which they rest,—assume, necessarily, a continuous linear aggregation. When two or more glaciers, thus edged with *lateral moraines*, unite to form a composite glacier, as is constantly the case in the higher regions,—just as the feeding branches of a river unite to form one greater stream,—the stony lists or borders, still retaining their positions relatively to the original glacier, constitute one or more central moraines having the primary linear aspect; and this aspect is the more strongly marked because *two* of the lateral moraines necessarily go to the formation of one of these *medial moraines*. The number of these medial or central moraines will be, of course, proportioned to the number of glaciers which have united to form the composite one. In the Miage these appear to be two or three; in the Mer de Glace at Chamouni, and on the great glacier of Monte Rosa, the Görnergletcher, they are four or five, as is very well seen in Plate I of the present work.

A very short distance below the extremity of the glacier of the Brenva, the pathway, following the river, takes a sudden turn to the right hand along

19 §

the base of Mont Chétif, and thenceforward leads directly south in the line of the Val d'Aosta, completely at right angles to the direction we had been hitherto advancing along the Allée Blanche. Before making this turn we have a fine view in the direction of our former course, up the Val Ferret, which is the continuation of the Allee Blanche and Val Veni along the south-western base of Mont Blanc. This valley of Ferret slopes towards the south-west, and sends down a large stream to meet the Doira just where it turns round the base of Mont Chétif and enters into the valley of Aosta. Into this valley we had now entered, and after proceeding some distance along the right bank of the river, we crossed it nearly opposite the baths of La Saxe, and then proceeded along its left bank till we reached Cormayeur, which we did about half-past four o'clock. We did not proceed into the village of Cormayeur, but took up our abode at the Hôtel du Mont Blanc, about half a mile above the village.

This hotel, as well as the others in the town, was well nigh in a state of disorganization, the season of the baths being just over and consequently the main requisites of hotels being no longer in demand. On this account, although we had a good apartment and clean beds, our dietetic relations were by no means satisfactory. It was evident that the artistes of the kitchen had departed with the landlord to Aosta. For the first time in our tour, we were supplied with river-water at table; and as the river supplying it was our near neighbour the Doira, the water was, of course, glacier-water from Mont Blanc, and therefore not very drinkable to men made fastidious by the excellence of the spring-water which they had been so long enjoying.

There is something very peculiar in the appearance and character of this water of the torrents which flow from glaciers. When seen in quantity, in a wooden vessel, it looks whitish, exactly like common water containing a minute proportion of milk : hence it is called by Schiller glacier-milk (*Gletscher-milch*).* In decanters as supplied to us at our present dinner, it has a whitish, glittering, luminous, opalescent look which immediately distinguishes it from common water. It is duller than spring-water, yet transparent, and without any discoverable opaque matter mechanically suspended in it. It is perfectly drinkable, and can hardly be said to be disagreeable, but it has a peculiar slight taste which renders it less palatable than good ordinary water : on which account, it is very rarely used in Switzerland, where the purest spring-water is so plentiful. On the present occasion, it was supplied to us, because *the spring* happened to be at a little distance from the hotel, and the ministering damsels of the house were rather indolent. Our remonstrances, however, soon procured for us the genuine beverage.

The cause of this peculiar character of glacier-

* " Den Durst mir stillend mit der Gletscher Milch
 Die in den Runsen schäumend niederquilt."
W. Tell.

water is not demonstratively ascertained.   That as-
signed by Professor Forbes seems most probable,
yet is not perfectly conclusive : he considers the
appearances above described to be owing to the
abrasion of the subjacent rock by the glaciers in
their downward progress, and consequent mechanical
suspension in the water from the melted ice, of some
of the extremely minute particles so abraded.   It is
certain that water derived from the melting of
glaciers *on their surface,* or to a depth short of the
supporting rock, has not this peculiar appearance.
And yet if it is derived from particles of rock in
mechanical suspension merely, these must be of
astonishing minuteness, as they produce hardly any
opacity, but rather a kind of opalescence, and are
not deposited after the water has stood for a long
time in a vessel.   The two strongest arguments in
favour of the theory of mechanical suspension, are
the following :——first, that *springs* issuing from the
face or base of mountains covered with glaciers, and
secondly, that the rivers issuing from lakes fed by
glacier streams, have none of this appearance.   In
the former case the water would appear to be filtered
clear in its passage through the earth ; in the latter
it has, no doubt, deposited its mechanical impregnation by standing.   The sole argument of weight
that I have heard advanced against this theory is one
which, if the facts are accurately stated, would seem
completely to overthrow it : it is this——that the same
character of water is seen in some of the mountain
torrents of Asia Minor, where glaciers do not exist.

After dinner, the evening being beautifully tranquil and mild, I walked into the small town of Cormayeur, which looked almost as deserted as its hotels. It contains a good many large houses huddled close on each other along very narrow and ill-paved streets, having an atmosphere tainted with those olfactory nuisances from the interior of houses, of which we have had such grave reasons for complaining even in the best inns of Switzerland. There are several saline springs, both hot and cold, in the vicinity of Cormayeur, much frequented during the summer by the inhabitants of Piedmont ; and there are several large boarding-houses in addition to the hotels, for the entertainment of the visitors.

As this valley is of considerable width, lies at so elevated a level (about 4000 English feet above the sea), is in itself so beautiful and is surrounded by such attractions for active exercise, I have no doubt but a residence here of a month or two in summer, must be productive of great benefit to persons exhausted by chronic ailments, or merely relaxed by the hot and heavy air of the plains of Piedmont : a benefit altogether independent of the mineral waters which are the ostensible attraction. And, indeed, to travellers who have time to spare and who have no need to consider the sanitary conditions of a locality, there are few places in the Alps which hold out greater attractions for a temporary residence than the vicinity of Cormayeur.

CHAPTER XXIX.

SUNRISE ON MONT BLANC — THE WATER-SHED OF MONT BLANC
— VALLEY OF AOSTA — ITS BEAUTY AND RICHNESS—VIEWS
FROM IT — AOSTA — ROMAN ANTIQUITIES—JOURNEY TO THE
GREAT ST. BERNARD—VALLEY OF THE BUTTIER—ST. REMY
—RECEPTION AT THE HOSPICE—A FREE AND INDEPENDENT
ENGLISHMAN — MILITARY OCCUPATION OF THE HOSPICE IN
1847—POLITICAL FEELING IN PIEDMONT — RECRUITING—RE-
ACTION FROM PARIS — NEW CONSTITUTION — RELIEF FROM
CLERICAL BURTHENS—LIBERTY OF THE PRESS.

September 6.——Having arranged over-night, with
the master of a one-horse char, to take us to the
city of Aosta in the morning (fare fifteen francs)
we got up before daylight, as we had a long day's
journey in prospect. We did not, however, leave
Cormayeur until half-past five. The Hôtel de Mont
Blanc, situated nearly midway between the two
mountains constituting the terminal boundaries of
the Val d'Aosta, commands a magnificent view of
that part of Mont Blanc called the Col de Géant,
through the gap of the valley of Entrêves and over
the summit of Mont Chétif, which, although really a
lofty mountain, seems almost to merit this depreciatory name, from contrast with its gigantic neighbour. We had also here in perfection that glorious
sight, the illumination of the summit of Mont
Blanc by the rising sun, which I had so thoughtlessly and so vainly looked for on the other side at

Sallanches. Not only were the mighty summits now seen bright as midday while the depth of the valley was yet in darkness, but the whole mass of Mont Blanc exposed to us, down to the brow of the vertical cliff constituting its base, put on the same brilliancy, while the summits of the mountains between us and it, particularly of Mont Chétif, were yet untinged with a ray of light : and it was a beautiful sight to see the sharp dark outline of the nearer range relieved against the bright ground beyond. Mont Blanc is so vast and massive in itself, and its south-eastern base of such great length, that it is only when we can thus compare it with other mountains that its unparalleled elevation can be justly appreciated.

In the course of this tour I have already described so many valleys—sweet smiling retreats shut in and sheltered by tremendous barriers of mountain cliff above and by soft wooded hills below, with their furious torrents rushing along through the rich slopes of their green but scanty meadows braided not overshadowed with the magnificent trees of the Alpine orchard, or with the blossoms and fruits of the wild coppice self-sown,—that if I attempted to delineate the features of that through which we were now passing, I should have merely to repeat what I fear I have already repeated too often. And yet it would be doing great injustice to the Val d'Aosta, if it were left unnoticed in a work whose professed object is mainly that of trying to delineate the natural beauties of Switzerland as far as seen by the author. Taken altogether, indeed, the valley of Aosta is certainly one of the finest—if not the finest yet seen by us. It is exceeded in picturesqueness and grandeur by many; but it is exceeded by none, and scarcely equalled by any, either in richness or beauty.

Like every other valley in the Alps that of Aosta is placed exactly where the requirements of the topography seem to indicate its necessary presence. But for it there would be no outlet for the streams that flow from the whole of the south-eastern side of Mont Blanc. The valley of the Allée Blanche with its continuation the Val Veni is, as we have seen, bounded on both sides by mountains of immense height, and at its upper extremity or origin, by the Col de la Seigne; and it slopes progressively downwards, with a considerable declivity until it reaches the Val d'Entrêves. Here it is met by the corresponding slope of the Val Ferret which descends precisely in the same way but in an opposite direction, bounded on both sides by the same range of mountains and terminated at its north-eastern extremity by the Col de Ferret, precisely as the Allée Blanche is terminated at its south-western extremity by the Col de la Seigne. These two valleys—or rather this one valley with two or three names—is full thirty miles in length. Where the two slopes meet at the lowest part of the valley, there is a huge gap in the south-eastern boundary through which the two streams now united make their escape at right angles to their former course. This gap is the commencement of the valley of Aosta, which may be described as the prolongation of the same gap through the mountains to the south and east for a distance of twenty or thirty miles. But for this channel for the escape of the waters that pour in such quantity from the innumerable glaciers that shoot from the south-eastern side of Mont Blanc, it is obvious that the continuous valleys of the Allée Blanche and Val Ferret must constitute a lake, the contents of which could have no outlet until they reached the height of one or other of the Cols at either extremity, or of the range of mountains that constitute its south-eastern boundary: and this they could not do until the mass of water was of the depth of 4000 feet. Whether this valley was ever so shut up and was only emptied of its waters by the formation (gradual or sudden) of the gap now leading into the Val d'Aosta, I pretend not to conjecture: I will only repeat, what I said above, that the existence of this valley is indispensable for the maintenance of the actual topographical relations of the district as to land and water.

The valley of Aosta is, generally speaking, very narrow, but in many places the bounding mountains recede sufficiently far to leave meadows of some extent: it is extremely irregular and winding, a circumstance which adds not a little to the roar and tumult of its river. At the commencement of the valley at the foot of Mont Blanc it still retains something of the roughness of the Allée Blanche and Val Ferret; but when we have descended only a short space it begins to assume a gentler and richer aspect, and this may be said to go on gradually increasing all the way to its eastern extremity. Soon after passing Cormayeur and St. Didier, the small tract of level ground on either side the river, begins to present a continuous succession of orchards of chesnut and walnut trees, which seem here to attain their greatest size and beauty; and as we advance, these become gradually intermixed with vineyards, which continue, in gradually increasing extent and richness, all the way to the city of Aosta. Even in those portions of the valley where it has most of the ravine-like character, and where, consequently, the direct rays of the sun are excluded by the proximity of the mountains for a considerable part of the day, the vineyards are numerous, and the crops excellent; the extreme heat of the sun's rays in the middle portion of the day, in so confined a locality, making full amends for the brevity of their presence.

And if the scenes through which we passed were, in our immediate vicinity and on our own level, rich and beautiful, the prospects we had on either side, and still more in our front and rear, offered for our admiration a spectacle still more attractive. The mountain boundaries on either side presented the general aspect so often described, of a wooded base, partially wooded flanks and fronts, interspersed with bare vertical cliffs here and there, and frequently crowned with the same. Before us, in the far distance, and rather on our right hand, we had for a long time a view of magnificent mountains, some completely covered with snow; and behind us, for the greatest part of our way, we had that magnificent and striking scene which I formerly attempted to describe in general terms, of a deep gap or vista along the tract of a valley, terminated and shut up, as it were, by a snowy mountain at the extremity. Of this peculiar kind of prospect, the present was the finest and grandest yet witnessed by us, inasmuch as the valley constituting the vista was the richest, the hills forming its lateral boundaries were the best wooded, and the terminal mountain was the monarch of mountains—the mighty Mont Blanc itself. So long as the course of the valley allowed us to see Mont Blanc at all, increased distance from it seemed in no way to diminish its altitude, size, or distinctness, to our observation, owing to its enormous vastness in relation to all other visible objects.

A few miles below Cormayeur we passed at a short distance on our right hand the village of St. Didier, situated on the right bank of the Doira, close under the mountains, and much frequented on account of the baths. The water here is of the temperature of 95° Fahrenheit, and is the only thermal spring in the neighbourhood.

In our journey down the valley we crossed the Doira twice, and passed through several villages and small towns, the principal of which are Morgex, Lasalle, L'Ivrogne, Villeneuve, St. Pierre, and Sarra. The towns are close, crowded, and impure, although all are rich in abundant supplies of running water. Great improvements, however, have already taken place, and more are in progress, in the way of new roads, bridges, &c.; and, indeed, it is but justice to the Sardinian government to say, that we had occasion to notice a similar spirit of amelioration in numerous instances since entering its territories.

At Sarra, about four miles from Aosta, what is properly called the valley of Aosta terminates, the tract of country from that point to the city being comparatively open and consisting of a series of vineyards.

We arrived at Aosta at half-past ten, and put up at the Hôtel de la Poste, a large hotel near the market-place. It is a busy bustling establishment, but does not possess any special attractions for the traveller. We remained at Aosta two hours, and saw all that could be inspected in so short a space of time——and, I believe, nearly all that was worth seeing. The town itself which is situated on a gently-sloping plain in the angle between the Doira and the Buttier, is of considerable size, is built entirely of stone, and contains many good houses and one fine square, the Place de Charles Albert. The streets are very narrow and without side pavement, but many of them have the delightful compensation of a stream of clear water running rapidly along them, supplied by the waters of the Buttier. It has a population of between six and seven thousand.

Aosta, as a town, can boast of great antiquity. It was the capital of the Salassi before their conquest and final extirpation by the Romans in the reign of Augustus. It was rebuilt by its new masters, and being peopled by a military colony, took the name of Augusta Prætoria; the word Aosta being evidently a corruption of Augusta. It still retains a few splendid memorials of its origin, and of the high consideration in which it was held by its founders : these, of course, we visited.

At the eastern side of the town a fine old Roman gate still remains, somewhat dilapidated, but sound and strong, and likely to last for centuries. It is of large size and massive architecture. It is double, with an interspace of some extent, and each front has three arches, two small and one large.

Further on, on the same road, just beyond the houses, there is a magnificent triumphal arch crossing the road, and in perfect preservation; retaining all the sharpness of its orignal outline, although it consists of a fine conglomerate or puddingstone, which one would expect to be liable to disintegration. It is stated by some antiquaries that this arch was originally cased with marble : I saw no evidence of this ; and as the gate consists of the same kind of stone and could hardly have been so lined, I am disposed to doubt the truth of the statement in regard to the arch. It appeared to me to be about half the size of the great Arc de l'Etoile at Paris, and of the same elegant proportions. It was, however, sadly disfigured by having a coarse wooden figure of Christ on the cross erected on a transverse beam and half-filling up the upper portion of the arch ; a miserable contrast, as far as relates to Art, between the taste of ancient and modern times.

A little further on, on the same road and beyond the present bridge over the Buttier, there is another fine relic of the Roman era, a bridge of a single arch constructed of massive blocks of stone, and in perfect preservation. This originally stood over the main stream of the Buttier, but this river has now its course three or four hundred feet to the west of it. A small stream, however, still runs under the old arch, apparently an artificial offset from what was once its own stream. The desertion of its old bed by this stream has permitted the houses of the suburb so to encroach on the old structure, that I had to go down into the cellar of a cottage to examine the western abutment of the arch.

The Roman amphitheatre is much less complete, but what still stands of it is solid and strong—consisting of one of the four walls. It is of great height and contains two stories of windows in its upper part. The interior base of the wall constitutes the back of several cottages, and what was its area is now filled with thriving gardens.

I paid a visit to the public hospital in hopes of meeting with some cretin patients, but was disappointed; none such being received into its wards. It is a neat, clean, and well-regulated establishment. I, however, saw some cretins in the town, particularly in the cottages in the suburbs, but not many : and here as elsewhere I was assured that the disease was greatly on the decline.

We set out on our journey to the Great St. Bernard at half-past twelve, in an open carriage, with a pair of horses which was to take us to St. Remy, and for which we paid twenty-five francs. Our route lay by the banks of the Buttier the whole way, along the valley of the same name, which runs nearly parallel to that of Aosta. The valley of the Buttier, however, has little of the exquisite beauty and picturesqueness of its fellow. It has nothing of the ravine character, until we reach its upper extremity, and its comparatively open slopes are all in the highest degree of cultivation. At its lower end these slopes are covered with vineyards, some of the exquisite produce of which we purchased from peasants on the roadside at a price which seemed to us, new men in lands of the vine, absurdly small. Higher up, the vineyards were superseded by cornfields, which spread themselves over every speck of surface which could possibly be cultivated, and indeed up slopes so steep as might have been thought to defy all cultivation. Most of the corn had been carried, but there still were shocks in many of the fields ; and in the more elevated, the corn still remained uncut. This gradual change in the condition of the vegetable products, as we ascended from the plain to the mountain, was a pleasing illustration of the progressive decrease of temperature.

We passed through a good many small towns and villages, and saw others on the opposite side of the valley. At Gignaud, about four miles from Aosta, the Buttier is joined by a large branch descending from the Valpellina, of which and of the mountains beyond we had here a fine but brief view. About five miles beyond this we crossed the river at the small town of Etroubles, and thenceforward kept on its left bank. Further on we stopped at St. Oyen, another small town, where we had to produce our passports. From this to St. Remy the road was extremely steep, but rendered easily practicable by a succession of zig-zags.

We arrived at St. Remy about half-past five. This is a small town containing a considerable number of solid stone houses, built in the very face of a steep slope. At the top of its precipitous street there is a good-sized modern hotel, where we stopped, and beyond which, indeed, no wheeled vehicle could proceed. Here, accordingly, we hired mules, paying three francs for each, and after waiting for them about half an hour, proceeded on our journey. By this time the sun had set to us behind the mountains on our left, and as we proceeded upwards on our zig-zag path overlooked by snowy peaks on either side, we found the air soon become rather cold in the increasing gloom.

All cultivation ceased at St. Remy; there being

nothing beyond but the scanty soil and coarse short turf characteristic of the higher Alpine slopes; and as we approached the end of our journey the path became more rugged and wild, and more closely overlooked by the snowy peaks on either hand. At length we came upon a steep path in the cliff looking down on a small lake in the hollow of the ravine on our right hand, and at the other extremity of this we could see amid the gloom the outlines of the Hospice, like a great barrack, just above us. As we approached it, we saw no light in the windows, heard no sounds of greeting, and met with no one to receive us : everything seemed as still and dead as the cold mountains around us. Uninvited, however, as we were, we ascended the door-steps with confidence, and pulled the bell; and its sound was no sooner heard in the interior, than a servant came to the door and ushered us at once into the refectory.

Being very cold (the temperature was 45°) we were glad to see the attendant immediately set about making a good fire of wood, and while this was being done one of the Brethren made his appearance in his neat clerical habit, and gave us a warm welcome to the Hospice. A hot supper was soon on the table, which we greatly enjoyed after our long journey and cold ride. It consisted of soup, two dishes of hot meat, neatly dressed, bread, cheese, wine, and a salad *grown in the garden of the Hospice*, with dessert. Nothing could exceed the polite kindness of our entertainer, who, though he did not eat with us

20

(having no doubt already dined), sat at table with us the whole time, and carved. This gentleman, M. de la Soit, had resided ten years in the Hospice; and here he had taught himself English, though the ordinary language of the Hospice is French.

There were no other guests at table but ourselves, as there had been no recent arrivals; but just as we had finished supper an English gentleman and his wife arrived, the latter half-spent with fatigue and cold, having *walked* the whole day up the valley of the Dranse from Orsières. The husband seemed averse to effeminacy and luxury, even on the part of his fair partner, as he himself carried the whole travelling stores of the family, in the shape of a small knapsack; and they appeared to have sought no assistance in their travels either from guides or mules. They were on their way to Turin. The husband seemed a genuine specimen of a " free and independent Englishman," and we all thought that his present course of proceeding was likely soon to make him independent of his better half, by walking her into the other world.

Our very intelligent and hospitable entertainer, M. de la Soit, favoured us with his company the whole evening, as well as in the morning, and contributed not a little, by his pleasing conversation and simple yet polished manners, to make our residence as agreeable as possible. Here, as elsewhere in Switzerland, the political condition of the neighbouring states had greatly lessened the number of visitors during the present year : still there were great numbers claiming hospitality daily. During the past year they had received at the Hospice not fewer than 19,000 persons. Of this number about 1800 were travellers of the better class, the remainder being either poor persons making a sort of pilgrimage to the Hospice, or crossing the Pass on business ; almost all of them receiving assistance without contributing to the funds. This vast disproportion between contributors and non-contributors shows the necessity of the former being liberal in their gratuities.

The previous year was an unfortunate year for the monks of St. Bernard, as the Sunderbund war invaded even their peaceful abode, and made these innocent apostles of benevolence and Christian charity suffer with the rest of the world. The notion had got abroad that the monks were extremely rich ; it being even reported that they had in their stronghold a mass of coined gold measuring a square fathom ! With the view of obtaining some part of this vast treasure in aid of their war-fund, the government of the Vallais took military possession of the Hospice. The brethren having warning of the attack, got all their more valuable furniture and plate conveyed out of the canton to Aosta——not money, for of this they had none——so that when the soldiers took possession of the Hospice, they found neither money nor money's worth, except the monks' stores of wine and provisions, of which they made free use.

They confined the brothers to their rooms for ten days, and then fairly turned them out of doors. They retired to Martigny, where they have another establishment, and after a short time were allowed to return to their Hospice without further moles- tation,—chiefly, as they believe, through the inter- vention of the British government.

We retired to bed early. The bedrooms are on the upper story, and open on either side of a long gallery traversing the house lengthwise. The rooms are very plainly furnished, but sufficiently comfort- able; and the beds are good. Even at this season the whole house felt chilly, except the room having a fire: and no wonder; considering that the Hospice is situated upwards of 8000 feet above the sea-level. At five o'clock next morning my thermometer in the bedroom stood at 50°, and in the open air at 40°. It is hardly necessary to say how terrible is the winter here. It lasts at least eight months, during which period the thermometer is frequently below zero. A minute account of the weather, and of the meteorological phenomena generally, is kept at the Hospice, which is regularly published in the 'Bib- liothèque de Genève.' It is understood that this Hospice is the highest inhabited spot in Europe.

During our last few days' journeying in the territories of his Sardinian Majesty, all the attrac- tions of external nature could not hinder our being interested by the opinions and feelings of the people. Everywhere we found the public mind agitated, as was natural, with the actual state of the country, and its political and social prospects. Everywhere there was a warm feeling for the independence of the kingdom, and a willingness to make sacrifices for this, prevalent; but the actual war, deemed one of aggression on the part of the king, not of self-defence, was most unpopular. The late disasters in Lombardy had disheartened the people generally; and the universal and most extensive recruiting, the consequence of these, brought the evils of war home to the hearth of every man. The extent of this recruiting may be judged by the fact that in the small commune of Cormayeur, containing only 1800 inhabitants, no fewer than one hundred men, between the ages of twenty-one and thirty-six, had recently been drawn by the conscription, and had already joined the army. As far as I could learn, not one of these men left their homes with good will: and no wonder: independently of the inherent evils of military service, the Sardinian soldier's pay is so absurdly small that it may be said to be next to nothing—not more than one-and-half sous per day!

Amid all its harsh inflictions, it was a comfort to know that the conscription was not altogether blind in its decimations: such men as could prove themselves the main stay of their respective families, even though of the fatal age, were exempted from service. Our driver from Cormayeur to Aosta, for instance, was in this happy predicament, from being the only son of his mother and the brother of several sisters.

It was curious to find in this small commune of Cormayeur——this out-of-the-way place at the foot of the distant Mont Blanc——how the recent revolution in France had made itself felt : a striking proof not merely of the " delirant reges plectuntur Achivi," but also of the universal sympathy of interests, so to speak, existing among the nations of modern times.   Not fewer than sixty-five individuals of Cormayeur were in good employment in Paris at the time of the breaking-out of the insurrection, chiefly as manufacturers of colours in the establishment of one of their countrymen grown rich there. Of these not fewer than thirty-two, dismissed for want of work, had actually returned to the commune, and of those who remained at Paris, the majority were glad to accept half the usual amount of wages.

The new constitution of Piedmont or Sardinia, promulgated by Charles Albert, was the theme of all, and immensely prized.   Whether granted willingly or no, whether intended to be permanent or not——and all seem to have strong doubts on these points——the general feeling was, that once granted it should be kept.   To preserve this, their Magna Charta, neither revolution nor war would be shrunk from——and all I spoke with seemed to be prepared to guarantee their new rights at all hazards.

The two great practical boons the common people seemed best to understand and most to prize were, the relief from clerical oppression and taxation, and the liberty of the press.   If I may trust to the fidelity and accuracy of my informants——and I obtained like statements from various quarters——it was indeed high time that the rule of the priests should receive a check in Piedmont; as it seems to have gone beyond all bounds of decency and moderation. The clerical fees seem to have been truly enormous, when the poverty of the people and the high value of money in that country are considered. I was assured that under the old regime, no less a sum than sixty francs had to be paid on the occurrence of a death in any family possessing the means to pay it, and this over and above the ordinary expenses for the coffin, &c. Out of the sixty francs some portion, as from five to eight francs, might go to cover a positive or ostensible outlay by the church, as for candles, mortcloth, &c., but all the rest went into the pocket of the priest of the commune. Sums proportionally great were paid for other offices of the church, as five francs for christening and twenty for marriage. These fines, to be sure, were the main source of the incomes of the clergy; but whether the resulting sums-total to the individual priests were little or much, it is self-evident that they were an intolerable burthen to the people. By the new constitution, the priests are to be paid directly by the state, out of the general taxes; and it is not doubted that their incomes will be much less than before.

The general ecclesiastical rule, also, seemed to be of like arbitrary severity. Indeed, until the recent change, the priests appear to have here preserved all the power and authority of the old times. One of my informants, at Cormayeur, an apparently mild and moderate man, and with all the signs of an honest man in his behaviour, assured me that one instance occurred within his own knowledge, where a man underwent nine months' imprisonment, by the award of the bishop on the representation of the parish priest, for the sole crime of contumacy in refusing to attend confession.

But all this abuse of power, and indeed almost all power whatever, of the clergy, is now at an end; and there is too much reason to fear that, for a time at least, religion itself will suffer in the correction of the misdoings of its ministers : it is certain that some of the dogmas and practices of the Roman Catholic church will from henceforth lose their influence and respect.   I myself had sufficient proof of this.   Many of the men of the lower ranks spoke with ridicule of confession, and still more of the power of the priest to forgive sins ; the women, however, were still unshaken in their faith.   Every one with whom I conversed seemed to be of opinion that the priests to a man desire the permanence of the old tyranny in the state as well as church, and, with this view, do all they can to prevent the instruction of the people. The Scriptures in their complete state are not forbidden in Piedmont, but they are not readily procurable, partly from their high price, and partly from want of facility of purchase : abridgments alone are in common use.

Since the promulgation of the constitution establishing liberty of the press, newspapers have become quite fashionable, and in Aosta they are eagerly devoured even by the common people. They had not, however, yet extended far into the country. For instance, neither before the constitution nor since, did any newspaper reach the commune of Cormayeur, at least any that was accessible to the working-classes : but here and elsewhere every one seemed to be aware of the nature and vast importance of a free press. Averse as every one seemed to war, there was only one sentiment on this head in relation to the constitution : they would fight for *it* and for Piedmont, but not for foreign objects.*

* *March,* 1849. The utter discomfiture of the Sardinian army, and the termination of the war by a single battle, of which accounts are just received, will surprise no one who had an opportunity of knowing the feelings of the people respecting Charles Albert and his wars.

CHAPTER XXX.

September 7.——We were roused from a sound
sleep between five and six, by the great organ of
the chapel of the Hospice vibrating through the
whole house. After dressing I descended to the
chapel where I found the whole brotherhood in their
stalls, with the exception of our host of the evening,
M. de la Soit, who was chanting the service. The
only auditors beside the brethren, were three gentlemen, travellers like myself, and about a dozen
visitors of the poorer class. There was something
wonderfully impressive in this scene, as well from its
physical concomitants as its moral associations : the
early hour,——the locality of the holy place on this
bleak and solitary Pass, amid the clouds and snows,
so far beyond the habitations of man,——the scanty
auditory,——the fine and tender voice of the priest
pouring out the holy words with a sort of rapturous

enthusiasm,—and, over all, the mighty organ making the whole fabric thrill with its louder strains. It was as impossible not to believe that the homage so expressively proffered could only come from the heart, as it was impossible not to sympathise with the mental mood in which it originated. The whole process, however artificial, seemed natural and spontaneous; an outpouring of the feelings from some irresistible impulse of the heart, like the matin song of birds in the wilderness.

The chapel is of considerable size and is very neatly fitted up. Beside the usual altar ornaments it contains several large pictures, relating to the founder St. Bernard; and the well-known marble monument of Desaix placed there by Napoleon. This monument is very large, occupying a dispro-portioned space on one of the walls. In the chapel there is a small box inscribed "Aux Aumones," for the reception of the gratuitous offerings of the guests of the Hospice. Up-stairs, not only is no money asked for or looked for, but the whole proceedings and manner both of the monks and servants seem regulated so as if to exclude the idea of the enter-tainment being a purchasable commodity. It is to be hoped, however, that no visitor who has the means will fail to deposit in the alms-box considerably more than he would have paid at the best hotel. He must consider that the funds of the establish-ment are almost entirely dependent on such offerings, and that of the numerous visitors relieved at the

Hospice, the proportion who can and do pay anything, is very small.

In the hall near the door of the refectory there is a large tablet of white marble, let into the wall, dedicated to Napoleon by the government of the Vallais in gratitude for his services to the canton, of which he is declared the regenerator. It is a simple slab of stone without any ornament, but contains a most laudatory inscription in Latin.*

It would be to repeat a tale a hundred-times told, to say aught of the exertions made by the monks of the Hospice, through the instrumentality of their servants, biped and quadruped, to save and assist travellers amid the dangers of the Pass in winter. But it is to be hoped that no one will forget this in his visit to the chapel. A more conclusive and striking evidence of the necessity of such charitable vigilance and hardy efforts, cannot well be supplied than by the two *morgues* or dead-houses in the vicinity of the Hospice, in which are deposited the shrivelled remains and bare bones of those whom neither vigilance nor courage could save from a premature death. It is a remarkable event, if a whole winter passes without some travellers being rescued; and also without some perishing whom no efforts could rescue.

* Having doubts both as to the precise meaning and lingual purity of the compound epithet *bis Italicus*, here applied to Napoleon, I subjoin the passage in which it occurs, for the judgment of the learned: "NAPOLEONI . . . . ÆGYPTIACO BIS ITALICO SEMPER INVICTO . . . . GRATA RESPUBLICA."

As important instruments in the search for and relief of these unhappy persons, the noble dogs of the Hospice, of course, attract the affectionate notice of all visitors. No one can look on their fine bearing and good-tempered countenance, without feeling the heart yearn towards them as benefactors of his race; and I think I can hardly pay a higher compliment to their masters than by saying that they resemble their quadruped friends in the utter absence of all seeming self-consciousness of the great and good deeds to the performance of which their best years are devoted, and their health and life too often sacrificed. That surest of charms in man or beast——the

"Unconscious fascination undesigned"

which characterises the human animal in the earlier periods of life at least, and the honest and faithful dog through the whole of his, is nowhere more prominent than on this "iced mountain's top"——where simplicity and charity and benevolence have made their home.

We set out on our route to Martigny at nine o'clock, all on foot, having sent on our knapsacks by a man whom we met with in the Hospice, and who promised to provide us with a char at some of the small towns in our way down the valley of Entremont. It was a lovely morning, with a bright sun and a cloudless sky; but at the Hospice the air was still so cold that one was glad to get to the lee-side of the house, while lounging about the doors with the dogs.   So soon, however, as we were fairly in action, and had descended below the summit of the Pass, we had no more reason to complain of chill, but were glad to part with. some of our clothing, now found oppressive in the hot sunshine.

Immediately below the Hospice, the valley of Entremont begins to form, and at its very commencement has already its stream, one of the branches of the Dranse, whose very source we passed, a huge patch of snow still remaining unmelted, at a very little distance from the convent.   At about the same short distance from it on the opposite side of the Pass, the Buttier, whose upward course we had traced yesterday, takes its origin ; the distance between their sources being hardly half a mile——or, to speak more correctly, the distance between their visible waters——for the same snows are the source of both. Their courses, however, are exactly the reverse of each other ; the one flowing to the south-east, and eventually into the Po ; the other to the north-west, into the Rhone.

A couple of miles below the Col, when the valley had assumed some width and spread out its green slopes on either side, we passed by a splendid herd of cows at feed, about seventy in number, which we were told belonged to the monks.   And a mile or so lower down, we passed through another of about the same size, which belonged to different individuals resident much further down the valley.   This last Alp was close to the hamlet of Cantine, consist-

ing of little more than the small inn and a few
neighbouring huts. Just above this hamlet, to the
east, but beyond the immediate boundaries of the
valley, Mount Velan rises to the height of very nearly
11,000 feet English; and only a few miles further to
the north-east, is the great Combin, upwards of
14,000 feet high : streams from the glaciers of both
these mountains cross our path as we descend, and
one of considerable size at St. Pierre. At the inn
at Cantine I saw several children who had been
sent from the lower valleys for change of air, with
the view of averting cretinism; and they could hardly
have a more promising locality than the fine open
Alps adjoining. At this village the carriage-road
commences, and here we overtook our porter or
guide, who proved to be an inhabitant of Liddes, a
town lower down the valley, and was now on his
return from the fair of Aosta, with a young mule
and some other purchases. He had left his horse
at this place on his way to the fair, and now proposed to convey us in his car to Liddes. As the
tract of country could be as well seen from a carriage
as on foot, I accepted the conveyance, but my companions preferred walking. They accordingly set
out at once, and although they had a very short
advance of us in point of time, they reached Liddes
before us.

The valley retains the narrow ravine-like character
for some miles below Cantine, and the road though
quite practicable for a narrow carriage, is extremely

precipitous in many places, and at others occupying
the very ledge of the cliff.   Both the valley and the
road, however, improve as we advance; and before
we reach the small town of St. Pierre, the former
has lost all its mountain wildness and roughness.
From hence, indeed, until it may be said to
terminate at St. Branchier, where it is joined by
the eastern Dranse from the Val de Bagnes; and
thenceforward all the way to within two miles of
Martigny; the valley of the Dranse may compare,
both in beauty and richness, with most of its Alpine
brethren.   All the way to St. Branchier, the ridges
of the bounding mountains on either side, are either
bare cliffs or are covered with fir trees to the
very top; while the whole of their base, which is
for the most part beautifully indented with rounded
slopes, is cultivated in the completest manner,
wherever soil can rest or corn can grow.   Over a
great extent of the valley, the mountains retire to
some distance from the river, leaving intermediate
haughs and small rounded hills, sometimes cultivated,
but oftener left in the natural condition of pasture
land or forest.   And such was the winding of the
valley in many places, particularly between Orsières
and St. Branchier, that, mile after mile, we seemed
to be shut up in some fairy hollow surrounded on
all sides by mountains, seeming at first sight impassable, but out of which we speedily escaped by
following the course of the river——but escaped only
to enter another, and make a like exit.

The little town of St. Pierre is the cantonal impost-station between the Vallais and Piedmont, and here I was detained a considerable time while my charioteer was settling the payment of the impost-tax on his mule and his oil, respecting the amount of which there was great difference of opinion and much angry wrangling. At Liddes it was our intention to take a char to Martigny, but as none could be got having springs, the proposed conveyance was changed for that of a mule, to be ridden by one of our party whose lameness was not yet quite removed; my other companion, who had already walked all the way from St. Bernard, preferred proceeding onwards on foot to Martigny; and I did the same. We left Liddes at half-past twelve and reached Martigny at half-past five. The walk was a very pleasant one, the road being excellent and all down-hill, the weather delightful, and the whole tract of country traversed, only a change of one kind of beauty for another. We halted neither at Orsières, where the large branch of the Dranse descending from the Col and Val de Ferret joins with that we had been tracing; nor at St. Branchier, where the still larger arm from the Val de Bagnes unites with both. All these together constitute a fine river, which from hence to Martigny, where it joins the Rhone, finds its way in nearly a direct course, and with all the force and fury of a true Alpine torrent: the road keeps close to it all the way from Orsières, and between this town and Martigny crosses it no less than six times.

Below St. Branchier, contrary to the more usual relations in descending rivers, the valley becomes narrower and more ravine-like, but with its bounding mountains more richly wooded. In one spot on the right bank, nearly midway between St. Branchier and Martigny, the cliff approaches the river so closely that it has been found necessary to cut a gallery through the rock for the roadway. It is very like that at the entrance of the Via Mala, and is nearly as extensive. As we advance towards Martigny, the beautiful and rich adornments of all the lower Swiss valleys, the stately walnut and chesnut trees, make their appearance in great abundance, as does also the vine on all the sunnier slopes.

All the way from St. Branchier, though our constant and close companion the Dranse retained uninterruptedly its precipitous and furious course, and though on some of the flatter shores it had left evidence of ravage here and there in a short stony beach, I cannot say that we could detect any very decisive indications of the fearful ravages of which it was the theatre in the year 1818, when it was suddenly inundated by the *débâcle* from the Val de Bagnes. In many places, no doubt, we saw projecting from its waters, or flanking them on either side, great square blocks of rock which looked somewhat foreign to the locality, but not, I think, to an extent which would have attracted attention from a traveller not on the outlook for such things. Compared with many other Alpine torrents which we had seen, and particularly the Aar in Oberhasli and the Visp, the whole bed of the Dranse might be said to be free and unobstructed. And nowhere above the banks could we trace any marks of the ravage either on the soil or on its vegetable productions. On the contrary, the whole valley on either side the stream was luxuriantly rich in all these : so beneficently, so admirably had the hand of Nature, in her own delightful way, healed all the wounds inflicted, and restored all the beauties lost, thirty years before.

As this inundation of the valley of the Dranse is so peculiarly an Alpine incident, and bears so striking an analogy, in its sublime magnitude and destructive horrors, to some other events already noticed in these pages—e. g., the falls of mountains and of avalanches—I should have been glad, had it been consistent with the nature of this work, to give a full account of it here as a sort of fellow or *pendant* to the Fall of the Rossberg and the Avalanche of Randa : I must, however, content myself with giving in the APPENDIX such brief notice of it as my limits will allow. Whoever desires a fuller account will find it in the original report of Escher Von der Linth, in the ' Bibliothèque Univ. de Genève,' tome viii, p. 291, from which I translate the chief particulars in an abridged form. M. Escher's report is dated from Berne, in the month of August in the same year (1818) in which the catastrophe occurred.

On reaching Martigny we put up at the splendid hotel called the Grande Maison, or Hôtel de la Poste, which proved an excellent house of accommodation.

September 8.——As to-day's proposed journey to Chamouni——either by the Col de Balme or the Tête Noire, as we might determine on our route——was comparatively short, we took our ease at our inn till eight o'clock, when we set off, I riding the mule, my companions walking. The morning was, as usual, very fine, and our lower level indicated by a much higher temperature, the thermometer being 57° at seven o'clock. Retracing our path of yesterday for about a couple of miles up the valley of the Dranse, we turned to the right at the Bourg de Martigny, and began immediately to climb the steep ascent to the Col de Trient. Our mule-path was everywhere richly shaded with fine trees——at first with the walnut and chesnut, and afterwards with forest trees,——and afforded from many points splendid views of the valley of the Rhone now left far behind and below us. From the highest point, about 5000 English feet above the sea, there was a rapid descent, but by a good path, to the deep valley of the Trient. As the day was very clear we decided on giving the preference to the route over the Col de Balme, as presenting finer views than that by the Tête Noire, and, accordingly, crossed the Trient a considerable way above the village of the same name, and not far below the glacier whence the torrent takes its rise. This is the stream which it will be remembered we saw issuing from a chasm in the rocky barrier on the left bank of the Rhone in our way from Martigny to St. Maurice. Immediately on passing the river we entered upon an extremely steep ascent on the other side, leading in zig-zags through a forest of pines which extends a long way up the mountain. This difficult passage was succeeded by a rugged and sterile tract, still steep but considerably less so, until we reached the summit of the Col de Balme, which we did at twelve o'clock.

The view of Mont Blanc from this point with its hundred peaks or needles (Aiguilles) as they are called, is in the highest degree magnificent and impressive; much finer, in my opinion, than that from the Col de la Seigne. In both cases, the great chain of Mont Blanc holds the same relation to the spectator, showing itself laterally on the left hand, as it rises precipitously from the valley which skirts its base, and along which the eye is carried in a direct line to an immense distance. On this side of Mont Blanc the peaks are much more numerous than on the other side, and the great central mass of the mountain is seen at a larger angle and consequently more fully than from the Col de la Seigne. Things are, however, reversed when we descend into the valleys, and track the respective lines of the mountains at their base; the nearer views being vastly grander and more picturesque in the Allée Blanche than in the Vale of Chamouni; while the glaciers in the latter, magnificent as they are, cannot be compared either in magnitude or beauty with those in the former. The general resemblance, however, of these two aspects of Mont Blanc and its valleys,

on its south-eastern and north-western flanks, is
very great; and it is curious that, in both cases, not
merely are there two Cols or Passes giving similar
lateral views and having the same precise relation
to the mountain, but also two valleys running at
right angles to the line of this, which give a direct
front view on either side——viz. the valley of the
Doira or Val d'Aosta, and the valley of the Arve——
(from Sallanches eastwards.) It will be seen from
the preceding pages, how grand and striking is the
view of the great summit of Mont Blanc along the
vista of either of these valleys.

In the very centre of the Pass or Col de Balme
there is a small inn, termed the Pavilion, where rest
and refreshment and even beds can be obtained;
and here we made our noontide halt. While my
companions were resting from the fatigue of their
severe walk, I ascended a steep green isolated hill
situated immediately to the north of the Pass between
it and the path by the Tête Noire. I do not know
the precise height of this hill above the Col; but
this may be judged of from its taking me twenty
minutes of very quick walking to reach its top. The
view of Mont Blanc, and all his court and kindred,
is considerably finer from this spot than from the
Col, and an entirely new and very splendid view is
obtained of the great snowy peaks of the Oberland
along the vista of the Rhone to the north-east.
The master of the Pavilion assured me that among
the mountains seen by me were the Jungfrau and

Finsteraarhorn; but a more experienced guide at Chamouni told me that the latter, at least, could not be seen from the point mentioned. The snowy peaks, however, were evidently of the first order of Alps, and, though distinctly seen in the clear light of this cloudless day, were manifestly at an immense distance. The distance of the Finsteraarhorn by Keller's map is full seventy miles from the Col de Balme. At any rate there can be no question of the superiority of the views over those from the Col; and as the ascent of the hill is easy, though somewhat steep, it is strongly recommended to all travellers crossing the Col de Balme, on a fine day, not·to omit ascending this specular mount.

After staying more than an hour on the Col de Balme, enjoying the endless variety of the sublime views presented by Mont Blanc, we descended into the vale of Chamouni. For some time the descent was steep and the path rugged, but shortly this became somewhat more level, and gradually softened until it ended in the cultivable and cultivated slopes of Le Tour and Argentière. In our descent we had a fine view of the glaciers which descend from the rocky gulfs dividing the Aiguilles of Mont Blanc—Le Tour, Argentière, the Mer de Glace, and, finest of all, the Bosson, gleaming in the sun far in our front. We passed close to the two first named in our descent, and from the magnificent Argentière we saw the principal source of the Arve rushing from its green vault, already a full-grown river.

This stream has its primary source much higher up in springs in the slope of the Col de Balme ; but its grand feeders are these two glaciers and the Mer de Glace——source of the Arveiron——a little below. This last glacier, as seen from the valley, is very inferior, both in size and beauty, to its neighbours.

We arrived at the village of Chamouni at half-past three, and took up our abode at the Hôtel de Londres et d'Angleterre, a splendid establishment kept by two brothers of the name of Tairraz.

Before arriving at Chamouni we had resolved, under the pressure of our fast-expiring Holiday, to spend only the remainder of this day here, and to start next morning in the Diligence for Geneva ; and this resolution seemed to have a deadening influence on our exertions, as, after arriving at the village, we contented ourselves with strolling about its little streets, looking at the collections of minerals in the shops, and gazing on the snowy summits rising sheer up from the valley at our feet. Having already seen Mont Blanc under so many aspects and from so many points——from Sallanches, from the valley of Nant Bourant and the Col de Bonhomme, from the Col de la Seigne and the Allée Blanche, from the Val d'Aosta, from the Col de Balme, and now from the depths of the vale of Chamouni, we thought we might, without much imputation on either our spirit of enterprise or our taste, leave the usual *sights* of Chamouni unvisited ——the Flegère, the Breven, and the Mer de Glace.

Accordingly, before dinner, we took our places in the Diligence which was to start for Geneva at seven next morning. Had we been so disposed, we had sufficient time after our arrival at Chamouni to pay a visit to the Glacier de Bosson, or even the Mer de Glace; but, as already said, we did not leave the village. We joined the table-d'hôte at the hotel, and partook of an excellent dinner in company with thirteen other persons—all English.

September 9.——The determination to which we had come of leaving Chamouni without further inspection of the wonders of Mont Blanc, weighed on my traveller-conscience as a deadly sin, and if it did not deprive me of a night's rest, it certainly disturbed my morning tranquillity. Had the day been rainy or even cloudy, I believe I should have quietly smothered my regrets and departed with the rest; but when I saw Mont Blanc displayed in all its glory before us, even to its highest peak, the whole blue heavens without a cloud, and the bright warm sunshine already flooding all the valley—I felt the attraction irresistible; and accordingly making up my mind during breakfast, and summoning a guide in haste, I started at seven to climb the Breven, at the very time my companions were starting for Geneva.

Being resolved to make the most of my day by visiting the Mer de Glace after my return, I did my best to climb the mountain with what vigour I could exert. There are two routes to the summit of the Breven, or, at least, to the base of the

21

vertical rock which constitutes the upper third of its mass——one very circuitous but practicable for mules, the other direct and only accessible on foot.   I chose the latter, which ascends in almost a straight line from the village of Chamouni.   This ascent, in point of steepness, exceeded all we had yet tried, except the Gemmi. For the first half of the journey the route——it cannot be called a path——winds in the usual zigzag manner along the rough grassy and slaty slope ; but the remaining third is a continuous scramble over and up huge fragments of slate fallen from the cliffs above, or up the fissures of the naked cliff itself, from which they have fallen.   In one spot termed the Chimney (Cheminée), the path, if such it may be called, is literally a fissure in the almost vertical cliff, and can only be mastered by resigning the Alpenstock to the guide, and scrambling on all-fours, and occasionally raising yourself by the aid of the guide's hand or staff extended from above. On surmounting the Cheminée——so called, I suppose, from the mode of ascent in it being analogous to that of the chimney-sweeper——the route, though still steep and over a wilderness of rugged rock without semblance of a path, and uncheered by a single blade of grass, is comparatively easy to the summit : this I reached a little before eleven, having made the ascent in ten minutes under four hours. The highest point of the Breven is somewhat more than 8300 English feet above the sea, or about 4700 above the village of Chamouni.

The toil of climbing the mountain was enhanced by the great heat, the sun setting directly on it, and by the absence of springs of water on the route to relieve thirst. The only spring which the guide calculated on, was found dry, and the journey was much more than half accomplished before we could have even the substitute of snow-water. A short way below the Chimney, however, we at length reached a huge patch of snow, and never did I enjoy a draught more than that which I collected from its scanty meltings; warm as I was, and in the highest degree, yet without the slightest feeling of exhaustion, I hesitated not to take a moderate supply, although the temperature of the water was only a degree below the freezing point. Beyond the summit of the cliff, on the northern side, there was a much more considerable mass of snow, feeding a small tarn amid the rocks; and here I again satisfied the longings of the system by repeated but moderate draughts taken slowly.

After all, it turned out that the labour of ascending the Breven might have been saved, as far as seeing Mont Blanc was concerned; as the summit which shone to us so clear from Chamouni, had become involved in a thick cloud of mist before we reached it. This mist was so dense that though Mont Blanc was only separated from us by the narrow valley of Chamouni, we could not see the smallest portion of it, either in front or on either side. The view to the north, however, and to the north-west along the

valley of the Arve, was clear.   After waiting half
an hour on the summit, and the guide assuring me
that the clearing away of the mist was an event
which could not be predicated with any degree of
certainty or even probability, I resolved to descend, in
order that I might have time to visit the Mer de Glace.

We descended by the same path as far as the
base of the cliff, and then took the circuitous mule-
track over the fine Alp of Planpra.   The descent of
the Chimney was found fully as difficult as the ascent,
and was not accomplished without many slippings
and slidings along surfaces not quite so soft or
smooth as Greenwich hill.   And yet the guide told
me that he had more than once attended ladies both
in the ascent and descent of this really perilous
passage.   More generally, however, not only ladies
but gentlemen, instead of mounting to the summit
of the Breven by this track, follow a circuitous route
round the base of the vertical cliff to the north side.

Had we remained only one half-hour longer on
the summit of the Breven, I should have perfectly
attained the object of my visit thither; as before we
had got half-way down to the pasturages, indeed
while not yet far below the Chimney, the mass of
mist suddenly was swept away from both Mont
Blanc and the Breven.   From the same spot we
had seen it in ascending, and a most magnificent
view it was, considerably more extensive than that
from the Flegère, which we saw lying far beneath
us to the left.   This view is considerably different

from that from the Col de Balme, and is on the whole finer; the display of pinnacles or aiguilles being much ampler, and the broad summit of Mont Blanc itself more manifestly the crowning glory of the whole. Plate IV shows the view from this point, and, small as it is, gives a much better idea of the whole scene than any verbal description, however graphic or minute, could possibly do.

After leaving the rocky descent, the route by the mule-track was comparatively easy, being for a considerable space over a moderate slope of Alpine pasture land, and then through a pine forest clothing a steeper declivity. Amid the pasture-ground we stopped half an hour in a herdsman's chalet or Sennhütte, still containing all the summer's store of cheese and butter, and made an excellent luncheon on sundry varieties of his produce. The master of the chalet and the flock was there—a tall strong man, with a young girl his daughter, and some boys his sons. He was, I found, " A NOBLE," according to the style of the common people in Piedmont, that is, a state pensioner on account of being the father of twelve living children.

I reached Chamouni a little after two, having accomplished the journey to the summit of the Breven and back, with an hour's rest inclusive, in little more than seven hours.

We were overtaken by a heavy shower in the latter part of our descent which wet us thoroughly, and there was a repetition of the same in a still

severer degree after I reached the hotel.   This
detained me a good while after I was ready to set
out for the Mer de Glace.   On this expedition I
rode a mule but was accompanied by the same
guide.   There is a very good mule-path all the way;
that portion of it up the mountain's breast being
through a forest of pine, and generally very steep
but very practicable.   We reached the Pavilion of
the Montanvert at half-past four, and having put up
the mule, immediately proceeded to the Mer de
Glace.   This glacier spreads out widely just below
the house in all its rugged grandeur; it is bounded
on every side by vertical walls of cliff, all splin-
tered at top, far up in the sky, into hundreds of
pointed pinnacles, well called needles.

After crossing a huge lateral moraine containing
many blocks of enormous size, we got upon the
glacier and walked a short distance upon it to see
its character.   It is very similar to the Grindelwald
glacier formerly described : with its huge hummocks,
and twisting ridges between the crevices; its deep
sea-green pools; its continuous heaps of rubbish and
rock constituting its unshed moraines—shapeless
and disfiguring close at hand, but when viewed from
a distance constituting a beautiful series of parallel
bands in the line of motion.

Standing on this mere shore of the icy sea, and
tracing with the eye its course upwards to bays still
more desolate, amid rocks and peaks yet grander,
it was impossible not to feel a strong desire to pene-

trate further amid the fascinating horrors concealed beyond; and I regretted much that my engagements did not allow me one day more, that I might at least make the excursion to the JARDIN, which, though far in the recesses of this dreary wilderness, is very commonly visited, being perfectly accessible, though not without fatigue. On the glacier the guide pointed out one great block of stone, which was of a marked character both as to shape and size, and was therefore recognised as a measurer of the progress of the icy stream on which it had so long rested. He said it had moved some hundred feet within his own knowledge; and at the side of the glacier he did not fail to point out the *Englishman's Stone,* celebrated as forming the only shelter afforded in this locality, when the glacier was visited in 1741 by Dr. Pocock and Mr. Wyndham, whose names are seen painted in fresh letters on it.

On returning from my visit to the Mer de Glace, I spent a short time in the Pavilion examining the collection of agates, rock-crystal, and other so-called products of Mont Blanc, and from which most travellers select something as a memorial of the Mer de Glace: I then set out on my return to Chamouni, as the twilight was making progress. Being rather chilly I preferred walking, and did not mount the mule until we had reached the chalet of Planatz almost at the bottom of the descent. I reached the Hôtel de Londres just in time to share in the late table-d'hôte, making an excellent dinner not unmerited by a good day's work.

CHAPTER XXXI.

September 10.——Having gone to bed betimes I was up early; and as the Diligence in which I had over-night taken my place for Geneva, did not profess to start till seven, and did not, in fact, start till near eight, I had time to enter in my note-book a few particulars respecting some things in the economy of the people of the Vallais and Piedmont, which had formed subjects of inquiry during the last few days. These notes I shall now transcribe, regardless of their connexion with each other or with the immediate business of the day.

1. I had heard so much of the inferior industrial habits of the Vallaisians, that I was agreeably surprised, in descending the valleys of the Dranse, to see such marked proofs of great industry and neatness; and I was fully satisfied by the information

communicated to me from various quarters, and especially by the intelligent guide who accompanied me for two days—from St. Bernard to Chamouni—that the inhabitants of that part of the canton, at least, are not in any respect inferior to their brethren in other parts of Switzerland. My guide, who was himself a man of some substance, having both cows and horses, and a very fair house in the town of Liddes, confirmed the impression already received in other parts of the country, that the rural population of Switzerland are, on the whole, in a much more satisfactory state, both as to their physical condition and mental comfort, than the great body of the agricultural population in England. If they fare rudely they have no actual deficiency of food; and they are not distressed by those terrible contrasts of superfluity and positive want, which form so unhappy a feature in the economy of our own country. There being no public provision for the poor, their relief is left to the natural workings of humanity,—which are never found to fail. No instance of positive want of food, much less of actual loss of life from such cause, was ever heard of in these valleys.

Education, also, is general, up to a certain moderate amount; and is, like the relief of the indigent and sick, left entirely to the spontaneous movements of society. I was assured that there are very few individuals who cannot both read and write. The education is almost restricted to the winter season, when the out-of-door operations are nearly all sus-

21 §

pended; as was the case in the agricultural districts
of the north of Scotland fifty years since,——and may
probably be the case still.   The teachers are persons
of their own humble class who happen to have
acquired a little more knowledge than the mass.
As may be believed, the fees paid to such instructors
are of the humblest kind.   In the summer season,
both teachers and pupils forsake books and benches
and betake themselves to the fields and pasturages,
to dig, to sow, to make hay, to herd the cows and
goats on the mountains——in a word, to attend to all
the manifold requirements of a mixed agricultural
and pastoral life.

2. The pastoral life of the Swiss peasantry forces
itself strongly on the attention of the Alpine traveller,
from the numerous herds of cattle which he meets
with on every pasturage in the mountains, and from
the frequent dairy-chalets or Sennhütte with their
plentiful produce, which greet him in the loneliest
spots.   The great staple of Swiss pastoral wealth are
cows and the produce of the dairy.   Sheep are comparatively rare; and even goats are seen in a proportion very inferior to that of cows.

Although some of the great mountain dairies and
the herds that supply them, are the property of one
or more individuals, by far the most common source
of such establishments, is the union of the smaller
properties of any particular hamlet or parish into
one, with the view of economising labour; a large
proportion of the *Alps* or mountain pasturages,

being *common lands* appertaining to the commune or parish. One or more cowherds is appointed and paid in common; and the dairy-staff, proportioned to the extent of the flock, is constituted in like manner. All the milk is kept in common, as well as all the butter and cheese produced from it; the apportioning of their share to the individual proprietors, being regulated by the award of inspectors appointed by the body of proprietors or by the commune. These inspectors attend the milkings occasionally so as to ascertain the exact average produce of each individual cow; and a division of the butter and cheese, proportioned to the number of cows and their respective amount of milk, is made at the end of the season.

3. It is a singular fact, and one I could not bring myself to believe, until I had it confirmed to me by repeated testimony, that the whole of the butter produced in any one of these Alpine pastures, is preserved sweet, or at least, perfectly fit for use, through the whole season, *without any admixture of salt*. The following is the way in which it is treated :——A narrow deal board, not more than four or five inches wide, is fixed horizontally in an open place in the dairy of the chalet : wooden pins, from two to three feet in length, are fixed in an upright position into this, their whole length projecting above its surface. As the butter is made it is placed daily around these pins (one at a time) beginning at their lower end, and in a mass not exceeding at first

the width of the board.　Every day as more butter is made it is added to the previous portion around the pin, the diameter of the growing mass being gradually enlarged *upwards* until the upper surface overhangs the base to a considerable extent, like an inverted beehive.　When one pin is filled, another is proceeded with in like manner, and so on.　The exposed surface of these masses gets soon covered with a sort of hard film which effectually excludes the access of the air; and this circumstance with two others—viz. the complete expression of milk from the butter, and the unobstructed circulation of a cool mountain air through the chalet,—will go far to explain how butter so treated can remain so long without becoming spoiled.

I should like this experiment to be tried in some of our English dairies.　The Swiss manipulators had no doubt of the trial succeeding, provided all the above-mentioned requisites of complete expression of the milk, a low temperature and a free circulation of air, were obtained.

It is very probable that if the butter thus preserved, from June or July to October, were then made use of as the supply of the daily breakfast, it might not be found exactly *good*, according to our acceptation of the term, as applied to so delicate an article of diet; yet there can be no doubt that butter so treated is preserved from all putrescency: and it is from it that the whole winter store of the inhabitants of Switzerland is obtained.

4. The mode of preparing this *winter store* of butter seems to me much more important; and I will here describe it in detail, as I believe it is little known in England, and ought to be more so. I refer to what is called in the Vallais and in Piedmont *boiled butter* (beurre cuit), the form in which this article of diet is universally used, at least for all purposes of cookery.

In looking at the horrid compound sold in England as *salt butter*, at least the cheaper sorts of it used by the poorer classes, I cannot but believe that its supercession by the boiled butter of Switzerland would be advantageous both to the comfort and health of a large proportion of our countrymen. It can hardly be believed that such an offensive, briny, and semi-putrid mass as the cheaper sorts of our salt butter, can be without serious detriment to the health of the consumers, any more than the salted meat formerly issued to our seamen was so. The only difference in the two cases, is the comparative quantity consumed in each case : in itself, I am disposed to regard the rancid butter as the more unwholesome of the two. The boiled butter, while infinitely more palatable, is neither saline nor rancid, and, consequently, is calculated to be more easily digested, and to produce a more wholesome material for absorption into the system.

I give the receipt for the process of making the boiled butter in the words I took it down from the mouth of my guide from the valley of Entremont, with the addition of some little variations in the process, as I obtained them from others learned in the same art.

Formula.——Into a clean copper pan [better, no doubt, tinned] put any quantity of butter, say from twenty to forty pounds, and place it over a very gentle fire, so that it may melt slowly ; and let the heat be so graduated, that the melted mass does not come to the boil in less than about two hours. During all this time the butter must be frequently stirred, say once in five or ten minutes, so that the whole mass may be thoroughly intermixed, and the top and bottom change places from time to time. When the melted mass boils, the fire is to be so regulated as to *keep* the butter at a *gentle boil* for about two hours more, the stirring being still continued, but not necessarily so frequently as before. The vessel is then to be removed from the fire, and set aside to cool and settle, still gradually ; this process of cooling being supposed also to require about two hours. The melted mass is then, while still quite liquid, to be carefully poured into the croc or jar in which it is to be kept. In the process of cooling, there is deposited a whitish cheesy sediment proportioned to the quantity of butter, which is to be carefully prevented from intermixture with the preserved butter.*

As might be expected, there are some variations in the process in the practice of different indivi-

---

* These caseous grounds are very palatable and nutrient, and are constantly used as food.

duals. One very experienced man assured me that a much shorter time than two hours need elapse between the setting of the vessel on the fire, and the period of bringing the butter to the boiling point.——Another said that the time should bear some relation to the quantity of materials used—— an average period of ten minutes being allowed for every pound. The same party told me that if the butter employed was not quite sweet, the addition of a slice of bread and a slice of onion will remove this; and also that the appearance of the *grounds* rising up to the top when the mass is stirred, is itself a proof that the coction is sufficient. My guide at Chamouni told me that his wife usually added a small portion of salt to the mass, in the early stage of the boiling.

Everybody agreed in asserting that butter so preserved will last *for years* perfectly good, without any particular precautions being taken to keep it from the air, or without the slightest addition of salt. Indeed, I myself tasted more than once butter so prepared full twelve months after preparation, and found it without the slightest taint. It wanted the flavour of fresh butter, but seemed to me infinitely more palatable than our coarse salted butter. This boiled butter, however, is not commonly used even in Switzerland as a condiment with bread, as fresh butter is, but merely as an article in cookery, for which purpose it is said to be even *better* than perfectly recent butter. I saw, at the Hôtel d'Angleterre in Chamouni, the very jar out of which all the butter used in the kitchen was taken; and certainly it would not be easy to find more delicate cookery than we here met with.

5. In my descent from the Breven, I found my *noble* friend in the chalet of Planpra making preparations for descending with his cows to a still lower pasture, although there appeared to me to be still excellent fare for his beasts in this locality; but no doubt he had good reasons for doing so. There is a regular system followed in Switzerland in relation to the feeding of the cattle, which, like all other agricultural and pastoral proceedings, has relation to the elevation and consequent temperature and vegetative power of the localities.

In the spring or early summer, so soon as the snow has disappeared from the pastures on the lower slopes of the mountains, the cattle are liberated from their winter durance in the stables, and sent to feed there. By the time the food is exhausted on them the snow has disappeared from the next range of Alps above, viz. in the early weeks of June, and the cattle are accordingly driven up to them. Here they remain about a month, and are then—or at least such of them as are not wanted for the more immediate supply of the inhabitants of the valleys—transferred to the highest pastures of all; on these they remain from six weeks to two months, according to the season and extent of pasture, and then descend towards the valleys, remaining, on their way, two or three weeks on their former ground.   They finally return to the inhabited valleys about the first or second week of October, picking up what they can there, until all vegetation is covered by the snow.   They are then perforce confined to their stables, where they consume that provender the procuring of which during the period of summer has formed so large a portion of the labour of the husbandman.

In the general language of the country a herd of cattle thus congregated on the mountain pastures is called *Senne* or *Sente*, the pastures themselves *Alpe* or *Sennenalpe*, and the keeper of the herd *Senn* or *Senner*, and the mountain-hut or chalet inhabited by him *Sennhütte*.   The phrase in common use for expressing the transport of the cattle to the upper pastures is " going, or gone to the Alp" (zu Alp fahren).   In these pasturages the cows at sunset return of their own accord to the neighbourhood of the Sennhütte or chalet, and there patiently await their turn to be milked.   It is the regular order or *rows* (Reihen) in which they stand during the process of milking, that has given the name (Kuhreihen) to the national song—more commonly known by its French name the *Rany* or *Ranz-des-Vaches*.

6. The fee to my Chamouni guide for his day's work was ten francs, the hire of the mule six. This guide was a very intelligent man, and gave me much interesting information in the course of our

twelve hours' association. Like almost all the people here, he spoke French, and spoke it fairly well. He initiated me into the economy of his own class, the Chamouni guides, who, probably, may be regarded as the first of their class in the country. The system adopted in regard to their organization and management seems very excellent and complete, and is rigidly adhered to under the authority of the government. The whole body is composed of sixty principal guides, and thirty aspirants who cannot be admitted as such until after an examination by a board of experienced guides. No person not belonging to the body is permitted to act as a guide by himself, but boys and lads are allowed to accompany their seniors with the view of studying their profession. Even the aspirants are only permitted to officiate alone when the whole of the guides are already engaged; but, in order that they may have complete scope for perfecting themselves in their duties, whenever four guides are wanted for any one party, as in ascending Mont Blanc or in carrying the luggage of a numerous company, every fourth man must be an aspirant. The guides can only be employed in turn, and the daily *roster* is under the immediate supervision of one of their seniors, who is paid by government, and designated chief guide. The guides are superannuated at a certain fixed age. A fund is formed by deducting a small tax from all fees, from which a certain allowance is made to the members during sickness, &c.

7. Being interested in a medico-statistical point of view, in the matter of the pensioning of the men vulgarly termed *Nobles*, that is, the fathers of large families, in the kingdom of Sardinia, and wishing to have some authentic information corroborative of what I obtained on the spot, on my return to England, I wrote to Dr. Bellingeri of Turin on the subject, who very kindly procured for me a communication from Signor Piotti, a distinguished engineer, the substance of which I here transcribe.

A law of Cristina, Duchess of Savoy, bearing date the 2d of June, 1648, enacted that all subjects of the House of Savoy, having twelve legitimate children should be exempted, during their lifetime, from all state contributions and public offices attaching to property, and from all taxes, whether royal, feudal or communal, on goods and provisions necessary for the maintenance of their family. In the royal constitution of April 1770 this privilege was confirmed. By royal letters patent of date 18th Feb. 1819, this privilege of the inhabitants of Piedmont was extended to the inhabitants of the dukedom of Genoa; but it was at the same time enacted that while the fathers of twelve children should still continue exempt from the tax on property, they should be subject, with others, to the payment of all other taxes (*Gabelle*), and receive, as an equivalent, an annual pension of 250 lire or francs. In July 1845 the law was again altered; no one being left exempt from the payment of all sorts of taxes; but the pension of 250 francs was still held payable to the fathers of twelve children—provided they were not rich (alle famiglie di 12 figli e bisognose). It is not requisite that all the twelve children should be of one mother. The number of families thus pensioned in the kingdom at the present time is 485, making a total of 5820 children in this number of families.

I learned from my Chamouni friends that the mode of proceeding in obtaining the pension is as follows: notice of the intended claim is given to the local authorities, and in due time a commission is sent to investigate its legitimacy. Before this commission the whole of the twelve children must be produced.

We started from Chamouni, as I have already stated, between seven and eight—nominally in the Diligence and with Diligence tickets, but in reality in an open caleche which transferred us to the veritable Diligence at Sallanches, beyond which it does not travel. The banks of the Arve retain something of the harshness characteristic of the higher Alpine valleys for some distance beyond Chamouni; but as we proceed onwards and at length turn our face northwards beyond the village of Ouches, the landscape gradually softens, and soon assumes all that boldness, picturesqueness and gentle beauty, which give such a combined charm to all the valleys of the Alps which are not beyond a certain elevation. The road crosses the Arve several times, giving the traveller ample opportunity of witnessing the splendid scenery on both sides of the valley, as well as the bold and furious descent and picturesque windings of the river itself. Some parts of the road are very steep, yet perfectly practicable and safe for a Swiss carriage drawn by Swiss horses and guided by a Swiss driver.

We found the Diligence waiting our arrival at Sallanches; and on our party joining it, it proceeded immediately on its way. It was a capital, well-appointed coach; and the day being extremely fine and the roads good, my comfortable front seat on its lofty top was really a position to be envied. For reviewing scenes so recently examined, the progress was hardly too rapid, while the passenger's independence of all the locomotive arrangements, left the mind entirely free for calm contemplation. The perfect ease and quiet of such a position was the more enjoyed from contrast with the active and exciting labours which had preceded. The traveller's real personal work was now felt to be done; and repose was acceptable both to the body and the mind.

We arrived at Geneva at half-past six. On rejoining my companions at the Couronne, I found that places were already engaged for us in the Diligence which was to start for Neuchatel at four the following morning.

September 11.—The Diligence started punctually at four, not without some exertion and difficulty on the part of the passengers to make good their personal

presence at the necessary time.   It was a pleasant
morning ; and as our route lay, all along, on the high
ground bounding the northern shore of the lake, we
had good views both of the water and of the mountains
to the south and east as the day dawned, and also
one of those glorious marvels of illumined clouds
which so often usher in the sunrise in lands of the
mountain and the flood.   But the glory of the sunrise was only a harbinger of bad weather, which set
in with a thunderstorm on the distant mountains,
and speedily reached us in the form of heavy rain
continuing throughout the day.   Passing through the
numerous small towns that line the northern shore
of Lake Leman——Coppet, Nyon, Rolle, Morges, &c.
——we reached Lausanne about breakfast-time, and
breakfasted in the classical Hôtel Gibbon ; then,
turning at right angles to our former course we
proceeded directly north till we reached Yverdun.
Here, rounding the south-western extremity of the
lake of Neuchâtel, the road henceforward took a
north-eastern direction, keeping the shore of this
lake as close on our right hand, the whole way, as
our previous route had kept Lake Leman.   We had
thus, from the most favorable point of view, the
range of hills high above their shores, an almost
continuous prospect of either the one piece of water
or the other, during the greater part of our journey.   We passed close to the Castle of Granson
built on the shore of the lake near its south-western
extremity : its fine, bold, feudal look harmonises

well with the great memories with which its towers are associated. We reached the town of Neuchâtel at half-past four and took up our abode at the Hôtel des Alpes, close on the shore of the lake. The evening being wet, we did not go out to examine the town.

September 12.——As the Diligence for Basel started at the same early hour of four, we had left Neu-châtel some time before daylight. We did not take the most direct road to Bienne, but rounding the north-eastern extremity of the lake proceeded on to Aarberg, to meet the Diligence coming from Berne. The Murtersee or lake of Morat lay at a short distance on our right hand, glorious in its unpicturesque locality. To pass it unvisited, was another of the few black stones that checquered the white records of our tour : but time, tide, and a Physician's Holiday, are things of fate. We breakfasted at Aarberg, and then proceeded in our new conveyance to Bienne.

From the time we left the valley of the Arve and the mountains of Faucigny, we may be said to have bidden farewell to all scenery truly Swiss ; the tract thenceforward, all the way to Bienne, having the character of an open champaign country or, at most, an expanse of gentle hills well cultivated and but little wooded. The only exception to this is the north-western shore of the lake of Neuchâtel, where the range of the Jura comes close upon our route. At Bienne, we had once more come upon the same

range ; and thenceforward were to penetrate into its
recesses through the greater part of our way to Basel.

The ascent of the Jura commences immediately
at Bienne, and so steeply that all the male passengers
left the Diligence to walk to the top of the first hill.
The day being sunny and cloudless we expected to
have from this point the well-known view of
the Grand Alps in all their snowy glory ; but we
were disappointed by a sort of sunny haze on the
southern horizon.   This, however, did not prevent
our enjoying the fine prospect near at hand of the
town of Bienne, with the lakes of Bienne, Neuchâtel,
and Morat, and the wide district stretching from
these lakes far to the north-east in the line of the Aar.

On surmounting this first ridge of the Jura we
descended its northern side by a steep but excellent
road, and, having crossed the river Suze, traced its
upward course, on its left bank, first to the north
and then to the west, for a considerable distance,
and in a direction almost opposite to our final destination, until we reached the village of Sonceboz.
Here, turning our backs on the river, which kept its
former direction along the Val St. Imier to the
south-west, we assumed our proper course to the
north-east, which we kept all the rest of the journey.
Ascending the ridge bounding the vale of St. Imier
on the north, we passed on its top through the famous
Pierre Pertuis and immediately descended, by a
gentle declivity, into the valley forming the commencement of Val Moutier or Münsterthal, which
gives its name to the district over an extent of many

miles. Just below the rock of the Pierre Pertuis the river Birs whose course we were henceforth to trace all the way to Basel, takes its origin in copious springs bursting from the face of the hill. Threading the depth of the valley all along, now on one side of the Birs now another, we passed through the small towns of Tavannes or Dachfeld; Malleray; Münster or Moutier Grand Val; Delement or Delsperg; Lauffen, &c., and reached Basel at half-past six,—making a stretch from Neuchâtel of about eighty-six English miles.

As I said a few pages back, we had taken leave of the characteristic scenery of Switzerland on parting with the Arve amid the mountains of Faucigny, I ought perhaps now to add that we had encountered it afresh in descending into the valleys of the Jura. And truly, the scenery through which we had this day passed—from Bienne to Basel—need not shrink from comparison with much that Switzerland can present. It has all its picturesqueness and beauty; but the comparative smallness of the scale deprives it of its grandeur and still more of its sublimity. All along the banks of the Suze the bounding hills are gently rounded and clothed with trees to the very top; the valley is narrow, but not precipitous, beautifully green, and rich with orchards. Every now and then, also, lateral valleys of precisely the same character, each with its little tributary stream, joined that in which we travelled, giving us

22

transitory glimpses of far-away beauties amid the recesses of the hills, as we hurried past.

After passing the Pierced Stone the scenery continued for some time of the same gentle character, and then assumed a wilder and more ravine-like aspect; the Birs running for miles—with intervals of gentler scenery—between lines of perpendicular rock, and so close as to leave, in many places, only just space enough for the river and the road. Although frequently quite bare, the majority of these cliffs were either covered or dotted over with pine trees, fixing themselves wherever the lines of stratification could give them a footing, and shooting up along the face of the cliff, with their straight white trunks and green pyramidal heads, in that elegant and beautiful manner which has been more than once noticed in these pages. And as we advanced, ever and anon the winding ravine would end abruptly in a wider space, forming a valley of a circular shape, bounded by walls of a gentler and more peculiar configuration. For instance, there would be, first, a green expanse of pasture-ground sloping gently from the river until met by the base of the bare cliff; then this cliff rising to a great height like a vertical wall; and, lastly, crowning this, a thick green wood of pines stretching steeply upwards and ending with its fringy margin relieved against the sky. Sometimes, as a variety, there would be seen in the very centre of one of these inclosed valleys, a low isolated hill, beautifully rounded and covered from top to bottom with beeches intermixed with pines.

Taken altogether, this whole tract of the Münsterthal is exquisite, and I think it would not be easy to find in nature a nearer approach to that matchless scene painted by Milton, where "the verdurous wall of Paradise upsprung," than in some of its more secluded valleys :—

> "A steep wilderness, whose hairy sides
> With thicket overgrown, grotesque and wild,
> Access denied; and overhead up-grew
> Insuperable height of loftiest shade,
> Cedar and pine and fir and branching palm,
> A sylvan scene; and, as the ranks ascend
> Shade above shade, a woody theatre
> Of stateliest view."

What adds greatly to the impression made on the mind by these beautiful scenes is their persistence for so lengthened a period beneath the eye,—the tract over which they are spread being almost fifty miles in extent.

It was growing dark before we left the valley of the Birs, and we had consequently (another black stone) but an imperfect glimpse as we passed, of the last of the glorious Swiss battle-fields we were to see—Dornach and Saint James. We arrived at Basel at half-past six, and took up our abode at the Three Kings.

Sept. 13.—Left Basel by the railway at six; arrived at Strasburg at half-past ten; embarked at once on board the steamer, which reached the Rhine by a canal two or three miles long, and, with the wind against us but the current in our favour, finally arrived at Mannheim at half-past six.   We lodged at the Hôtel de l'Europe, a splendid establishment of immense size, and affording admirable accommodations.

Sept. 14.——Left Mannheim in the steamer at six a.m., and reached Köln about seven p.m.

Sept. 15.——Left Köln by the railway at seven, a.m., and reached Ostend about the same hour in the evening.   We went immediately on board the English steamer in the harbour, where we found supper prepared for a large company of passengers.

Sept. 16.——Left Ostend by the early morning tide, and reached Blackwall at one p.m.   Here we were most vexatiously detained more than two hours by the Custom House, so that we did not reach our home in London until after four.

In accordance with a principle kept constantly in view while writing out the particulars of the HOLIDAY now concluded, viz. to give to those who may follow the same or a similar tract, such economical and financial details as may be useful to them, I may here state that the total expenses of the tour— from the moment of departure to that of return— was, as near as may be, ONE GUINEA *per diem* to each of the travellers.

APPENDIX.

Mont Pleureur abuts by an extremely steep descent on the Val de Bagnes, and forms with Mont Mauvoisin, directly opposite, a rather long and very narrow ravine, in which the Dranse is confined in a channel not more than from twenty to forty feet wide. The rocky walls of the ravine are vertical, and about one hundred feet high; and on these the bridge of Mauvoisin has been built, about eighty feet above the bed of the river. Adjoining Mont Pleureur is Mont Getroz; and at the top of the narrow and deep channel lying between them, the glacier of Getroz is situated. From this glacier there has always been a great flow of water in the form of cascades; and this, for some years previously to 1818, owing to the advance of the extremity of the glacier, had been constantly intermixed with huge masses of ice, which descended quite into the bed of the Dranse. During the five years previously to 1818, a sort of supplementary glacier, of a conical form, had been formed by these icy avalanches, its point lying up in the Getroz channel about five hundred feet above the level of the river, and its base abutting against the vertical base of Mont Mauvoisin on the other side of the Dranse. This mass was further augmented by the annual fall of avalanches of snow; and so soon as it attained a size sufficient to resist the melting power of the summer heats, it, of necessity, increased from year to year. The Dranse had found a passage below this obstacle until 1817, in which year its waters were blocked up for a short time; and when they suddenly escaped, they did considerable damage to the valley below. In April, 1818, the same event occurred on a greater scale, an artificial lake being formed half a league in length.

To avert the danger of the sudden emptying of such a mass of water, it was determined to pierce the obstructing mass of ice by a tunnel, at such a height above the actual surface of the lake as the water might be calculated to attain by the time the tunnel was complete. It was expected that when an outlet was once given to the water, its flow would gradually wear away the ice over which it ran, and thus evacuate the whole contents of the lake without danger. The operation was committed to M. Venetz, the engineer. The tunneling process commenced on the 10th of May, and was completed on the 13th of June, during which time the lake rose sixty-two feet, but still some feet lower than the upper opening of the tunnel. In consequence, the floor of this had to be cut away downwards until it was on the level with the surface of the water. The tunnel was six hundred feet in length.

On the 13th of June, the day of the completion of the work, the length of the lake was from 10,000 to 12,000 feet; its mean breadth about 700 feet at the surface, and about 100 feet at the bottom; its mean width was 400 feet, and its mean depth 200 feet; its total contents being at least 800,000,000 cubic feet of water.

During the first day after the water began to flow the lake rose a little; but then the floor of the gallery beginning to melt, the augmented discharge produced a gradual diminution of the mass of water, and consequently of the surface of the lake, until, by the 16th of June, the lowering of the surface amounted to forty-five feet, equivalent to a decrease of the sum total of water by 270,000,000 cubic feet, leaving, consequently, 530,000,000.

Partly by the gradual melting of the floor of the gallery, and by the partial rupture *en masse* of the great body of ice from the infiltration of the water, the tunnel not merely lost substance in its floor, but still more in its length ; so that it was reduced from 600 feet to only eight feet from end to end.

And yet it was not the weakness of this narrow barrier that, after all, was the immediate cause of the *débâcle*. When the channel formed in the ice by the flow of the water had reached quite down to the bottom (some hundred feet in depth), it then attacked the surface of Mont Mauvoisin, consisting here merely of a thick mass of earth and stones, and at length carried the whole of this off down to the solid rock, and so opened a direct passage into the lake, which, consequently, discharged itself all at once, breaking down, with a horrible crash, the whole of the icy barrier yet remaining : the lake was completely emptied in half an hour.

The escape of the water into the valley would have been still more rapid, but for the narrowness of the gorge immediately below it (over which the bridge of Mauvoisin stood) which afforded a temporary obstacle to the water's progress. The flood carried away this bridge, though ninety feet above the usual level of the river, and rose several fathoms above the projecting portion of Mont Mauvoisin on which it stood. The inundation then spread itself over the more open part of the valley below, carrying everything before it—forests, detached rocks, houses, barns, cultivated fields, &c. Arrived at the village Chable, the flood was obstructed for a time by the abutments of a solid bridge rising more than fifty feet above the usual level of the Dranse; but fortunately for the safety of the village, it at length gave way, and, together with the houses on either side, was swept down the stream. This once more spread itself over the valley, until it reached the narrow ravine which continues from St. Branchier all the way to Martigny, carrying destruction with it through its whole course, covering the whole plain of Martigny with a thick mud, and with millions of unrooted trees, the ruins of houses and furniture, the dead bodies of men and animals, until it finally fell in divided streams into the Rhone.

According to the unanimous testimony of the spectators, the flood occupied nearly half an hour in passing all the places where observation was made: there consequently passed 300,000 cubic feet of water per second, which is five times more water than the Rhine contains below Basel when at the fullest, the river being calculated to carry only 60,000 cubic feet per second.

The flood took thirty-five minutes to reach Chable, a distance of about 70,000 feet; consequently the water, charged as it was with all its solid materials, flowed at the rate of thirty-three feet per second. This is vastly greater than that of the most rapid rivers. The rapidity of the swiftest stream is only from six to ten feet per second; very few ever reach the velocity of thirteen feet: in the straight channel of the Linth and Mollis, the river, when at its highest, flows at the rate of only twelve feet per second.

The velocity of the *débâcle*, consequently, when taken in connexion with its half-solid contents, easily explains the immense force which it exerted on everything it touched.

From Chable to Martigny the time occupied by the flood was about fifty-five minutes, a distance of about 60,000 feet; consequently, the main rapidity of the current was here about eighteen feet per second. From Martigny to St. Maurice, the *débâcle*, then occupying the wide bed of the Rhone, flowed in seventy minutes a distance of about 50,000 feet, showing a velocity of eleven to twelve feet per second. Finally, from St. Maurice to the lake of Geneva, a distance of about 80,000 feet, the flow took about two hundred and thirty minutes, giving a velocity of six feet per second.

M. Escher gives it as his opinion that the effect of the tunneling, though unhappily not so completely successful as was hoped, was yet most beneficial; as, had it not been effected, he calculates that the water would have probably accumulated for a full month longer, and would then have amounted to 1,700,000,000 of cubic feet——the sudden discharge of which enormous mass must have not only entirely destroyed every town and village on its banks, including Martigny, but would have ravaged the whole country as far as the lake of Geneva, almost as severely as the actual flood ravaged the valley of the Dranse.*

The effects of this flood on the village of Martigny are graphically described by two of our countrymen who visited the spot soon after the catastrophe, viz. Mr. John Murray of Edinburgh, and Capt. Basil Hall.

* Notice sur le Val de Bagne et sur le Catastrophe qui en a devasté le fond, en Juin 1818.

" I arrived at Martigny," says Mr. Murray, " on the morning of the 21st, only five days after this terrible catastrophe. . . . I walked from Geneva to Martigny: all the roads were destroyed, and I had to *wade for half a mile*, where the Rhone had inundated the road from having overflowed its banks. At Martigny I found all the fountains destroyed, and the approach to the fragment of the town that remained was marked by the most pitiable scene of desolation; what had once been fields were sand-banks, sparkling with particles of mica, and clothed with myriads of grasshoppers; I observed some trees decorticated to the height of ten feet, so that the water must have rushed through Martigny at that depth."*

" I arrived at Martigny," says Capt. Hall, " on the 5th of August, just seven weeks after the catastrophe above described. Many of the houses had been swept away, and all the remaining habitations gave token of having been invaded by the flood, which even at the lower extremity of the town where the valley is widest, had risen to the height of ten feet, as we could remark by the traces left on the walls. Higher up the torrent had been much deeper; and the inhabitants pointed out to us the manner in which a considerable district of houses had been saved from destruction by the intervention of the village church, a compact stone building placed—perhaps not accidentally—with one of its corners directed towards the adjacent gorge, out of which the overcharged torrent of the Dranse burst with such violence on the 16th of June. Had the side or end of the church faced the stream, it is supposed that not only it must have given way, but, in its

* A Glance at some of the Beauties of Switzerland, p. 97; Edin. 1839.

train, all that quarter of the village would have been overwhelmed. . . . . .

"All the hedges, garden-walls, and other boundary lines and landmarks of every description were of course obliterated, under one uniform mass of detritus, which had levelled all distinctions in a truly sweeping and democratic confusion.   In every house, without exception, there lay a stratum of alluvial matter several feet in thickness, so deposited that passages were obliged to be cut through it, along the streets, as we see roads cut in the snow after a storm.   On that side of every building which faced up the valley, and consequently against which the stream was directed, there had been collected a pile of large stones under all, then a layer of trees, with their tattered branches lying one way, and their roots the other.   Next came a network of timber-beams of houses, broken doors, fragments of mill-wheels, shafts of carts, handles of ploughs, and all the wreck and ruin of the numerous villages which the *débâcle* had first torn to pieces, and then swept down the valley in one undistinguishable mass.   The lower part of the bark had been completely stripped off all the trees still standing, each one being charged on the side next the torrent with a singular accumulation of rubbish, consisting chiefly of uprooted trees and those wooden portions of the buildings which were bolted together.   I ought to mention, also, that from every house, and behind every tree, circumstanced as I have described, there extended down the valley a long tail or train of diluvial rubbish, deposited in the swirl, or as a sailor would say, in the eddy, under the lee of these obstacles.   All over the plain, large boulders or erratic blocks lay thickly strewed.   These varied in size from a yard to a couple of yards in diameter."

Captain Hall revisited Martigny only fifteen years afterwards, and then he could hardly find any traces of the ravages which had impressed him so strongly on the former occasion. Indeed his account of the scene might apply exactly as it presented itself to us after double the period. " The only circumstance," he says, " which I could now discover to mark the event of which I supposed the visible effects were to exist for ages, consisted in a black line painted on the wall of one of the hotels, at the height of ten feet from the ground, to point out to travellers that such was the limit to which the inundation had reached ! The fields were all again matted thickly with verdure ; the hedges and dividing walls appeared never to have been disturbed ; flower-gardens, and kitchen-gardens, and grass-plots smiled on every side of the happy valley; apple trees laden with fruit, and rows of tall poplars, marked out many lines of new and better roads than before, leading from new bridges, which formerly had no existence !*

* Patchwork, vol. i, pp. 46-7, Second edit. ; Lond. 1841.

INDEX.

THE END.

C. AND J. ADLARD, PRINTERS,
BARTHOLOMEW CLOSE.

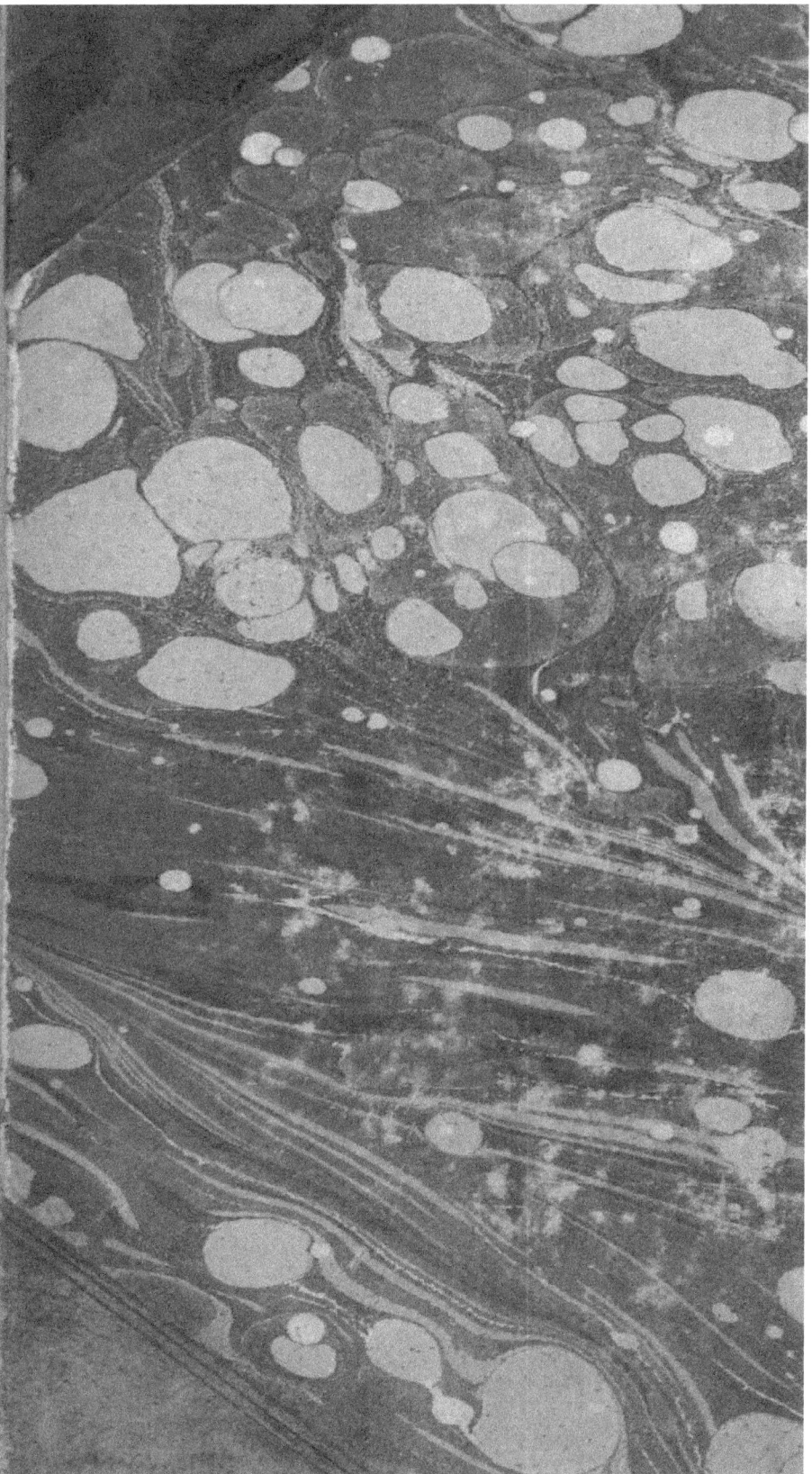

Im The Story

personalised classic books

"Good thought, lovely book, well executed, close read art"

Why We Love It By

UNIQUE GIFT

FOR KIDS, PARTNERS AND FRIENDS

Timeless books such as:

Alice in Wonderland • The Jungle Book • The Wonderful Wizard of Oz
Peter Pan & Wendy • Robin Hood • The Prince and the Pauper
The Railway Children • Treasure Island • A Christmas Carol

Romeo and Juliet • Dracula

Add Inscriptions

Visit
Im The Story .com
and order yours today!